AIA

Foundation Level

CORPORATE GOVERNANCE AND AUDIT
LEARNING & PRACTICE WORKBOOK

In this edition

- A **user-friendly format** for easy navigation
- **Exam-centred topic coverage**, directly linked to AIA's syllabus
- **Exam focus points** showing you what the examiner will want you to do
- Regular **fast forward** summaries emphasising the key points in each chapter
- **Questions** and **quick quizzes** to test your understanding
- **Practice question bank** containing exam-standard questions with answers
- **Exam question bank** containing recent exam questions with answers
- 2 Mock exams
- A full index

FOR EXAMS FROM MAY 2025

Second edition November 2024
ISBN 9781 0355 2572 0
eISBN 9781 0355 2600 0

British Library Cataloguing-in-Publication Data
A catalogue record for this book
is available from the British Library

Published by
BPP Learning Media Ltd
BPP House, Aldine Place
142-144 Uxbridge Road
London W12 8AA

learningmedia.bpp.com

Printed in the United Kingdom

Your learning materials, published by BPP Learning Media Ltd, are printed on paper obtained from traceable sustainable sources.

All rights reserved. No part of this publication may be reproduced, stored in a retrieval system or transmitted in any form or by any means, electronic, mechanical, photocopying, recording or otherwise, without the prior written permission of BPP Learning Media.

Contains public sector information licensed under the Open Government Licence v3.0.

The contents of this book are intended as a guide and not professional advice. Although every effort has been made to ensure that the contents of this book are correct at the time of going to press, BPP Learning Media makes no warranty that the information in this book is accurate or complete and accept no liability for any loss or damage suffered by any person acting or refraining from acting as a result of the material in this book.

We are grateful to the Association of International Accountants for permission to reproduce past examination questions.

The suggested solutions in the exam answer bank have been prepared by BPP Learning Media Ltd.

BPP Learning Media is grateful to the IASB for permission to reproduce extracts from the International Financial Reporting Standards including all International Accounting Standards, SIC and IFRIC Interpretations (the Standards). The Standards together with their accompanying documents are issued by:

The International Accounting Standards Board (IASB)
30 Cannon Street, London, EC4M 6XH, United Kingdom.
Email: info@ifrs.org Web: www.ifrs.org

Disclaimer: The IASB, the International Financial Reporting Standards (IFRS) Foundation, the authors and the publishers do not accept responsibility for any loss caused by acting or refraining from acting in reliance on the material in this publication, whether such loss is caused by negligence or otherwise to the maximum extent permitted by law.

©
BPP Learning Media Ltd
2024

A note about copyright

Dear Customer

What does the little © mean and why does it matter?

Your market-leading BPP books, course materials and e-learning materials do not write and update themselves. People write them on their own behalf or as employees of an organisation that invests in this activity. Copyright law protects their livelihoods. It does so by creating rights over the use of the content.

Breach of copyright is a form of theft – as well as being a criminal offence in some jurisdictions, it is potentially a serious breach of professional ethics.

With current technology, things might seem a bit hazy but, basically, without the express permission of BPP Learning Media:

- Photocopying our materials is a breach of copyright
- Printing our digital materials in order to share them with or forward them to a third party or use them in any way other than in connection with your BPP studies is a breach of copyright.

You can, of course, sell your books, in the form in which you have bought them – once you have finished with them. (Is this fair to your fellow students? We update for a reason.) Please note the e-products are sold on a single user licence basis: we do not supply 'unlock' codes to people who have bought them secondhand.

And what about outside the UK? BPP Learning Media strives to make our materials available at prices students can afford by local printing arrangements, pricing policies and partnerships which are clearly listed on our website. A tiny minority ignore this and indulge in criminal activity by illegally photocopying our material or supporting organisations that do. If they act illegally and unethically in one area, can you really trust them?

NO AI TRAINING. Unless otherwise agreed in writing, the use of BPP material for the purpose of AI training is not permitted. Any use of this material to "train" generative artificial intelligence (AI) technologies is prohibited, as is providing archived or cached data sets containing such material to another person or entity.

Copyright © IFRS Foundation

All rights reserved. Reproduction and use rights are strictly limited. No part of this publication may be translated, reprinted or reproduced or utilised in any form either in whole or in part or by any electronic, mechanical or other means, now known or hereafter invented, including photocopying and recording, or in any information storage and retrieval system, without prior permission in writing from the IFRS Foundation. Contact the IFRS Foundation for further details.

The Foundation has trade marks registered around the world (Trade Marks), including 'IAS®', 'IASB®', 'IFRIC®', 'IFRS®', the IFRS® logo, 'IFRS for SMEs®', IFRS for SMEs® logo, the 'Hexagon Device', 'International Financial Reporting Standards®', NIIF® and 'SIC®'.

Further details of the Foundation's Trade Marks are available from the Licensor on request.

Contents

Page

Introduction

> The introductory pages contain lots of valuable advice and information. They include tips on studying for and passing the exam, also the content of the syllabus and what has been examined.

How the BPP Learning Media Learning & Practice Workbook can help you pass – Help yourself study for your AIA exams – Syllabus – Command words and learning outcomes – The exam paper

Part A The Foundations of Governance

1	Corporate governance and agency theory	3
2	Overview of corporate governance	15
3	The board	27
4	Board members (directors)	37
5	Board committees	49
6	Stakeholders, corporate social responsibility and sustainability	61
7	Risk and control	93

Part B The Foundations of Auditing

8	The nature and purpose of auditing	107
9	Regulation of audit	131
10	The audit process	143
11	Risk assessment	145
12	Internal controls	159
13	Audit evidence	173
14	Tests of controls	187
15	Auditing and governance	209

Answers to end of chapter questions 221
Practice question bank 227
Practice answer bank 281
Exam question bank 299
Exam answer bank 333
Mock exam 1 355
Mock exam 2 365
Bibliography 375
Index 379

How the BPP Learning Media Learning & Practice Workbook can help you pass

> It provides you with the knowledge and understanding, skills and application techniques that you need to be successful in your exams

This Learning & Practice Workbook has been targeted at the **Corporate Governance and Audit** syllabus.

- It is **comprehensive**. It covers the syllabus content. No more, no less.
- It is written at the **right level**. Each chapter is written with AIA's syllabus in mind.
- It is aimed at the **exam**. We have taken account of recent exams, guidance the examiner has given and the assessment methodology.

> It allows you to study in the way that best suits your learning style and the time you have available, by following your personal Study Plan (see page vii)

You may be studying at home on your own or you may be attending a course. You may like to read every word, or you may prefer to do a fast read through and learn through doing practice questions the rest of the time. However you study, you will find the BPP Learning Media Learning & Practice Workbook meets your needs in designing and following your personal Study Plan.

INTRODUCTION

Help yourself study for your AIA exams

Exams for professional bodies such as AIA are very different from those you have taken at college or university. You will be under **greater time pressure before** the exam – as you may be combining your study with work. Here are some hints and tips.

The right approach

1   Develop the right attitude

Believe in yourself	Yes, there is a lot to learn. But thousands have succeeded before and you can too.
Remember why you're doing it	You are studying for a good reason: to advance your career.

2   Focus on the exam

Read through the Syllabus	This tells you what you are expected to know and is supplemented by **Exam focus points** in the Workbook.
Study the Exam paper section	Past papers are likely to be good guides to what you should expect in the exam.

3   The right method

See the whole picture	Keeping in mind how all the detail you need to know fits into the whole picture will help you understand it better. • The **Introduction** of each chapter puts the material in context. • The **Syllabus content** and **Exam focus points** show you what you need to **grasp**.
Use your own words	To absorb the information (and to practise your written communication skills), you need to **put it into your own words**. • Take **notes**. • Answer the **questions** in each chapter. • Draw **mind maps**. • Try '**teaching**' **a subject** to a colleague or friend.
Give yourself cues to jog your memory	The Learning & Practice Workbook uses **bold** to **highlight key points**. • Try **colour coding** with a highlighter pen. • Write **key points** on cards.

4   The right recap

Review, review, review	Regularly reviewing a topic in summary form can **fix it in your memory**. The Learning & Practice Workbook helps you review in many ways. • **Chapter roundups** summarise the 'Fast forward' key points in each chapter. Use them to recap each study session. • The **Quick quiz** actively tests your grasp of the essentials. • Go through the **Examples** in each chapter a second or third time.

Developing your personal Study Plan

BPP recommends that you follow a study plan. Planning and sticking to the plan are key elements of learning successfully.

Step 1 **How do you learn?**

What types of intelligence do you display when learning? You might be advised to brush up on certain study skills before launching into this Learning & Practice Workbook but refer to the 'tackling your studies' section below which will help.

Step 2 **What do you prefer to do first?**

If you prefer to get to grips with a theory before seeing how it is applied, we suggest you concentrate first on the explanations we give in each chapter before looking at the examples and case studies. If you prefer to see first how things work in practice, read through the detail in each chapter, and concentrate on the examples and case studies, before supplementing your understanding by reading the detail.

Step 3 **How much time do you have?**

Work out the time you have available per week, given the following:

- The standard you have set yourself
- The other exam(s) you are sitting
- Practical matters such as work, travel, exercise, sleep and social life

Note your time available in box A.

	Hours
A	

Step 4 **Allocate your time**

- Take the time you have available per week for this Learning & Practice Workbook shown in box A, multiply it by the number of weeks available and insert the result in box B.

B	

- Divide the figure in box B by the number of chapters in this Workbook and insert the result in box C.

C	

Remember that this is only a rough guide. Some of the chapters in this book are longer and more complicated than others, and you will find some subjects easier to understand than others.

Step 5 **Implement**

Set about studying each chapter in the time shown in box C, following the key study steps in the order suggested by your particular learning style.

This is your personal **Study Plan**. You should try to combine it with the study sequence outlined below. You may want to modify the sequence to adapt it to your **personal style**.

INTRODUCTION

Tackling your studies

The best way to approach this Learning & Practice Workbook is to tackle the chapters in order. Taking into account your individual learning style, you could follow this sequence for each chapter.

Key study steps	Activity
Step 1 **Topic list**	This topic list helps you navigate each chapter; each numbered topic is a numbered section in the chapter.
Step 2 **Introduction**	This sets your objectives for study by giving you the big picture in terms of the context of the chapter. The content is referenced to the syllabus, and Exam guidance shows how the topic is likely to be examined. The Introduction tells you **why** the topics covered in the chapter need to be studied.
Step 3 **Fast forward**	Fast forward boxes give you a quick summary of the content of each of the main chapter sections. They are listed together in the roundup at the end of each chapter to help you review each chapter quickly.
Step 4 **Explanations**	Proceed methodically through each chapter, particularly focusing on areas highlighted as significant in the chapter introduction, or areas that are frequently examined.
Step 5 **Key terms and Exam focus points**	• Key terms are definitions of important concepts that you really need to know and understand before the exam. • Exam focus points highlight areas or topics that may be examined.
Step 6 **Note taking**	Take brief notes, if you wish. Don't copy out too much. Remember that being able to record something yourself is a sign of being able to understand it. Your notes can be in whatever format you find most helpful; lists, diagrams, mind maps.
Step 7 **Examples**	Work through the examples very carefully as they illustrate key knowledge and techniques.
Step 8 **Case studies**	Study each one and try to add flesh to them from your own experience. They are designed to show how the topics you are studying come alive in the real world.
Step 9 **Questions**	Attempt each one, as they will illustrate how well you've understood what you've read.
Step 10 **Answers**	Check yours against ours, and make sure you understand any discrepancies.
Step 11 **Chapter roundup**	Review it carefully, to make sure you have grasped the significance of all the important points in the chapter.
Step 12 **Quick quiz**	Use the Quick quiz to check how much you have remembered of the topics covered and to practise questions in a variety of formats.
Step 13 **Question practice**	Attempt the multiple choice questions contained in the question bank at the end of this Learning & Practice Workbook.

AIA Achieve Academy

AIA provides an interactive course of study AIA Achieve Academy, which offers students the tools, resources and learning environment to study for the exams. The study tools include a course of study e-book, marked practice questions, marked mock exam paper and feedback and technical advice via an e-Tutor. Contact the Study Support team at: Achieve@aiaworldwide.com

Moving on...

When you are ready to start revising, you should still refer back to this Learning & Practice Workbook.

- As a source of **reference** (you should find the index particularly helpful for this)
- As a way to review (the Fast forwards, Exam focus points, Chapter roundups and Quick quizzes help you here)

PQ Qualification Syllabus

The assessment requirements in the AIA exams at the Foundation, Professional 1 and 2 stages reflect a progression of cognitive levels which successful students are expected to demonstrate in satisfying each stage of the qualification. The levels progress from an emphasis on 'knowledge and comprehension' at the Foundation stage, to a predominance of 'application and analysis' at the subsequent Professional 1 and 2 stages and incorporate 'synthesis and evaluation' at the Professional 2 stage.

Indicative weightings for the cognitive levels at each stage of the qualification are defined in the following table.

Stage of qualification	Cognitive levels of learning*			Associated learning outcomes
	Knowledge and comprehension	Application and Analysis	Synthesis and evaluation	
Foundation Level	90%	10%	0%	Outcomes consistent with the International Education Standards Board (IAESB) standards
Professional 1 Level	50%	50%	0%	
Professional 2 Level	10%	70%	20%	

The cognitive levels of learning are associated with the following:

'Knowledge and comprehension' refer to

The acquisition of concepts, ideas, terms, facts, practices and techniques in accounting and related disciplines and understanding of how they relate to the conduct, management, reporting and assessment of the activities of business and other organisations.

'Application and analysis' refer to

The ability to apply knowledge and comprehension to actual circumstances and situations and to identify constituent components involved (concepts, ideas, terms, facts, practices, and techniques) and the relationship between these elements.

'Synthesis and evaluation' refer to

The ability to bring together a variety of components in order to form a coherent whole, and to form judgements about the application of and value of those components in a particular context or for a particular purpose.

Foundation Level Syllabus

The Foundation level examination is intended to establish that students have attained the necessary knowledge of accounting in its economic context and relevant skills to be permitted to commence study for the first Professional stage examinations of the Association. It does so by assessing students in four foundational areas of knowledge and understanding relevant for prospective professional accountants; offered within the Foundation Unit: Financial Accounting, Corporate Governance and Audit, Management Accounting and Business Management.

In designing the syllabus and the related examination papers AIA has employed 'intended learning outcomes' as the means to communicate expectations to potential students and stakeholders and to inform the specification requirements to be tested in the assessment of students.

The use of learning outcomes:

- Is consistent with what is commonly acknowledged as good practice in the higher education sector; and
- Is consistent with the approach embodied in International Accounting Education Standards

At the Foundation Level students are expected to demonstrate that they are able to achieve the following:

Intended Learning Outcomes[1] – Description of expectations	
Foundation level	At the Foundation level students are expected to demonstrate that they: • Understand basic principles and concepts underpinning accounting and related practices in organisations • Understand the role of accounting and related practices within the financial and governance context of organisations • Know and can execute basic recording and measurement techniques relevant to accounting, management and assurance • Are able to analyse financial information and interpret it for the purpose of supporting decision making

Foundation level syllabus components

The Foundation Unit is made up of four components:

- Section A: Financial Accounting
- Section B: Corporate Governance and Audit
- Section C: Management Accounting
- Section D: Business Management

---

[1] The description of the levels of proficiency supports the IAESBs use of learning outcomes in its International Education Standards (IESs) 2, 3, and 4.

Relationship to Qualification Structure

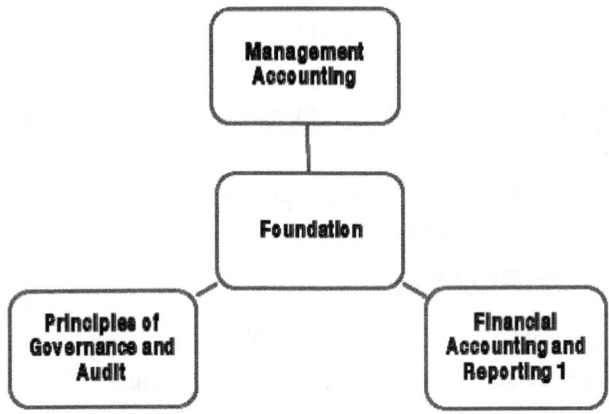

Demonstrating that the learning outcomes associated with the Foundation syllabus have been met is a requirement for all students before they are permitted to proceed to Professional level studies.

Students able to demonstrate they have met the learning outcomes based on prior study and educational qualification can be granted exemption from the Foundation Examination. For those students unable to do so, passing the Foundation Examination is a core requirement to Professional levels studies.

Aims

The aim of Foundation Level paper is to develop and examine the candidate's knowledge and understanding of:

1. The theory of accounting and its application to the practical situations indicated in the syllabus
2. The fundamental elements of corporate governance and audit and the inter-relationship between these areas
3. The fundamentals of management and cost accounting and their application in cost ascertainment, the control of operations, and the provision of information to assist management decision-making and policy formulation
4. Business management and the role of the manager in modern business organisations

Foundation Level learning outcomes

In order to successfully complete this paper, candidates will demonstrate that they are able to:

FINANCIAL ACCOUNTING

1. Explain and identify accounting concepts and the regulatory purpose of accounting standards and sustainability standards
2. Describe, prepare and summarise basic accounting records
3. Identify accounting concepts in presenting financial statements for sole traders and limited companies
4. Describe and explain the financial position and performance of an organisation

CORPORATE GOVERNANCE AND AUDIT

5. Identify and explain the purpose of corporate governance and auditing
6. Explain the inter-relationship between corporate governance and auditing
7. Relate the contribution of corporate governance and auditing to the safeguarding of capital markets

INTRODUCTION

MANAGEMENT ACCOUNTING

8   Explain the role of management and cost accounting within an organisation

9   Describe the nature of costs and how and why they are classified in different ways for different purposes

10 Calculate material, labour, expense and overhead costs for products, processes, services and functions

11 Identify and discuss appropriate principles and techniques to advise managers on short-term and long-run decision-making

BUSINESS MANAGEMENT

12 Describe the major schools of management thought, their development and their implications

13 Explain the key aspects of organisational structure and design

14 Identify the nature and importance of managerial control, including the main elements and types of control in the business organisation and the role and importance of management information in the control process

15 Describe the use of information technology in modern business management

This Learning & Practice Workbook covers **Section B: Corporate Governance and Audit**.

Detailed learning outcomes for Section B: Corporate Governance and Audit

B1   THE FOUNDATIONS OF GOVERNANCE (LEARNING OUTCOMES 5 and 7)

Topic weighting 50%

- The agency problem and agency theory
- Stakeholder theory, the main stakeholder groups and the objectives of each group
- Sustainability, corporate social responsibility and stakeholder theory
- The meaning of corporate governance, its scope and its development
- Different approaches to corporate governance
- The development of corporate governance codes both in the UK and worldwide
- Characteristics of effective boards
- The board of directors and the importance of the non-executive director
- The function and purpose of the sub-committees of the board
- Introduction to alternative board structures
- The relationship between corporate governance and sustainability
- The meaning of corporate social responsibility and its importance
- Risk and its management

B2   THE FOUNDATIONS OF AUDITING (LEARNING OUTCOMES 5, 6 and 7)

Topic weighting 50%

- Overview of the role and purpose of auditing and different types of audit
- The scope of the financial statement audit function
- Audit regulation
- Basic concepts of auditing
- The audit process
- The audit approach
- Audit risk and assessment
- Audit and internal control
- The audit evidence
- The interrelationship between auditing, governance and sustainability

Structure of the Foundation Level exam

Assessment is by a three-hour 15 minute examination (including 15 minutes reading time) consisting of 100 questions. There are 25 objective test style questions in the form of multiple-choice questions covering each component area of the syllabus. All questions are compulsory.

The assessment covers the learning outcomes for each of the four component areas of study in the foundation syllabus.

The coverage of questions will reflect the weighting of different areas of syllabus content as specified in the Foundation examination syllabus, but the format of questions associated with each area of study may vary between sittings of the examination.

Relationship to qualification structure

This paper provides the necessary knowledge and skills to progress to studying for the first professional stage of the examinations.

Ethics

Candidates are advised that the standards outlined in The Code of Ethics for Professional Accountants issued by the International Ethics Standards Board for Accountants (IESBA Code) are implicit in, and examinable throughout, the AIA syllabus. The Code can be accessed via the AIA website at www.aiaworldwide.com.

Recommended reading

AIA International Accountant Magazine
ISSN: 1465 5144

AIA Learning and Practice Workbooks
Foundation Unit
Publisher: BPP Learning Media

Four books one for each component:

Financial Accounting
ISBN: 9781035525737 / eISBN 9781035526017

Management Accounting
ISBN: 9781035525744 / eISBN 9781035526024

Corporate Governance and Audit
ISBN: 9781035525720 / eISBN 9781035526000

Business Management
ISBN: 9781035525713 / eISBN 9781035525997

Other recommended texts for each component

Financial Accounting (15th Edition 2021)
Business Accounting Volume 1
Author: Wood, F, Sangster, A and Gordon, L
Publisher: Pearson Education Limited
ISBN: 9781292365435

Free website providing comprehensive information about IFRS: www.iasplus.com

INTRODUCTION

Corporate Governance: Principles Policies and Practices (4th Edition)
Author: Bob Tricker
Publisher: Oxford University Press
ISBN: 9780198809869

Corporate Governance and Accountability (5th Edition)
Author: Jill Solomon
Publisher: Wiley
ISBN: 9781119561200

Auditing (12th Edition)
Author: Millichamp, A and Taylor, R
Publisher: Cengage Learning EMEA
ISBN: 9781473778993

Modern Auditing (3rd Edition 2009)
Author: Cosserat, G Wand Rodda, N
Publisher: Wiley
ISBN: 9780470319734

The Audit Process: Principles practice and cases (7th Edition)
Author: Gray, L, Manson, S and Crawford, L
Publisher: Cengage Learning
ISBN: 9781473760189

Management Accounting and Business Management and Cost Accounting (7th Edition 2019)
Author: Bhimani A. Horngren, Datar, S, Rajan, M
Publisher: Pearson
ISBN: 9781292232669

Management Accounting (UK Edition 2013)
Author: Burns, J., Quinn, M., Warren, L., Oliveira, J
Publisher: McGraw-Hill Education/Europe, Middle East & Africa
ISBN: 9780077121617

Management and Cost Accounting, (11th Edition 2020)
Author: Drury, C
Publisher: Cengage Learning EMEA
ISBN: 9781473773615

Management (1st International Edition 2016)
Author: Daft, R L and Benson, A
Publisher: Cengage Learning EMA
ISBN: 9781408063859

ISEContemporary Management (12th Edition 2021)
Author: Jones, G. and George, J
Publisher: McGraw-Hill
ISBN: 9781264972432

Organisational Behaviour in the Workplace (12th Edition 2019)
Author: Mullins, L. J
Publisher: Pearson
ISBN: 9781292245485

Management (15th Edition 2020)
Author: Robbins, S. P. and Coulter, M
Publisher: Pearson
ISBN: 9781292340883

The Foundations of Governance

Corporate governance and agency theory

Topic list	Syllabus reference
1 Agency theory in a corporate context	B1.1
2 Stakeholder theory	B1.2
3 Resource dependency theory	B1.2
4 Shareholder activism	B1.2

Introduction

Corporate governance is considered in more detail in subsequent chapters but, at its simplest, corporate governance is all about making sure that companies are managed and supervised properly. In this chapter we consider the relationship which a company has with those people working on its behalf, known as agents. We also consider the relationships a company has with its stakeholders, essentially those parties who have a valid interest in its activities. We look at the impact of resource dependency theory on the board of directors and the reasons for increasing levels of shareholder activism.

PART A THE FOUNDATIONS OF GOVERNANCE

1 Agency theory in a corporate context

FAST FORWARD

> In corporate entities the **separation of ownership from control** arises from shareholders, the firm's **principals**, being different people from the firm's managers, the paid **agents** of the shareholders.

Nowadays, very few large businesses are managed by their owners. In the case of larger companies, there are large numbers of shareholders and they are unlikely to wish to take part in the management of the company, viewing it simply as a vehicle for investment. Even where ownership is concentrated, large companies tend to be managed mostly by professional managers who have little ownership interest, if any. This **separation of ownership from control** has arisen for several reasons.

(a) Limited liability structure does not give shareholders power to manage the company (unless they are also managers); their influence normally extends only to proposing and voting on resolutions at company meetings.

(b) It is impracticable for a large number of shareholders to exercise managerial powers jointly; to be effective, power must be concentrated.

(c) Many shareholders are not interested in being managers, and are content to employ professional managers, so long as their investment prospers.

(d) Many organisations are so large or complex, or deal with such advanced technology, that they can only be managed effectively by suitably qualified professionals.

Separation of ownership from control has been a feature of business for over a century and brings with it a recurring problem: the business should be managed so as to promote the economic interest of its owners (shareholders) as a body, but the power to manage the business lies in the hands of people who may use it to promote their own interests. How can the managers be made to favour the interest of the owners rather than their own?

This question provides the context of agency theory. **Agency theory** is concerned with resolving the problems between principals (such as shareholders) and agents (such as company executives.)

A following key concepts are vital in understanding agency theory:

(a) An **agent** is employed by a **principal** to carry out a task on their behalf. The relationship between a principal and their agent is known as agency.

(b) **Accountability** – By agreeing to undertake a task on their behalf, an agent becomes accountable to the principal by whom they are employed. So, in the context of a firm, the executives and managers of the firm are accountable to the shareholders to act in their best interests.

(c) **Agency costs** are incurred by principals in ensuring that agents act in the best interests of the principal. So, in the context of a firm, shareholders will provide reward incentives (such as performance bonuses or share options) to try to ensure that agents execute their duties in a way which increases shareholder value, thereby aligning the interests of principals and agents.

Agency theory addresses two key problems:

(a) The problems which arise when the **objectives or goals of the principal and the agent differ**, or are in conflict, and it is difficult or expensive for the principal to verify what the agent is actually doing. For example, the managers in a company may be motivated to grow a company in a way which maximises their personal power and wealth, rather than in a way which generates value for the shareholders.

(b) The problems which arise when principals and agents have **different attitudes to risk** and therefore may be inclined to take different actions, or to think that different courses of action are acceptable.

More generally, the issues of agency and accountability highlight the **need for effective corporate governance** in firms, and we will consider corporate governance in more detail in the next section of this chapter.

However, the problems addressed in agency theory are not confined only to the management of companies: they are the general problems of the **agency relationship**, and occur whenever one person (the **principal**) gives another (the **agent**) power to deal with their affairs. This separation of ownership from control is known as a **principal-agent problem**.

1.1 Resolving the agency problem

> **FAST FORWARD**
>
> The **agency problem** refers to the problem that agents will pursue their personal interests, sometimes at the expense of making profits for the principals. This can be addressed by **incentivisation**, basing the earnings of agents on the profits given to principals.

A common approach to ensuring that company managers act in the owners' interest is to offer them **reward incentives** that depend on the achievement of ownership goals. Thus, it is common for the remuneration of a CEO to depend, at least in part, on satisfactory achievement in such matters as profit and share price. At lower levels, **bonus schemes** can be based on achieving targets that support good overall performance, such as improved sales or reduced costs. **Profit sharing schemes** that provide shares to large numbers of employees are intended to align employees' interests with those of the wider body of shareholders.

Unfortunately, these types of approach can be flawed, in that they have to be designed. The designers themselves are in an agency relationship with the owners, such that their objectives may conflict with the owners' (shareholders') objective of profitability. Thus executive remuneration schemes have been criticised for emphasising the wrong targets or for setting the targets too low.

Critics of bonus schemes based on annual profits argue that such bonuses may encourage short-term, risky behaviour which maximises profits in the short term but could potentially be loss-making in the longer term.

1.2 Alternative managerial goals

Under the conditions of the agency relationship between owners and managers, the goal of profit maximisation might not fully explain management behaviour, because managers have interests of their own.

Managers will not necessarily make decisions that will maximise profits.

(a) They may have no **personal interests** at stake in the size of profits earned, except in so far as they are accountable to shareholders for the profits they make.

(b) There may be a **lack of competitive pressure** in the market to be efficient, minimise costs and maximise profits, for example where there are few firms in the market.

It has been suggested that price and output decisions will be taken by managers with **managerial objectives** in mind. Rather than seeking to **maximise** profits, managers may choose to achieve a **satisfactory** profit for a firm: this is called **satisficing**. Satisficing is also a common managerial response when there are multiple objectives, such as boosting share price, and achieving revenue growth. Similarly, if directors' remuneration schemes are based on non-financial criteria such as growth in market share or improving corporate social responsibility performance, then they are unlikely to make the maximisation of profit their sole objective.

1.3 Agency theory and corporate governance

> **FAST FORWARD**
>
> **Agency** is extremely important in corporate governance, as often the directors/managers are acting as agents for the owners. Corporate governance frameworks aim to ensure directors/managers **fulfil their responsibilities** as agents by requiring disclosure and suggesting they be rewarded on the basis of performance.

We will consider corporate governance in more detail in Chapters 2 to 6. Corporate governance is all about making sure that companies are properly supervised and controlled to protect the interests of shareholders and other stakeholders.

Agency problems are dealt with in corporate governance codes in a number of ways, for example:

- The problem of conflicting goals may be alleviated by aligning directors' remuneration with corporate performance (see Chapter 4)
- Different attitudes to risk may be alleviated by requiring disclosure of risk management processes (see Chapter 7)
- Accountability may be enhanced by the creation of committees (sub-committees of the Board) (see Chapter 5)

1.4 Other agency relationships

1.4.1 Shareholder-auditor relationship

The shareholder-auditor relationship is another agency relationship on which corporate governance guidance has focused. The shareholders are the principals, auditors are the agents and the audit report the key method of communication.

1.4.2 Shareholder-auditor relationship in public companies

An agency problem with auditors is that auditors may not be independent of the management of the companies that they audit. They become too close to management or are afraid that management will not give them non-audit work.

Corporate governance codes have sought to address this problem. However, the shareholder-auditor relationship in public companies imposes its own complexities. The auditors are acting as shareholders' agents in **monitoring the stewardship of directors.** However the (non-executive) directors, who are on the audit committee (see Chapter 5) effectively also act as shareholders' agents in their role of **monitoring the auditors**.

A problem arises if there is conflict between auditors and non-executive directors.

2 Stakeholder theory

> **FAST FORWARD**
>
> **Stakeholder theory** highlights that firms need to be accountable to a wide range of stakeholder groups, and not just to their shareholders.

2.1 An introduction to stakeholder theory

The notion of corporate social responsibility (CSR) highlights that, when making business decisions, firms need to consider the implications of those decisions on a range of different stakeholders – not just for their shareholders. We look at CSR in detail in Chapter 6.

This idea is captured more generally through the notion of stakeholder theory. Stakeholder theory highlights that the extent of the impact firms have on society is so significant that firms need to **be accountable to many more groups in society (stakeholder groups) than just their shareholders.**

The traditional, shareholder-based, view of the firm argues that a firm's primary objective is to meet the needs of its owners (shareholders) and to generate value for them.

However, stakeholder theory argues that there is a much wider range of parties (stakeholders) who have legitimate interests in a firm, and who can affect it or are affected by it. Consequently, a firm's management needs to give due consideration to the interests of those groups. Potential stakeholder groups in a firm include employees, customers, suppliers, banks and other finance providers, local communities, government or government bodies, trades unions, and environmental agencies – as well as the firm's shareholders.

Consequently, the logic of stakeholder theory suggests that, instead of viewing business as a way of creating value solely for shareholders, we should see business as a way of **creating value for the much wider range stakeholders**. Importantly, in the context of business economics, stakeholder theory suggests that a firm's business decisions cannot be seen simply in terms of maximising profits for its shareholders, but also in relation to considering the needs of other stakeholder groups – for example, managing relationships with customers and suppliers, and maintaining employee motivation.

2.2 Stakeholders in corporate governance

FAST FORWARD

Directors and managers need to be aware of the **interests of stakeholders** in governance.

2.2.1 Stakeholders

Key term

Stakeholders are any entity (person, group or possibly non-human entity) that can **affect** or **be affected by** the achievements of an organisation's objectives. It is a **bi-directional** relationship. Each stakeholder group has different **expectations** about what it wants and different **claims** upon the organisation.

There is an overview of some important points about stakeholders in corporate governance in the sections that follow. Later in the Workbook, in Section 3 of Chapter 6 (Managing Stakeholders) we discuss the different groups of stakeholders in detail, including stakeholder objectives and risks.

2.2.2 Stakeholder claims

The definition above highlights the important point for both business ethics and strategy, that stakeholders do not only just exist, they also have claims on an organisation. Some stakeholders want to influence what the organisation does. Others are mainly concerned with how the organisation affects them and may want to increase or decrease this effect.

2.2.3 Importance of recognition of stakeholder claims

Knowledge of who stakeholders are and what claims they make is a vital part of an organisation's **risk assessment**, since the **claims** made by the stakeholder can affect the achievement of objectives. Stakeholders also have **influences** over the organisation. It is important to identify what these are and how significant they are, since it may determine the organisation's decision if it has to decide between competing stakeholder claims.

2.2.4 Stockholder theory (shareholder theory)

The theory that focuses on the interests of shareholders is known as stockholder theory, since it is mostly discussed in American literature.

Stockholder theory states that shareholders alone have a legitimate claim to influence over the company. It uses agency theory to argue that shareholders (as principals) own the company. Hence directors as agents have a moral and legal duty only to take account of shareholders' interests. As it is assumed that shareholders wish to maximise their returns, then directors' sole duty is to pursue profit maximisation.

2.2.5 Problems with stockholder view

Modern corporations have been seen as **so powerful, socially, economically and politically**, that **unrestrained use of their power** will inevitably **damage other people's rights**. For example, they may blight an entire community by closing a major factory, inflicting long-term unemployment on a large proportion of the local workforce. They may use their purchasing power or market share to impose unequal contracts on suppliers and customers alike. They may exercise undesirable influence over government through their investment decisions. There is also the argument that corporations exist within society and are **dependent upon it for the resources** they use. Some of these resources are obtained by direct contracts with suppliers but others are not, being provided by government expenditure.

2.2.6 Stakeholder theory

Stakeholder theory proposes **corporate accountability** to a broad range of stakeholders. It is based on companies being so large, and their impact on society being so significant that they cannot just be responsible to their shareholders.

What stakeholders want from an organisation will vary. Some will actively seek to influence what the organisation does and others may be concerned with limiting the effects of the organisation's activities upon themselves.

Relations with stakeholders can also vary. Possible relationships can include conflict, support, regular dialogue or joint enterprise.

2.2.7 Examples of stakeholders

The following is a non-exhaustive list of potential stakeholders in a company:

- Executive directors
- Non-executive directors
- Company secretary
- Sub-board managers
- Employees
- Suppliers
- Customers
- External auditors
- Regulators
- Government
- Stock exchanges
- Institutional investors
- Small investors

2.2.8 Other stakeholders

The list above typifies an **anthropocentric approach**, which puts human interests above those of others. Increasingly animals and other non-human interests are being recognised as stakeholders. For example the research paper *Acknowledging non-human stakeholders in designing for sustainable food systems* (2014) (Authors: Jessica Frawley and Laurel Dyson) considered co-operative farming philosophies which could more meaningfully represent both farmer and animal stakeholders, taking account of the rights of chickens in agriculture.

3 Resource dependency theory

FAST FORWARD
Resource dependency theory considers the power relationships between providers of resources and those who require those resources. This theory has implications for the composition of the board of directors.

3.1 Introduction to resource dependency theory

There is a tendency to consider firms as self-contained, stand-alone entities. However, resource dependency theory (RDT) challenges this approach. Instead of characterising firms as autonomous units, it argues that we should view firms as being **constrained and affected by inter-dependencies with other organisations and the context of their external environment**.

RDT argues that:

- Firms require resources (eg capital, materials, labour, know-how)
- Resources originate from the firm's environment
- There are other firms in the environment
- The resources upon which a firm depends are under the control of other organisations (eg loan capital is controlled by banks, raw materials controlled by suppliers) which give power to the controller
- Power and resource dependence are directly linked: if A is a supplier and B a purchaser then A's power of B is equal to B's dependence on A's resources
- Firms will attempt to reduce others' power over them, while often attempting to increase their own power over others.

Two particularly important aspects of resources are **criticality** (how critical a resource is) and **scarcity** (how easily available the resource is, or not). Critical resources are those which a firm must have in order to operate. (For example, a petrol station cannot operate without a supply of petrol). However, a firm can adopt different strategies to deal with this criticality – on the one hand it may develop links with more suppliers, or it may integrate vertically or horizontally.

RDT and this pursuit of power relationships tells us that profit maximisation is not the only objective which firms have.

3.2 Resource dependency theory and boards of directors

Resource dependency theory can also be useful when assessing the **size and composition of a company's board** of directors (something we will consider in more detail in the context of corporate governance, in subsequent chapters.)

The size and composition of a board indicate the board's ability to provide strategic management resources to a firm. One of the main benefits which directors bring to organisations is the information they offer, in the form of advice or recommendations (know-how).

RDT suggests that board size and composition are not random or independent factors, but rather, are rational organisational responses to the external environment. This implies that firms with higher degrees of interdependence also require a higher ratio of 'outsider' (non-executive) directors with relevant experience.

'Insiders' are members of firm's top management who also serve on the board of directors. 'Outsiders' are members of the board of directors who are not otherwise employed by the firm. 'Independent outsiders' are outsiders who have no business connections with the firm.

Another perspective is that the number of other directorships each director holds can also be benefit, suggesting that 'resource-rich' directors (who have experience from sitting on the boards of a number of companies) can share their experience from one company to another. As such, it is not the just the number, but the type of directors which is important.

PART A THE FOUNDATIONS OF GOVERNANCE

Similarly, if firms are able to attract powerful members of the community onto their boards, this can help to acquire critical resources from the environment.

This approach is consistent with corporate governance recommendations for the composition of the board which we will consider in Chapter 3.

4 Shareholder activism

> **FAST FORWARD**
>
> There have been many high-profile incidents of shareholder activism as shareholders try to influence the way companies are managed.

4.1 Purpose of shareholder activism

Key term

> **Shareholder activism** is 'the way shareholders can assert their power as owners of the company to influence its behaviour.' [European Corporate Governance Institute]

Activism covers a broad spectrum of activities. The overriding rationale behind shareholder activism is to make companies more accountable to shareholders and to increase shareholders' influence over a company's strategy generally.

(**Note.** In this context, the shareholders we are considering are external investors; not directors who also hold shares in a company, for example as a result of their share options maturing).

Although shareholders don't manage a company, there are still ways for them to influence its board of directors and senior management. In some cases shareholders may engage in dialogue with a company's management to raise concerns they have about a particular issue, while in other cases formal proposals are voted on at an annual general meeting.

The notion of shareholders (as owners of a company) wanting to assert their power is not new, but historically they had done so in private – through discussions with management behind closed doors. However, shareholder activism has become more apparent to the outside world as shareholders have adopted higher profile tactics in their efforts to determine a company's course of action or strategy.

The profile of shareholder activism has also been heightened by the increased use of social media. For example, blogs and posts allow shareholder activists to have a public voice, and to publicise their issues or concerns about a company's performance or about management's performance.

The growing demand from stakeholders and the general public has increased the expectation on companies to manage and disclose Environmental, social and governance (ESG) impacts (covered in more detail in Chapter 6). This has led to the emergence of an increasing level of ESG shareholder activism. The two case studies that follow demonstrate this.

Case Study

An article in the New York Times published in May 2021 (updated September 2021) described how oil giant Exxon Mobil was defeated 'when shareholders of Exxon Mobil elected at least two board candidates nominated by activist investors who pledged to steer the company toward cleaner energy and away from oil and gas.'

The report went on to say: 'The success of the campaign, led by a tiny hedge fund against the nation's largest oil company, could force the energy industry to confront climate change and embolden Wall Street investment firms that are prioritising the issue. Analysts could not recall another time that Exxon management had lost a vote against company-picked directors.'

(Source: New York Times (2021) *Climate Activists Defeat Exxon in Push for Clean Energy* [Online]. Available from: https://www.nytimes.com/2021/05/26/business/exxon-mobil-climate-change.html [Accessed 3 July 2024]).

Case Study

Another article in the New York Times published in January 2023 reports on a deal that technology giant Apple reached with investors to audit labour practices.

The article reported the action taken by the company after pressure from investors and stated that 'as part of its agreement with the coalition of investors …. Apple agreed to hire a third-party firm to conduct the assessment.'

The report contained details that the action was taken after the coalition of investors filed a shareholder proposal 'urging Apple to hire an outside firm to assess whether the company was following through on its stated commitment to labour rights.'

This is another example of shareholder activism and, at the time of publication of the article, it demonstrated that investors with approximately $7 billion worth of Apple stock were able to influence a company with a market capitalisation of more than $2 trillion.

(Source: New York Times (2023) *Apple Reaches Deal With Investors to Audit Its Labor Practices* [Online]. Available from: https://www.nytimes.com/2023/01/17/business/economy/apple-labor.html [Accessed 3 July 2024]).

4.2 Drivers for shareholder activism

Shareholder activists can be motivated by many different factors. The UK Institutional Shareholders' Committee has identified a number of reasons why shareholders might want to intervene:

(a) To raise concerns about the strategy being pursued, in terms of products, markets and investments, and/or to ensure a different strategy is pursued in order to improve performance and profitability

(b) To influence the outcome of a takeover or other merger and acquisition activity

(c) Poor operational performance, particularly if one of more key business segments (or business units) has persistently underperformed. (In this respect, shareholders may also seek the disposal of under-performing assets).

(d) Major failures in internal controls; particularly in sensitive areas such as health and safety, pollution or quality.

(e) Poor attitudes towards corporate social responsibility and management of ESG impacts and dependencies; for example, poor working conditions in a company's factories, or across its supply chain or failure to reduce emissions and waste that is harmful to the environment.

(f) Failure to comply with laws and regulations, or corporate governance codes

(g) The company's management is being dominated by a small group of executive directors, and the non-executive directors are failing to hold management to account

(h) Excessive levels of directors' remuneration, or concerns that directors' remuneration packages do not reward value creation

(i) To ensure changes to a company's board – either removing individual directors, or replacing the board as a whole.

4.3 Implications of shareholder activism

Despite the potential reasons for it, shareholder activism remains controversial. Proponents argue that companies with active and engaged shareholders are more likely to be successful in the long term than those whose shareholders are passive and do not hold the board to account for a company's performance. For example, by forcing a debate about a company's strategy and leadership, shareholder activism could potentially help to improve the company's performance.

Opponents of shareholder activism say that it is disruptive, arguing that the uninformed actions of shareholders, and their hostility to management, can weaken strong companies. Also, some critics view shareholder activists as 'corporate raiders' who aren't interested in the long term future of the company, but buy shares in a company they perceive to be undervalued and then push through changes in order to increase share value. This then enables them to generate a massive return on their shares.

Ultimately, though, the issues around shareholder activism again link back to the agency problem. Although shareholders do not manage the company, to what extent should they be able to influence the board of directors and the company's management? This question becomes even more important if a company (or its management) is under-performing. If shareholders feel a company is underperforming – and not maximising the value it generates for them as owners – why should they not be entitled to voice their concerns about this? Similarly, shareholders who consider that the company is failing in its corporate social concerns, for example by causing pollution, should be entitled to voice their concerns.

In this respect, discussions around shareholder activism perhaps also highlight the need for improved relations and communications between boards and shareholders – and this also has potential implications for corporate governance.

We build on the knowledge from this chapter when we look at managing stakeholders later in this book.

Chapter roundup

- In corporate entities the **separation of ownership from control** arises from shareholders, the firm's **principals**, being different people from the firm's managers, the paid **agents** of the shareholders.

- The **agency problem** refers to the problem that agents will pursue their personal interests, sometimes at the expense of making profits for the principals. This can be addressed by **incentivisation**, basing the earnings of agents on the profits given to principals.

- **Agency** is extremely important in corporate governance as often the directors/managers are acting as agents for the owners. Corporate governance frameworks aim to ensure directors/managers **fulfil their responsibilities** as agents by requiring disclosure and suggesting they be rewarded on the basis of performance.

- **Stakeholder theory** highlights that firms need to be accountable to a wide range of stakeholder groups, and not just to their shareholders.

- Directors and managers need to be aware of the **interests of stakeholders** in governance.

- Resource dependency theory considers the power relationships between providers of resources and those who require those resources. This theory has implications for the composition of the board of directors.

- There have been many high-profile incidents of shareholder activism as shareholders try to influence the way companies are managed.

Quick quiz

1. In a modern business corporation, who are the agents and who are the principals?

2. Which of these statements about agency relationships are true?

    (a) Auditors are the agents of the directors
    (b) Directors are the agents of the shareholders
    (c) Shareholders are the agents of the company

3. Suggest three reasons why shareholders may not be able to control the decisions of the firms they have invested in.

4. What does the term 'stakeholders' mean?

5. Match the stakeholder with the reason why they are interested in a company

Stakeholder	Reason
(1) Customer	(a) To assess whether rules are being followed
(2) Employees	(b) To assess likelihood of continuing supply and quality
(3) Regulator	(c) To assess likelihood of company continuing, assess whether salaries are fair

6. What are the two factors which influence the importance of particular resources to an organisation?

7. Suggest three ways in which shareholders can regain control over firms.

Answers to quick quiz

1. The agents are the paid managers of the business who are supposed to be acting in the best interests of their principals. The principals are the shareholders of the business.

2. Only (b) is true. (a) is false because auditors are the agents of the shareholders, not the directors. (c) is false because shareholders are principals, not agents.

3. Shareholders may be unable to control firms due to infrequent shareholder meetings, lack of information from management about what the firm is doing, and the desire of managers to do things to benefit themselves rather than the things that will benefit the shareholders.

4. The stakeholders of an organisation are people or organisations who have a legitimate interest in the strategy and behaviour of that organisation.

5. 1 (b)
   2 (c)
   3 (a)

6. **Criticality** (how critical a resource is) and **scarcity** (how easily available the resource is).

7. Shareholders can regain control by more effective scrutiny of management decisions, providing incentives to management linked to profits, and by strengthening some of the measures of corporate governance.

End of chapter questions

1.1 Which of the following statements is false?

   A   Directors are the agents of the shareholders
   B   External auditors are the agents of the shareholders
   C   Internal auditors are the agents of the external auditors
   D   Shareholders are the agents of neither directors or auditors

1.2 Which of the following is an agency problem?

   A   Directors may not be competent
   B   Directors and shareholders may have different attitudes to risk
   C   External auditors may not be competent
   D   There is separation of ownership and management

1.3 Which of the following correctly defines a stakeholder?

   A   Those who own shares in the company
   B   Those who have a financial interest in the company
   C   Those who can affect or be affected by the achievements of the company's objectives
   D   Those who act on behalf of the company

1.4 Which two factors determine the importance of a resource to a firm under resource dependency theory?

   A   Scarcity and power
   B   Criticality and dependence
   C   Power and dependence
   D   Scarcity and criticality

1.5 Which of the following is not an agency cost?

   A   Dividends paid to shareholders
   B   Audit fee
   C   Directors' bonuses
   D   Legal fees

Overview of corporate governance

Topic list	Syllabus reference
1 The corporate governance problem	B1.3
2 The historical development of corporate governance	B1.4
3 Approaches to corporate governance	B1.4, B1.5
4 Reporting on corporate governance	B1.3, B1.4

Introduction

In this chapter we provide an overview of corporate governance. In Section 1 we consider the reason why corporate governance guidance is required and in Section 2 we consider the historical development of corporate governance guidance.

Section 3 considers different approaches towards corporate governance and Section 4 follows on to consider how corporate governance compliance or noncompliance may be reported.

PART A   THE FOUNDATIONS OF GOVERNANCE

1 The corporate governance problem

FAST FORWARD

> Good corporate governance is important because the owners of a company and the people who manage the company are not always the same people. Good corporate governance will help to protect the interests of shareholders and other stakeholders.

1.1 What is corporate governance

Key term

> '**Corporate governance** is the system by which companies are directed and controlled.'
> (Report of the Cadbury Committee (UK))
>
> **Corporate governance** involves a set of relationships between a company's management, board, shareholders and stakeholders. Corporate governance also provides the structure and systems through which the company is directed and its objectives are set, and the means of attaining those objectives and monitoring performance are determined.
> (Organisation for Economic Co-operation and Development (OECD))

1.2 The driving forces of governance development

Corporate governance issues came to prominence originally during the 1970s. The main, but not the only, drivers associated with the increasing demand for the development of governance were:

- **Increasing internationalisation and globalisation** meant that investors, and institutional investors in particular, began to invest outside their home countries..

- Issues concerning the fairness and transparency **financial reporting** were raised by many investors and were the focus of much debate and litigation.

- An increasing number of **high profile corporate scandals** and collapses prompted the development of governance codes in the early 1990s. However other scandals since then have raised questions about further measures that may be necessary.

> You may have heard have of some famous corporate scandals, such as Enron, Madoff, Lehman Brothers. The following link has brief details of corporate scandals going back to 1494:
> https://en.wikipedia.org/wiki/List_of_corporate_collapses_and_scandals

1.3 The advantages of corporate governance

Good corporate governance has several advantages:

- It provides a **framework** for an organisation to pursue its strategy in an **ethical and effective** way and **offers safeguards against misuse of resources**, human, financial, physical or intellectual.

- It can help to **attract new investment** into companies, particularly in developing nations, because it should mean that shareholders can **trust** those responsible for running and monitoring the company.

- It increases **accountability** to shareholders and other stakeholders.

- It **helps to increase the confidence of capital markets in companies.**

1.4 Risks of poor corporate governance

Corporate scandals over a number of years have highlighted the need for guidance to tackle the various risks and problems that can arise in organisations' systems of governance.

1.4.1 The board of directors

Boards that have failed to manage companies effectively have been a key aspect of governance scandals. Common problems include:

- Boards dominated by a single senior executive, with other board members merely acting as a rubber stamp.
- Appointments being made by personal recommendation rather than a formal, objective process. This could lead to directors lacking the knowledge or skills necessary to contribute effectively.
- Boards that meet irregularly or fail to consider systematically the organisation's activities and risks.
- Board failure to properly supervise employees.

1.4.2 Directors' remuneration

Complaints over directors' remuneration levels have not only focused on remuneration levels but on the unwillingness of those who can challenge remuneration packages effectively to do so. Problems include:

- **Excessive remuneration levels**
- Directors being **rewarded for failure**, for example receiving bonuses when their companies have performed poorly and receiving **significant compensation payments** when they lose office
- **Remuneration arrangements** providing incentives for directors to allow excessive risk-taking

1.4.3 Accounts and audit

Many companies involved in scandals have had glaring weaknesses in internal control that had not been picked up by those monitoring control. These weaknesses included:

- A **lack of internal audit**. As we shall see in Chapter 15, internal audit is a key function within a company which oversees systems and controls.
- A **lack of adequate technical knowledge** in key roles, for example in the audit committee or in senior accounting positions.
- A **lack of proper scrutiny** by external auditors, perhaps because of fears of losing the audit.

2 The historical development of corporate governance

> **FAST FORWARD**
>
> The UK Corporate Governance Code is typical of many codes around the world.

2.1 A history of corporate governance in the UK

The UK Corporate Governance Code (formerly known as The Combined Code on Corporate Governance) is a good example of a typical corporate governance code. We will be looking at corporate governance approaches and provisions later in this chapter and in subsequent chapters. The following table provides a short history of corporate governance in the UK.

PART A   THE FOUNDATIONS OF GOVERNANCE

Name of report/Code*	Date	Main areas covered
Cadbury	1992	Composition and role of board, audit committees
Greenbury	1995	Directors' remuneration
Hampel	1998	Recommended production of Combined Code based on previous reports
Combined Code	1998	Board, remuneration, accountability and audit, risk assessment
Turnbull	1999	Risk management and internal control
Smith	2003	Audit committees
Higgs	2003	Non-executive directors
UK Corporate Governance Code	2010	The Combined Code became the UK Corporate Governance Code in 2010.
UK Stewardship Code 2020	2019	Guidance on good practice for investors. The original Stewardship Code was published in 2010 and was last updated in 2019 to become the UK Stewardship Code 2020.
UK Corporate Governance Code 2024	2024	The Code has been updated several times since it was first published in 2010. 2024 is the most recent revision.

* These are all published by the Financial Reporting Council (FRC) and can be found on the FRC website (www.frc.org.uk). The reports/Codes included are just selected parts of the full history which can be found in the overview of corporate governance provided on the FRC website (https://www.frc.org.uk/library/standards-codes-policy/corporate-governance/corporate-governance-overview/ [Online]. Last accessed 9 July 2024).

The UK Corporate Governance Code applies to all companies with a **premium listing of equity shares in the UK**, whether incorporated in the UK or elsewhere.

The updated 2024 Code applies to accounting periods beginning on or after 1 January 2025, with the exception of Provision 29. This provision is applicable for accounting periods beginning on or after 1 January 2026.

As we progress through the rest of this chapter and the rest of the chapters in part A of this Workbook we will look at the provisions of the UK Corporate Governance Code 2024 relevant to each topic being covered.

The FRC has also published further Audit Committee specific guidance to assist with applying provisions of the UK Corporate Governance Code relating to audit committees. Audit committees are covered in Chapter 5.

A point to note is, although the FRC currently regulates auditors, accountants and sets the UK's Corporate Governance and Stewardship Codes, the UK government had indicated that the FRC would be replaced by a regulator with greater powers (the Audit, Reporting and Governance Authority, or ARGA). However, due to delays in putting in place the necessary legislation to create AGRA, the timetable for the transition from the FRC to ARGA remains unclear. For the purposes of your exam you should assume the FRC remains in place.

2.2 Corporate governance codes internationally

Because of increasing international trade and cross-border links, there is significant pressure for the development of internationally comparable practices and standards.

2.2.1 G20/OECD Principles of Corporate Governance

FAST FORWARD

The OECD has developed a set of principles to assist in the development of corporate governance codes around the world.

The Organisation for Economic Co-operation and Development (OECD) has carried out an extensive consultation with member countries, and developed a **set of principles of corporate governance** that countries and companies should work towards achieving.

'The G20/OECD Principles of Corporate Governance provide guidance to help policy makers evaluate and improve the legal, regulatory and institutional framework for corporate governance, with a view to supporting market confidence and integrity, economic efficiency, sustainable growth and financial stability' (G20/OECD Principles of Corporate Governance 2023).

The **Principles of Corporate Governance** were issued in 1999 and revised in 2015 and then underwent a **comprehensive review** between 2021-2023 to reflect recent evolutions in corporate governance and capital markets. The revised Principles were adopted by the OECD Council in June 2023 and endorsed by G20 Leaders in September 2023.

The Principles aim to provide a robust but flexible reference for policy makers and market participants in each country to **develop their own frameworks for corporate governance**. They are **non-binding** and do not aim to provide detailed prescriptions for national legislation.

The OECD principles cover six areas.

G20/OECD Principles of Corporate Governance
I Ensuring the basis for an effective corporate governance framework   The corporate governance framework should promote **transparent and fair markets**, and the **efficient allocation of resources**. It should be consistent with the rule of law and support effective supervision and enforcement.
II The rights and equitable treatment of shareholders and key ownership functions   The corporate governance framework should **protect and facilitate the exercise of shareholders' rights and ensure the equitable treatment of all shareholders**, including minority and foreign shareholders.   All shareholders should have the opportunity to obtain effective redress for violation of their rights at a reasonable cost and without excessive delay.
III Institutional investors, stock markets, and other intermediaries   The corporate governance framework should provide sound **incentives** throughout the investment chain and provide **for stock markets to function in a way that contributes to good corporate governance**.
IV Disclosure and transparency   The corporate governance framework should ensure that **timely and accurate disclosure is made on all material matters** regarding the corporation, including the financial situation, performance, ownership, and governance of the company.
V The responsibilities of the board   The corporate governance framework should ensure the **strategic guidance** of the company, the **effective monitoring** of management by the board, and the board's accountability to the company and the shareholders.
VI Sustainability and resilience   The corporate governance framework should provide incentives for companies and their investors to **make decisions and manage their risks, in a way that contributes to the sustainability and resilience of the corporation**.

(OECD, 2023)

The G20/OECD Principles can be found on the OECD website at: https://doi.org/10.1787/ed750b30-en

PART A   THE FOUNDATIONS OF GOVERNANCE

2.2.2 Significance of international codes and guidance

International guidance such as the OECD principles have been developed from best practice in a number of jurisdictions. As such, they can be seen as **representing an international consensus**. They stress global issues that are important to companies operating in a number of jurisdictions.

Although the OECD code is **non-binding**, its principles have been incorporated into national guidance by a number of countries including Greece and China. The OECD principles have also been used by organisations such as the World Bank as a basis for assessing the corporate governance frameworks and practices in individual countries. These assessments are used to determine the level of policy dialogue with, and technical assistance given to, these countries.

When applying the G20/OECD principles, countries may take a hybrid approach and make some elements of corporate governance mandatory and some voluntary.

2.2.3 Other country codes: Sarbanes-Oxley

FAST FORWARD

> The Sarbanes-Oxley legislation requires directors to report on the effectiveness of the controls over financial reporting, limits the services auditors can provide and requires listed companies to establish an audit committee. It adopts a rules-based approach to governance.

One of the most significant scandals in America this century was the **Enron** scandal, when one of the country's biggest companies filed for bankruptcy. The scandal also resulted in the closure of Arthur Andersen, one of the Big Five accountancy firms who had audited Enron's accounts. Enquiries into the scandal exposed a number of weaknesses in the company's governance:

- Lack of transparency in the accounts. There were methods of, for example, over-inflating revenues and offloading debt that were not properly disclosed.

- Ineffective board. The management team was criticised for being arrogant and over ambitious, the CEO had too much influence and the non-executive directors were weak.

- Inadequate scrutiny by the external auditors; Arthur Andersen failed to identify/question dubious accounting treatments and there were allegations of conflicts of interest.

- Executive compensation methods seemed to encourage the overstatement of short-term profits.

The US government response to the Enron scandal was the **Sarbanes-Oxley Act 2002**. The Act applies to all companies that are required to file periodic reports with the Securities and Exchange Commission (SEC) and also has implications for overseas subsidiaries of those companies.

Sarbanes-Oxley shifts responsibility for financial integrity and accuracy to the board's **audit committee**, which typically comprises three independent directors, one of whom has to meet certain financial literacy requirements.

Sarbanes-Oxley also requires companies to increase their financial statement **disclosures**, to have an internal **code of ethics** and to impose **restrictions on share trading** by, and **loans to**, corporate officers.

The Sarbanes-Oxley Act led to the formation of **The Public Company Accounting Oversight Board (PCAOB),** to oversee the audit of public companies that are subject to the securities laws. The Board **oversees** the work done by auditors for these companies and has **inspection and disciplinary powers** over firms.

3 Approaches to corporate governance

FAST FORWARD

Many governance codes have adopted a **principles-based approach**, allowing companies flexibility in interpreting the codes' requirements and to explain if they have departed from the provisions of the code. Other codes have a rules-based approach.

3.1 Principles-based vs. rules-based

A continuing debate on corporate governance is whether the guidance should predominantly be in the form of principles, or whether there is a need for detailed laws or regulations.

Regardless of the approach taken, most corporate governance codes worldwide are designed to achieve the following:

- Adherence to and satisfaction of the **strategic objectives** of the organisation
- Reinforcing the local **statutory and listing requirements** relating to governance.
- Assisting companies in **minimising risk**, especially financial, legal and reputational risks.
- Promoting **ethical behaviour**.
- Underpinning **investor confidence**.
- Fulfilling **responsibilities to all stakeholders** and minimising **potential conflicts of interest**.
- Establishing **clear accountability** at senior levels within an organisation.
- Maintaining the **independence** of non-executive directors, and internal and external auditors.
- Providing accurate and timely reporting of **financial and operational data**.
- Encouraging more proactive **involvement** of owners/members in the effective management of the organisation.

3.2 Characteristics of a principles-based approach

(a) **Focus on aims**

The approach focuses on **objectives** (for example the objective that shareholders holding a minority of shares in a company should be treated fairly) rather than the **mechanisms** by which these objectives will be achieved.

(b) **Flexibility**

A principles-based approach can lay stress on those elements of corporate governance to which rules **cannot easily be applied** as circumstances will be different in different organisation, for example the internal controls that are required.

(c) **Breadth of application**

Principles-based approaches can applied across **different legal jurisdictions** rather being founded in the legal regulations of one country.

(d) **Comply or explain**

Recommendations are usually enforced on a **comply or explain basis** (see Section 4).

(e) **Role of capital markets**

Principles-based approaches are often adopted in jurisdictions where **stock market regulators** have had the prime role in developing corporate governance.

3.3 Characteristics of a rules-based approach

(a) **Emphasis on achievements**

Rules-based systems place more emphasis on **achieving targets,** however there may be little incentive to **achieve more** than is required by the rules.

(b) **Compulsory compliance**

There is **no flexibility** for different circumstances, for organisations of varying size or in different stages of development.

(c) **Visibility of compliance**

It should be **easy to see** whether there has been compliance with the rules, but only where the rules are **unambiguous and the evidence is clear.**

(d) **Limitations of rules**

Enforcers may find it difficult to deal with **questionable situations** that are not covered sufficiently in the rulebook. Keeping legislation up-to-date to keep loopholes closed is a reactive and probably costly process.

(e) **Criminal sanctions**

Rules-based approaches tend to be found in legal jurisdictions and cultures that lay great emphasis on **obeying the letter of the law** rather than the spirit. They often take the form of legislation themselves, for example the Sarbanes-Oxley Act. The amount of legislation may give rise to **significant compliance costs.**

3.4 Advantages of a principles-based approach

Possible advantages of basing corporate governance codes on a series of principles are:

- Avoids inflexible legislation with costly compliance
- Allows companies to develop their own more appropriate report
- More flexibility, for example can allow for transitional arrangements and unusual circumstances
- Emphasis on explanations; businesses can explain why they have departed from the specific provisions if they feel it is appropriate.
- Emphasis on investor decisions; allows investors to make their own decisions

Example

Can you think of an example of an unusual circumstance where flexibility may be required?

Solution

A non-executive director may resign suddenly meaning that the company may have an insufficient number of non-executive directors to comply with corporate governance requirements until a replacement can be appointed.

3.5 Criticisms of a principles-based approach

There are a number of potential problems with a principles-based approach:

- Principles may be so broad that they are of very little use as a guide to best corporate governance practice.
- Investors cannot be confident of consistency of application with a principles-based approach.

- There may be confusion over what is compulsory and what isn't, for example Stock Exchange requirements.
- Some explanations may be inadequate.
- Investors may misunderstand the impact of companies failing to comply.

4 Reporting on corporate governance

FAST FORWARD

Many countries adopt a 'comply or explain' approach in their corporate governance codes.

4.1 Principles-based vs rules-based

How companies report on corporate governance is linked to whether codes are principles-based or rules-based. If codes are rules-based, then companies must comply with those rules or risk penalties. This could be termed a 'comply or else' approach'. For example, US listed companies must comply with the Sarbanes-Oxley legislation or face penalties of up to $1m together with up to ten years in prison for the corporate officer concerned. This has led to high Sarbanes-Oxley compliance costs.

4.2 Comply or explain

Many countries have adopted a concept known as 'comply or explain'. This essentially means that listed companies have to comply with corporate governance provisions or provide an explanation if they have not.

The thinking behind this approach is that, since investors generally disapprove of companies failing to comply with corporate governance, any failure to comply without good reason is likely to have a negative impact on share price. These market forces would therefore encourage companies to comply or risk a falling share price.

4.3 An example of comply or explain – the UK situation

All companies with a premium listing of equity shares in the UK are required under the Listing Rules to report on how they have applied the Principles of the UK Corporate Governance Code in their annual report and accounts (regardless of whether the company is incorporated in the UK or elsewhere).

The Code contains **broad Principles** and more **specific Provisions** which seek to apply the Principles. Listed companies have to report how they have applied the principles and either confirm that they have applied the provisions or, if they have not, provide an explanation as to why this has not been done. This is an illustration of the '**comply or explain**' concept.

The board can only choose not to comply with a specific provision if they believe that complying with the specific provision would have meant that they fail to comply with the broad principle. However the reasons for not complying with the specific provision should be clearly and fully explained to the shareholders. Any explanation must include details as to how actual practices are consistent with the overall broad principle to which a specific provision relates.

4.4 Alternatives to comply or explain

There are subtle differences in the wording used by different corporate governance codes, but the meaning is broadly similar to comply or explain. For example, the King Report in South Africa used the term 'apply or explain' which seemed to reflect that these were principles being applied rather than rules being complied with. A later version of the King Report, released in 2016, uses the term 'apply AND explain', the idea being that there is a presumption that the principles in the code will be applied. The Australian corporate governance code uses the term "if not, why not", meaning that companies must state why they have failed to follow a recommendation.

PART A   THE FOUNDATIONS OF GOVERNANCE

Chapter roundup

- Good corporate governance is important because the owners of a company and the people who manage the company are not always the same people. Good corporate governance will help to protect the interests of shareholders and other stakeholders.
- **Corporate governance** is the system by which companies are directed and controlled.'
- **The UK Corporate Governance Code is typical of many codes around the world.**
- The OECD has developed a set of principles to assist in the development of corporate governance codes around the world.
- The **Sarbanes-Oxley legislation** requires directors to **report on the effectiveness of the controls over financial reporting, limits the services auditors can provide** and requires listed companies to establish an **audit committee**. It adopts a **rules-based** approach to governance.
- Many governance codes have adopted a **principles-based approach**, allowing companies flexibility in interpreting the codes' requirements and to explain if they have departed from the provisions of the code. Other codes have a rules-based approach.
- Many countries adopt a 'comply or explain' approach in their corporate governance codes.

Quick quiz

1. An advantage of voluntary codes is that they are flexible and therefore suit different kinds of companies in different situations. True or false?

2. Corporate governance is a set of _____ between a company's _____, its _____ and other _____.

3. The Sarbanes-Oxley legislation requires directors to report on the effectiveness of the _____ over _____, limits the _____ auditors can provide and requires listed companies to establish _____.

4. The Sarbanes-Oxley legislation is principles-based. True or false?

5. In terms of reporting on corporate governance, the UK Code requires companies to _____ or _____ .

6. What is the name of the South African report on corporate governance?

Answers to quick quiz

1 True

2 Corporate governance is a set of relationships between a company's directors, its shareholders and other stakeholders.

3 The Sarbanes-Oxley legislation requires directors to report on the effectiveness of the controls over financial reporting, limits the services auditors can provide and requires listed companies to establish an audit committee.

4 False. Sarbanes-Oxley is rules-based.

5 In terms of reporting on corporate governance, the UK Code requires companies to comply or explain.

6 The King Report.

End of chapter questions

2.1 Which of the following is not an advantage of corporate governance?

    A   It helps to increase the confidence of capital markets
    B   It helps to prevent misuse of resources
    C   It increases accountability to shareholders and other stakeholders
    D   It provides an independent opinion on whether the accounts give a true and fair view.

2.2 Which publication provides a point of reference for policy makers and market participants in each country to develop their own frameworks for corporate governance?

    A   The UK Corporate Governance Code
    B   The Hampel Report
    C   The G20/OECD Principles of Corporate Governance
    D   The King Report

2.3 Which of the following best describes Corporate Governance?

    A   The system by which annual financial statements are produced
    B   The system by which companies assess business risks
    C   The system by which companies are directed and controlled
    D   The system by which stakeholders are kept informed by the board of directors

2.4 Which one of the following does not describe a G20/OECD principle of corporate governance?

    A   To protect directors' rights and ensure all directors are treated fairly.
    B   To promote transparent and fair markets and the efficient allocation of resources
    C   To ensure timely and accurate disclosure of material matters
    D   To ensure companies are effectively guided and monitored

2.5 Which of the following is not a characteristic of a principles-based approach?

    A   Comply or explain
    B   Criminal sanctions
    C   Flexibility
    D   Focus on aims

PART A THE FOUNDATIONS OF GOVERNANCE

The board

Topic list	Syllabus reference
1 Role of the board	B1.4, B1.6
2 Board structures	B1.5, B1.7, B1.8
3 Effective boards	B1.4, B1,6

Introduction

In Chapter 1, we considered agency theory and the fact that management of companies is delegated to the directors, who act as agents of the shareholders. In Chapter 2 we introduced the subject of corporate governance and noted that many corporate governance problems are caused by the board not doing its job properly.

In this chapter we look at the board in more detail. In Section 1 we consider the role of the board, in Section 2 we consider approaches worldwide to structuring the board, and in Section 3 we look at what makes a board effective.

1 Role of the board

FAST FORWARD

The board should be responsible for taking major **policy** and **strategic** decisions.

1.1 Definition of board's role

Corporate governance is all about making sure companies are properly managed, and the board of the company represents the most senior level of management. In order for the board to be effective, and to do the job it is supposed to do, its role must be defined carefully.

We will consider directors in more detail in Chapter 4, but note, for the purposes of understanding this chapter, that there are two types of directors; **executive directors** are those who have a functional responsibility (eg sales director) in the company and are part of the management team, whereas **non-executive directors** have no functional responsibility, are part-time and part of the supervisory function.

Case Study

The South African King Report provides a good summary of the role of the board.

> To define the purpose of the company and the values by which the company will perform its daily existence and to identify the stakeholders relevant to the business of the company. The board must then develop a strategy combining all three factors and ensure management implements that strategy.

The King Report stresses that the board is responsible for assets and for ensuring the company follows its strategic plan. For management to be held properly responsible, there must be a system in place that allows for **corrective action** and **penalising mismanagement**. Responsible management should do, when necessary, whatever it takes to set the company on the right path.

The UK Corporate Governance Code provides details of the roles undertaken by a strong board within corporate governance principles included in Section 1 *Board leadership and company purpose*.

These principles are covered later in this Chapter when we look at what makes an effective board.

1.2 Matters for board decision

The board should have a **formal schedule of matters** specifically reserved to it for decision at board meetings. Some decisions such as **mergers and takeovers** are **fundamental** to the business and hence should not be taken solely by executive managers. Other decisions include **acquisitions and disposals of assets of the company** or its subsidiaries that are material to the company, **investments, capital projects, bank borrowing** facilities, **loans**, foreign currency transactions, all **above a set size** (to be determined by the board).

1.3 Other tasks

- Monitoring the Chief Executive Officer
- Overseeing strategy
- Monitoring risks, control systems and governance
- Monitoring the human capital aspects of the company eg succession, morale, training, remuneration etc.

- Monitoring sustainability-related risks and dependencies (covered in Chapter 6)
- Managing potential conflicts of interest
- Ensuring that there is effective communication of its strategic plans, both internally and externally

1.4 Role of the board in strategy setting

Although boards are responsible ultimately for strategy, they can manage strategic development in different ways.

- Boards can be actively involved with executive management in strategic development. However the primary role of non-executive directors is to **monitor decision-making** by executive directors and there is a conflict of interests if they are also significantly involved in decision-making.
- Boards adopt more of a **stewardship role** – directors approve strategic plans developed by senior managers. There is a danger that the board is too permissive and allows managers to act in their own interests rather than protecting the interests of shareholders and other stakeholders.

2 Board structures

FAST FORWARD

> There are different structures of board in different parts of the world. The two most common are the unitary structure and the two-tier structure.

There are two main models of board structure – the **unitary structure** (or board of directors) and the **two-tier structure**. We will also touch on the Japanese 'keiretsu' model and the Asian family-based model.

2.1 Unitary structure

The **unitary structure** is the dominant model in corporate governance systems, and is commonly found in the United States, UK, Ireland, Australia, Canada, Japan and Russia. The board of directors consists of executive directors (managers of the company) and **independent** non-executive directors. The biggest advantage of this structure is the better communication between executives and non-executives and the ready access to corporate data and information by the non-executive directors.

The disadvantages relate mainly in the very powerful position of the CEO who, in a significant proportion of large companies, holds the chair function at the same time, thereby fully controlling the board's work. However, more and more companies are splitting this role. This will be covered in more detail in Chapter 4.

2.2 Two-tier structure

The **two-tier model** is used in Germany and many other European countries. The two-tier board system is based on two main bodies: the **supervisory board** and the **management board** (the executives). The supervisory board is exclusively comprised of independent non-executive directors, who may include representatives from employees and lenders. The supervisory board appoints the CEO, structures executive remuneration, selects the auditor and follows corporate strategy.

The major weakness of the two-tier system lies in the **limited access to corporate data** by the supervisory level, which has to be provided by the management board. The relative separation of board members and executives is mitigated by regular meetings and committees. This system may also be more expensive as more people may be involved.

2.3 The Japanese business network model ('Keiretsu')

Keiretsu is the term given to a structure in which organisations (usually buyers and suppliers) are linked by **taking small stakes in each other** to reinforce their already close business relationship. The rationale

behind this structure is that businesses are more likely to reach a way of working that is of mutual benefit if they have such close ties. The boards of such organisations are formal in structure and large in size. Independent external directors are unacceptable as it is felt that they will not understand the company culture.

South Korea's **chaebol** are industrial groupings that are modelled closely on the keiretsu. Outside Japan, the word keiretsu has become attached to any loose network of alliances between more than two organisations.

2.4 The Asian family-based model

Firms that are structured this way are centred on the family, with close family control. These organisations still operate under the relevant corporate governance model (such as the unitary board structure under the Anglo-Saxon model) and have to comply with relevant codes and, if relevant, listing rules. However, in family-based firms management may be centred on the dominance and control of a central figure. Boards may consist largely of family members, and the number of independent non-executive directors may be limited. A major risk in this model is the difficulty for the board to act as independent body.

3 Effective boards

> In order to have an effective board, one that achieves its objectives, it's important for the board to have capable and competent people.
>
> Directors should have a **mix of skills** and their **performance** should be assessed regularly.
>
> Appointments should be conducted by formal procedures administered by a **nomination committee**.

3.1 Characteristics of an effective board

Effective board behaviour can be achieved if the board possesses the following six traits:

- **Commitment** – diligently performing duties and devoting enough time to company affairs.
- **Character** – an effective board will comprise of a diverse mix of trustworthy individuals that possess high levels of integrity and professionalism.
- **Collaboration** – the directors should support and trust each other.
- **Competence** – the board should possess the collective knowledge and skills required to govern the company effectively, including core skills in finance, law, governance and human resources as well as commercial acumen.
- **Creativity** – the board should look for new ways of working, new commercial developments, and new ways to respond to the challenges presented by the environment.
- **Contribution** – all members should be empowered to and take the initiative to contribute effectively.

3.2 Composition of the board

Key issues for consideration are:

- **Size** – with greater size can come greater opportunities for representation of varied views. However this can be at the expense of ease of operation and coherence of decision-making.
- **Inside/outside mix** – what proportion should be executive decision-makers whose main employment is by the company and what proportion should be outsiders?
- **Diversity** – the issues here include male/female mix, representation from ethnic minorities, representatives from professions other than business (for example academia).

3.2.1 Board size

A large board provides significant opportunities for **varied views** to be put forward. However a large board can make it difficult to achieve ease of operation and coherence of decision-making.

A large board will mean that directors are not overloaded, for example by committee work, which may be a particular risk for non-executive directors with limited time. A complex company operating in a complicated environment may need a bigger board to have access to a wide range of skills and experience. On the other hand a company operating in a fast-moving environment where rapid decision-making is required may be better served by a smaller board.

3.2.2 Inside/outside mix

It is advantageous for a company to have a balance of executive and non-executive directors to prevent power being concentrated in the hands of a few executive directors, enabling them to abuse their powers.

We will consider this issue in detail in Chapter 4.

3.2.3 Board diversity

Categories of diversity include age, race, ethnicity, gender education, experience.

Diversity of expertise and backgrounds can help the board to function efficiently.

Advantages include:

- Access to the best talent available
- A broad range of knowledge from the variety of directors
- The board is more representative of different stakeholders

Further detail of a trend in increased board diversity and the related positive effects are highlighted in the case studies that follow.

Case Study — **Board diversity**

Spencer Stuart's US Board Index 2023 examined the latest data and trends in board composition, board governance practices and director compensation among S&P 500* companies.

The reported highlights from the 2023 index stated that 'S&P 500 boards are becoming more diverse. Directors who self-identify as women and/or an underrepresented minority and/or LGBTQ+ represent a significant majority of directors joining S&P 500 boards and make up a growing percentage of S&P 500 directors overall. They now make up 33% and 24% of boards, respectively'.

The full details of the findings can be found at the link below and include industry comparisons, new director and diversity recruiting trends, and director compensation information.

(Source: Diversity, 2023 *US Spencer Stuart Board Index* [Online]. Available from: https://www.spencerstuart.com/research-and-insight/us-board-index [Accessed 28 June 2024].)

*The S&P Index is a market-capitalisation-weighted index of 500 leading publicly traded companies in the USA.

Case Study: FRC - Board Diversity and Effectiveness

The FRC published a report in 2021 on board diversity and effectiveness in FTSE 350 companies.

It reported an increase in the level of board diversity and evidence of the positive effects of board diversity. The following graphic summarising the effect of diversity is taken from the executive summary of the report.

Effects of Diversity

- Boardroom culture becomes more relationship focused and collaborative
- Better future financial performance (as measured by EBITDA margin), especially after three years
- Higher stock returns, especially when diversity is well managed
- Boards less likely to experience shareholder dissent

(Source: The full FRC *Board Diversity and Effectiveness in FTSE 350 Companies* report is available at: https://media.frc.org.uk/documents/FRC_Board_Diversity_and_Effectiveness_in_FTSE_350_Companies.pdf [Accessed 2 July 2024].)

3.3 Competence

> **FAST FORWARD** Boards will be more effective if the directors are competent. The likelihood of competence is increased if appointment, training, and appraisal of directors is well-managed.

3.3.1 Appointment

It is important that the best qualified candidates are appointed to the board, rather than directors be appointed due to their relationships with existing directors. One way to achieve this is to establish a nomination committee to oversee the appointment of directors. This will be considered in Chapter 5.

3.3.2 Training

> **FAST FORWARD** Even if directors are very experienced, they still need to be given information about the particular business and to keep their knowledge and skills up to date.

It is important for every director to receive appropriate training when first appointed to a board and subsequently as necessary. Training should include the general responsibilities of being a director and industry-specific issues.

Case Study

The UK Higgs Report provides detailed guidance on the development of an induction programme tailored to the needs of the company and individual directors.

Build an understanding of the nature of the company, its business and its markets	<ul><li>The company's culture and values</li><li>The company's products or services</li><li>Group structure/subsidiaries/joint ventures</li><li>The company's constitution, board procedures and matters reserved for the board</li><li>The company's principal assets, liabilities, significant contracts and major competitors</li><li>Major risks and risk management strategy</li><li>Key performance indicators</li><li>Regulatory constraints</li></ul>
Build a link with the company's people	<ul><li>Meetings with senior management</li><li>Visits to company sites other than headquarters, to learn about production and services, meet employees and build profile</li><li>Participating in board's strategy development</li><li>Briefing on internal procedures</li></ul>
Build an understanding of the company's main relationships including meetings with auditors	<ul><li>Major customers</li><li>Major suppliers</li><li>Major shareholders and customer relations policy</li></ul>

To remain effective, directors should **extend their knowledge and skills** continuously.

A variety of approaches to training may be appropriate, including lectures, case studies and networking groups.

3.3.3 Appraisal of board and individual directors

Appraisal of the board's performance is an important control over it, aimed at **improving board effectiveness, maximising strengths and tackling weaknesses**. It should be seen as an essential part of the **feedback** process within the company and may prompt the board to change its **methods** and/or **objectives**. The UK Corporate Governance Code recommends that **performance of the board, its committees, the chair and individual directors** should be formally **assessed once a year**. The assessment should be by an external third party who can bring **objectivity** to the process.

The external reviewer should be identified in the annual report and a statement made about any other connection it has with the company or individual directors.

In order to be conducted effectively, the appraisal of the whole board will need to include:

- A review of the board's systems (conduct of meetings, work of committees, quality of written documentation)
- Performance measurement in terms of the standards it has established, financial criteria, and non-financial criteria relating to individual directors
- Assessment of the board's role in the organisation (dealing with problems, communicating with stakeholders)

Additionally individual directors should have some form of individual appraisal.

3.4 Resources

> **FAST FORWARD**
>
> Boards should have sufficient time allocated to fulfil their role, and must be provided with high-quality information.

Boards must **meet sufficiently frequently**. Companies should amend their constitutions to provide for online and videoconference meetings if necessary.

Directors should have **sufficient time** to fulfil their responsibilities. The time commitment for non-executive directors should be set out when they are appointed, and they should undertake to have sufficient time to discharge their role.

It is important for the chair of the board to decide what information should be made available and for the directors to satisfy themselves that they have **appropriate information** of **sufficient quality** to make sound judgements. The South African King Report highlights the importance of the board receiving **relevant non-financial information** in addition to financial and quantitative information.

We conclude this chapter by looking at the principles of the UK Corporate Governance Code relating to board leadership and company purpose.

Case Study

Principles of the UK Corporate Governance Code (for listed UK companies)

Board Leadership and Company Purpose

A   A successful company is led by an effective and entrepreneurial board, whose role is to promote the long-term sustainable success of the company, generating value for shareholders and contributing to wider society. The board should ensure that the necessary resources, policies and practices are in place for the company to meet its objectives and measure performance against them.

B   The board should establish the company's purpose, values and strategy, and satisfy itself that these and its culture are all aligned. All directors must act with integrity, lead by example and promote the desired culture.

C   Governance reporting should focus on board decisions and their outcomes in the context of the company's strategy and objectives. Where the board reports on departures from the Code's provisions, it should provide a clear explanation.

D   In order for the company to meet its responsibilities to shareholders and stakeholders, the board should ensure effective engagement with, and encourage participation from, these parties.

E   The board should ensure that workforce policies and practices are consistent with the company's values and support its long-term sustainable success. The workforce should be able to raise any matters of concern.

(FRC *UK Corporate Governance Code 2024*: Section 1)

Chapter roundup

- The board should be responsible for taking major **policy** and **strategic** decisions.
- There are different structures of board in different parts of the world. The two most common are the unitary structure and the two-tier structure.
- In order to have an effective board, one that achieves its objectives, it's important for the board to have capable and competent people.
- Directors should have a **mix of skills** and their **performance** should be assessed regularly.
- Appointments should be conducted by formal procedures administered by a **nomination committee**.
- Boards will be more effective if the directors are competent. The likelihood of competence is increased if appointment, training, and appraisal of directors is well-managed.
- Even if directors are very experienced, they still need to be given information about the particular business and to keep their knowledge and skills up to date.
- Boards should have sufficient time allocated to fulfil their role, and must be provided with high-quality information.

Quick quiz

1. The board should be responsible for taking major _____ and _____ decisions.
2. The two main models of board structure are the _____ structure and the _____ structure.
3. What is the name of the Japanese business network model?
4. A large board provides significant opportunities for _____ to be put forward.
5. Experienced non-executive directors do not require any training when they join a board. True or false?
6. An advantage of diversity in the board is that there should be access to _____ .

PART A   THE FOUNDATIONS OF GOVERNANCE

Answers to quick quiz

1   The board should be responsible for taking major policy and strategic decisions.

2   The two main models of board structure are the unitary structure and the two-tier structure.

3   Keiretsu

4   A large board provides significant opportunities for varied views to be put forward.

5   False. Even experienced directors should have an induction about the particular characteristics of the company.

6   An advantage of diversity in the board is that there should be access to the best talent available.

End of chapter questions

3.1   Which of the followings are tasks that should be performed by the board of directors?

   (1)   Monitoring the Chief Executive Officer
   (2)   Overseeing strategy
   (3)   Monitoring risks, control systems and governance
   (4)   Preparing the financial statements

   A   (1), (2) and (3)
   B   (2), (3) and (4)
   C   (1), (3) and (4)
   D   (1), (2) and (4)

3.2   Which of the following board structures is more likely to be found in a country with accounting and laws based on the Anglo-Saxon model?

   A   Chaebol
   B   Unitary
   C   Two-tier
   D   Keiretsu

3.3   Which of the following C's is not a characteristic of an effective board?

   A   Character
   B   Competence
   C   Contribution
   D   Communication

3.4   Which committee should be set up to select and appoint directors?

   A   Audit committee
   B   Remuneration committee
   C   Nomination committee
   D   Risk management committee

3.5   In which of these countries are you mostly likely to see a two-tier board structure?

   A   USA
   B   Japan
   C   UK
   D   Germany

Board members (directors)

Topic list	Syllabus reference
1 Executive directors	B1.6
2 Non-executive directors	B1.6
3 Directors' remuneration	B1.6, B1.7

Introduction

In Chapter 3 we said that the board should consist of both executive and non-executive directors. The role of non-executive directors is to oversee how the executive directors manage the company and to prevent the executive directors abusing their powers.

In this chapter we look in more details at directors and their role. In Section 1 we consider executive directors and in Section 2 we consider non-executive directors. In Section 3 we look at directors' remuneration and measures that can be taken to prevent directors paying themselves too much.

PART A   THE FOUNDATIONS OF GOVERNANCE

1 Executive directors

> **FAST FORWARD**
> Executive directors are those who have functional management responsibilities within the business.

1.1 Who are executive directors

Executive directors are those who have functional management responsibilities within the business, for example the finance director, the sales director, the production director. They have a lot of power over day to day decisions. It is important that the executive directors are competent and have the appropriate qualifications, as we discussed in Chapter 3, to contribute towards the effectiveness of the board.

An executive director of particular importance is the Chief Executive Officer (CEO) or Managing Director.

1.2 The Chief Executive Officer (CEO)

> **FAST FORWARD**
> The CEO is responsible for leading the management team at and below board level.

The CEO is responsible for **running the organisation's business** and for **proposing and developing the group's strategy** in consultation with the directors and the board. The CEO is also responsible for **implementing the decisions of the board** and its committees.

The CEO is the senior executive in charge of the management team and is answerable to the board for the team's performance.

Case Study

The FRC's Corporate Governance Code Guidance published in January 2024 sits alongside the UK Corporate Governance Code. It describes **the role of the executive directors and the CEO** in particular. Some of the key points are summarised below

(a) Executive directors have the same duties as other members of a unitary board. These duties extend to the whole of the business, and not just that part of it covered by their individual executive roles so they are able to bring a wider perspective when engaged in board business.

(b) As the most senior executive director, the chief executive is responsible for proposing company strategy and for delivering the strategy as agreed by the board. The chief executive's relationship with the chair is a key influence on board effectiveness.

(c) The **chief executive** has primary responsibility for setting an example to the company's workforce and for communicating to them the expectations in respect of the company's culture. They are responsible for supporting the chair to make certain that appropriate standards of governance permeate through all parts of the organisation. They ensure the board is made aware of views gathered via engagement between management and the workforce.

(d) It is the responsibility of the chief executive to ensure the board knows the views of the senior management on business issues in order to improve the standard of discussion in the boardroom and, prior to a final decision on an issue, explain in a balanced way any divergence of view.

(e) The chief executive is also responsible for ensuring that management fulfils its obligation to provide board directors with:
- Accurate, timely and clear information in a form and of a quality and comprehensiveness that will enable it to discharge its duties.
- The necessary resources for developing and updating their knowledge and capabilities.
- Appropriate knowledge of the company, including access to company operations and members of the workforce.

(f) Executive directors should welcome constructive challenge from non-executive directors as an essential aspect of good governance and a way of drawing on wider experience outside the company.

(FRC *Corporate Governance Code Guidance 2024*, paras. 70-75)

The FRC *Corporate Governance Code Guidance* in the preceding case study talks broadly about the role of the CEO in a corporate governance context. A guidance note that used to supplement the UK Combined Code (which became the UK Corporate Governance Code) suggested some specific responsibilities of the CEO.

(a) **Business strategy and management**

The CEO will take the lead in **developing objectives and strategy** having regard to the organisation's stakeholders, and will be responsible to the board for ensuring that the organisation achieves its objectives, optimising the use of resources.

(b) **Investment and financing**

The CEO will **examine major investments**, capital expenditure, acquisitions and disposals and be responsible for identifying new initiatives.

(c) **Risk management**

The CEO will be responsible for **managing the risk profile** in line with the risk appetite accepted by the board. He will also be responsible for ensuring that appropriate planning, operational, and control systems and internal controls are in place and operate effectively. The CEO has ultimate ownership of the control systems and should take the lead in establishing the control environment and culture.

(d) **Establishing the company's management**

The CEO will provide the nomination committee with his view on the **future roles and capabilities** required of directors, and make recommendations about the recruitment of individual directors. He will also be responsible for recruiting and overseeing the management team below board level.

(e) **Board committees**

The CEO will make **recommendations** to be discussed by the board committees on **remuneration policy**, **executive remuneration** and **terms of employment**.

(f) **Liaison with stakeholders**

Like the chair, part of the CEO's role will be to deal with those interested in the company. The chairman's focus though will often be on dealing with shareholder concerns, whereas the CEO will also be **concerned with other major stakeholders** who impact upon the company's operations, for example its most important customers.

2 Non-executive directors

FAST FORWARD

Division of responsibilities at the head of an organisation is most simply achieved by separating the roles of chair and chief executive.

Non-executive directors are directors who do not have day-to-day operational responsibility for the company. They are not employees of the company or affiliated with it in any other way.

Independent non-executive directors have a key role in governance. Their number and status should mean that their views carry significant weight.

2.1 Who are non-executive directors, and why are they necessary?

There is a risk that the executive directors, who are in charge of the management of the company, could abuse their powers and take actions that are in their best interests rather than those of the shareholders and other stakeholders.

Key term

> **Non-executive directors** are directors who do not have day-to-day operational responsibility for the company. They are not employees of the company or affiliated with it in any other way.

Non-executive directors should provide a **balancing influence**, and play a key role in **reducing conflicts of interest** between management (including executive directors) and shareholders. They should provide **reassurance** to shareholders, particularly institutional shareholders, that management is acting in the interests of the organisation.

2.2 Role of non-executive directors

Case Study

The FRC's Corporate Governance Code Guidance describes **the role of the non-executive directors**, with a focus on what is expected of non-executive directors and the time and information that should be made available to them.

(a) When appointed, non-executive directors are expected to devote time to a comprehensive, **formal and tailored induction** that generally extends beyond the boardroom. Initiatives such as partnering a non-executive director with an executive board member may speed up the process of them acquiring an understanding of the main areas of business activity, especially areas involving significant risk.

(b) Non-executive directors need **sufficient time** available to discharge their responsibilities effectively. The time commitment to engage with shareholders and other key stakeholders and get to know the business can be significant. Non-executive directors assess the demands of their portfolios and other commitments carefully before accepting new appointments, devoting time to developing and refreshing their knowledge and skills, to ensure that they continue to make a positive contribution to the board.

(c) Non-executive directors need timely, high-quality information sufficiently in advance so that there can be thorough consideration of the issues prior to, and informed debate and challenge at, board meetings. They seek clarification or amplification from management where they consider the information provided is inadequate or lacks clarity.

(d) Non-executive directors do not operate exclusively within the confines of the boardroom but have a good understanding of the business and its relationships with significant stakeholders. Accordingly, it is advisable for them to take opportunities to meet other stakeholders from all levels of the organisation.

(FRC's *Corporate Governance Code Guidance 2024,* paras. 76-79)

4: BOARD MEMBERS (DIRECTORS)

The UK's Higgs Report which was later revised and updated by the FRC to form the *Guidance on Board Effectiveness* in 2018, before again being revised and incorporated into the Corporate Governance Code in 2024, provided a useful summary of the some responsibilities of non-executive directors.

(a) **Strategy**

Non-executive directors should contribute to, and challenge the direction of, strategy. They should use their own business experience to reinforce their contribution.

(b) **Scrutiny**

Non-executive directors should scrutinise the performance of executive management in meeting goals and objectives.

(c) **Risk**

Non-executive directors should satisfy themselves that financial information is accurate and that financial controls and systems of risk management are strong.

(d) **People**

Non-executive directors are responsible for determining appropriate levels of remuneration for executives, and are key figures in the appointment and removal of senior managers.

2.3 Advantages of non-executive directors

Non-executive directors can bring a number of advantages to a board of directors.

(a) **Experience and knowledge**

They may have **external experience and knowledge** from many different fields **which executive directors do not possess.**

(b) **Perspective**

Non-executive directors can provide a **wider perspective** than executive directors who may be more involved in detailed operations.

(c) **Reassurance**

Good non-executive directors are often a **comfort factor** for third parties such as investors or creditors.

2.4 Independence of non-executive directors

FAST FORWARD — The role and effectiveness of non-executive directors will be enhanced if they are also independent.

Exam focus point

You could be examined on which directors described in a short scenario would be considered as independent.

Imagine the case of a company where the CEO appointed his son as a non-executive director. The son would be a non-executive director but, because he is not independent he may not properly fulfil his role in scrutinising the performance of the independent directors, including his father.

Non-executive directors' contribution is likely to be enhanced if they are **independent**. Independence means **independence of management** and freedom from any other business relationship that could interfere with the exercise of their unfettered and independent judgement.

Non-executive directors should have **no business**, **financial** or other **connection** with the company.

Case Study

The UK Corporate Governance code states that At least half the board, excluding the chair, should be non-executive directors whom the board considers to be **independent**. Circumstances identified by the Code which are likely to impair, or could appear to impair, a non-executive director's independence include, but are not limited to, whether a director:

- Is or has been an employee of the company or group within the last five years;
- Has, or has had within the last three years, a material business relationship with the company, either directly or as a partner, shareholder, director or senior employee of a body that has such a relationship with the company;
- Has received or receives additional remuneration from the company apart from a director's fee, participates in the company's share option or a performance-related pay scheme, or is a member of the company's pension scheme;
- Has close family ties with any of the company's advisers, directors or senior employees;
- Holds cross-directorships or has significant links with other directors through involvement in other companies or bodies;
- Represents a significant shareholder; or
- Has served on the board for more than nine years from the date of their first appointment.

(FRC *UK Corporate Governance Code 2024*: Section 2)

2.5 Number of non-executive directors

Most corporate governance codes acknowledge the importance of having a significant presence of non-executive directors on the board. As mentioned in the case study in 2.4, the UK Corporate Governance Code states that at least half the board, excluding the chair should be independent.

The Code also states that the board should appoint one of to be the **senior independent director** in order to provide a sounding board for the chair and serve as an intermediary for the other directors and shareholders

2.6 The chair

Key term

> The role of the **chair** is to lead the board of directors. It is important that the same individual should not be both CEO and chair otherwise that person would have too much power.

2.6.1 Role of chair

The Case study that follows picks out the guidance from the UK Corporate Governance Code relating to the role of chair, including the detail set out in the supporting UK Corporate Governance Code Guidance published in January 2024 (last updated in September 2024 at the time of writing of this Workbook).

 **Case Study**

The UK Corporate Governance Code 2024 and supporting guidance gives details of the role the chair should play to help make the board as effective as it can be.

It states that the chair should set clear expectations concerning the style and tone of board discussions, ensuring the board has effective decision-making processes and applies sufficient and constructive challenge to major proposals.

It is up to the chair to make certain that all directors are aware of their responsibilities and to **hold meetings with the non-executive directors without the executives present** to facilitate a full and frank airing of views.

The Code gives details of what a chair's role should include:

- Setting a board agenda primarily focused on strategy, performance, value creation, culture, stakeholders and accountability, and ensuring that issues relevant to these areas are reserved for board decision
- Shaping the culture and diversity in the boardroom
- Encouraging all board members to engage in board and committee meetings by drawing on their skills, experience and knowledge
- Fostering relationships based on trust, mutual respect and open communication – both in and outside the boardroom – between non-executive directors and the executive team
- Developing a productive working relationship with the chief executive, providing support and advice, while respecting executive responsibility and offering constructive challenge
- Providing guidance and mentoring to new directors as appropriate
- Leading the annual board performance review
- Commissioning regular external board performance reviews.

(FRC *UK Corporate Governance Code 2024 Guidance*: Section 2)

The UK Corporate Governance Code summarises and brings together the concepts we have discussed in this chapter in the principles it includes in section 2 on the division of board responsibilities.

PART A THE FOUNDATIONS OF GOVERNANCE

Case Study

Principles of the UK Corporate Governance Code (for listed UK companies)

Division of Responsibilities

F   The chair leads the board and is responsible for its overall effectiveness in directing the company. They should demonstrate objective judgement throughout their tenure and promote a culture of openness and debate. In addition, the chair facilitates constructive board relations and the effective contribution of all non-executive directors, and ensures that directors receive accurate, timely and clear information.

G   The board should include an appropriate combination of executive and non-executive (and, in particular, independent non-executive) directors, such that no one individual or small group of individuals dominates the board's decision-making. There should be a clear division of responsibilities between the leadership of the board and the executive leadership of the company's business. (Detailed provision 11 states that at least half the board, excluding the chair, should be non-executive directors whom the board considers to be independent.)

H   Non-executive directors should have sufficient time to meet their board responsibilities. They should provide constructive challenge, strategic guidance, offer specialist advice and hold management to account.

I   The board, supported by the company secretary, should ensure that it has the policies, processes, information, time and resources it needs in order to function effectively and efficiently.

(FRC *UK Corporate Governance Code 2024*: Section 2)

3 Directors' remuneration

FAST FORWARD

Directors' remuneration should be set by a **remuneration committee** consisting of independent non-executive directors.

Remuneration should be aligned with company values and long-term strategy for sustainable success. Remuneration packages should be linked to the successful delivery of the company strategy.

Financial statements should disclose the **remuneration policy** and (in detail) the **remuneration packages of individual directors.**

3.1 Purposes of directors' remuneration

Clearly adequate remuneration has to be paid to directors in order to **attract and retain** individuals of **sufficient calibre**. Remuneration packages should be designed to ensure that individuals are **motivated to achieve performance levels** that are in the company and shareholders' best interests as well as their own personal interests.

3.2 Need for guidance

Directors being paid excessive salaries and bonuses has been seen as one of the major corporate abuses for a large number of years. A distinction should be made between reasonable rewards, that are justified by performance, and high rewards that are not justified and are seen as unethical.

The **Greenbury committee** in the UK set out principles which are a good summary of what remuneration policy should involve.

- Directors' remuneration should be set by **independent members** of the board. The **remuneration committee** will be covered in Chapter 5.
- Any form of bonus should be related to **measurable performance** or enhanced shareholder value.
- There should be **full transparency of directors' remuneration** in the financial statements.

The UK Corporate Governance Code 2024 also has a section (Section 5) dedicated to remuneration. We will consider the topic of remuneration further in Chapter 5 when we look at Remuneration Committees.

PART A THE FOUNDATIONS OF GOVERNANCE

Chapter roundup

- Executive directors are those who have functional management responsibilities within the business.
- The CEO is responsible for leading the management team at and below board level.
- **Division of responsibilities** at the head of an organisation is most simply achieved by separating the roles of chair and chief executive.
- **Non-executive directors** are directors who do not have day-to-day operational responsibility for the company. They are not employees of the company or affiliated with it in any other way.
- **Independent non-executive directors** have a key role in governance. Their number and status should mean that their views carry significant weight.
- The role and effectiveness of non-executive directors will be enhanced if they are also independent.
- The role of the chair is to lead the board of directors. It is important that the same individual should not be both CEO and chair otherwise that person would have too much power.
- Directors' remuneration should be set by a **remuneration committee** consisting of independent non-executive directors.
- Remuneration should be **aligned with company values and long-term strategy** for sustainable success. Remuneration packages should be linked to the successful delivery of the company strategy.
- Financial statements should disclose the **remuneration policy** and (in detail) the **remuneration packages of individual directors**.

Quick quiz

1. Executive directors are those who have _____ _____ _____ within the business.

2. The CEO is responsible for running the _____ _____ and for proposing and developing the group's strategy in consultation with the _____ _____ _____ _____.

3. Division of responsibilities at the head of an organisation is most simply achieved by _____ the roles of chair and chief executive.

4. Non-executive directors are directors who do not _____ _____ _____ _____ for the company.

5. The CEO should be a non-executive director. True or false?

6. Directors' remuneration should be set by a remuneration committee consisting of _____ _____ _____.

Answers to quick quiz

1 Executive directors are those who have functional management responsibilities within the business.

2 The CEO is responsible for running the organisation's business and for proposing and developing the group's strategy in consultation with the directors and the board.

3 Division of responsibilities at the head of an organisation is most simply achieved by separating the roles of chair and chief executive.

4 Non-executive directors are directors who do not have day-to-day operational responsibility for the company.

5 False. The CEO is an executive director, in charge of the company's strategy.

6 Directors' remuneration should be set by a remuneration committee consisting of independent non-executive directors.

End of chapter questions

4.1 Which of the following roles is not that of an executive director?

    A   Finance director
    B   Chair
    C   CEO
    D   Production director

4.2 Which of the following would not be responsibility of the CEO?

    A   Developing objectives and strategy
    B   Liaison with stakeholders
    C   Managing the board
    D   Examining major investment possibilities

4.3 Which of the following are advantages of having non-executive directors?

    (1)   Varied experience and knowledge
    (2)   Wider perspective available
    (3)   Reassurance to banks
    (4)   Cost effectiveness

    A   (1), (2), (3) and (4)
    B   (1), (2) and (3) only
    C   (1), (2) and (4) only
    D   (3) and (4) only

4.4 Which of the following would be independent non-executive directors under the UK Corporate Governance Code 2024?

    A   A person who was the company's lawyer four years ago
    B   A person who was an employee of the company four years ago
    C   A person who owns 40% of the shares in the company
    D   A person who is an employee of another company in the group

4.5 Which of the following should be performed by the chair of the board?
(1) Setting board agendas
(2) Developing corporate strategy
(3) Addressing the development needs of the board
(4) Deciding on the remuneration of non-executive directors

A (1) and (2)
B (3) and (4)
C (1) and (3)
D (2) and (4)

Board committees

Topic list	Syllabus reference
1 Audit committee	B1.7
2 Nomination committee	B1.7
3 Remuneration committee	B1.7
4 Sustainability committee	B1.7, B1.9

Introduction

In this chapter we consider the committees of the board:

- **Audit committee:** responsible for liaising with external audit, supervising internal audit and reviewing the annual accounts and internal controls. We will consider this in Section 1.

- **Nomination committee:** responsible for recommending the appointments of new directors to the board. We will consider this in Section 2.

- **Remuneration committee:** responsible for advising on executive director remuneration policy and the specific package for each director. We will consider this in Section 3.

- **Sustainability committee:** responsible for overseeing the development of the organisation's Environmental, Social and Governance strategy and framework. We discuss this briefly in Section 4 but look at its role in more detail in Chapter 6.

PART A   THE FOUNDATIONS OF GOVERNANCE

1 Audit committee

FAST FORWARD

> An audit committee can help a company maintain objectivity with regard to financial reporting and the audit of financial statements.

Exam focus point

> Committees of the board required by corporate governance codes and the compositions of them (executive and non-executive directors) is commonly examined. You should know which committees are required for listed companies and the balance of executive and independent non-executive directors each committee should have.

1.1 The audit committee

FAST FORWARD

> An audit committee of independent non-executive directors should liaise with external audit, supervise internal audit, review the annual accounts, and review the risk management and internal control framework.

Key term

> An **audit committee** is a sub-committee of the board of directors, usually containing a number of independent non-executive directors.

The role and function of the audit committee is described in the UK Corporate Governance Code:

Extract of UK Corporate Governance Code provisions relating to the audit committee

Provision 24:

'The board should establish an **audit committee of independent non-executive directors**, with a minimum membership of three, or in the case of smaller companies, two.

The chair of the board should **not** be a member. The board should satisfy itself **that at least one member** has recent and relevant **financial experience**.

The committee as a whole shall have competence relevant to the sector in which the company operates.'

Provision 25:

'The main role and responsibilities should be set out in **written terms of reference** and should include:

- **Monitoring the integrity of the financial statements** of the company and any formal announcements relating to the company's financial performance, and reviewing significant financial reporting judgements contained in them
- **Providing advice** on whether the **annual report and accounts**, taken as a whole, is fair, balanced and understandable, and provides the information necessary for shareholders to assess the company's position and performance, business model and strategy
- Following the *Audit Committees and the External Audit: Minimum Standard**
- **Reviewing the company's risk management and internal control framework**, unless expressly addressed by a separate board risk committee composed of independent non-executive directors, or by the board itself
- Monitoring and reviewing the effectiveness of the company's **internal audit function** or, where there is not one, considering annually whether there is a need for one and making a recommendation to the board
- Reporting to the board on how it has discharged its responsibilities

> **Provision 26:**
>
> 'The annual report should describe the work of the audit committee, including:
>
> - The matters set out in the *Audit Committees and the External Audit: Minimum Standard*
> - Where there is no internal audit function, an explanation for the absence, how internal assurance is achieved, and how this affects the work of external audit.'
>
> * The FRC issued the Standard *Audit Committees and the External Audit: Minimum Standard* in May 2023. It should be read in conjunction with the UK Corporate Governance Code and the FRC Guidance on Audit Committees. Further details are given in the next subsection.

1.1.1 Audit Committees and the External Audit: Minimum Standard

The FRC have provided a standard, *Audit Committees and the External Audit: Minimum Standard,* that sits alongside the UK Corporate Governance Code intended to enhance performance and ensure a consistent approach across audit committees within the FTSE 350 when **overseeing and assessing the entity's external audit** process.

Summary extracts of FRC Audit Committees and the External Audit: Minimum Standard
Responsibilities *(para. 4)*
<ul><li>Requiring that the company manages its non-audit relationships with audit firms to **ensure that it has a fair choice of suitable external auditors at the next tender**.</li><li>**Conducting the tender process and making recommendations** to the board, about the appointment, reappointment and removal of the **external auditor**, and approving the remuneration and terms of engagement of the external auditor.</li><li>Engaging with shareholders on the scope of the external audit, where appropriate.</li><li>Ensuring that the **external auditor has full access to company staff and records**.</li><li>Inviting challenge by the external auditor, **giving due consideration to points raised** and making changes to financial statements in response, where appropriate.</li><li>Reviewing and monitoring the **external auditor's independence and objectivity**.</li><li>Reviewing the **effectiveness of the external audit process**, taking into consideration relevant UK professional and regulatory requirements.</li><li>Developing and implementing policy on the engagement of the external auditor to supply **non-audit services**, ensuring there is prior approval of non-audit services and considering the **impact this may have on independence.**</li><li>Reporting to the Board and the members of the company on how it has discharged its responsibilities with respect to the external audit.</li></ul>
Oversight of Auditors and Audit *(paras. 15-17)*
<ul><li>The Audit Committee is responsible for overseeing and **assessing the entity's external audit** and its auditors.</li><li>It should work to create a **culture which** recognises the work of, and **encourages challenge** by, the auditor.</li><li>The Committee should **review and monitor the external auditor's independence and objectivity**.</li><li>They should also assess the effectiveness of the audit process including an **assessment of external audit quality,** asking the auditor to **explain the risks to audit quality** they have identified and how they have been addressed.</li><li>They should also review whether the auditor has met the agreed audit plan and **understand the reasons for any changes**, including changes in perceived audit risks.</li></ul>

Note that under the FRC standard the annual report of the company should describe the work of the audit committee, which includes an **explanation of how it has assessed the independence and effectiveness of the external audit process** and the approach taken to the appointment or reappointment of the external auditor.

(**Note:** The full standard including all of the reporting requirements can be found on the FRC website: https://media.frc.org.uk/documents/Audit_Committees_and_the_External_Audit_Minimum_Standard.pdf [online], last accessed 11 July 2024).

1.2 Advantages and disadvantages of audit committees

The key advantage to an auditor of having an audit committee is that a committee of independent non-executive directors provides the auditor with an independent point of reference other than the executive directors of the company, in the event of disagreement arising.

Other **advantages** that are claimed to arise from the existence of an audit committee include:

(a) It will lead to **improved quality** of financial reporting and **increased confidence** in the credibility and objectivity of financial reports. This is because an audit committee should have at least one member with financial expertise and is particularly important for listed companies and companies seeking listing.

(b) By specialising in the problems of financial reporting the internal auditors will be able to assist the directors, allowing the **executive** directors to **devote their attention to management**.

(c) In cases where the interests of the company, the executive directors and the employees conflict, the audit committee might provide an **impartial body** for the auditors to consult. It will also provide a channel for international and external auditors to communicate through.

(d) The internal auditors will be able to report to the audit committee, rather than the main board, **enhancing their independence and objectivity**.

(e) The audit committee can be a **'critical friend'** to the board in ensuring that the company keeps up to date with corporate governance requirements.

Opponents of audit committees argue that:

(a) The executive directors **may not understand** the purpose of an audit committee and may perceive that it detracts from their authority.

(b) There may be **difficulty selecting** sufficient non-executive directors with the necessary competence in auditing matters for the committee to be really effective.

(c) The establishment of such a **formalised reporting procedure** may **dissuade** the **auditors** from raising matters of judgement and limit them to reporting only on matters of fact.

(d) Costs may be increased.

2 Nomination committee

The nomination committee is responsible for recommending the appointments of new directors to the board. This should help to ensure that individuals of sufficient calibre are appointed. The nomination committee would be made up **wholly or mainly** of independent non-executive directors.

In Chapter 3 we discussed the fact that boards will only be effective if the directors are competent and capable. A key factor in achieving this is the establishment of a nomination committee.

2.1 Members of the nomination committee

A key purpose of the nomination committee is to ensure that directors are appointed based on their qualifications and experience rather than because of their relationship with the executive directors. Ideally, therefore, the nomination committee would be made up **wholly or mainly** of independent non-executive directors.

The UK Corporate Governance Code states, for example, that a **majority of members** of the committee should be independent non-executive directors. It adds that the chair of the board should not chair the nomination committee when it is dealing with the appointment of their successor as chair of the board.

2.2 Factors for the nomination committee to consider

The nomination committee needs to consider:

- The **balance** between executives and independent non-executives
- The **skills**, **knowledge** and **experience** possessed by the current board
- The **need for continuity** and succession planning
- The desirable **size** of the board
- The need to attract board members from a **diversity** of backgrounds

The UK Higgs Report made a number of suggestions about possible sources of non-executive directors:

- Companies operating in international markets could benefit from having at least one non-executive director with international experience
- Lawyers, accountants and consultants can bring skills that are useful to the board
- Listed companies should consider appointing directors of private companies as non-executive directors
- Including individuals with charitable or public sector experience but strong commercial awareness can increase the breadth of diversity and experience on the board.

The UK Corporate Governance Code recommends that an **external search consultancy** and **open advertising** should be used, particularly when appointing a non-executive director or chair.

The nomination committee should ensure that appointments to the board are made using **objective criteria**. However, the criteria should not be so restrictive that it limits too greatly the number of candidates.

2.3 Other factors

As well as considering these issues when appointments are made, the nomination committee should regularly review the **structure, size** and **composition** of the board, and keep under review the **leadership needs** of the company.

It should also consider whether non-executive directors are spending **enough time** on their duties and other issues relating to re-election and reappointment of directors, also membership of board committees.

2.4 Re-election

> **FAST FORWARD**
>
> Directors should be re-elected at regular intervals.

If directors are appointed indefinitely, they may not perform well in the longer term. It is therefore important that they are re-elected at regular intervals.

Case Study

The UK Corporate Governance Code states that all directors should be **subject to annual re-election**. The board should document the specific reasons why their contribution is, and continues to be, important to the company's long-term sustainable success.

3 Remuneration committee

FAST FORWARD

Directors' remuneration should be set by a **remuneration committee** consisting of independent non-executive directors.

3.1 Role and function of remuneration committee

The remuneration committee plays the key role in establishing remuneration arrangements. In order to be effective, the committee needs both to **determine** the organisation's **general policy** on the **remuneration of executive directors** and **specific remuneration packages** for each director.

The UK Corporate Governance Code suggests measures to ensure that the committee is **independent**, including requiring the committee to be staffed by **independent non-executive directors in order to ensure** that executive directors do not set their own remuneration levels.

Case Study

The UK Corporate Governance Code includes provisions stating what the composition of the remuneration committee should be and how remuneration packages should be determined.

(a) The board should establish a remuneration committee of **independent non-executive directors**, with a minimum membership of **three**, or in the case of smaller companies, two. The chair of the board can only be a member if they were independent on appointment and they cannot chair the committee. Before appointment as chair of the remuneration committee, the appointee should have served on a remuneration committee for at least 12 months.

(b) The remuneration committee should have delegated responsibility for determining the policy for **executive director remuneration** and setting remuneration for the chair, executive directors and senior management. It should review workforce remuneration and related policies and the alignment of incentives and rewards with culture, taking these into account when setting the policy for executive director remuneration.

(c) The remuneration of non-executive directors should be determined in accordance with the Articles of Association or, alternatively, by the board. Levels of remuneration for the chair and all non-executive directors should reflect the **time commitment** and **responsibilities** of the role. Remuneration for all non-executive directors should **not** include share options or other performance-related elements.

(d) Remuneration schemes should promote long-term shareholdings by executive directors that support alignment with long-term shareholder interests. Only basic salary should be pensionable.

(FRC *UK Corporate Governance Code 2024:* Provisions 32-34, 36, 39)

3.2 Elements of remuneration packages

FAST FORWARD

> Packages will need to **attract, retain and motivate directors** of sufficient quality.

Packages will need to attract, retain and motivate directors of sufficient quality, whilst at the same time taking into account shareholders' interests as well.

Important factors to take into account in determining packages include:

- The **market rate**, ie what would a director earn if he/she moved elsewhere.
- **Legal, fiscal or regulatory constraints** such as a compulsory multiple between the highest and lowest paid in an organisation.
- **Previous performance in the job** and the **outcome of performance reviews**.
- **Stakeholder opinion and ethical considerations**, for example salaries in organisations with charitable objectives might be lower.

3.3 Balancing of different elements

In order to achieve a fairly-balanced package, the remuneration committee needs to consider how the package is balanced in different ways.

- **Fixed and variable elements.** Part of the package should be performance-related.
- **Immediate and deferred elements.** The idea is that directors are not rewarded excessively for gains in performance that turn out to be temporary.
- **Long-term and short-term elements.** Packages should be designed to promote the success of companies over time.
- **Cash and non-cash elements,** such as benefits and pensions.

4 Sustainability committee

FAST FORWARD

> The sustainability committee is responsible for overseeing the development of the organisation's Environmental, Social and Governance (ESG) strategy and framework. An increasingly large number of companies have established a dedicated sustainability committee to manage ESG and advise on ESG issues.

4.1 Increase in sustainability committees

As we will see in Chapter 6, sustainability is now at the forefront of the minds of stakeholders and is a key business driver. This has meant that companies have needed to adapt their business structures so that they can properly oversee the organisation's Environmental, Social and Governance (ESG) strategy and framework.

As a result, many companies have chosen to set up a board level committee dedicated to management of sustainability and ESG issues. This helps to increase the level of expertise in this critical area and results in more accountability in relation to sustainability.

Although sustainability (or ESG) committees are not yet a requirement for listed companies under corporate governance codes applied under listing rules, establishing one has been seen by a large proportion of listed entities as the best way to respond to ESG-related risks and opportunities. Regulators have reacted by including sustainability committees in guidance that sits alongside corporate governance codes, or by issuing separate governance guidance for sustainability.

PART A   THE FOUNDATIONS OF GOVERNANCE

Case Study: The rise of the sustainability committee

The Chartered Governance Institute UK & Ireland is a professional body for governance and qualifying and membership body for governance professionals.

In April 2024 they reported a steady rise in the number of UK organisations choosing to set up committees dedicated to ESG and sustainability issues at board level. The report stated that 51 of the FTSE 100 have such a committee (as of Q1 2024), and that the trend is not confined to the UK's largest companies.

A survey of the institute's members included 130 governance professionals across organisations of all sizes and sectors. In the responses, 41% said that their organisation already has a sustainability committee, and another 5% reported an intention to establish one. The responses represent large and small, publicly listed and private companies, finance and insurance firms, not-for-profits, educational bodies, and local authorities.

The report stated that the increasing focus on sustainability in the press, amongst investors and in society generally, has raised its profile to one that many organisations feel they simply cannot ignore.

This is because companies are facing:

- High volume and increased complexity of ESG-related regulation
- Expectations from investors and other stakeholders for increased transparency and reporting about sustainability
- Reputational impacts associated with environmental and social practices, which can extend to shareholder activism or litigation
- Deeper understanding that ESG risks and opportunities translate to financial risks and opportunities
- Greater emphasis on ESG performance in capital allocation and investment decisions

The Chartered Governance Institute UK & Ireland, 2024

At the time of writing, the full report could be accessed at:
https://www.cgi.org.uk/knowledge/research/governing-sustainability-apr24 (Accessed 11 July 2024).

We will consider the makeup and the role of this committee in detail in Chapter 6, but as with other committees we have looked at, members of the committee should have the relevant mix of skills, experience and diversity. The membership should include a mix of executive and non-executive directors and ideally the majority of the members should be non-executive directors.

4.1.1 Alternatives to sustainability committees

FAST FORWARD

> Some companies have taken an alternative approach by keeping ESG as the responsibility of the full board and moving it up the agenda, or by placing accountability for sustainability with an existing committee such as the audit committee.

Some companies choose not to set up a sustainability committee, but instead seek different ways to address management of ESG strategy.

The alternatives that may be adopted are:

- Sustainability remains the responsibility of the full board and make sure it is made a prominent issue in board meetings.
- Accountability for sustainability is placed with an existing committee such as the audit committee. This could be in the form of a sub-committee sitting under the existing committee.

Chapter roundup

- An audit committee can help a company maintain objectivity with regard to financial reporting and the audit of financial statements.
- An audit committee of independent non-executive directors should liaise with external audit, supervise internal audit, review the annual accounts, and review the risk management and internal control framework.
- The nomination committee is responsible for recommending the appointments of new directors to the board. This should help to ensure that individuals of sufficient calibre are appointed.
- The nomination committee would be made up **wholly or mainly** of independent non-executive directors.
- Directors should be re-elected at regular intervals.
- Directors' remuneration should be set by a **remuneration committee** consisting of independent non-executive directors.
- Packages will need to **attract, retain and motivate directors** of sufficient quality.
- The sustainability committee is responsible for overseeing the development of the organisation's Environmental, Social and Governance (ESG) strategy and framework.
- An increasingly large number of companies have established a dedicated sustainability committee to manage ESG and advise on ESG issues.
- Some companies have taken an alternative approach by keeping ESG as the responsibility of the full board and moving it up the agenda, or by placing accountability for sustainability with an existing committee such as the audit committee.

Quick quiz

1. An audit _____ is a sub-committee of the _____ _____ _____ usually containing a number of _____ _____ directors.

2. When a company cannot easily find non-executive directors it should not have an audit committee. True or false?

3. How many members of the audit committee must have recent and relevant financial experience?

4. The nomination committee should be made up _____ or _____ of _____ _____ directors.

5. The remuneration committee should determine the organisation's _____ _____ on the remuneration of executive directors and _____ _____ _____ for each director.

6. Match the committee with the responsibility

Committee	Responsibility
(1) Audit committee	(a) Determine the pay of the CEO
(2) Nomination committee	(b) Oversee ESG strategy
(3) Remuneration committee	(c) Recommend appointees to the board
(4) Sustainability committee	(d) Monitor the effectiveness of internal audit

Answers to quick quiz

1 An audit committee is a sub-committee of the board of directors, usually containing a number of independent non-executive directors.

2 False. It should have an audit committee if required, or if the directors feel it is in the best interests of the shareholders, even if it is difficult to find non-executive directors.

3 At least one.

4 The nomination committee should be made up wholly or mainly of independent non-executive directors.

5 The remuneration committee should determine the organisation's general policy on the remuneration of executive directors and specific remuneration packages for each director.

6 1d, 2c, 3a, 4b

End of chapter questions

5.1 Which of the following does **not** form part of an audit committee's objectives?

   A   Safeguarding the privacy of whistleblowers
   B   Appointing the external auditor
   C   Monitoring the independence of the external auditor
   D   Implementing a policy on the supply of non-audit services by the external auditor

5.2 Which of the following statements best describes why having an audit committee could help a company raise additional finance by addressing concerns its bank has about its financial viability?

   A   The independent non-executive members of the audit committee can provide guarantees to the bank concerning the company's financial viability.
   B   The audit committee will have at least one member who has relevant financial experience, so that they can monitor the integrity of the financial statements.
   C   The audit committee will review all the available evidence to substantiate information in financial reporting, thus improving the credibility of the financial statements.
   D   The audit committee will have at least one member who has relevant financial experience. This person will be able to stand in as the company's finance director in an emergency.

5.3 The tasks of which body include: monitoring the CEO; formulating strategy; and ensuring that there is effective communication of the strategic plan?

   A   The shareholders
   B   The audit committee
   C   The board of directors
   D   The nomination committee

5.4 What is the purpose of a nomination committee of the board of directors?

   A   To put forward nominations for new appointments to the board
   B   To nominate the directors who should stand for re-election at each annual general meeting of the company
   C   To review nominations for appointments to senior executive posts and the position of company secretary
   D   To decide whether to accept nominations for new appointments to the board, put forward by the chair or the chief executive officer

5.5 Which of the following structures for the composition of an audit committee for a listed company is **least likely** to meet requirements for good practice in corporate governance?

- A A committee consisting entirely of independent directors
- B A committee consisting entirely of non-executive directors
- C A committee with an executive director chair and all other members who are non-executive directors
- D A committee with a non-executive chair, one representative of management and other members who are non-executive directors

5.6 Which of the following is true in relation to sustainability committees?

- A They are mandatory for all listed and public interest entities
- B Members of the sustainability committee should have a balance of appropriate skills, experience and diversity
- C Due to the nature of the sustainability committee the majority of its members should be executive directors
- D The trend over time is a decrease in the number of companies establishing sustainability committees and instead delegating responsibility to existing committees

PART A　　THE FOUNDATIONS OF GOVERNANCE

Stakeholders, corporate social responsibility and sustainability

Topic list	Syllabus reference
1 Corporate social responsibility (CSR)	B1.10
2 Sustainability reporting and governance	B1.9
3 Managing stakeholders	B1.2

Introduction

Corporate social responsibility (CSR) refers to the expectation in society that companies are accountable for the social and ethical effects of their actions. CSR issues are often covered by legal regulations (eg Environmental regulations and human rights).

Consumers are demanding that producers of the products and services they use do more than simply comply with laws; they expect companies to carry out sustainable activities, to consider the impact of the business on society and to behave ethically.

Understanding the way in which companies manage sustainability related risks and opportunities has become crucial for investors and other stakeholders. This has seen the rapid development of improved sustainability reporting frameworks and a demand for assurance over these reports.

Corporate governance frameworks need to address the stakeholder demand for a sustainable long-term strategy and related reporting. This has led to an increase in the number of companies establishing a sustainability committee.

At the centre of all discussions in this chapter are stakeholders and the final part of this chapter looks at managing stakeholders.

1 Corporate social responsibility (CSR)

FAST FORWARD

Corporate social responsibility (CSR) refers to the expectation in society that companies are accountable for the social and ethical effects of their actions. Some argue however that businesses already contribute enough to society via the taxes on their profits.

1.1 Corporate social responsibility

The term corporate social responsibility (CSR) is used to describe a wide range of obligations that an organisation may feel it has towards its stakeholders, including the society in which it operates.

If it is accepted that businesses currently do not bear the total social cost of their activities, it could be suggested that corporate social responsibility might be a way of recognising this.

Key terms

Social costs: Social costs are defined as the tangible and intangible costs and losses sustained by third parties or the general public as a result of economic activity, for example pollution by industrial effluent.

Social responsibility: Social responsibility is the principle that organisations should act in a manner which benefits society as well as meeting strategic and financial objectives.

The primary purpose of a business organisation is to make profits, thereby increasing the wealth of its owners, the shareholders. Businesses do not, however, exist in splendid isolation; they are dependent on the society in which they operate, and they should therefore contribute to that society.

Corporate social responsibility includes **economic** and **legal issues**, as well as **ethical ones**, reflecting the whole range of stakeholders who have an interest in an organisation.

1.2 Corporate social responsibility stances

Corporate social responsibility (CSR) is concerned with the ways in which an organisation exceeds its minimum, legally required obligations to stakeholders (Johnson, Scholes and Whittington, 2007, p.146).

Therefore, CSR is more closely associated with contemporary business issues, and concerns organisations giving something back to society, and being good citizens.

In contrast to ethics, CSR is socially mediated and likely to be specific to the time and culture in which it is considered. For example, CSR could include:

- Staff development via training and education
- Equal opportunities statements
- Written anti-discrimination policies
- Commitment to reporting on CSR
- Policies for restricting the use of child labour by suppliers
- Policies on fair trade
- Commitment to the protection of the local community

However, the approaches organisations take to CSR can vary significantly, and this will influence the way organisations act, and the way they judge their performance.

Johnson, Scholes and Whittington (2007, p.146) identify four typical CSR 'stances' which illustrate the different approaches organisations can take to CSR:

(a) Short-term shareholder interest
(b) Long-term shareholder interest
(c) Multiple stakeholder obligations
(d) Shaper of society

1.2.1 CSR: Short-term shareholder interest

An organisation might limit its CSR stance to taking responsibility for short-term shareholder interest on the grounds that it is for government alone to impose regulations and wider constraints using a code of corporate governance. This means some organisations take a minimal approach to CSR in the short term as there is little pressure to do more.

For example, organisations may focus only on direct profit-making activities and not invest in any activities which benefit local communities as there is no requirement to do so.

1.2.2 CSR: Long-term shareholder interest

In the longer term, many organisations can identity the value and benefits of investing in CSR in the longer term.

The rationale behind an 'enlightened self-interest' stance is that there can be a long-term benefit to shareholders from well-managed relationships with other stakeholders. Therefore, the justification for social action is that it makes good business sense and can contribute to long-term shareholder value.

There are two reasons why an organisation might take a wider view of social responsibilities when considering the **longer-term interest of shareholders**.

(a) **Corporate image** may be enhanced by an assumption of wider responsibilities. The cost of undertaking such responsibilities may be justified as essentially promotional expenditure.

(b) The responsible exercise of corporate power may prevent a build-up of social and political **pressure for legal regulation**. Freedom of action may be preserved, and the burden of regulation lightened by acceptance of social and ethical responsibilities.

1.2.3 CSR: Multiple stakeholder obligations

Organisations adopting this stance accept the **legitimacy of the expectations of stakeholders other than shareholders** and build those expectations into the organisation's stated purposes. Such organisations recognise that, without appropriate relationships with groups such as suppliers, employees and customers, they would not be able to function.

However, organisations adopting a 'multiple stakeholder obligations' stance also argue that performance should not be measured simply through the financial bottom line. They argue that the key to long-term survival is dependent on social and environmental performance as well as economic (financial) performance and, therefore, it is important to take account of the views of stakeholders with interests relating to social and environmental matters.

1.2.4 Shaper of society

Shapers of society regard financial considerations as being of secondary importance to changing society or social norms. For such organisations, ensuring that society benefits from their actions is more important than financial and other stakeholder interests.

1.3 Corporate social responsibility and corporate citizenship

Corporate citizenship refers to an organisation's responsibilities toward society. The goal of corporate citizenship is to produce higher standards of living and quality of life for the communities that surround them and still maintain profitability for stakeholders.

It involves the social responsibility of businesses and the extent to which they meet legal, ethical, economic and environmental responsibilities, as established by shareholders and other stakeholders.

The concept of corporate citizenship personalises an organisation as part of the community, so a board of directors considers the impact of business operations on the environment and socially as well as on profit and take actions which limit harm.

Corporate citizenship includes complying with best practice and being responsive to ethical concerns. An organisation's reputation as a good corporate citizen may be thought to be worth the extra costs incurred in order to maximise long term sustainable strategic objectives and performance.

Corporate citizenship is important as investors, potential employees, customers, suppliers, banks and other stakeholders are seeking out companies that have socially responsible orientations such as their environmental, social, and governance (ESG) practices.

1.4 Corporate social responsibility and sustainability reporting

Consumers are increasingly concerned about the impact of business activities on the environment. There has been an increase in the use of the environmental approach to market products. 'Dolphin friendly' tuna and paper products from managed forests are good examples. Companies now monitor the impact they have on the environment as part of their CSR obligations due the significant impact environmental issues can have.

Sustainability reporting and governance is explored further in Section 2.

1.5 CSR Strategy

A business that has a strategy in place to demonstrate its corporate social responsibility will have a deliberate plan with specific activities identified. Examples of CSR activities might include:

- Making donations to charity
- Contributing to the activities on non-governmental organisations (NGOs)
- Supporting local good causes
- Including stakeholders in key decisions
- Managing the social and environmental impacts of the business

Having a strategy means making choices, providing funding for the CSR initiatives chosen, and monitoring the outcomes.

To assist with development of a strategy organisations sometimes carry out corporate social responsibility audits. This generally involves:

- Recognising a firm's rationale for engaging in socially responsible activity
- Identifying programmes which are congruent with the mission of the company
- Setting objectives and priorities related to this programme
- Specifying the nature and range of resources required
- Evaluating company involvement in such programmes (past, present and future)

1.6 CSR initiatives to meet CSR strategic goals

It could be argued that CSR activities should reflect the ethos of the business, which leads to the concept of strategic CSR. When CSR activities become strategic, they are concerned with the long-term success of the business and should therefore be beneficial to the business as well as to society. The increasing prevalence of strategic CSR is linked to the development of frameworks such as the Integrated Reporting framework, which places an emphasis on the long-term success of an organisation and is covered in more detail later in this chapter.

Examples of strategic CSR initiatives might include:

- A pharmaceutical company funding the training of medical staff, in the hope that when qualified they will source drugs from that company

- A bank providing free internet training for senior customers, who might then be disposed to buying financial products

- Encouraging employees to nominate and get involved in good causes, in order to develop loyalty to the company

- Sponsoring sports teams in return for advertising space on shirts, other merchandise, and at the ground.

The decision as to whether CSR should be strategic is an ethical one. From a pristine capitalist point of view, all CSR activities should be strategic since all of a company's money should be used to benefit

shareholders. On the other hand, a deep green perspective would argue that, because businesses take from society, they should give something back.

One difference between 'CSR strategy' and 'strategic CSR' is the extent to which an organisation will promote the support given to a CSR cause, making it more likely that strategic CSR will be more visible. Consequently, the ethical viewpoint most likely to support this could be that of the expedient (promoting strategic CSR in a way that benefits the organisation).

1.7 Pressures on organisations

Organisations face a number of pressures from different directions to be socially responsible.

1.7.1 Governance requirements

The South African King report emphasises the importance of **sustainability**, linking it with the value of ethics and improved ethical standards. The King report stresses that sustainability is a business opportunity to eliminate or minimise adverse consequences for the company, on the community and on the environment and to improve the impact of the company's operations on the economic life of the community. The triple bottom line (economic, social and environmental responsibilities) enables a company to be relevant to society and the natural environment.

1.7.2 Stakeholder expectations

Pressures on organisations to widen the scope of their corporate public accountability come from **increasing expectations of stakeholders** and **knowledge** about the **consequences of ignoring such pressures**. The King report stresses the importance of engagement with external stakeholders, and individual workers and stakeholders being able to communicate openly.

Stakeholders include communities (particularly those where operations are based), customers, suppliers, supply chain participants and competitors. Issues such as plant closures, pollution, job creation and sourcing can have powerful **social effects** on these stakeholders.

1.7.3 Reputation risk

Increasingly, a business must have the reputation of being a **responsible business** that enhances long-term shareholder value by addressing the needs of its **stakeholders**.

1.8 Significance of corporate social responsibility

Businesses, particularly large ones, are subject to increasing expectations that they will exercise corporate social responsibility. Carroll's model of social responsibility suggests there are four levels of social responsibility.

1.8.1 Economic responsibilities

Companies have economic responsibilities to shareholders demanding a good return, to employees wanting fair employment conditions and customers who are seeking good-quality products at a fair price. Businesses are set up to be properly functioning economic units and so this responsibility forms the basis of all others.

1.8.2 Legal responsibilities

Since laws **codify society's moral views**, obeying those laws must be the foundation of compliance with social responsibilities. Although in all societies corporations will have a minimum of legal responsibilities, there is perhaps more emphasis on them in continental Europe than in the Anglo-American economies where the focus of discussion has been on whether many legal responsibilities constitute excessive red tape.

1.8.3 Ethical responsibilities

These are responsibilities that require corporations to act in a **fair and just way** even if the law does not compel them to do so.

1.8.4 Philanthropic responsibilities

According to Carroll, these are **desired** rather than being required of companies. They include charitable donations, contributions to local communities and providing employees with the chance to improve their own lives.

1.9 Corporate social responsibility and stakeholders

Inevitably, discussion on corporate social responsibilities has been tied in with the stakeholder view of corporate activity, the view that as businesses benefit from the goodwill and other tangible aspects of society, that they owe it **certain duties** in return, particularly towards those affected by its activities.

As previously discussed, organisations need to identify and classify stakeholders systematically and decide on how they will respond to stakeholder claims. The Mendelow model (which we look at later in Section 3.4) is one method of assessing the power and interest of stakeholders.

1.9.1 Problems of dealing with stakeholders

Whatever the organisation's view of its stakeholders, certain problems in dealing with them on corporate social responsibility may have to be addressed.

(a) Collaborating with stakeholders may be **time consuming** and **expensive**.

(b) There may be **culture clashes** between the company and certain groups of stakeholders, or between the values of different groups of stakeholders with companies caught in the middle.

(c) There may be **conflict between the company and stakeholders** on certain issues when they are trying to collaborate on other issues.

(d) **Consensus** between different groups of stakeholders may be difficult or impossible to achieve, and the solution may not be economically or strategically desirable.

(e) Influential stakeholders' **independence** (and hence ability to provide necessary criticism) may be compromised if they become too closely involved with companies.

(f) Dealing with certain stakeholders (eg public sector organisations) may be complicated by their being **accountable in turn to the wider public**.

1.10 Impact of corporate social responsibility on strategy and corporate governance

Social responsibilities can impact on what companies do in a number of ways.

1.10.1 Objectives and mission statements

If the organisation publishes a mission statement to inform stakeholders of strategic objectives, **mention** of **social objectives** is a sign that the board believes that they have a significant impact on strategy.

1.10.2 Ethical codes of conduct

As part of their guidance to promote **good corporate behaviour** among their employees, some organisations publish a **business code of ethics**.

1.10.3 Corporate social reporting and social accounts

Organisations, as part of their reporting on operational and financial matters, report on **ethical or social conduct**. Some go further, **producing social accounts** showing quantified impacts on each of the organisation's stakeholder constituencies.

1.10.4 Corporate governance

Impacts on corporate governance could include representatives from key stakeholder groups on the board, or perhaps even a **stakeholder board of directors**. It also implies the need for a binding corporate governance code that regulates the rights of stakeholder groups.

1.11 Ownership and corporate social responsibility

Having talked about the social responsibilities of companies, we also need to consider the responsibilities of shareholders in companies. This is complicated by the nature of ownership of shares. Shareholders are not buying something tangible that they can use as they please and regulate how others use it. Instead shareholders are buying a **right to participate in risks and rewards** from a separate legal entity.

One view is that shareholders have **responsibilities arising directly out of their rights**, particularly the rights to vote in an annual general meeting. The argument is that they should use the voice they have at this meeting. If they own a large block of shares, they should make the most of the influence this gives them to ensure good corporate governance and accountability for decisions made.

A wider view is that shareholders, by buying shares in the hope of an opportunity of greater returns than they could achieve from a safe investment, also have a responsibility to society in the same way as they would be responsible for controlling tangible property that they owned. They should be insisting that those managing the company carry out a policy that is consistent with the **public welfare**. Institutional investors can help achieve this by having publicly-stated policies that they will only invest in companies that demonstrate corporate social responsibility.

One of the main problems with this view in relation to large corporations is the **wide dispersion of shareholders**. This means that shareholders with small percentage holdings have negligible influence on managers. In addition, the ease with which shareholders can **dispose of shares** on the stock markets arguably loosens their feeling of obligation in relation to their property. This then raises the question of why the speculative (and possibly short-term) interests of shareholders should prevail over the longer-term interests of other stakeholders.

In corporate governance discussions, the idea of ownership responsibilities has had a significant influence because of the importance of **institutional shareholders**. Not only do they have the level of shareholdings that can be used as a lever to pressure managers, but they themselves have **fiduciary responsibilities** as trustees on behalf of their investors.

2 Sustainability reporting and governance

FAST FORWARD

> Sustainability reporting is now a key part of a company's dialogue with its stakeholders. The stakeholder desire for and expectation of such information is so strong that companies which fail to provide sustainability disclosures will be at a significant disadvantage in terms of attracting and retaining investors and appealing to wider stakeholders.

Sustainability reporting is currently the biggest focus in corporate reporting. However, it has been difficult to navigate, for both preparers and stakeholders, due to the many different sources of guidance and regulatory requirements across the world. The IFRS Foundation has sought to address this issue through the formation of the **International Sustainability Standards Board (ISSB)** and the issue of **IFRS Sustainability Disclosure Standards**.

In this section, we will consider first the concepts of sustainability and of impacts and dependencies, before looking at some existing reporting frameworks for sustainability. We will also look at the IFRS Sustainability Disclosure Standards.

Sustainable development was defined by the United Nations Brundtland Commission.

PART A   THE FOUNDATIONS OF GOVERNANCE

Key terms

> **Sustainability:** Development that 'meets the needs of the present without compromising the ability of future generations to meet their own needs' (UN, 1987)

It is important to recognise that sustainability is not just about environmental issues. Sustainability is generally recognised to encompass issues of:

- Environment
- Society
- Economics
- Governance

As sustainability continues to be a key global issue, there is increasing pressure on entities from investors and other stakeholders to both conduct their operations in a sustainable way and to report on how they are doing this.

2.1 The Sustainable Development Goals (SDGs)

In 2015, the United Nations member states pledged commitment to the 2030 Agenda for Sustainable Development as 'a plan of action for people, planet and prosperity' (UN, 2015). At the heart of the agenda are the 17 Sustainable Development Goals (SDGs), which include:

- **No Poverty**: End poverty in all its forms everywhere.
- **Decent Work and Economic Growth**: Promote sustained, inclusive, and sustainable economic growth, full and productive employment, and decent work for all.
- **Reduced Inequality**: Reduce inequality within and among countries.
- **Climate Action**: Take urgent action to combat climate change and its impacts.
- **Life Below Water**: Conserve and sustainably use the oceans, seas, and marine resources for sustainable development.
- Manage forests, combat desertification, halt and reverse land degradation, and halt biodiversity loss.

(UN, 2015)

The full list of SDGs, including details on target and indicators can be found at: https://sdgs.un.org/goals.

The SDGs set the priorities for governments and apply to all nations. To meet the goals, it will require effort from all aspects of society, including businesses.

Case Study   IKEA

IKEA, the Swedish home furnishing store, has a sustainability strategy called People & Planet Positive. The strategy uses the UN Sustainable Development Goals as its 'compass to mobilise change in our work' (IKEA, 2022).

IKEA has identified three main challenges that are relevant for its business: climate change, unsustainable consumption and rising inequality. The three main focus areas of IKEA's sustainability strategy relate to these challenges:

- **Healthy and sustainable living** – IKEA's ambition is 'By 2030 ... to inspire and enable more than 1 billion people to live a better everyday life within the boundaries of the planet' (IKEA, 2022)
- **Circular and climate positive business** – IKEA's ambition is 'By 2030 ... to become climate positive and regenerate resources while growing the IKEA business' (IKEA, 2022)
- **Fair and equal** – IKEA's ambition is 'By 2030 ... to play our full part in contributing to a fair and equal society by respecting human rights, creating a positive impact for people across our value chain and contributing to resilient societies' (IKEA, 2022)

IKEA publishes an annual sustainability report which details how it has followed its sustainability strategy and the challenges it has faced. Read more online in the reports section of the IKEA website: https://www.ikea.com/global/en/our-business/reports/.

2.2 Sustainability impacts and dependencies

There are two fundamental aspects of sustainability as it relates to business: impacts and dependencies.

Description	Examples
Impacts: Refers to the effect that an entity has on its stakeholders, society, the economy and the natural environment, through the resources it uses and the relationships it has in its value chain	• Worker rights • Human rights • Waste • Greenhouse gas emissions • Water use
Dependencies: Refers to the reliance an entity has on its stakeholders, society, the economy and the natural environment through the resources it uses and the relationships it has in its value chain.	• Worker health • Diversity • Climate risks • Resource availability • Consumer expectations • Regulatory risks

Information on dependencies is typically more useful for investors, lenders and creditors as dependencies create risks and opportunities which can affect the entity's prospects.

Information on impacts is typically more useful for broader stakeholders, such as governments, consumers, employees and wider society who want to know how the entity's actions and future strategy will impact both people and planet.

However, it is of course more nuanced than this, as investors, lenders and creditors are increasingly interested in whether the companies they provide capital to are socially and environmentally responsible, and an entity's impacts may therefore form part of the investing or lending decision.

Additionally, an entity's impacts may also create risks and opportunities that affect the entity's prospects, and information on these impacts is therefore useful to investors, lenders and creditors. For example, an entity may have a poor record in terms of worker rights or pollution, both of which are impacts of its actions, but these impacts could result in risk to the entity's reputation, which would ultimately affect its future prospects.

2.3 Environmental, Social and Governance (ESG) vs Sustainability

The language surrounding sustainability issues can be confusing as there is not one source of globally understood definitions. Often the terms 'ESG' (Environmental, Social and Governance) and 'sustainability' are used interchangeably, however, it is generally understood that ESG is a sub-category of sustainability, considering risks and opportunities related to the environment, society and governance issues and how these can affect enterprise value.

ESG tends therefore to be more about an entity's dependencies than its impacts and so is more useful for investors and creditors than broader stakeholders. Sustainability is a broader concept that includes a company's commitment to responsible business practices and is relevant to a wider range of stakeholders.

Environmental, social and governance (ESG) is also referred to as the three pillars of sustainability and the Principle of Responsible Investment (PRI) defines ESG issues as follows:

(**Source:** https://www.unpri.org/Uploads/i/m/n/maindefinitionstoprireportingframework_127272_949397.pdf)

- **Environmental**: "Issues relating to the quality and functioning of the natural environment and natural systems. These include biodiversity loss; greenhouse gas (GHG) emissions, climate change, renewable energy, energy efficiency, air, water or resource depletion or pollution, waste management, stratospheric ozone depletion, changes in land use, ocean acidification and changes to the nitrogen and phosphorus cycles."

- **Social:** "Issues relating to the rights, well-being and interests of people and communities. These include human rights, labour standards in the supply chain, child, slave and bonded labour, workplace health and safety, freedom of association and freedom of expression, human capital management and employee relations; diversity; relations with local communities, activities in conflict zones, health and access to medicine, HIV/AIDS, consumer protection; and controversial weapons."

- **Governance:** "Issues relating to the governance of companies and other investee entities. In the listed equity context these include board structure, size, diversity, skills and independence, executive pay, shareholder rights, stakeholder interaction, disclosure of information, business ethics, bribery and corruption, internal controls, and risk management, and, in general, issues dealing with the relationship between a company's management, its board, its shareholders and its other stakeholders. This category may also include matters of business strategy."

Organisations recognise that sustainability and good ESG practice and reporting creates shareholder value. ESG and sustainability governance, strategy setting, and risk management are now standard practice in boardrooms. Some global stock exchanges mandate listed companies to prepare an annual sustainability report, in addition to its financial report. A sustainability report is a report published by a company about the economic, environmental, and social impacts caused by its business activity and operations and can include the reporting of ESG related targets and key performance indicators (KPIs). Increasingly, sustainability reporting is becoming mandatory for companies which are listed on global stock exchange.

2.4 Sustainability reports

Sustainability reports generally focus on three key factors: environment, social and governance. The addition of sustainability reporting to financial reporting provides a more comprehensive picture of the issuer: statements of financial position and profit or loss and other comprehensive income provide a snapshot of the present and an account of the past year, while sustainability reports of environmental, social and governance factors ('ESG factors') show the risks and opportunities within sight, managed for future returns. Taken together, the combined financial and sustainability reports enable a better assessment of the issuer's financial prospects and quality of management.

A sustainability report should comprise the following primary components:

- **Material ESG factors.**

    In broad terms, the following factors should be included:

    - **Environmental factors:** Materials, energy, water usage, emissions, effluents and waste, as well as environmental complaint mechanisms
    - **Social factors:** Health and safety, product responsibility, employment practices, labour rights (such as collective bargaining), and supplier assessments

- **Governance factors** relate to the procedures that the issuers have in place to manage economic, environmental and social performance. Anti-corruption and diversity factors could be included in governance or social factors.

- **Climate-related disclosures:** For example, listed companies in some countries have an obligation to report on climate risks and opportunities annually, on a comply or explain basis.

- **Policies, practice and performance:** In relation to the material ESG factors identified, providing descriptive and quantitative information on each of the factors for the reporting period. Actual performance should be described against targets.

- **Targets:** The issuer should set out its targets for the forthcoming year in relation to each material ESG factor.

- **Sustainability reporting framework:** The issuer should select an appropriate sustainability reporting framework (see section 2.5).

- **Board statement:** Disclosures included in the board statement should include the actions taken by the board to consider sustainability issues, to determine the material factors, and to oversee the management and monitoring of material factors.

2.4.1 ESG key performance indicators

A sustainability report should include a balance of short- and longer-term ESG related targets, specific measurable targets for all material topics and clear linkages between ESG targets and the company's financial performance and business strategy.

Examples of ESG key performance indicators (KPIs) are included in the table below:

Example	Suggested ESG Metric
Environment	
Greenhouse gas emissions ("GHG")	• Absolute emissions • Emission intensity
Energy consumption	• Energy consumption intensity
Water consumption	• Total water consumption • Water consumption intensity
Waste generation	• Total waste generated
Social	
Gender diversity	• Current employees by gender • New hires and turnover by gender
Age-based diversity	• Current employees by age • New hires and turnover by age
Employment	• Total turnover • Total number of employees
Development and training	• Average training hours per employee • Average training hours per employee per gender
Occupational health & safety	• Fatalities • High-consequence injuries • Recordable injuries • Recordable work-related ill health cases
Governance	
Board composition	• Board independence • Balance between the skills, experience, gender, race, and tenure of board members.
Management diversity	• Balance between the skills, experience, gender, race within the management team.
Ethical behaviour	• Anti-corruption disclosures • Anti-corruption training for employees
Certifications	• List all sustainability or ESG-related certification
Alignment with frameworks	• The issuer needs to give priority to using globally recognised frameworks and disclosure practices to guide its sustainability reporting.

PART A   THE FOUNDATIONS OF GOVERNANCE

Example	Suggested ESG Metric
Assurance	• Disclose whether sustainability report has undertaken: (a) External independent assurance; (b) Internal assurance; or (c) No assurance. • Provide scope of assurance if organisation has undertaken external or internal assurance.

2.5 Reporting frameworks

The increased global interest in sustainability and the demand for transparency from investors on sustainability-related issues resulted in the emergence of different regulatory and voluntary sustainability disclosure frameworks.

The many different sources of guidance and regulatory requirements that emerged caused difficulties for preparers who were not sure which guidance to apply, and for investors, who reported inconsistency between entities and variation in the quality and quantity of information provided.

The table below summarises some of the prominent frameworks for sustainability reporting.

Framework	Reporting on:	Most useful to:
Global Reporting Initiative (see section 2.5.1)	Impacts	Broader stakeholders, including investors and others who are interested in impacts
Task Force on Climate-related Financial Disclosures (TCFD)	Climate-related risks and opportunities (arising from impacts and dependencies); some information on climate-related impacts where specified	Investors and other providers of capital
Taskforce on Nature-related Financial Disclosures (TNFD)	Nature-related risks and opportunities (arising from impacts and dependencies); nature-related impacts	Both investors and other providers of capital as well as broader stakeholders
European Sustainability Reporting Standards (ESRSs) (see section 2.5.2)	Impacts; sustainability related risks and opportunities (arising from impacts and dependencies)	Both investors and other providers of capital as well as broader stakeholders
ISSB – IFRS Sustainability Disclosure Standards (see section 2.5.3)	Sustainability-related risks and opportunities (arising from impacts and dependencies); some information on climate related impacts where specified	Investors and other providers of capital

You will learn more about sustainability reporting frameworks at Professional Level 1, but the following sections give a brief overview of the three sets of standards from the GRI (GRI Standards), the EU (ESRs) and the ISSB (IFRS Sustainability Disclosure Standards).

2.5.1 Global Reporting Initiative (GRI)

The GRI Standards are currently the most widely used set of sustainability reporting standards in the world (GRI, no date).

The objective of sustainability reporting using the GRI Standards is to provide transparency on how an entity contributes or aims to contribute to sustainable development (GRI, 2021). The GRI standards focus on reporting the entity's impacts on the economy, the environment and people and how the entity manages these impacts. A principle of the GRI standards is stakeholder inclusiveness and requires businesses to identify stakeholders beyond investors and lenders.

The focus of the GRI Standards is on reporting an entity's impacts, and not its dependencies. Therefore, it is limited in its usefulness to investors when they are assessing the future prospects of an entity.

The GRI Standards are structured as a system of interrelated standards that are organised into three series:

- GRI Universal Standards,
- GRI Sector Standards, and
- GRI Topic Standards.

The *Universal Standards* are used by all organisations when reporting in accordance with the GRI Standards. Organisations use the *Sector Standards* according to the sectors in which they operate, and the *Topic Standards* according to their list of material topics.

Case Study — Reporting under the GRI Standards

The GRI reported in October 2022 that four-in-five of the largest global companies were reporting sustainability in accordance with GRI. (Source: https://www.globalreporting.org/news/news-center/four-in-five-largest-global-companies-report-with-gri/ [online] last accessed 3 July 2024)

An example of a large global company reporting under GRI is global energy company Shell. The sustainability report for Shell for 2023 can be filtered by GRI sector topics. You can have a look at an example of the extensive reporting on sustainability provided by Shell under the GRI standards (see https://reports.shell.com/sustainability-report/2023/ [online] last accessed 3 July 2024).

2.5.2 European Union's Corporate Sustainability Reporting Directive (CSRD)

The CSRD, which seeks to significantly expand the reporting on sustainability by companies in order to help stakeholders, was adopted by the EU in 2022. The first reporting under the CSRD, using the recently issued European Sustainability Reporting Standards (ESRSs), relates to accounting periods commencing 1 January 2024, with a phased implementation for certain companies over three years. ESRS 1 *General Requirements* requires certain sustainability information to be included in a company's annual report, in a dedicated section of the management report. The structure of the reporting is specified in ESRS 1. The sustainability information must be subject to external assurance.

Under the ESRSs, companies must report on four areas: governance; strategy; impact, risk and opportunity management; and metrics and targets, over three topics:

- **Environment** – encompassing climate change, pollution, water and marine resources, biodiversity and ecosystems, resource use and circular economy
- **Social** – encompassing own workforce, workers in the value chain, affected communities, consumers and end users
- **Governance** – business conduct

(KPMG, 2023)

The ESRSs specify some mandatory disclosures, which must be made by all entities, and other disclosures which are only required if they are **material**. We consider the concept of materiality in the context of audit in Chapters 8 and 10, which is mostly concerned with a single materiality assessment as to whether financial misstatements would significantly impact the users of the financial statements.

Materiality in the context of sustainability reporting requires a **double materiality** assessment. This means considering both impact materiality and financial materiality from a sustainability perspective.

- **Impact materiality** considers whether a company's activities (direct or indirect) significantly impact on people and planet.
- **Financial materiality** considers the risks and opportunities arising from sustainability issues which may have a material impact on the company's value in the short, medium or long term.

2.5.3 IFRS Sustainability Disclosure Standards

IFRS Sustainability Disclosure Standards are issued by **the International Sustainability Standards Board (ISSB)**, formed by the IFRS Foundation. The ISSB seeks to create of a comprehensive global set of **sustainability standards** that are focussed on meeting the information needs of investors. IFRS Sustainability Disclosure Standards are also known as 'ISSB Standards'.

In addition to the information needs of investors, the ISSB focus is also on providing information to capital markets. This focus is likely to mean that the impacts of the entity are not fully reported and may be limited to the extent that they affect investors and the capital markets. This is a narrower scope than the requirements of the EU CSRD.

The ISSB issued the first two IFRS Sustainability Disclosure Standards in June 2023:
- IFRS S1: *General Requirements for Disclosure of Sustainability-related Financial Information*
- IFRS S2: *Climate-related Disclosures*

IFRS S1 sets out the general requirements for disclosing sustainability-related information. IFRS S1 refers companies to other ISSB Standards or to other sources for detailed requirements on different topics. IFRS S1 provides a framework for entities to disclose sustainability-related information that is material to their financial performance and prospects. This information can help investors and other stakeholders make informed decisions.

For climate-related disclosures that are reasonably expected to affect the entity's prospects, **entities should apply IFRS S2**. As there are currently no other issued ISSB Standards, an entity should use other sources for guidance on what to disclose on other sustainability-related topics.

An entity must apply both standards in order to comply with IFRS Sustainability Disclosure Standards.

The standards are effective for reporting periods beginning from 1 January 2024, though earlier adoption is permitted provided both standards are applied together.

The ISSB Standards can be accessed on the IFRS Foundation website here: https://www.ifrs.org/issued-standards/ifrs-sustainability-standards-navigator.

Note that application of the standards is on a **voluntary basis** unless jurisdiction authorities decide to require application. However, it is anticipated a number of jurisdictions will enforce the application of the standards and a large number of companies will voluntarily apply the standards, such is the global demand for transparent and credible sustainability reporting.

2.5.4 Assurance over sustainability reporting and disclosures

Part B of this Workbook looks at assurance in relation to the statutory audit of an entity's financial statements.

At the time of writing this Workbook, the audit of sustainability related disclosures in annual reports or separate sustainability reports presented with the financial statements is **not mandatory**.

However, the proportion of companies seeking assurance on their sustainability disclosures continues to rise, as does the demand for statutory assurance on sustainability reporting.

We cover the assurance engagements in this area along with any guidance available for assurance providers expressing opinions over sustainability reporting in Chapter 8.

2.5.5 IFRS Sustainability reporting standards and statutory audit

We have already noted that, at the time of writing, the application of IFRS S1 and IFRS S2 is not compulsory, and nor is obtaining assurance over the sustainability disclosures.

However, there is likely to be widespread adoption of the standards and disclosures are likely to be presented alongside the financial statements in the annual reporting process, increasingly in separate sustainability reports. This means there are going to be implications for the statutory audit.

(a) Under International Standards on Auditing (ISAs) auditors are required to read information presented with the financial statements being audited (including the sustainability related reporting) and report any inconsistencies in it with the financial statements. If it turns out there is an error is in the financial statements it will increase the work to be completed and may impact on their overall audit opinion if unresolved (we look at the audit opinion in Chapter 8).

(b) The sustainability information reported under IFRS S1 and S2 may indicate risks of material misstatement (or even going concern issues) within the financial statements. The auditor should have identified sustainability related risks (including due to climate change) during the risk assessment process. However, they should consider the information disclosed under any sustainability reporting framework and consider if further risks arise as well as what audit procedures might be needed. Types of audit procedures are covered in part B of this Workbook.

(c) The auditor should consider the potential financial impact of any information reported under IFRS S1 and S2. For example, if it becomes clear that environmental or human rights legislation has not been complied with, there are likely to be substantial fines payable and damage to the company's reputation causing a loss of business.

2.6 Sustainability and governance

In Chapter 5 you saw how the increasing prominence of sustainability has led to companies adapting their business structures so that they can properly oversee the organisation's Environmental, Social and Governance (ESG) strategy and framework. In some cases accountability has been placed with an existing committee (such as the audit committee) but increasingly companies have been and are establishing dedicated sustainability committees, sometimes referred to as, or named, ESG committees.

In the following section we examine the importance of the work of this committee, the composition of the membership and the tasks or duties that are typically assigned to the committee.

2.6.1 Establishing a sustainability committee

Chapter 5 highlighted the steady increase in the proportion of companies establishing sustainability committees voluntarily. Formation of a robust sustainability committee has been increasingly prioritised due to the value it is considered to add to the business.

Benefits of establishing a sustainability include:

- **Sending a clear message to investors** that the company is responding to stakeholder demand to appropriately manage ESG impacts and dependencies, as well as reporting more about sustainability.

- **Incorporating sustainability into business strategy**. ESG will cover multiple business areas including compliance, human resources, procurement and development. A sustainability committee can help integrate sustainability into all of these and increase collaboration across these different business areas.

- **Increasing ESG expertise** and accountability. This helps the company to better understand sustainability related issues and take the appropriate action to add value and minimise risks.

- **Committing appropriate time to a key business driver.** The full board has an array of pressures and duties, and if responsibility remained with them sustainability may not be given the essential and appropriate time and care needed.

- **Taking advantage of commercial opportunities**. ESG if unmanaged can result in risks to reputation and regulatory risk, but with good governance it also provides potential opportunities for businesses to position themselves as leaders or supply profitable goods/services in times of transition to, for example, a zero-carbon economy.

- **Enhancing the reputation of the entity.** The increased focus on sustainability along with transparent reporting of ESG by the company will become associated with the company brand and over time can enhance the reputation of the company amongst different stakeholder groups, particularly consumers.

However, if implementation of the committee is not properly managed there can be drawbacks to the formation of a separate sustainability committee.

- **Duplication of work** if other committees are also assigned similar tasks or communication of roles is poor.
- **Over-reliance on the committee** if the rest of the board think that by establishing a committee, then sustainability issues are automatically dealt with.
- **Greenwashing.** This is where the committee is established to 'tick a sustainability box' and there is sustainability reporting stating that a company has an active sustainability committee and is managing sustainability effectively, when in reality little action is taken and the impact is minimal.

2.6.2 The role of the sustainability committee

The role and duties of a sustainability committee can vary from one organisation to another but based on good practice among organisations leading on ESG management and disclosures, some duties are generally accepted as falling under the remit of the sustainability committee.

Case Study — Sustainability committee duties

Duties categorised by key sustainability related areas were highlighted in the Chartered Governance Institute UK & Ireland 2024 report *'Governing Sustainability: Are sustainability committees the answer?*

Sustainability related area	Duties
ESG strategy or framework	- Oversee development of the ESG strategy/framework - Ensure the strategy is aligned with regulations, good practice and the company's business plan, values and objectives - Oversee the execution of the ESG strategy - Review the effectiveness of governance and processes in place to ensure the ESG strategy is delivered - Advise on the risks and opportunities for the organisation's operations and reputation in relation to ESG - Oversee materiality assessments, climate scenario analysis, and cost-benefit analyses of different courses of action - Support the long-term sustainable success of the organisation, through long-term strategic and net zero transition planning
Goals and metrics	- Advise on appropriate ESG strategic goals, and short- and long-term science-based targets - Advise on and oversee ESG metrics and key performance indicators (KPIs) - Monitor annual and long-term progress against previously set ESG objectives - Oversee the ongoing measurement and reporting of performance against ESG metrics and KPIs - Monitor the organisation's performance against peers and/or external benchmarks - Explore options for external accreditation of ESG goals and metrics
Reporting and disclosures	- Review the content, integrity and completeness of external statements and disclosures about ESG - Review ESG-related reporting prior to approval, including the annual sustainability report - Evaluate the extent and effectiveness of external reporting on ESG performance

Sustainability related area	Duties
	• Regularly review the requirement for assurance of ESG-related matters and appoint parties to provide assurance where necessary
Horizon scanning	• Identify current and emerging ESG-related issues, standards, good practice, and regulatory or legislative development • Determine how these should be reflected in the organisation's ESG objectives, policies and reporting • Oversee compliance with relevant ESG-related legislation and regulation, including any training or external consultation needed
Policies and procedures	• Monitor the establishment of appropriate ESG-related policies, procedures • Encourage high standards of ethical behaviour and decision-making
Social issues	• Advise the board on the organisation's appetite and tolerance with respect to environmental and social risk • Identify material ESG-related risks and ensure they are captured in the organisation's risk management framework • Articulate the risks of taking no action to tackle ESG issues or to mitigate ESG-related risks
Resourcing ESG projects	• Make recommendations to the board in relation to the required resourcing and funding of ESG-related activities

2.6.3 Composition of the sustainability committee

The number of members on a sustainability committee should be comparable with other board-level committees to ensure it receives the necessary attention. Members of the committee should have an appropriate mix of skills and experience to ensure that the organisation and its board are prepared to respond to ESG-related risks and opportunities.

Where corporate governance codes are established and enforced they recommend that **all, or the majority**, of any committee at board level should be made up of **independent non-executive directors**.

For example, the FRC's Guidance that sits alongside the 2024 UK Corporate Governance Code states that members of any board-level committee should be independent non-executive directors (FRC's *Corporate Governance Code Guidance* 2024, para. 87).

In practice, one or more executive directors will often be found on sustainability committees, but it is important that membership includes significant representation of independent non-executive directors.

Ensuring **diversity and equality** within board and committee composition is an important factor, including genre, ethnicity and age considerations.

Case Study — Sustainability committee diversity

Spencer Stuart's UK Board Index 2023 looked at the largest 150 FTSE companies and found the following:

(a) 64% of sustainability committee chairs are women. This indicates significant gender diversity, compared to other committees. For example, women make up 34% of audit committee chairs and 18% of nomination committee chairs.

(b) Women make up 45% of the total membership of sustainability committees.

(c) Directors with an ethnic minority background make up approximately 17% of the members of sustainability committees according to Spencer Stuart's 2023 Index, compared to 13% of directorships across FTSE 150 boards as a whole.

These findings seem to indicate that sustainability committees are on average slightly more diverse than the full board.

(Source: Diversity, 2023 UK Spencer Stuart Board Index (Sustainability and ESG committees. Accessed 28 June 2024 [online] https://www.spencerstuart.com/research-and-insight/uk-board-index/sustainability)

2.6.4 Sustainability: Corporate governance codes and guidance

This is an evolving area and guidance on ESG governance is emerging within or alongside established corporate governance best practice guidance.

Case Study — FRC Corporate Governance Code Guidance

The FRC's Guidance accompanying the 2024 UK Corporate Governance Code includes a section on the role of sustainability committees.

You can access this section of the guidance at https://www.frc.org.uk/library/standards-codes-policy/corporate-governance/corporate-governance-code-guidance/#role-of-sustainability-committees-44cea40c.

You will notice the references to assessing the need for 'external assurance on the effectiveness of policies, processes and reporting on sustainability and environmental social and governance matters' (FRC *Corporate Governance Code Guidance* 2024, para. 148).

Assurance over sustainability related matters was discussed in Section 2.5.3 and is considered further in Chapter 8.

3 Managing stakeholders

FAST FORWARD

> Different groups of stakeholders have different objectives which can lead to conflicts between competing groups. By understanding the different stakeholders and their needs and goals, then an organisation can determine strategies to resolve stakeholder conflicts which may prevent an organisation from achieving its strategic objectives.

Where companies are poorly governed and where they fail to properly meet their social responsibilities, then it is their stakeholders who will be affected by this. In recent years, the spotlight has fallen on wealth inequality and climate change as areas in which companies are failing. This has contributed to the development of the sustainability reporting frameworks we looked at in Section 2.

Climate change is a key problem facing modern societies and provides a good illustration of the difficulties involved with governing a privately-owned corporation whose actions affect society as a whole. Most carbon emissions (the drivers of climate change) are made by private companies; these affect the whole of society, but the benefits of these carbon-intensive activities are reaped only by specific parties (eg customers, employees, shareholders). Stakeholder theory therefore provides a useful perspective on the issue – if society as a whole is considered a stakeholder, then it is argued that companies ought to take into account their impact on the environment if they are to be responsible corporate citizens.

Stakeholder theory itself has been covered in Chapter 1. In this section, we will now move to consider the objectives and roles of stakeholders, as well as managing stakeholder expectations.

3.1 Objectives of stakeholder groups

When formulating and evaluating financial strategies, it is important to bear in mind the organisation's stakeholders. These are people or groups who have an interest in the organisation's activities. Depending on the precise relationship between the organisation and the stakeholder group the success of the financial strategy can be affected significantly by the stakeholder group.

The various groups of internal and external stakeholders of an organisation will have diverse goals. They will exercise different levels of influence on the organisation and, in some cases, will affect the organisation's financial strategy. For example, an organisation's lenders have significant legal rights that have to be fulfilled by an organisation. Failure on the company's part to satisfy their obligations in relation to this powerful stakeholder group could lead to the company being liquidated.

Stakeholders were defined in Chapter 1 and a summary of typical stakeholders is provided in the following diagram.

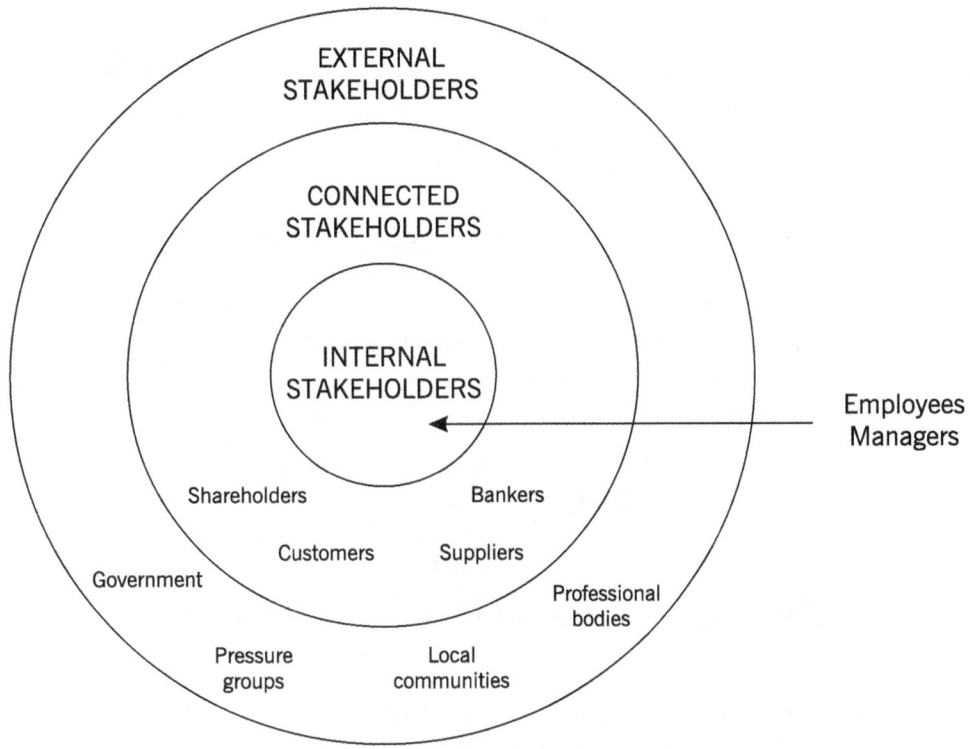

The following table is a summary of wider stakeholder objectives:

Stakeholder goals	
Shareholders	Providers of risk capital, aim to maximise wealth
Suppliers	Often other businesses, aim to be paid full amount by date agreed, but want to continue long-term trading relationship, and so may accept later payment
Long-term lenders	Wish to receive payments of interest and capital on loan by due date for repayment
Employees	Maximise rewards paid to them in salaries and benefits, also prefer continuity in employment
Government	Political and economic objectives such as sustained economic growth and high employment
Community	Wish to have a good 'corporate neighbour'. Source of stable employment and income for the local community. Economic regeneration
Management	Maximising their own rewards, safeguarding career prospects

The actions of stakeholder groups in pursuit of their various goals can exert influence on strategy. The **greater** the **power** of the **stakeholder**, the greater their influence will be.

Many managers acknowledge that the interests of some stakeholder groups (eg themselves and employees) should be recognised and provided for, even if this means that the interests of shareholders might be adversely affected. Not all stakeholder group interests can be given specific attention in the decisions of management, but those stakeholders for whom management recognises and accepts a responsibility are referred to as **constituents** of the firm.

All organisations have a range of stakeholders or stakeholder groups. Some stakeholders may be relatively passive or lack influence. However, some organisations have stakeholders whose influence can be disruptive of the achievement of strategic goals.

3.2 Stakeholder objectives

The **stakeholder view** is particularly important in the business context, where shareholders own the business but employees, customers and government also have particularly strong claims to having their interests considered.

3.2.1 Stakeholder objectives

The following are some examples of stakeholders' objectives. These examples are not intended to be comprehensive, more to demonstrate why organisations are driven to improve business performance, adapt to external markets or innovate and diversify.

(a) **Employees and managers**

   (i) Job security (over and above legal protection)
   (ii) Good conditions of work (above minimum safety standards)
   (iii) Job satisfaction
   (iv) Career development and relevant training
   (v) Personal achievement

(b) **Customers**

   (i) Products of a certain quality at a reasonable price
   (ii) Products that should last a certain number of years
   (iii) A product or service that specifically meets customer needs.
   (iv) A product or service which is new, innovative or provides a seamless customer experience

(c) **Suppliers**: Regular orders in return for reliable delivery and good service

(d) **Shareholders**: Long-term wealth enhancement within acceptable risk levels

(e) **Providers of loan capital (stockholders):** Reliable payment of interest and capital repayments due and maintenance of the value of any security

(f) **Society as a whole**

   (i) Control environmental pollution, reduce energy consumption and increase usage of renewable resources
   (ii) Provide fair wages, employment rights and conditions, training and advancement opportunities
   (iii) Provide a regular source of tax to profits
   (iv) Financial assistance to charities, sports and community activities
   (v) Co-operate with government in identifying and preventing health hazards

Organisations which communicate with the different stakeholder group will understand the specific expectations on business performance and this often helps management to pursue an optimal strategy for the organisation.

It is suggested that modern corporations are so powerful, socially, economically and politically, that unrestrained use of their power will inevitably damage other people's rights. For example, they may blight an entire community by closing a major facility, thus enforcing long-term unemployment on a large proportion of the local workforce.

However, organisations are now much more cautious about how there are perceived and as a response some organisations invest in corporate communications departments specifically to manage brand image and perception, media briefings, press statements and direct communications with stakeholders.

The exercise of corporate social responsibility (CSR) constrains the organisation to act at all times as a good citizen.

3.2.2 Stakeholder risks

Each group of stakeholders will react to the severity of the risk it faces, for example, employees will strike if they fear their employments rights are being threatened. Organisations can analyse the various risks to stakeholders to understand and respond to likely stakeholder reactions.

Stakeholder	Risk (Interests to defend)	Stakeholder response to risk
Internal Managers and employees (eg restructuring, relocation)	• Jobs/careers • Money • Promotion • Benefits • Satisfaction	• Pursuit of systems goals rather than shareholder interests • Industrial action • Negative power to impede implementation • Refusal to relocate • Resignation
Connected Shareholders (corporate strategy)	• Increase in shareholder wealth, measured by profitability, P/E ratios, market capitalisation, dividends and yield • Risk	• Sell shares (eg to predator) or replace management
Bankers (cash flows)	• Security of loan • Adherence to loan agreements	• Denial of credit • Higher interest charges • Receivership
Suppliers (purchase strategy)	• Profitable sales • Payment for goods • Long-term relationship	• Refusal of credit • Court action • Wind down relationships
Customers (product market strategy)	• Goods as promised • Future benefits	• Buy elsewhere • Sue
External Government	• Jobs, training, tax	• Tax increases • Regulation • Legal action
Interest/pressure groups	• Pollution • Rights • Other	• Publicity • Direct action • Sabotage • Pressure on government

How stakeholders relate to the management of the company depends very much on what type of stakeholder they are: internal, connected or external: and on the level in the management hierarchy at which they are able to apply pressure. Clearly a company's management will respond differently to the demands of, say, its shareholders and the community at large.

The way in which the relationship between company and stakeholders is conducted is a function of the parties' relative stakeholder bargaining strength and the philosophy underlying each party's objectives.

Stakeholders' bargaining strength can be shown by means of a spectrum as illustrated in the following diagram.

	Weak			Stakeholders' bargaining strength			Strong
Company's conduct of relationship	Command/ dictated by company	Consultation and consideration of stakeholders' views	Negotiation	Participation and acceptance of stakeholders' views	Democratic voting by stakeholders	Command/ dictated by stakeholders

Illustration of stakeholders' bargaining strength

The relative stakeholder bargaining strength exerted by each of the various stakeholder groups can shape strategic decisions made by its management as well as the overall strategic direction of an organisation as they seek to meet the various stakeholder needs.

For example. stakeholders, such as shareholders or government, impose specific targets for the organisation to achieve. For example, a 5% rise in the share price or dividend or a 20% reduction in CO_2 emissions.

Without ethical safeguards in place and under pressure to meet performance targets, organisations can make decisions and implement policies which prioritise financial performance and profitability. This can sometimes result in unethical practises which can cause harm to individuals, to the environment, to the community or other stakeholder groups.

Here, stakeholders perform an important role in regulating company behaviour by making clear the expectations in terms of adhering to ethical principles or responding when unethical practices become known.

3.3 Stakeholder roles and responsibilities

We have considered how stakeholders can influence the **strategy** of an organisation. Now we consider how stakeholders can affect the **performance** of an organisation. We use specific examples of stakeholder groups to show how these affect the performance of organisations.

3.3.1 Employees and management

Employees and management are internal stakeholders. They may exert considerable power over the performance of the organisation. Organisations should aim to align the interests of their staff with those of the organisation.

In other words, organisations should look at ways of motivating their employees and managers to perform better by agreeing to organisational objectives, such as:

- **Motivation for employees** to perform well comes in a variety of guises. Some will work harder and better for more money whereas others prefer benefits or promotion. Many employees rank the environment in which they work as important for their well-being and productivity.

- **Performance measurement** for managers is usually designed so that by attaining targets set by the organisation, they earn rewards. These targets can be negotiated or imposed depending on the culture of the organisation. The rewards are linked to the attainment of the targets using various means.

- **Simple bonuses** can be paid on the achievement of a target return or profit.

- **Share options** can be granted whereby the reward is linked to the growth in the share price of the organisation. Thus, on the exercise of the option, and receipt of the shares, any growth in the share price from the date of grant is realised by the employee if they sell the shares or earn income from dividends on shares received.

However, there is a danger of dysfunctional behaviour where individuals concentrate on attaining just the measure that leads to the reward to the exclusion of other activities. There is also a risk of the measure being manipulated so that it is achieved whatever the consequences. A good example of this manipulation is return on capital employed (ROCE) where the return can be improved by retaining older written down assets thereby keeping the capital employed figure low. This may not be the optimum replacement policy for assets but will improve the measure of ROCE.

3.3.2 Shareholders

Shareholders represent a class of connected stakeholder, which provides funds for investment. They often take a short-term view of their involvement in an organisation.

Shareholders can be influential stakeholders, encouraging management to improve performance, by their decision to hold or sell shares.

Institutional shareholders often have significant holdings in companies. They usually hold shares for capital growth or their revenue stream, so they tend to monitor performance closely and dispose of under-performing shares. They can be a strong influence on the decisions made by the organisation in which they hold their shares.

Profit-making organisations tend to focus on financial performance in general and on the interests of shareholders in particular.

The traditional argument for this is that shareholders are the legal owners, the company belongs to them and so their interests are paramount. This means:

(a) Maximising shareholder wealth is a long-term goal for an organisation, inevitably managers must decide between what funds they want to disburse now and what funds need to be maintained in the business to ensure the prospects of long-term profitability.

(b) Shareholders own the business, and so the directors of the company have a duty to safeguard their interests.

(c) What the shareholders require as a return is used to judge the validity of investment projects.

(d) Shareholders assess the quality of management by how well the business performs financially.

(e) Shareholders are the principal source of capital investment in an organisation. They provide funds on share issues or permit managers to retain profits for investment.

A company's senior management should remain aware of who its major shareholders are, and it will often help to retain shareholders' support if the chairman or the managing director meets occasionally with the major shareholders, to exchange views.

(a) The company's management might learn about shareholders' preferences for either high dividends or high retained earnings for profit growth and capital gain.

(b) For public companies, changes in shareholdings might help to explain recent share price movements.

(c) The company's management should be able to learn about shareholders' attitudes to both risk and gearing. If a company is planning a new investment, its management might have to consider the relative merits of seeking equity finance or debt finance, and shareholders' attitudes would be worth knowing about before the decision is taken.

(d) Management might need to know its shareholders in the event of an unwelcome takeover bid from another company, to identify key shareholders whose views on the takeover bid might be crucial to the final outcome.

3.3.3 Consumer groups

Consumer groups are a connected group representing consumers' interests. They exist to ensure that products give good value. They promote safeguards for consumers against unethical business practice.

Consumerism reflects the increased importance and power of consumers. It appears in organised consumer groups, and the recognition by producers that consumer satisfaction is the key to long-term profitability.

3.3.4 Suppliers

Suppliers are a connected group of stakeholders. They can influence the cost and quality of goods and services. Suppliers can directly influence the performance of an organisation through the quality of the goods and services that they supply to an organisation. Poor quality goods will affect the saleability of the product to the customer, depressing sales and revenues.

The prices that suppliers charge will also affect the profitability of the end product if margins are eroded.

Organisations have developed a number of strategies for controlling price and quality from their suppliers. The best known of these is just-in-time that commits suppliers to supply on-demand zero-defect parts. If an organisation has confidence in its supplier, a long-term relationship will be established.

3.3.5 Government

Government is an external stakeholder group. Central government sets the regulatory framework in which organisations operate. Local government has devolved powers and can raise local revenues from business.

Question — Identifying stakeholders

You work as a senior advisor to the board of a large, listed organisation that operates in the construction industry. The services offered range from homebuilding to large civil engineering projects, such as bridges and dams, and can be undertaken for central and local government bodies as well as other profit-making companies. All projects are carried out by staff who require formal accreditation by their professional body.

Required

Draft a list of stakeholders for the board and briefly explain the nature of each stakeholder's claim.

Answer

The list of stakeholders is likely to include the following (with their claims in brackets)

- **Shareholders** who require a return on their investment – (this is a direct claim because they are in contact with the organisation already)
- **Lenders** who require their loans to be serviced in full and on time (also direct)
- **Customers** who require good quality projects to be completed (also direct)
- **Suppliers** who require being paid on time (also direct)
- **Employees** who require good working conditions and being paid on time (also direct)
- **The general public** who requires no adverse effects from the organisation and its projects (such as safe housing, reliable infrastructure)(direct/indirect)
- **The government** which requires tax to be paid on corporate profits and other expenses, plus the ideal of maximising employment levels in the economy (probably also direct)
- **Professional bodies** which require the organisation's accreditation process to be robust to maintain their reputation (also direct)
- **Plants and animals** whose natural environment is affected by civil engineering projects being built – (they require a clean, unspoilt environment to live in, but their claims are indirect because they did not ask to be affected by the organisation's projects)
- **People living near a construction project** (whether housing or some other kind) who require a quiet, clean and safe environment in which to live but who may be adversely affected by either the construction process or the finished asset (again, likely to be indirect)

3.4 Stakeholder analysis

Different stakeholder groups will assess differently the risk a strategy poses to their interests due to their attitude and appetite to for risk. Some stakeholders are able to exercise power over management to direct strategic direction to actively manage this.

It is helpful for management to understand which stakeholders are likely to exert most influence. Stakeholder mapping may be used to analysis the influence of various stakeholder groups.

Stakeholder analysis (sometimes referred to as stakeholder mapping) uses Mendelow's matrix (Johnson, Scholes & Whittington, 2007) and helps an organisation establish its priorities in relation to managing stakeholder expectations. The matrix classifies stakeholders in terms of the power they can exert on the organisation, and the likelihood that they will show an interest in the organisation's activities (and therefore exert that power).

These factors (power and interest) will help define the type of relationship the organisation should seek with its stakeholders.

	Level of interest	
	Low	High
Power High	Keep satisfied	Key players
Power Low	Minimal effort	Keep informed

(**Source:** Johnson, Scholes & Whittington, 2007, p.156)

- **Stakeholders with high level of power and interest are key players.** An organisation's strategy must be acceptable, and they need to be managed closely. An example of a key player could be a major customer.

- **Stakeholders with a high power, but low interest, must be treated with care.** Although they are currently passive, they are capable of becoming key players if their level of interest increases. Therefore, they need to be kept satisfied. Large institutional shareholders could be an example of this type of stakeholder: with increasing levels of shareholder activism in recent years also demonstrating their potential to move from 'keep satisfied' to 'key players'.

- **Stakeholders with low power and high interest must be kept informed.** These stakeholders have little ability to influence strategy in their own right, but their views could be important in influencing more powerful stakeholders: perhaps by lobbying, for example. They should therefore be kept informed.

- **Stakeholders with low power and low interest require** minimal effort is expended on stakeholders who have both low power and low interest.

Stakeholder analysis is used to assess the significance of stakeholder groups. This in turn has implications for the organisation.

- The framework of **corporate governance** should recognise stakeholders' levels of interest and power.
- It may be appropriate to seek to **reposition** certain stakeholders and discourage others from repositioning themselves, depending on their attitudes.
- Key **blockers** and **facilitators** of change must be identified.

Stakeholder analysis can also be used to establish **political priorities**. A map of the current position can be compared with a map of a desired future state. This will indicate critical shifts that must be pursued.

Stakeholder analysis, or also referred to as stakeholder mapping, demonstrates that different stakeholders can have varying degrees of influence on management and the strategy of an organisation. Specific groups of stakeholders are motivated by different aims. In the next section, we will look at the role of the management accountant in helping management to analyse the different needs and provide management with analysis to support business performance and meet specific performance targets.

We can look in detail at the stakeholder groups that not only have an **interest** in an organisation but also **power** over it.

The external coalition	The internal coalition
• Owners (who hold legal title) • Associates (suppliers, customers, trading partners) • Employee associations (unions, professional bodies) • Public (government, media)	• The chief executive and board at the strategic apex • Line managers • Operators • Support staff • Ideology (ie culture and formal and informal power structures)

Each of these stakeholder groups has three basic choices:

1. **Loyalty.** Stakeholders can follow decisions and/or do as they are told.
2. **Exit.** Stakeholders can exit by selling their shares or getting a new job, for example.
3. **Voice.** Stakeholders can stay and try to change the system. Those who choose voice are those who can, to varying degrees, influence the organisation. Influence implies a degree of power and willingness to exercise it.

Existing structures and systems can channel stakeholder influence.

- They are the location of power, giving groups of people varying degrees of influence over strategic choices.
- They are conduits of information, which shape strategic decisions.
- They limit choices or give some options priority over others. These may be physical or ethical constraints over what is possible.
- They embody culture.
- They determine the successful implementation of strategy.
- The firm has different degrees of dependency on various stakeholder groups. A company with a cash flow crisis will be more beholden to its bankers than one with regular cash surpluses.

Different stakeholders will have their own views as to strategy. As some groups have negative stakeholder power, in other words power to impede or disrupt the decision, their likely response might be considered.

Strategic options pose varying degrees of risk to the **interests** of the different stakeholders. It is possible that they may respond in such a way as to reduce the attractiveness of the proposed strategy.

3.5 Enhancing stakeholder engagement

Key terms

Stakeholder engagement: Stakeholder engagement is the process of involving all parties affected by a company's operations in its decision-making processes.

Integrating sustainability into business practice requires a robust framework of corporate accountability and proactive stakeholder engagement.

We looked at the increasing prominence and demand for sustainable development and reporting in Section 2. Organisations that embrace sustainability best practice not only enhance their reputations and build trust but also drive long-term sustainable value for all stakeholders. By doing so, they contribute to a more sustainable and equitable world, addressing critical global challenges such as climate change, social inequality, and environmental degradation. Stakeholder engagement helps to alleviate the need for shareholders to launch shareholder activism attacks of the type discussed in Chapter 1. This is because the views of stakeholders (including minority investors) are captured early and factored into corporate decision making.

3.5.1 Donaldson and Preston's stakeholder engagement theory

According to Donaldson and Preston's stakeholder engagement theory, businesses have a duty to consider the interests of all their stakeholders, not just shareholders and argue that organisations have a responsibility to balance the needs and expectations of these diverse groups of stakeholders to achieve sustainability. (**Source:** Donaldson, T., & Preston, L. E. (1995). "The Stakeholder Theory of the Corporation: Concepts, Evidence, and Implications." Academy of Management Review, 20(1), 65-91.)

Donaldson and Preston (1995) theory to stakeholder engagement is divided into three interrelated perspectives:

Perspectives of stakeholder engagement	Description
Normative approach	The **normative approach** asserts that considering stakeholders' interests is inherently the right thing to do. It is based on ethical principles and the intrinsic value of treating all stakeholders with respect and fairness.
Descriptive Approach	The **descriptive approach** describes how companies actually operate, showing that businesses naturally interact with various stakeholders and that these interactions influence corporate behaviour.
Instrumental Approach	The **instrumental approach** perspective suggests that attending to stakeholders' interests can lead to better business outcomes, such as increased loyalty, improved reputation, and long-term profitability.

3.5.2 Enhancing stakeholder engagement

Effective stakeholder engagement enhances corporate accountability by ensuring that boards of directors take stakeholder expectations and feedback seriously which means a company actions are much more likely to align with stakeholder needs and wider societal values.

Conversely, by implementing corporate accountability practices delivers the drivers for organisations to invest in meaningful stakeholder engagement.

Therefore, organisations require a methodology to achieve effective stakeholder engagement. Donaldson and Preston (1995) theory of stakeholder engagement recommends the following three stages.

1   **Identify key stakeholders**

    Organisations must recognise the diverse groups affected by their actions, including employees, customers, suppliers, local communities, and investors.

2   **Deploy stakeholder engagement strategies**

    Effective stakeholder engagement involves open communication, transparency, and responsiveness. Organisations use various methods such as surveys, public consultations, and social media platforms to engage with stakeholders.

3   **Integrate stakeholder feedback to organisation's strategic and operational objectives**

    Organisations should evaluate then incorporate feedback from stakeholders into their strategic planning and operations.

3.6 Managing stakeholder conflict

> **FAST FORWARD**
>
> The fundamental objective of a profit making organisation is normally the maximisation of shareholders' wealth. In its purest sense, this means pursuing the maximum amount of profit from the organisation's operations. A threat to this objective is conflicting shareholder objectives.

Organisations must consider the interests of managers and owners may conflict so areas of conflict can be effectively managed. Shareholder wealth may be maximised by reducing the local workforce or changing the nature of the work done due to new technology being available. This would be perceived as a conflict with the goals of employee.

In Chapter 1 we looked at the separation of ownership (shareholders) from control (management) which resulted in the agency problem.

Examples of conflicts of interest between managers and shareholders include:

- **Short-termism:** There is evidence that in many companies the primary driver of decision-making has been to increase share prices and hence managerial rewards in the short term. The longer-term benefits of investment in research and development may be ignored in the short-term drive to cut costs and increase profits thus jeopardising the long-term prospects of the company.

- **Sales maximisation:** This strategy is often employed by managers to increase market share and therefore the importance of the company within its sector. An increase in importance for the company will mean greater status for management but will not necessarily be in the best interests of the shareholders.

- **Overpriced acquisitions:** Takeovers is another manifestation of the non-alignment of the interests of shareholders and managers. Managers have motives other than shareholder value maximisation and may choose to acquire another business to seek growth and status.

- **Resistance to takeovers:** The management of a company may tend to resist takeovers if they feel that their position is threatened even if in doing so shareholder value is also reduced.

- **Relationships:** Many companies' pursuit of short-term cost reduction may lead to difficult relationships with their wider stakeholders. Relationships with suppliers may be disrupted by demands for major improvements in terms and in reduction of prices. Employees may be made redundant in a drive to reduce costs and customers may be able to buy fewer product lines and have to face less favourable terms. These policies may aid short-term profits, but in the long-term suppliers and employees are able to take full advantage of market conditions and move to other companies, and customers can shop elsewhere or over the internet.

- **Avoiding risk:** In order to maximise shareholder wealth in the long-term a company needs to evolve which means some risk must be taken. When managers' attitudes are conservative and risk-averse they are seeking the easiest path. Risk-averse managers seeks to avoid conflict or change because of the disruption it could cause. However, this may not be in the best interests of the shareholders.

- **Dividend policy:** Managers may decide to maintain high dividend pay-outs in order to avoid resistance from the shareholders. This is not necessarily the best thing for shareholder wealth maximisation in the long-term as it may be better to invest in new technology so that new products can be made, or existing products made more effectively and efficiently.

3.6.1 Conflict between stakeholders

Although we have just discussed the conflict between managers and owners, there are other areas of potential conflict between managers, owners and other stakeholders who provide capital, namely the debt holders. The relationship between the long-term creditors (payables) of a company, the management and the shareholders of a company encompasses the following factors:

- Management may decide to raise finance for a company by taking out long-term or medium-term loans.

- Investors who provide debt finance will rely on the company's management to generate enough net cash inflows to make interest payments on time, and eventually to repay loans. Long-term creditors (payables) will often take security for their loan, perhaps in the form of a fixed charge over an asset (such as a mortgage on a building). Debentures are also often subject to certain restrictive covenants, which restrict the company's rights to borrow more money until the debentures have been repaid.

- The money that is provided by long-term creditors (payable) will be invested to earn profits, and the profits (in excess of what is needed to pay interest on the borrowing) will provide extra dividends or retained profits for the shareholders of the company. In other words, shareholders will expect to increase their wealth using the borrowed money.

Sometimes the needs of shareholders and debtholders may conflict:

- Managers may be tempted to take risky decisions using debtholders' money to finance them, knowing that the benefits of these decisions will accrue to the shareholders. If the projects go badly and the company fails, the debtholders may suffer a greater loss than the equity shareholders.

- In many jurisdictions there are rules limiting the proportion of company assets that can be paid out as dividends. However, it may still be possible to pay out lawfully considerable sums as dividends, enough to jeopardise the company's future and hence the amounts that the debtholders have advanced, should trading results turn bad in the near future.

- Shareholders and managers may wish to prolong the company's life as long as possible, whereas debtholders may wish to safeguard the amount loaned and realise their security as soon as the company appears to be getting into difficulties.

- Managers may attempt to undermine the position of debtholders by seeking further loan capital, committing the company to an increased interest burden and hence greater risk of insolvency. The additional loan capital may also have superior claims on the company's assets to the original amounts borrowed.

3.6.2 Strategies to manage stakeholder conflict

We will now show how ensuring goal congruence and enforcing corporate governance best practice can help manage conflict between different groups of stakeholders.

- **Reward systems:** Agency theory sees employees of businesses, including managers, as individuals, each with their own objectives. Within a department of a business, there are departmental objectives. Goal congruence between managers, directors and shareholders may be better dealt with by giving managers some profit-related pay, or by providing incentives which are related to profits or share price.

    Examples of such remuneration incentives are:

    (a) **Profit-related/economic value-added pay**

    Pay or bonuses related to the size of profits or economic value added

    (b) **Rewarding managers with shares**

    This might be done when a private company 'goes public' and managers are invited to subscribe for shares in the company at an attractive offer price. This means that directors and employees, as well as shareholders, have a stake in the long-term profitability of an organisation.

    (c) **Executive share options plans**

    In a share option scheme, selected employees are given a number of share options, each of which gives the holder the right after a certain date to subscribe for shares in the company at a fixed price. The value of an option will increase if the company is successful, and its share price goes up.

Note. When considering remuneration, incentives and benefits packages for the board, remuneration committees will need to take account of corporate governance best practice and align remuneration with the company's long-term strategy and link it to achievement of long-term sustainable goals. We covered this in Chapter 5.

- **Separation of roles and corporate governance:** Complying with corporate governance principles ensured that not too much power accrues to a single individual within an organisation which increases the risk of disagreement between a chief executive and the board of directors, the company shareholders and the employees. Also, the adoption of a corporate governance framework of decision making will restrict the power of managers and increase the role of independent non-executive directors in key decisions. We looked at this in Chapter 4.

- **Negotiation:** Stakeholder conflict between shareholders and directors can be resolved by negotiating contracts that allow the principal to control the agent in such a way to ensure that the agent will operate in the interests of the principal. Also, a board of directors may schedule regular investors updates which allow key investors to voice their concerns and to provide feedback on strategic decisions made by a board of directors. Differences of opinion between a company and its customers or suppliers can also be resolved by negotiation of contractual terms, price or deliverables.

- **Self-regulation:** A voluntary code of conduct is a statement by an organisation of the standards by which it seeks to do business. Codes are usually developed by a trade association and individual members incorporate the code into the dealings they have with their customers. Organisations in some business sectors self-regulate their dealings by voluntary codes of conduct. Voluntary codes usually include a mechanism for resolving disputes through arbitration.

Chapter roundup

- **Corporate social responsibility (CSR)** refers to the expectation in society that companies are accountable for the social and ethical effects of their actions. Some argue however that businesses already contribute enough to society via the taxes on their profits.

- **Sustainability reporting** is now a key part of a company's dialogue with its stakeholders.

- The stakeholder desire for and expectation of such information is so strong that **companies which fail to provide sustainability disclosures will be at a significant disadvantage** in terms of attracting and retaining investors and appealing to wider stakeholders.

- **Different groups of stakeholders have different objectives** which can lead to conflicts between competing groups.

- By understanding the different stakeholders and their needs and goals, then an organisation can **determine strategies to resolve stakeholder conflicts** which may prevent an organisation from achieving its strategic objectives

- The fundamental objective profit making organisations is normally the maximisation of shareholders' wealth. In its purest sense, this means pursuing the maximum amount of profit from the organisation's operations. A threat to this objective is conflicting shareholder objectives.

Quick quiz

1. Fill in the blanks:

    ……………... ……………….. are defined as the tangible and intangible costs and losses sustained by third parties or the general public as a result of economic activity.

    ……………... ……………….. is the principle that organisations should act in a manner which benefits society as well as meeting strategic and financial objectives.

2. Which two of the following are sustainability dependencies?

    (a) Consumer expectations
    (b) Emissions
    (c) Water usage
    (d) Diversity

3. The Corporate Sustainability Reporting Directive (CSRD) developed the IFRS Sustainability Disclosure Standards which all organisations worldwide must apply under international law.

    True ☐ False ☐

4. A sustainability committee should ideally be made up of independent non-executive directors.

    True ☐ False ☐

5. A stakeholder which has high interest but low power should be ……….. ………….. .

PART A   THE FOUNDATIONS OF GOVERNANCE

Answers to quick quiz

1   **Social costs** are defined as the tangible and intangible costs and losses sustained by third parties or the general public as a result of economic activity.

   Social responsibility is the principle that organisations should act in a manner which benefits society as well as meeting strategic and financial objectives.

2   (a) Consumer expectations and (d) Diversity are sustainability dependencies. (b) Emissions and (c) Water usage are sustainability impacts.

3   **False.** The first reporting under the CSRD, using the recently issued European Sustainability Reporting Standards (ESRSs) relates to accounting periods commencing 1 January 2024. The IFRS Sustainability Disclosure Standards are instead issued by the International Sustainability Standards Board (ISSB) and are not mandatory at the time of writing this Workbook.

4   **True.** Where corporate governance codes are established and enforced they recommend that **all, or the majority, of any committee** at board level (which would include the sustainability committee) should be made up of independent non-executive directors.

5   A stakeholder which has high interest but low power should be **kept informed**.

End of chapter questions

6.1   Which of the following is being demonstrated when companies aim to produce higher standards of living and quality of life for the communities that surround them and still maintain profitability for stakeholders?

   A   Compliance with laws and regulation
   B   Corporate citizenship
   C   Reporting of sustainability related impacts
   D   Stakeholder analysis

6.2   Which of the following statements about the ISSB and the IFRS Sustainability Disclosure Standards is true?

   A   Application of the disclosure standards is mandatory for all organisations.
   B   The disclosures described in the standards must be included in the notes to the financial statements.
   C   The focus of the ISSB and the IFRS Sustainability Disclosure Standards is on the information needs of wider range of stakeholders than those targeted by the EU's European Sustainability Reporting Standards.
   D   An entity must apply all current IFRS Sustainability Disclosure Standards in order to comply with IFRS Sustainability Disclosure Standards.

6.3   Which of the following best describes the process of involving all parties affected by a company's operations in its decision-making processes?

   A   Stakeholder engagement
   B   Stakeholder analysis
   C   Stakeholder theory
   D   Stakeholder conflict

Risk and control

Topic list	Syllabus reference
1 Risk and the organisation	B1.11
2 Risk management	B1.11
3 Risk management responsibilities	B1.11

Introduction

A key part of the role of senior management is managing the risks facing the organisation which could affect the achievement of its objectives.

In Section 1 we consider what types of risks may impact on an organisation. In Section 2 we consider how risks are identified, assessed and managed. In Section 3 we consider the parties who are responsible for risk management and what those responsibilities are.

PART A THE FOUNDATIONS OF GOVERNANCE

1 Risk and the organisation

FAST FORWARD

Risk in an organisation is the possibility of something bad happening that could affect the business.

1.1 What is risk?

There are many ways that risk could be defined. A simple definition might be as follows:

The possibility of something bad happening

(Source: Cambridge English dictionary)

Managers are concerned with the possibility that bad things may happen that could have a detrimental effect on the business. Risks they will be interested in include:

Key terms

> **Business risks** are threats that an event or action will adversely affect a business's ability to achieve its ongoing objectives. These can arise due to external and internal factors.
>
> **Strategic risks** are risks that relate to the fundamental decisions that the directors take about the future strategic direction of the organisation.
>
> **Operational risks** relate to matters that can go wrong on a day-to-day basis while the organisation is carrying out its business.

Question — Risks

What sort of risks might an organisation face?

Answer

Make your own list, specific to the organisations that you are familiar with. Here is a list extracted from an article by Tom Jones 'Risk Management' (Administrator, April 1993). It is illustrative of the range of risks faced and is not exhaustive. It's worth noting that this article was written some time ago and nowadays businesses would also need to consider risks relating to the internet, social media, and technological processes that were not relevant in 1993. This illustrates that businesses need to keep their risk assessment up to date.

- Fire, flood, storm, impact, explosion, subsidence and other disasters
- Accidents and the use of faulty products
- Error: loss through damage or malfunction caused by mistaken operation of equipment or wrong operation of an industrial programme
- Theft and fraud
- Breaking social or environmental regulations
- Political risks (the appropriation of foreign assets by local governments or of barriers to the repatriation of overseas profit)
- Computers: fraud, viruses, and espionage
- Product tamper
- Malicious damage

94

1.2 Why is risk important?

As we can see from the definitions above, risks can adversely affect the business's ability to achieve its objectives. For most firms the main strategic objective is **profit maximisation** so risks arise from events or actions that can damage the firm's ability to make profits.

Risks may be externally and/or internally driven, as shown in the following diagram.

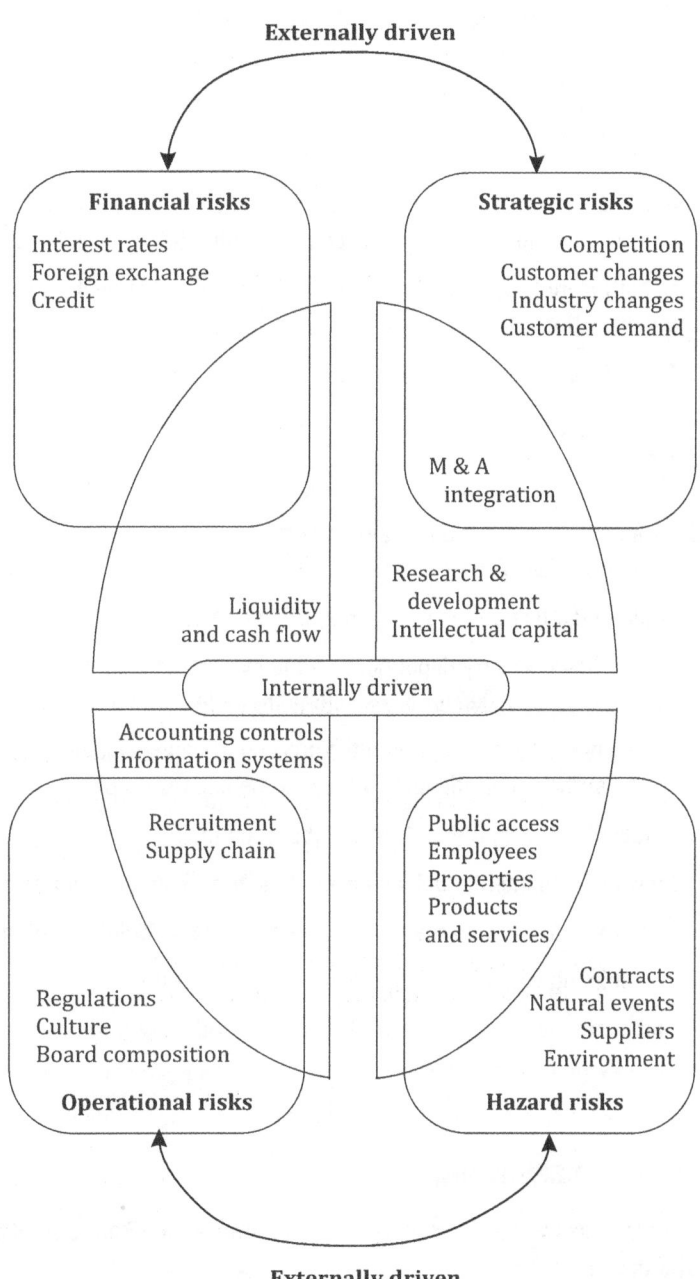

Source: Institute of Risk Management – A Risk Management Standard

If the management does not appropriately manage risks that can affect profits, its operations may be damaged to the extent that it becomes **unable to carry on business**. Risk management is therefore a critical aspect of management and corporate governance.

You may notice that some of the risks in the diagram above relate to **financial issues and accounting systems**. They are therefore of interest to the **auditors** of a company, as we will see in the second part of this Workbook.

2 Risk management

FAST FORWARD

The process of risk management has three stages:

- Risk identification (covered in Section 2.1)
- Risk assessment (covered in Section 2.2)
- Risk management (covered in Section 2.3)

Identified risks will be assessed to estimate the likelihood of the risk events their occurring and the impact if they do.

2.1 Risk identification

Risk identification is generally performed using:

- A "top-down" approach is where those at the top of the business consider the objectives of the business and identify risks that could threaten those objectives.
- A 'bottom-up" approach is where those at the operational level of the business identify risks facing the operations.
- A combination of the two.

Case Study

ABC Co is an owner-managed IT training company based in Singapore. It is planning to expand into other locations in South East Asia.

The risks identified using the top-down approach include:

1. The company is very dependent on the owner-manager to drive the company forward. If she retires, dies or makes poor decisions then the company's performance will suffer.
2. The owner-manager has a limited amount of capital available to inject into the business, which may not be sufficient to adequately finance the expansion plans.

The risks identified using the bottom-up approach include:

3. Movable equipment, such as computers and fixtures, could be damaged or stolen.
4. Cash (which students may use to pay their fees) could be stolen
5. The building could be completely destroyed in a fire.
6. The company may not be able to recruit a sufficient number of competent trainers.

2.2 Risk assessment

The identified risks will then be assessed to **estimate** the **likelihood** of the risk events occurring and the **impact** if they do.

2.2.1 Likelihood

A simple approach would be to categorise risks as high, medium, or low probability. Alternatively risks could be categorised in terms of the estimated frequency of the risk event occurring, for example once in 50 years, once in 10 years, every year.

2.2.2 Impact

This is the estimated impact on the business if the risk event occurred. Impacts could be categorised in qualitative terms (for example manageable, difficult, catastrophic) or quantitative (for example less than $10,000, $10,000–$50,000, more than $50,000.

2.2.3 Risk matrix

As part of the decision how to manage the identified risks, a risk matrix may be useful.

A risk matrix has two axes, one for likelihood and another for impact, and each risk is plotted on the matrix.

A simple risk matrix could look like this:

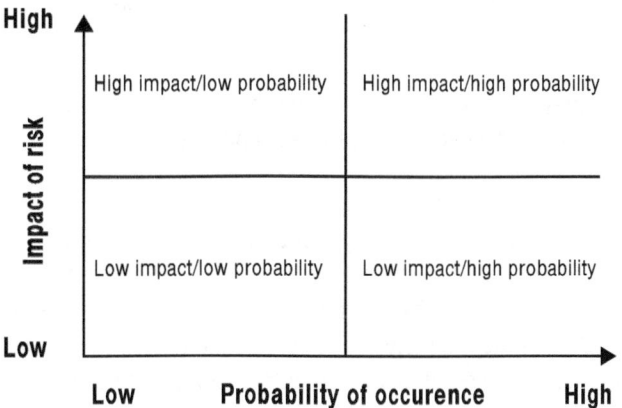

A more complicated risk matrix might look like this:

IMPACT of risk			1	2	3	4	5
	Extreme	5	M	M	H	H	H
	High	4	L	M	M	H	H
	Medium	3	L	L	M	M	H
	Low	2	L	L	L	M	M
	Negligible	1	L	L	L	L	M
			1	2	3	4	5
			Rare	Unlikely	Possible	Likely	Almost certain
			PROBABILITY of risk				

This matrix identifies which of the combinations result in the highest levels of risk to be managed.

PART A   THE FOUNDATIONS OF GOVERNANCE

2.3 Risk management

FAST FORWARD

> The most common types of **risk management techniques** include avoidance, mitigation, transfer, and acceptance.

The most common types of risk management techniques include:

- Avoidance
- Mitigation
- Transfer
- Acceptance

Different risk management techniques will be appropriate in different circumstances. A concept that should always be borne in mind is cost vs. benefit, ie whether the cost of introducing a risk management technique exceeds the benefit (the financial impact avoided).

Avoidance

Some risks may be managed by avoiding the activity that leads to the risk. For example, in the case study above ABC Co could avoid risk (2) by deciding not to expand into South East Asia.

Mitigation

Mitigation means doing something to reduce the risk by, for example, introducing internal controls (see below). For example, in the case study above risk (3) could be managed by locking the training rooms and premises after use and (4) by putting cash in a safe and then banking it soon after receipt. Risk (1) could be mitigated by hiring a deputy to the owner-manager, who can be trained up in how to manage the business, or appointing some non-executive directors to give the benefit of their experience.

Transfer

The most obvious example of risk transfer is by insurance. In the case study above, risks (3), (4) and (5) are obvious examples of risks that can be insured. However insurance is best used for risks that have a low probability of occurring but a serious impact on the business if they do, for example the fire in risk (5). Although risks (3) and (4) could be insured, since the likelihood of occurrence is higher but the impact smaller, insurance may not be cost-effective; it may be more cost-effective for ABC Co to introduce the controls mentioned in the mitigation section. Note that risk (1) could also be mitigated by insurance, by ABC Co taking out "key-man insurance."

Acceptance

Some risks have such low likelihood of occurrence or such minor impacts if they do occur that the most cost-effective thing to do is simply to accept the risk as the cost of acceptance may be lower than other options. This might be a sensible approach to risk (6).

2.4 The system of internal control

We will consider internal controls in detail in Chapter 11, but a brief mention will be given here.

Key term

> The **system of internal control** is the system designed, implemented and maintained by those charged with governance, management, and other personnel to provide reasonable assurance about the achievement of an entity's objectives with regard to reliability of financial reporting, effectiveness and efficiency of operations and compliance with applicable laws and regulations.
>
> *(ISA 315 (Revised): para. 12)*

Internal controls are essential to management, as they contribute to

- Safeguarding the company's assets
- Helping to prevent and detect fraud
- Therefore, safeguarding the shareholders' investment

In this Workbook, we will be primarily concerned with financial controls, but controls are wider than this and are any processes and procedures designed to protect the business.

A few examples include:

- **Internal audit** – this is a function that oversees the systems operating within the company to make sure things run smoothly.
- **Training** – having well trained staff means they are less likely to make mistakes that cause loss to the company.
- **Keeping valuable assets in secure locations** – this reduces the chance of theft.
- **Authorisation of purchases** – this is the process whereby senior staff approve purchase orders and invoices to try to ensure that staff do not buy unnecessary goods or goods for their own use.
- **Arithmetical checks** – for example, checking the payroll calculations to ensure they are correct.
- **Passwords** – this prevents unauthorised access to computer records.

As you can see from this short list, there are many and varied processes and procedures that can be internal controls in a business. We will revisit this topic in Chapters 12 and 14.

3 Risk management responsibilities

FAST FORWARD

> The **board** has overall responsibility for **risk management** as an essential part of its corporate governance responsibilities. Responsibilities below board level will depend on the extent of delegation to **line managers** and whether there is a **separate risk management function**.

3.1 Responsibilities for risk management

Everyone who works for the organisation has responsibilities for risk management. Primary responsibility belongs with the board of directors. In larger organisations there may be a separate risk management department or a risk management committee. The role of risk specialists is considered below.

3.2 The board

As we have seen, the board's role in managing risk is one of its most important. The board is responsible for **determining risk management strategy and monitoring risks** as part of its responsibility for the organisation's overall strategy and its responsibilities to shareholders and other stakeholders. It is also responsible for **setting appropriate policies on internal controls** and **seeking assurance** that the internal control system is **functioning effectively**. It should also communicate the organisation's strategy to employees.

The FRC sets out these responsibilities in its 2014 report *Guidance on Risk Management, Internal Control and Related Financial and Business Reporting* as follows:

- Design and implement appropriate risk management and internal control systems that identify the risks faced by the company and enable the board to make a robust assessment of the principal risks.
- Determine the nature and extent of the principal risks faced and those it is prepared to accept to meet its strategic objectives (set the risk appetite).
- Embed an appropriate culture and rewards system throughout the organisation.
- Establish how to manage or mitigate principal risks to reduce the impact and likelihood of risks.
- Monitor and review the risk management and internal control systems.

- Ensure sound internal and external information and communication processes.
- Take responsibility for external communication on risk management and internal control.

The board also must determine whether to adopt the going concern basis of accounting and make related disclosures of material uncertainties in the financial statements.

3.3 Risk management committee

Boards also need to consider whether there should be a separate board committee, with responsibility for monitoring and supervising risk identification and management. If the board doesn't have a separate committee, under the UK Corporate Governance Code the audit committee will be responsible for risk management.

> **Principles of the UK Corporate Governance Code (for listed UK companies)**
>
> The main roles and responsibilities of the **audit committee** should include..... **reviewing the company's risk management and internal control framework**, unless expressly addressed by a separate board risk committee composed of independent non-executive directors, or by the board itself.
>
> (FRC *UK Corporate Governance Code*: Section 4, Provision 25)

Arguments in favour of having a separate risk management committee:

(a) **Staffing:** A risk management committee can be staffed by executive directors, whereas an audit committee should be staffed by non-executive directors.

(b) **Breadth of remit:** The audit committee may focus too much on financial risks.

(c) **Leadership:** A risk management committee can take the lead in promoting awareness and driving changes in practice, whereas an audit committee will have a purely monitoring role.

(d) **Investigations:** A risk management committee can carry out special investigations, particularly in areas not related to the accounting systems

3.4 Role and function of risk committee

A risk management committee will be far more effective if it has clear terms of reference, which could include:

- Approving the organisation's risk management strategy and risk management policy.
- Reviewing reports on key risks prepared by business operating units, management and the board.
- Monitoring overall exposure to risk and ensuring it remains within limits set by the board.
- Assessing the effectiveness of the organisation's risk management systems.
- Providing early warning to the board on emerging risk issues and significant changes in the company's exposure to risks.
- In conjunction with the audit committee, **reviewing the company's statement on internal control** with reference to risk management, prior to endorsement by the board.

Note that the focus is on supervision and monitoring rather than the committee having responsibility for day-to-day decision-making and implementation of policies.

3.5 Internal audit

Setting up an internal audit department is a control that will help to mitigate some of the risks faced in the company. The internal audit department will also assist in monitoring of the effectiveness of the controls in mitigating risks by testing those controls. Internal audit is covered in more detail in Chapter 14.

3.6 External audit

Auditors need to consider risks that could lead to material misstatement when designing their audit approach. For example, there could be a business risk that managers are awarded a bonus based on sales so may be tempted to achieve sales by aggressive and unethical techniques. This would also lead to a risk affecting the financial statements, in that the directors could overstate sales in order to increase their bonuses. We consider this in more detail in Chapter 11.

> **Principles of the UK Corporate Governance Code (for listed UK companies)**
>
> - The board should establish and maintain an effective risk management and internal control framework, and determine the nature and extent of the principal risks the company is willing to take in order to achieve its long-term strategic objectives.
>
> (FRC *UK Corporate Governance Code*: Section 4)

PART A   THE FOUNDATIONS OF GOVERNANCE

Chapter roundup

- Risk in an organisation is the possibility of something bad happening that could affect the business.
- Business risk is the threat that an event or action will adversely affect a business's ability to achieve its ongoing objective. It can arise due to external and internal factors.
- Strategic risks are risks that relate to the fundamental decisions that the directors take about the future of the organisation.
- Operational risks are risks: relate to matters that can go wrong on a day-to-day basis while the organisation is carrying out its business.
- If management does not appropriately manage risks that can affect profits, its operations may be damaged to the extent that it becomes **unable to carry on business**.
- The process of risk management has three stages:
    - Risk identification
    - Risk assessment
    - Risk management
- Identified risks will be assessed to estimate the likelihood of the risk events their occurring and the impact if they do.
- The most common types of **risk management techniques** include avoidance, mitigation, transfer, and acceptance.
- The **board** has overall responsibility for **risk management** as an essential part of its corporate governance responsibilities. Responsibilities below board level will depend on the extent of delegation to **line managers** and whether there is a **separate risk management function**.

Quick quiz

1. Is the below a definition of business risk, strategic risk or operational risk?

   The risk that something can go wrong on a day-to-day basis while the organisation is carrying out its business

2. What is the strategic objective of most firms?

3. What are the three stages of risk management?

4. Match the categorisations with the factors used to assess risk (two categorisations for each factor):

Factor	Categorisation
(1) Likelihood	(a) Manageable, difficult, catastrophic
	(b) High, medium, low
(2) Impact	(c) Once in 50 years, once in 10 years, every year
	(d) < $10,000, $10,000–$50,000, > $50,000

5. What would be the most appropriate way to manage a low likelihood, high impact risk?

6. Who has overall responsibility for risk management in a company? The CEO, the board, or the risk management committee?

Answers to quick quiz

1 Operational risk, as it relates to the day-to-day operations of the company.

2 Profit maximisation, therefore business risks are those that affect the business's ability to do that.

3 Risk identification, risk assessment, risk management

4 1b, 1c, 2a, 2d

5 Transfer of the risk, perhaps by insurance. As the impact is high the company may not be able to afford to bear the potential impact itself but, because there is low likelihood of it occurring, the premiums should be relatively affordable.

6 The board as a whole has overall responsibility, although some of the tasks associated with risk management may be delegated to the CEO or risk management committee.

End of chapter questions

7.1 The implementation of a system of internal control aids a business in risk management.

Which of the following best describes a system of internal control?

- A The system designed, implemented and maintained to provide absolute assurance about the achievement of the organisation's objectives including operational effectiveness, reliability of financial reporting and compliance with laws and regulations
- B The system designed, implemented and maintained to provide reasonable assurance about the achievement of an entity's objectives with regard to reliability of financial reporting, effectiveness and efficiency of operations and compliance with applicable laws and regulations.
- C The system designed to ensure that controls deficiencies are not identified by the external auditors during the annual audit
- D The system by which companies are directed and controlled

7.2 Ultimate responsibility for the effectiveness of a company's system of internal control lies with:

- A The board of directors
- B The shareholders
- C The auditors
- D The accounting staff

7.3 ABC Co has decided not to do anything in response to a particular risk facing its business as the cost of doing so exceeds the benefit. What is the name of this type of response?

- A Avoidance
- B Acceptance
- C Transfer
- D Manage

7.4 Which is the correct order of the stages of the risk management process?

- A Assessment, identification, management
- B Management, identification, assessment
- C Identification, management, assessment
- D Identification, assessment, management

7.5 Which of these statements is appropriate in terms of risk management?

- A High likelihood, high impact risks should be avoided
- B High likelihood, low impact risks should be insured
- C Low likelihood, high impact risks should be accepted
- D Low likelihood, low impact risks should be managed

The Foundations of Auditing

The nature and purpose of auditing

Topic list	Syllabus reference
1 History of the audit	B2.1
2 The purpose of auditing	B2.1
3 The objective of an external audit	B2.1, B2.2
4 Audits and other engagements	B2.3, B2.4
5 Fraud, laws and regulations	B2.2, B2.4
6 Benefits and limitations	B2.1, B2.2

Introduction

In the first section of this chapter we consider the historical development of auditing.

We then move on to the objectives of an external statutory audit before looking at other non-statutory assurance engagements. We also look at audit scope and levels of assurance here.

In Section 5 we consider the extent of the auditor's responsibility for detecting fraud and illegal acts. Finally the chapter looks at the advantages of audit and the inherent limitations which result in the expectations gap.

PART B   FOUNDATIONS OF AUDITING

1 History of the audit

FAST FORWARD

Directors are agents of the shareholders and manage the company on their behalf. Auditors are also the agents of the shareholders, and their role is to help ensure that the directors are properly fulfilling their responsibility to manage the company's finances (the 'stewardship' function). This has become more critical over the years as corporate organisations have increased in size and number of shareholders.

1.1 Auditors as agents

In Chapter 1 we considered the fact that directors are agents of the shareholders and manage the company on their behalf. Auditors are also the agents of the shareholders, and their role is to help ensure that the directors are properly fulfilling their responsibility to manage the company's finances (the 'stewardship' function).

1.2 Early auditing

There is evidence that auditing procedures existed in the economic activities of many of the earliest civilisations, including those of Rome and ancient Egypt. Sometimes property owners who wanted to verify the activities of their employees undertook the task. In Britain in medieval times independent auditors who were employed by landowners carried out the job. The objective was to verify that the landowners were receiving the correct returns from the tenant farmers who worked on the estates. Early auditing also existed in government, usually related to the collection of taxation revenues.

1.3 Evolution of corporate organisations

In the nineteenth century in the UK and its empire, the **evolution of corporate organisations significantly separated ownership from management**, as discussed above. This brought about the need to account to the shareholders of companies by means of published accounts, as well as the corresponding need to verify the quality of the content of the statements.

The Joint Stock Companies Act of 1844 was the first enactment to require all incorporated companies to have their annual financial statements audited. In most cases, the auditor was one of the shareholders, elected by them. The audit report was to state whether the balance sheet (now called the statement of financial position) gave a 'full and fair view' of its state of affairs. In addition there was another major audit objective – to detect fraud and error in the company's accounting records.

The Companies Act 1856 removed the requirement for a statutory audit, but audits continued to be conducted on a voluntary basis. The government also retained the requirement for audit for industries with particularly bad records of dishonest managerial practices, such as the railways and banks.

In 1900 the requirement for an audit was restored for every company. The auditor was still not required to be a professional accountant, although he could not be a director of officer of the company being audited. However, as transactions became more complex, there grew a need for auditors with an accounting expertise sufficient to cope with the increasing complexity of accounting record keeping.

Until the 1920s, **fraud and error detection** continued to be the dominating factor in company audits. Gradually, however, there was a growing awareness of the usefulness of accounting information to investors, and more emphasis than before was placed on the information content of company accounts. The role of the auditor began to be viewed in terms of lending credibility to the financial statements, rather than certifying that they are free from fraud and error.

1.4 Accountancy profession develops

Along with this change in audit emphasis came the **emergence of a self-regulated accountancy profession**, whose members were educated and trained sufficiently to take responsibility for the corporate audit. If we take the UK as an example, these changes were formally recognised in the Companies Act 1948, which introduced for the first time the requirement that the auditor was to express an opinion as to the truth and fairness of the statement of profit or loss and other comprehensive income (also known as the 'income statement' or the 'statement of profit or loss') as well as the statement of financial position. In addition, the auditor was required to possess a recognised professional qualification, and detailed provisions were included regarding their duties, powers and responsibilities. This Act has been amended by subsequent Companies Acts, but its main requirements remain substantially unchanged.

In the late 1940s the first **UK accounting practice guidelines** began to be issued by the Institute of Chartered Accountants of England and Wales. In 1961 the first formal guidance for auditors was issued. For the first time, audit practice was no longer a matter for individual auditors' professional judgement.

In 1980, the main accounting bodies introduced a new series of Auditing Standards and Guidelines intended to set out the basic principles and practices which auditors were expected to follow. We will look more at such regulation of auditing in Chapter 9.

1.5 Modern audit

The emphasis of today's company audit has switched from the detailed checking of individual transactions, to an **overall review and evaluation of the systems** in operation by an **examination of the records and the financial statements**. The detection of fraud is no longer the main objective of the audit, although material discrepancies should be picked up as a result of normal audit procedures. Technology is increasingly used to assist with all stages of the audit process.

2 The purpose of auditing

FAST FORWARD

> An audit provides **assurance** to the shareholders and other stakeholders of a company on the financial statements because it is **independent and impartial**.

The key reason for having an audit can be seen by working through the following case study.

Case Study

Vera decides to set up a business selling flowers. She gets up early in the morning, visits the market and then sets up a stall by the side of the road. For the first year, all goes well. She sells all the flowers she is able to buy and she derives some income from the business.

However, Vera feels that she could sell more flowers if she was able to transport more to the place where she sells them, and she also knows that there are several other roads nearby where she could sell flowers, if she could be in two places at once. She could achieve these two things by buying a van and by employing people to sell flowers in other locations.

Vera needs more money to achieve this expansion of her business. She decides to ask her rich friend Peter to invest in the business.

Peter can see the potential of Vera's business and wants to invest, but he doesn't want to be involved in the management of the business. He also does not want to have ultimate liability for the debts of the business if it fails. He therefore suggests that they set up a limited company. He will own the majority of the shares and be entitled to dividends. Vera will be managing director and be paid a salary for her work.

At the end of the first year of trading as a limited company, Peter receives a copy of the financial statements. Profits are lower than expected, so his dividend will not be as large as he had hoped. He knows that Vera is paid a salary so does not care as much as him that profits are low.

Peter is concerned by the level of profits and feels that he wants further assurance on the accounts. He doesn't know whether they give a true reflection on the last year's trading, particularly as the profits do not seem as high as those Vera had predicted when he agreed to invest.

The solution is that the **assurance** Peter is seeking can be given by an independent **audit or review** of the financial statements. An auditor can provide the two things that Peter requires:

- A **knowledgeable review** of the company's business and of the accounts
- An **impartial view**, since Vera's view might be biased

Other people will also view the company's accounts with interest, for example:

- Creditors of the company
- Taxation authorities

The various parties interested in the accounts of a company are sometimes referred to as **stakeholders**. Although they will each judge the accounts by different criteria, they will all **gain assurance** from learning that the accounts they are reading have been subject to an independent report.

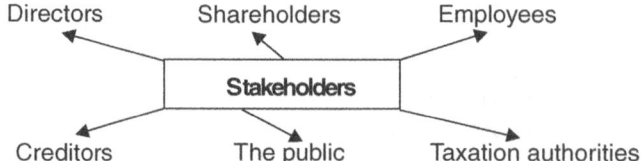

The example above is a simple one. In practice companies may have thousands of shareholders who may not know the management personally. It is therefore important that directors are **accountable** to shareholders. Directors act as **stewards** of the shareholders' investments. They are **agents** of the shareholders.

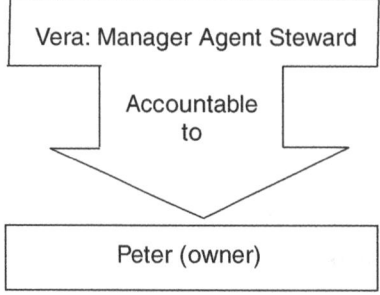 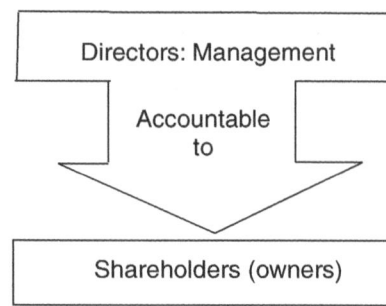

Key terms

Accountability is the quality or state of being accountable, that is, being required or expected to justify actions and decisions. It suggests an obligation or willingness to accept responsibility for one's actions.

Stewardship refers to the duties and obligations of a person who manages another person's property.

Agents are people employed or used to provide a particular service. In the case of a company, the people being used to provide the service of managing the business also have the second role of trying to maximise their personal wealth in their own right.

You may ask, 'what are the directors accountable for?' It is important to understand the answer to this question. The directors are accountable for the **shareholders' investment**. The shareholders have bought shares in that company (they have invested). They **expect a return** from their investment. As the **directors** manage the company, they are **in a position to affect that return**.

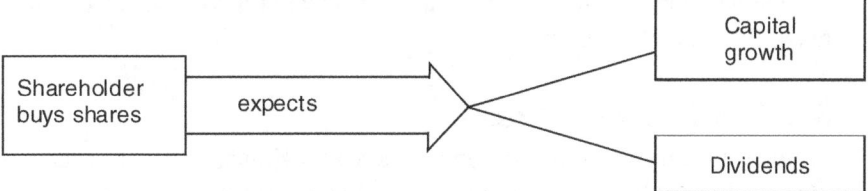

The exact nature of the return expected by the shareholder will depend on the type of company he or she has chosen to invest in: that is part of his or her investment risk analysis. Certain issues are true of any such investment. For example, if the directors **mismanage** the company, and it goes **bankrupt**, it will neither provide a source of future dividends, nor will it create capital growth in the investment – indeed, the opposite is true and the original investment may even be lost.

Accountability therefore covers a range of issues:

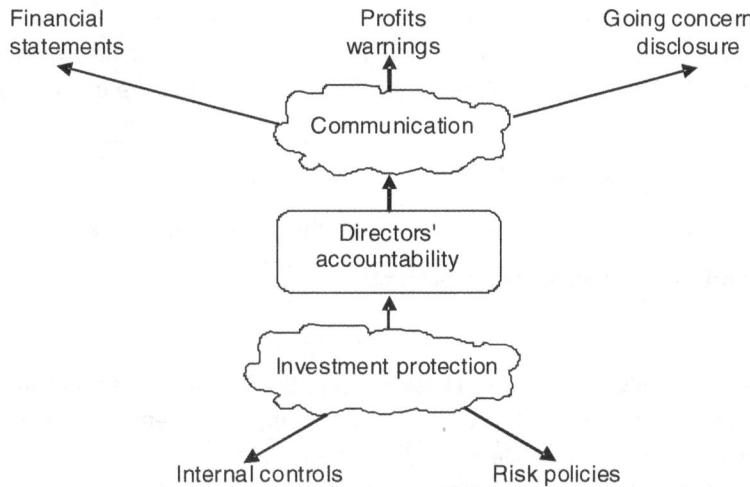

These issues are often discussed under the umbrella title '**corporate governance**', where 'governance' indicates the management (governing) role of the directors, and 'corporate' indicates that the issue relates to companies (bodies corporate). This is illustrated by our scenario, where we saw Vera taking up a corporate governance position in relation to Peter. We introduced corporate governance previously in this Workbook.

3 The objective of an external audit

FAST FORWARD

> The purpose of an external audit is to enable auditors to **give an independent opinion** on the financial statements.

3.1 Objectives of the auditor

Key term

> In conducting an audit of financial statements, the overall **objectives of the auditor** are:
>
> (a) To obtain reasonable assurance about whether the financial statements as a whole are free from material misstatement, whether due to fraud or error, thereby enabling the auditor to express an opinion on whether the financial statements are prepared, in all material respects, in accordance with an applicable financial reporting framework; and
>
> (b) To report on the financial statements, and communicate as required by the ISAs, in accordance with the auditor's finding.

The purpose of an external audit is to enable auditors to **give an opinion** on the financial statements. While an audit might produce by-products such as recommendations to the directors on improvements to the internal control systems, its objective is **solely to report to the shareholders on the truth and fairness of the financial statements.**

3.2 Truth and fairness

External auditors give an opinion on the **truth and fairness** of financial statements. This is not an opinion of absolute correctness. 'True' and 'fair' are not defined in law or audit guidance, but the following definitions are generally accepted.

Key terms

> **True** is information that is factual and conforms with reality. In addition the information conforms with required standards and law. The financial statements have been correctly extracted from the books and records.
>
> **Fair** is information that is free from discrimination and bias and in compliance with expected standards and rules. The accounts should reflect the commercial substance of the company's underlying transactions.

Below is an example of an auditor's report on an entity's financial statements. This is a report with an **unmodified** opinion (which means the financial statements are true and fair and properly prepared).

INDEPENDENT AUDITOR'S REPORT

To the shareholders of ABC Company [or other appropriate addressee]

Report on the audit of the financial statements

Opinion

We have audited the financial statements of ABC Company (the Company), which comprise the statement of financial position as at 31 December 20X1, and the statement of comprehensive income, statement of changes in equity and statement of cash flows for the year then ended, and notes to the financial statements, including a summary of significant accounting policies.

In our opinion, the accompanying financial statements present fairly, in all material respects, (or **give a true and fair view of**) the financial position of the Company as at 31 December 20X1, and (of) its financial performance and its cash flows for the year then ended in accordance with International Financial Reporting Standards (IFRSs).

Basis for opinion

We conducted our audit in accordance with International Standards on Auditing (ISAs). Our responsibilities under those standards are further described in the *Auditor's Responsibilities for the Audit of the Financial Statements* section of our report. We are independent of the Company in accordance with the International Ethics Standards Board for Accountants' *Code of Ethics for Professional Accountants* (IESBA *Code*) together with the ethical requirements that are relevant to our audit of the financial statements in [jurisdiction], and we have fulfilled our other ethical responsibilities in accordance with these requirements and the IESBA *Code*. We believe that the audit evidence we have obtained is sufficient and appropriate to provide a basis for our opinion.

Key audit matters

Key audit matters are those matters that, in our professional judgment, were of most significance in our audit of the financial statements of the current period. These matters were addressed in the context of our audit of the financial statements as a whole, and in forming our opinion thereon, and we do not provide a separate opinion on these matters.

[Description of each key audit matter in accordance with ISA 701.]

Other information

Management is responsible for the other information. The other information comprises the [information included in the X report, but does not include the financial statements and our auditor's report thereon.]

Our opinion on the financial statements does not cover the other information and we do not express any form of assurance conclusion thereon.

In connection with our audit of the financial statements, our responsibility is to read the other information and, in doing so, consider whether the other information is materially inconsistent with the financial statements or our knowledge obtained in the audit or otherwise appears to be materially misstated. If, based on the work we have performed, we conclude that there is a material misstatement of this other information, we are required to report that fact. We have nothing to report in this regard.

Responsibilities of management and those charged with governance for the financial statements

Management is responsible for the preparation and fair presentation of the financial statements in accordance with IFRSs and for such internal control as management determines is necessary to enable the preparation of financial statements that are free from material misstatement, whether due to fraud or error.

In preparing the financial statements, management is responsible for assessing the Company's ability to continue as a going concern, disclosing, as applicable, matters related to going concern and using the going concern basis of accounting unless management either intends to liquidate the Company or to cease operations, or has no realistic alternative but to do so.

Those charged with governance are responsible for overseeing the Company's financial reporting process.

Auditor's responsibilities for the audit of the financial statements

Our objectives are to obtain reasonable assurance about whether the financial statements as a whole are free from material misstatement, whether due to fraud or error, and to issue an auditor's report that includes our opinion. Reasonable assurance is a high level of assurance, but is not a guarantee that an audit conducted in accordance with ISAs will always detect a material misstatement when it exists. Misstatements can arise from fraud or error and are considered material if, individually or in the aggregate, they could reasonably be expected to influence the economic decisions of users taken on the basis of these financial statements.

As part of an audit in accordance with ISAs, we exercise professional judgment and maintain professional scepticism throughout the audit. We also:

- Identify and assess the risks of material misstatement of the financial statements, whether due to fraud or error, design and perform audit procedures responsive to those risks, and obtain audit evidence that is sufficient and appropriate to provide a basis for our opinion. The risk of not detecting a material misstatement resulting from fraud is higher than for one resulting from error, as fraud may involve collusion, forgery, intentional omissions, misrepresentations, or the override of internal control.

- Obtain an understanding of internal control relevant to the audit in order to design audit procedures that are appropriate in the circumstances, but not for the purpose of expressing an opinion on the effectiveness of the Company's internal control.

- Evaluate the appropriateness of accounting policies used and the reasonableness of accounting estimates and related disclosures made by management.

- Conclude on the appropriateness of management's use of the going concern basis of accounting and, based on the audit evidence obtained, whether a material uncertainty exists related to events or conditions that may cast significant doubt on the Company's ability to continue as a going concern. If we conclude that a material uncertainty exists, we are required to draw attention in our auditor's report to the related disclosures in the financial statements or, if such disclosures are inadequate, to modify our opinion. Our conclusions are based on the audit evidence obtained up to the date of our auditor's report. However, future events or conditions may cause the Company to cease to continue as a going concern.
- Evaluate the overall presentation, structure and content of the financial statements, including the disclosures, and whether the financial statements represent the underlying transactions and events in a manner that achieves fair presentation.

We communicate with those charged with governance regarding, among other matters, the planned scope and timing of the audit and significant audit findings, including any significant deficiencies in internal control that we identify during our audit.

We also provide those charged with governance with a statement that we have complied with relevant ethical requirements regarding independence, and to communicate with them all relationships and other matters that may reasonably be thought to bear on our independence, and where applicable, related safeguards.

From the matters communicated with those charged with governance, we determine those matters that were of most significance in the audit of the financial statements of the current period and are therefore the key audit matters. We describe these matters in our auditor's report unless law or regulation precludes public disclosure about the matter or when, in extremely rare circumstances, we determine that a matter should not be communicated in our report because the adverse consequences of doing so would reasonably be expected to outweigh the public interest benefits of such communication.

Report on other legal and regulatory requirements

[The form and content of this section of the auditor's report would vary depending on the nature of the auditor's other reporting responsibilities prescribed by local law, regulation, or national auditing standards. The matters addressed by other law, regulation or national auditing standards (referred to as "other reporting responsibilities") shall be addressed within this section unless the other reporting responsibilities address the same topics as those presented under the reporting responsibilities required by the ISAs as part of the Report on the Audit of the Financial Statements section. The reporting of other reporting responsibilities that address the same topics as those required by the ISAs may be combined (ie included in the Report on the Audit of the Financial Statements section under the appropriate subheadings) provided that the wording in the auditor's report clearly differentiates the other reporting responsibilities from the reporting that is required by the ISAs where such a difference exists.]

The engagement partner on the audit resulting in this independent auditor's report is [name].

[Signature in the name of the audit firm, the personal name of the auditor, or both, as appropriate for the particular jurisdiction]

[Auditor Address]

[Date]

3.3 Reasonable assurance

The auditor's report refers to the fact that the audit is planned and performed to obtain 'reasonable assurance' whether the financial statements are free from material misstatement. This is because the auditor cannot check everything and therefore can only provide 'reasonable' not 'absolute' assurance.

Key term

> An auditor's report gives the reader **reasonable assurance** on the truth and fairness of the financial statements, which is a high, but not absolute, level of assurance. The auditor's report does not guarantee that the financial statements are correct, but that they are true and fair within a reasonable margin of error.

One reason an auditor does not give absolute assurance is because of the **inherent limitations** of an audit. We discuss these limitations later in this chapter.

3.4 Materiality

Misstatements which are significant to readers may exist in financial statements and auditors will plan their work focussing on these material (significant/important) items. This is the concept of **materiality**.

Key term

> Misstatements, including omissions, are considered to be **material** if they, individually or in the aggregate, could reasonably be expected to influence the economic decisions of users taken on the basis of the financial statements. Judgements about materiality are made in light of surrounding circumstances, and are affected by the size or nature of a misstatement, or a combination of both.

The auditors' task is to decide whether the financial statements show a **true and fair view**. The auditors are not responsible for establishing whether the financial statements are correct in every particular. This is because it can take a great deal of time and trouble to check the accuracy of even a very small transaction and the resulting benefit may not justify the effort. Also financial accounting inevitably involves a degree of estimation which means that financial statements can never be completely precise.

Although the definition of materiality refers to the decisions of the addressees of the auditor's report (the company's members), materiality levels may well be influenced by other entities that use the financial statements, for example, the bank.

We will look at materiality in more detail when we cover planning the audit later in this Workbook.

3.5 Modified opinions

Where there are **material misstatements** in the financial statements or when the auditor has **been unable to obtain sufficient appropriate audit evidence** the auditor's report will contain a **modified** opinion.

The following table summarises the different types of modified opinion:

Nature of Matter Giving Rise to the Modification	Auditor's Judgement about the Pervasiveness of the Effects or Possible Effects on the Financial Statements	
	Material but not Pervasive	**Material and Pervasive**
Financial statements are materially misstated	Qualified opinion	Adverse opinion
Inability to obtain sufficient appropriate audit evidence	Qualified opinion	Disclaimer of opinion

Pervasiveness is a term used to describe the effects or possible effects on the financial statements of misstatements or undetected misstatements (due to an inability to obtain sufficient appropriate audit evidence). There are three types of pervasive effect:

- Those that are not confined to specific elements, accounts or items in the financial statements
- Those that are confined to specific elements, accounts or items in the financial statements and represent or could represent a substantial portion of the financial statements
- Those that relate to disclosures which are fundamental to users' understanding of the financial statements

4 Audits and other engagements

> **FAST FORWARD**
>
> A **statutory external audit** is just **one type of assurance engagement** that is carried out by an auditor to give an independent opinion on a set of financial statements.

4.1 Statutory and non-statutory engagements

In most countries, audits are required under national statute for many undertakings, including limited liability companies. Other organisations and entities requiring a statutory audit may include charities, investment businesses and trade unions. In the UK for example, under registered companies' legislation (currently the Companies Act 2006), most companies are required to have an audit.

The statutory audit can bring various advantages to the company and shareholders. The key benefit to shareholders is the impartial view provided by the auditors. However, the company also benefits from professional accountants reviewing the accounts and systems as part of the audit. Advantages might include recommendations being made in relation to accounting and control systems and the possibility that auditors might detect fraud and misstatements.

A statutory external audit is just one type of assurance engagement that is carried out by an auditor to give an independent opinion on a set of financial statements. **Non-statutory assurance engagements** are performed by independent auditors because the company's owners, proprietors, members, trustees, professional and governing bodies or **other interested parties want them, rather than because the law requires them**. In consequence, assurance may extend to every type of undertaking which produces accounts, including clubs, charities (some of these may require statutory audits as well), sole traders and partnerships. Some of these organisations do not operate for profit, and this has a specific impact on the nature of their assurance.

The internal audit function at a company is another example of a non-statutory assurance engagement. This is discussed in more detail in Section 4.3 below.

Earlier in this Workbook when covering sustainability reporting we highlighted the increasing demand for assurance from professionals in relation to sustainability reports and disclosures. A number of companies have already obtained (or are seeking to obtain) assurance on their sustainability reporting to enhance the degree of confidence stakeholders have in the facts and measures reported.

We look at sustainability assurance engagements in Section 4.4.

4.2 Levels of assurance

> **FAST FORWARD**
>
> The **degree of assurance** given by the auditor will depend on the nature of the engagement.

Audits are an example of an assurance engagement.

Key term

> **Assurance engagement** is an engagement in which a practitioner aims to obtain sufficient appropriate evidence in order to express a conclusion designed to enhance the degree of confidence of the intended users other than the responsible party about the subject matter information (that is, the outcome of the measurement or evaluation of an underlying subject matter against criteria).

A key factor of an assurance engagement is a three-party relationship between:

- A practitioner
- A responsible party
- An intended user

In the case of an audit, this means:

- The auditor
- The directors
- The shareholders

'Assurance' here means **the auditors' satisfaction as to the reliability of the assertion made by one party for use by another party**.

Directors prepare financial statements for the benefit of members. They **assert** that the financial statements give a true and fair view. The auditors provide **assurance** on that assertion. To provide such assurance, the auditors must:

- Assess risk
- Plan audit procedures
- Conduct audit procedures
- Assess results
- Express an opinion

The degree of satisfaction achieved and, therefore, **the level of assurance which may be provided** is **determined by** the **nature** of **procedures performed** and their results.

An **external audit** can be distinguished from other assurance engagements in the following ways.

(a) **External audit engagement:** the auditor provides a high, but not absolute, level of assurance that the information audited is free of material misstatement. This is expressed positively in the auditor's report as **reasonable assurance.**

(b) **Review engagement:** the auditor provides a **limited** level of assurance that the information subject to review is free of material misstatement. This is expressed in a negative form. The auditor gives an assurance that nothing has come to their attention which indicates that the financial statements have not been prepared according to the framework. In other words, he gives limited assurance in the absence of any evidence to the contrary.

The following table summarises the different types of engagement that can be carried out by practitioners.

Type of assurance provided	Typical form of conclusion provided	Example
Reasonable	Positive	Statutory external audit
Limited	Negative	Review of interim financial statements

4.3 Internal audit reviews

Up to now we have discussed assurance services where an independent outsider provides an opinion on financial information. Assurance can also be provided to management (and by implication, to other parties) by **internal auditors**.

Key term

> **Internal auditing** is a function of an entity that performs assurance and consulting activities designed to evaluate and improve the effectiveness of the entity's governance, risk management and internal control processes.
> (ISA 610: para. 14)

As part of good corporate governance all directors are advised to review the effectiveness of the company's risk management and internal control systems. They should also consider the need for an **internal audit function to help them carry out their duties.**

Larger organisations may therefore appoint full-time staff whose **function is to monitor and report on the running of the company's operations**. Internal audit staff members are one type of control. There are a number of assignments that may be carried out by internal auditors and these include:

(a) **Value for money (VFM) audits** which examine the **economy**, **efficiency** and **effectiveness** of activities and processes.

(b) An **information technology (IT) audit**, which is a test of controls in a specific area of the business.

(c) **Best value audits**. 'Best value' is a performance framework introduced into local authorities by the UK government in 2000. They are required to publish annual best value performance plans and review all of their functions over a five year period and internal audit can carry out this review.

(d) **Financial audits**, which involve reviewing all the available evidence to substantiate information in management and financial reporting. The substantive procedures and tests of controls employed by external audit are also used by internal audit.

(e) **Operational audits**, which are audits of the operational processes of the organisation.

(f) **Procurement** audits. Procurement is the process of **purchasing** for the business. A procurement audit will therefore concentrate on the **systems** of the purchasing department(s).

(g) **Compliance audits.** These are audits to confirm whether an organisation complies with rules and regulations.

(h) **Social and environmental audits**: Audits to check whether the company has met stated social and environmental performance measures.

Note. Although we have listed these as activities performed by internal audit, an organisation may also hire an external audit firm to perform them. However, apart from (d), they are not part of the statutory audit.

We will consider internal audit in more depth in Chapter 15.

4.4 Sustainability assurance engagements

In Chapter 6 we mentioned that at the time of writing this Workbook, the audit of sustainability related disclosures in annual reports or separate sustainability reports presented with the financial statements is **not mandatory**.

However, the demand for assurance over the reporting is evident and there has been a sharp increase in non-statutory engagements in this area.

This means there is a clear need for guidance for firms carrying out sustainability assurance engagements. Normally the sustainability related information will either be within a section of the annual report or presented as a separate sustainability report. The disclosures which we described in Chapter 6, both qualitative and quantitative, would potentially be covered in an assurance engagement agreed between a client and a practitioner.

Case Study — ED 5000

The need for guidance for sustainability assurance engagements prompted the International Audit and Assurance Standards Board (**IAASB**) to draft an **International Standard on Sustainability Assurance** 5000 *General Requirements for Sustainability Assurance Engagements*.

In June 2023, the IAASB prepared an exposure draft (ED) of its proposed standard. Comments on ED-5000 were to be submitted by 1 December 2023. At the time of writing this workbook the final standard had not been published but it is expected to be released in late 2024.

Under the proposed standard, assurance providers will evaluate disclosures that are the responsibility of the reporting entity. The structure of the assurance report under the proposed standard is similar to that of an auditor's report on a set of financial statements.

ED-5000 is **principles-based** in order to accommodate:

- A **broad range of sustainability topics** that could be reported by any organisation
- Variety in **the way such topics are disclosed**
- The ability to use **different criteria and methodologies** (for example, the GRI, the ISSB standards or the EU's Corporate Sustainability Reporting Directive (CSRD))
- **Intended users with different requirements** (investors, policy makers and other stakeholders: it is noted that ED-5000 recognises the term '**double materiality**' - covered in Chapter 6)
- The availability of **accurate and complete evidence** may vary, meaning that sufficiency and appropriateness of evidence may be subjective
- The ability to issue a conclusion which delivers either **limited assurance or reasonable assurance** to suit the jurisdiction
- A **range of assurance providers** with different skills and resources

As the case study above states, the materiality used by the assurance provider when carrying out sustainability assurance engagements will be consistent with double materiality concept we looked at in Chapter 6.

As a reminder this means considering both impact materiality and financial materiality from a sustainability perspective.

- **Impact materiality** considers whether a company's activities (direct or indirect) significantly impact on people and planet.
- **Financial materiality** considers the risks and opportunities arising from sustainability issues which may have a material impact on the company's value in the short, medium or long term.

5 Fraud, laws and regulations

FAST FORWARD

When carrying out risk assessment procedures, the auditors should also consider the risk of **fraud** and **non-compliance with law and regulations,** causing a misstatement in financial statements.

5.1 What is fraud?

Key terms

Fraud is an **intentional act** by one or more individuals among management, those charged with governance (management fraud), employees (employee fraud) or third parties involving the use of deception to obtain an unjust or illegal advantage. Fraud may be perpetrated by an individual, or **colluded** in, with people internal or external to the business.

Fraud risk factors are events or conditions that indicate an incentive or pressure to commit fraud or provide an opportunity to commit fraud.

(ISA 240: paras. 11(a) and 11(b)).

It is **primarily** the **responsibility of those charged with governance of the entity and management** to **prevent and detect fraud**. This responsibility is discharged **through the use of internal controls**, such as segregation of duties, and having **an internal audit function.** We look at the responsibilities of those charged with governance in more detail in Section 5.2.1.

ISA 240 *The Auditor's Responsibilities Relating to Fraud in an Audit of Financial Statements* states that the **auditor** is responsible for **obtaining reasonable assurance that the financial statements are free from material misstatement, whether caused by fraud or error** (ISA 240: para. 5).

Therefore the **auditor's main concern** is with **fraud** that **causes a material misstatement** in the financial statements. Fraud is distinguished from error, which is when a material misstatement is caused by mistake, for example, in the misapplication of an accounting policy. The auditor must be aware that ISA 240 clearly places a responsibility on them to detect fraud which would have a **material** impact on the financial statements of an entity and design audit procedures accordingly. We look at the responsibilities of the auditor under ISA 240 in more detail in section 5.2.2.

It should be noted that there is a common misconception held by the public in relation to the responsibilities of the auditor in relation to the prevention and detection of fraud. Members of the public sometimes assume the primary role falls to the auditor, whereas we have seen that the **primary responsibility** rests with those charged with governance, and that the auditors are responsible for obtaining reasonable assurance that the financial statements are free from material misstatement caused by fraud. This misconception is called the '**expectations gap**'.

There are two types of fraud causing material misstatement in financial statements:

- Fraudulent financial reporting
- Misappropriation of assets

5.1.1 Fraudulent financial reporting

This may include:

- Manipulation, falsification or alteration of accounting records/supporting documents
- Misrepresentation (or omission) of events or transactions in the financial statements
- Intentional misapplication of accounting principles

Such fraud may be carried out by overriding controls that would otherwise appear to be operating effectively, for example, by recording fictitious journal entries or improperly adjusting assumptions or estimates used in financial reporting.

5.1.2 Misappropriation of assets

This is the theft of the entity's assets (for example, cash, inventory). Employees may be involved in such fraud in small and immaterial amounts, however, it can also be carried out by management for larger items who may then conceal the misappropriation, for example by:

- Embezzling receipts (for example, diverting them to private bank accounts)
- Stealing physical assets or intellectual property (inventory, selling data)
- Causing an entity to pay for goods not received (payments to fictitious vendors)
- Using assets for personal use

5.2 Responsibilities with regard to fraud

5.2.1 Responsibilities of those charged with governance

As discussed earlier, **management and those charged with governance** at an entity are primarily responsible for preventing and detecting fraud. It is up to them to put a strong emphasis within the company on fraud prevention. The directors at an entity should to take reasonable steps to prevent and detect fraud. This includes:

- Ensuring that the activities of the company are conducted honestly and that its assets are safeguarded.

- Implementing procedures designed to deter fraudulent or other dishonest conduct and to detect any that occurs.
- Ensuring that, to the best of their knowledge and belief, financial information is reliable.

To prevent and detect fraud, the directors should:

- Develop an appropriate control environment within the company;
- Implement a Code of Conduct which is clearly communicated to employees, monitor compliance and take appropriate disciplinary action in cases of non-compliance; and
- Implement systems of internal control, regularly monitoring their effectiveness and taking corrective action where necessary.

An **internal audit function** and an **audit committee** will help those charged with governance and management to meet their responsibilities with regards to detecting and preventing fraud.

Since it is the responsibility of **directors** to prepare financial statements that give a true and fair view of the state of affairs of the company, where material error or fraud has occurred, whether detected by the directors or the auditors, the directors must correct the accounting records and ensure that the matter is appropriately reflected and/or disclosed in the financial statements.

5.2.2 Responsibilities of the auditor

Auditors are responsible for carrying out an audit in accordance with international auditing standards, one of which is ISA 240 *The Auditor's Responsibilities Relating to Fraud in an Audit of Financial Statements*, the details of which we shall look at now.

The auditors' approach to the possibility of fraud is similar to the approach to the possibility of misstatement. The objectives of ISA 240 are as follows:

(a) To **identify and assess the risks of material misstatement** of the financial statements **due to fraud**

(b) To **obtain sufficient appropriate audit evidence** regarding the assessed risks of material misstatement due to fraud

(c) To **respond appropriately** to fraud or suspected fraud identified during the audit

An overriding requirement of the ISA is that auditors are aware of the possibility of there being misstatements due to fraud. The team must have **professional scepticism** and must discuss the possibility of material misstatements due to fraud (how fraud could be perpetrated and by whom, and how unpredictability could be added into the audit).

5.2.3 Risk assessment procedures

The auditor would undertake risk assessment procedures as set out in ISA 315 (Revised) *Identifying and Assessing the Risks of Material Misstatement* which would include assessing the risk of fraud. These procedures will include:

- Inquiries of management, those charged with governance and internal auditors (where present)
- Evaluation of fraud risk factors present
- Consideration of unusual or unexpected results of analytical procedures
- Consideration of any other relevant information that indicates risk of material misstatement due to fraud

In identifying the risks of fraud, the auditor is required by the ISA to make specific enquiries of management regarding fraud (for example, what they think the risk is, what their process for identifying and responding to fraud is, and management communications on the topic).

Auditors are also required to enquire of management, internal audit or others whether any alleged, actual or suspected fraud has taken place.

While obtaining their understanding of the entity, they should consider whether any fraud risk factors are present. For example, management may have an incentive to report fraudulently if profitability is threatened by market conditions or as a result of new accounting standards, alternatively there may be pressure to meet certain targets to impress shareholders or to retain funding.

5.3 Reporting

The ISA states:

> 'If the auditor has identified a fraud or has obtained information that indicates that a fraud may exist, the auditor shall communicate these matters on a timely basis to the appropriate level of management in order to inform those with primary responsibility for the prevention and detection of fraud of matters relevant to their responsibilities'.

In addition, 'if the auditor has identified or suspects fraud involving:

- Management
- Employees who have significant roles in internal control, or
- Others, where the fraud results in a material misstatement in the financial statements

the auditor shall communicate these matters to **those charged with governance** on a timely basis.'

The auditor should also make relevant parties within the entity aware of material weaknesses in the design or implementation of controls to prevent and detect fraud which have come to the auditor's attention, and consider whether there are any other relevant matters to bring to the attention of those charged with governance with regard to fraud.

The auditor may have a **statutory duty** to report fraudulent behaviour to **regulators** outside the entity. For example, in the UK, money laundering is covered by the Money Laundering Regulations 2017 (amended 2022). If no such legal duty arises, the auditor must consider whether to do so would breach his **professional duty of confidence**. In either event, the auditor should take **legal advice**.

5.4 Laws and regulations

FAST FORWARD

> The auditor's responsibility is to obtain reasonable assurance that the financial statements are free from material misstatement whether due to fraud or error and, in this respect, the auditor must take into account the legal and regulatory framework within which the entity operates.

The auditor is also required to consider the issue of laws and regulations in the audit. Auditors are given guidance in ISA 250 (Revised) *Consideration of Laws and Regulations in an Audit of Financial Statements*.

5.4.1 Responsibilities of management and the auditor

It is management's responsibility to ensure that the entity complies with the relevant laws and regulations.

The auditor's responsibility is to obtain reasonable assurance that the financial statements are free from material misstatement whether due to fraud or error and, in this respect, the auditor must take into account the legal and regulatory framework within which the entity operates.

The auditor has differing responsibilities in relation to compliance with two different categories of laws and regulations:

(a) Those that have a **direct effect** on the determination of **material amounts** and disclosures in the financial statements (such as tax or pension laws and regulations)

(b) Those that **do not have a direct effect** on the determination of material amounts and disclosures in the financial statements but where compliance may be fundamental to the **operating aspects**, ability to **continue in business**, or to avoid **material penalties** (such as regulatory compliance or compliance with the terms of an operating licence)

For the first category, the auditor's responsibility is to obtain sufficient appropriate audit evidence about **compliance** with those laws and regulations.

For the second category, the auditor's responsibility is to undertake specified audit procedures to help **identify non-compliance** with laws and regulations that may have a **material effect** on the financial statements. These include enquiries of management and inspecting correspondence with the relevant licensing or regulatory authorities.

If non-compliances are suspected or identified by the auditor, the auditor will need to respond appropriately with suitable audit procedures or actions.

5.4.2 Audit procedures

In accordance with ISA 315 (Revised), the auditor shall obtain a general understanding of:

- The applicable legal and regulatory framework
- How the entity complies with that framework

(ISA 250: para. 13)

The auditor can achieve this understanding by using their **existing understanding** and updating it, and making **enquiries of management** about other laws and regulations that may affect the entity, and about its policies and procedures for ensuring compliance and about its policies and procedures for identifying, evaluating and accounting for litigation claims.

The auditor shall remain alert throughout the audit to the possibility that **other audit procedures** may bring instances of non-compliance or suspected non-compliance to the auditor's attention. These audit procedures could include:

- Reading minutes
- Making enquiries of management and in-house/external legal advisers regarding litigation, claims and assessments
- Performing substantive tests of details of classes of transactions, account balances or disclosures

5.4.3 Audit procedures when non-compliance is identified or suspected

The following table summarises audit procedures to be performed when non-compliance is identified or suspected.

Non-compliance: audit procedures
Obtain an understanding of the nature of any acts and circumstances
Obtain further information to evaluate the possible effect on the financial statements
Discuss with management and those charged with governance unless laws and regulations in the jurisdiction concerned prohibit such communication (for example, avoiding tipping off in cases of suspected money laundering) meaning legal advice may need to be sought by the auditor before proceeding with such enquiries
Consider the need to obtain legal advice (or consult with others inside or connected to the firm) anyway if sufficient information is not provided and the matter is material
Evaluate the effect on the auditor's opinion if sufficient information is not obtained
Evaluate the implications of any identified or suspected non-compliance on risk assessment and the reliability of any written representations (especially if the auditor possesses evidence of either management or those charged with governance being involved in this non-compliance in some way)

5.4.4 Reporting identified or suspected non-compliance

The auditor shall communicate with **those charged with governance**, but, if the auditor suspects that those charged with governance are involved, the auditor shall communicate with the next highest level of authority, such as the **audit committee or supervisory board**. If this does not exist, the auditor shall consider the need to obtain **legal advice**.

The auditor shall consider the impact of any identified or suspected non-compliance.

6 Benefits and limitations

> **FAST FORWARD**
>
> While having many advantages, the statutory audit also has limitations which may not be understood by users. This leads to what is termed the **expectations gap**.

6.1 Advantages of the statutory audit

We have discussed already the principal aim of the external audit – to provide an **independent opinion** on the truth and fairness of the financial statements for the owners of a business. This is particularly important where the owners are separate from the day-to-day management or directors of a business.

An external audit may **enhance the credibility** of the financial statements to **outsiders** as they will have been examined independently. Banks and other lenders often ask to view the audited accounts before making an investment decision. An individual thinking of joining a partnership may also view the audited accounts as part of their decision-making process. Additionally, tax authorities are more likely to accept figures being used for the basis of a tax calculation if they have been audited.

The external audit can highlight other issues as a result of work relating to the financial statements such as **deficiencies in the internal control system** of the entity, which can be improved by the entity's management. We will look at this aspect later in this Workbook. A company may be able to take advantage of other professional services offered by the audit firm, such as tax advice and corporate finance. It is worth noting that other professional services can only be undertaken by the audit firm if the correct ethical guidance is followed.

An audit may also **prevent misstatements and fraud**. The fact that an audit is being carried out may make the staff preparing the subject matter more careful in its preparation and reduce the chance of misstatements or fraudulent reporting arising. In this way, audit services may act as a deterrent.

An audit is important in more general terms by helping to ensure that high quality, reliable information exists, leading to effective markets that investors trust. Audit adds to the reputation of organisations and countries so that investors are comfortable investing in them.

For these reasons, even where entities are not obliged to undergo an external audit, they may choose to do so, regardless of the costs involved (time and money) because the benefits outweigh those costs.

6.2 Limitations of audit

> **FAST FORWARD**
>
> External audits give **reasonable assurance** that the financial statements are free from material misstatement. This assurance can never be **absolute**.

The assurance given by auditors is governed by the fact that auditors use **judgement** in deciding what audit procedures to use and what conclusions to draw, and also by the **limitations** of every audit. These are illustrated in the following diagram.

8: THE NATURE AND PURPOSE OF AUDITING

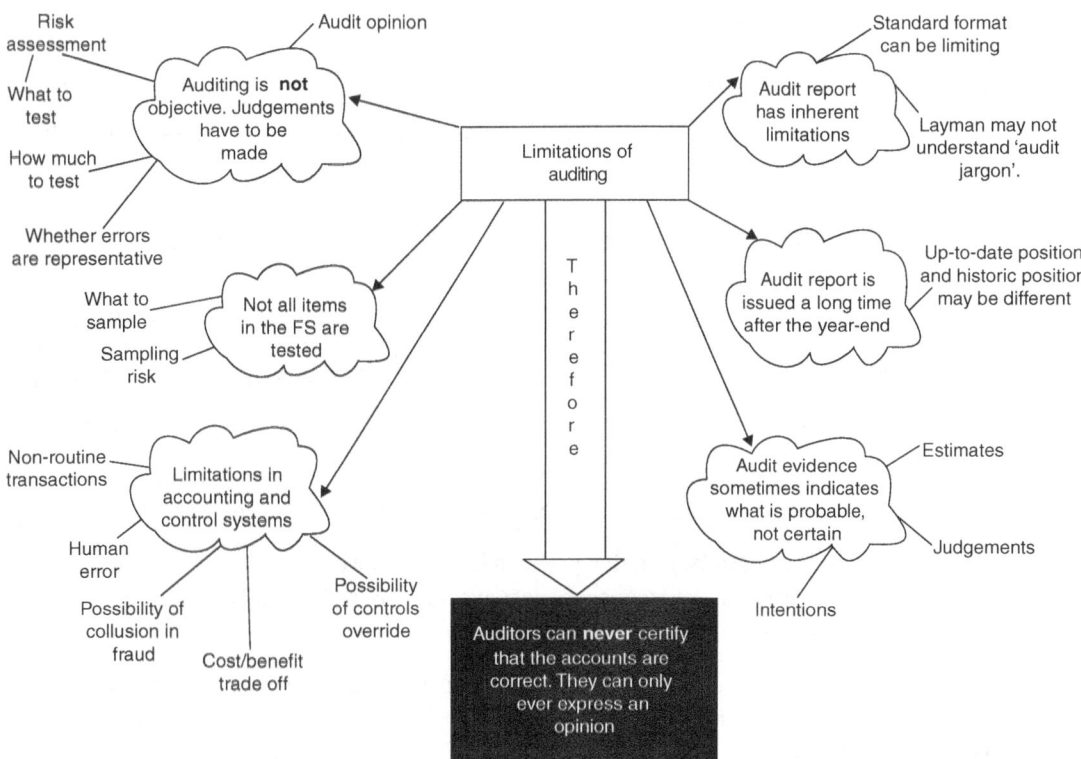

6.3 Implied information

FAST FORWARD

> Auditors report by **exception**. The report says much by **implication**. This difference between what is stated and what is implied in the auditor's report affects public perception and is part of what is called the '**expectations gap**'.

Auditor's reports with unmodified opinions may not appear to give a great deal of information. The report says much, however, by implication. Remember that the auditors report **by exception** on a number of issues, so a standard auditor's report in the UK tells the user that, for example:

- **Adequate accounting** records have been **kept**.
- The **accounts agree** with the **records**.
- The **auditors** have **received** all **necessary information**.
- All **directors' transactions** have been **disclosed**.

The real problem here is that, unfortunately, most users do not know that this is what an auditor's report tells them. This issue is also confused by the fact that many users do not understand the responsibilities of either the auditors or the directors in relation to the financial statements.

This difference between the actual and the public perception is part of what is called the '**expectations gap**'.

6.4 Expectations gap

This difference between the actual and the public perception is part of what is called the '**expectations gap**', defined as the difference between the apparent public perceptions of the responsibilities of auditors on the one hand (and hence the assurance that their involvement provides) and the legal and professional reality on the other. The question remains: how can we make the **meaning** of an unqualified auditor's report clear to the user?

The above definition of the expectations gap is not definitive but we can highlight some specific issues.

(a) **Misunderstandings of the nature of audited financial statements**, for example that:
- The statement of financial position provides a fair valuation of the reporting entity.
- The amounts in the financial statements are stated precisely.
- The audited financial statements will guarantee that the entity concerned will continue to exist.

(b) **Misunderstanding as to the type and extent of work undertaken by auditors**

(c) **Misunderstanding about the level of assurance provided by auditors**, for example that:
- An unmodified auditor's opinion means that no frauds have occurred in the period.
- The auditors provide absolute assurance that the figures in the financial statements are correct (ignoring the concept of materiality and the problems of estimation).

Different countries have tackled this problem in different ways. The role of auditors has been included in the debate on corporate governance in many western countries, leading to further rules which are nevertheless voluntary, not mandatory.

The expectations gap has been discussed and explained for many years by leading authors in different audit related publications, such as within Chapter 18 of the *Principles of External Auditing* (2014), by Brenda Porter (Author), Jon Simon (Author), David Hatherly (Author), Wiley, 4th edition. The chapter discusses the '**Audit Expectation-Performance Gap**' and suggested proposals at the time for reforming the external audit function.

Chapter roundup

- Directors are agents of the shareholders and manage the company on their behalf. Auditors are also the agents of the shareholders, and their role is to help ensure that the directors are properly fulfilling their responsibility to manage the company's finances (the 'stewardship' function). This has become more critical over the years as corporate organisations have increased in size and number of shareholders.

- An audit provides **assurance** to the shareholders and other stakeholders of a company on the financial statements because it is **independent and impartial**.

- The purpose of an external audit is to enable auditors to **give an independent opinion** on the financial statements.

- A **statutory external audit** is just **one type of assurance engagement** that is carried out by an auditor to give an independent opinion on a set of financial statements.

- The **degree of assurance** given by the auditor will depend on the nature of the engagement.

- Auditors must consider the risk that fraud or non-compliance with law and regulations could cause a misstatement in the financial statements.

- The auditor's responsibility is to obtain reasonable assurance that the financial statements are free from material misstatement whether due to fraud or error and, in this respect, the auditor must take into account the legal and regulatory framework within which the entity operates.

- While having many advantages, the statutory audit also has limitations which may not be understood by users. This leads to what is termed the **expectations gap**.

- External audits give **reasonable assurance** that the financial statements are free from material misstatement. This assurance can never be **absolute**.

- Auditors report by **exception**. The report says much by **implication**. This difference between what is stated and what is implied in the auditor's report affects public perception and is part of what is called the 'expectations gap'.

PART B FOUNDATIONS OF AUDITING

Quick quiz

1 Complete the definition of the objectives of the auditor:

   The overall objectives of the auditor are to obtain .... about whether the financial statements as a whole are free from ...., whether due to fraud or error, thereby enabling the auditor to express an .... on whether the financial statements are prepared, in all material respects, in accordance with an applicable financial reporting framework; and to .... on the financial statements, and communicate as required by the ISAs, in accordance with the auditor's findings.

2 Give four examples of a non-statutory assurance engagement.

3 Link the correct definition to each term.

   (i)   Accountable   (iv) True
   (ii) Steward   (v)   Fair
   (iii) Agent   (vi) Materiality

   (a) An expression of the relative significance or importance of a particular matter in the context of the financial statements as a whole.

   (b) A person employed to provide a particular service.

   (c) Factual and conforming with reality. In conformity with relevant standards and law and correctly extracted from accounting records.

   (d) A person employed to manage other people's property.

   (e) Free from discrimination and bias and in compliance with expected standards and rules. Reflecting the commercial substance of underlying transactions.

   (f) Being required or expected to justify actions and decisions.

4 Reasonable assurance is a high, but not absolute, level of assurance.

   True [ ]   False [ ]

5 Name four items of information implied by a standard auditor's report.

6 Auditors have a duty to detect fraud.

   True [ ]   False [ ]

7 Auditors should always report suspected fraud to management.

   True [ ]   False [ ]

Answers to quick quiz

1. The overall objectives of the auditor are to obtain reasonable assurance about whether the financial statements as a whole are free from material misstatement, whether due to fraud or error, thereby enabling the auditor to express an opinion on whether the financial statements are prepared, in all material respects, in accordance with an applicable financial reporting framework; and to report on the financial statements, and communicate as required by the ISAs, in accordance with the auditor's findings.

2. Any from the following:
   - Local authority audit
   - Insurance company audit
   - Bank audits
   - Pension scheme audits
   - Charity audits
   - Solicitors' audits
   - Social auditing
   - Environmental audits
   - Internal audit
   - Value-for-money audit
   - Due diligence
   - Circulation reports (eg for magazines)
   - Web assurance

   Note. This is not an exhaustive listing.

3. (i)   (f)   (iv) (c)
   (ii) (d)   (v)   (e)
   (iii) (b)   (vi) (a)

4. True

5. See Section 6.3

6. False

7. False. If the auditor suspects management is involved it should be reported to those charged with governance or legal advice should be sought.

PART B FOUNDATIONS OF AUDITING

End of chapter questions

8.1 Which of the following statements best defines the external audit?

- A The external audit is an exercise carried out by auditors in order to give an opinion on whether the financial statements of a company are fairly presented (give a true and fair view).
- B The external audit is an exercise carried out in order to give an opinion on the effectiveness of a company's internal control system.
- C The purpose of the external audit is to identify areas of deficiency within a company and to make recommendations to mitigate those deficiencies.
- D The external audit provides negative assurance on the truth and fairness of a company's financial statements.

8.2. ABC & Co has a client, XYZ Co, which operates a chain of restaurants. There are strict hygiene regulations in the restaurant industry.

Which of the following statements best describes ABC & Co's responsibility regarding XYZ's compliance with hygiene regulations?

- A ABC & Co should actively prevent and detect non-compliance with the regulations.
- B ABC & Co should perform specific audit procedures to identify possible non-compliance.
- C ABC & Co should obtain sufficient appropriate audit evidence about XYZ's compliance with the regulations as they have a direct effect on the financial statements.
- D ABC & Co does not have any responsibility as the hygiene regulations do not have a direct effect on the financial statements.

8.3 The level of assurance provided by an external audit is:

- A Reasonable
- B Negative
- C Absolute
- D Limited

8.4 ABC & Co has been engaged to comment on whether XYZ & Co has met its carbon emissions targets. What type of audit is this?

- A Statutory audit
- B Internal audit
- C Social and environmental audit
- D Systems audit

8.5 Which of these best describes auditors' responsibility for fraud?

- A The auditor is responsible for preventing material frauds
- B The auditor must gain reasonable assurance as to whether the financial statements are materially misstated as a result of fraud
- C The auditor must gain reasonable assurance as to whether the financial statements are misstated as a result of fraud
- D The auditor has no responsibility with respect to fraud

Regulation of audit

Topic list	Syllabus reference
1 Importance of regulation	B2.3
2 Professional regulation	B2.3
3 Statutory regulation	B2.3

Introduction

This chapter looks at the regulation of the audit profession and process and why it is important. We consider professional regulation in Section 2 and look at the internal bodies regulating audit, as well as what individual firms do.

Section 3 explores the regulations and guidelines surrounding the appointment, resignation and dismissal of auditors.

1 Importance of regulation

We saw in the first half of this book that corporate governance codes were developed in response to corporate scandals and were an attempt to repair public faith in company management.

The audit profession also came in for a lot of criticism in many of these scandals. It is important, therefore, that auditors do their work competently and with integrity in order to maintain public faith in the accounting profession. This will also help to narrow the expectation gap, which we considered in the previous chapter.

Auditors are partly regulated by statute; there are statutory regulations in most countries governing some aspects of auditors. However, the audit profession has always been keen to self-regulate as far as possible, so as to minimise the impact of governmental involvement. In Section 2 we will consider professional regulation and in Section 3 statutory regulation.

2 Professional regulation

In this section we will consider:

- Regulation of auditing processes through International Standards on Auditing (ISAs)
- International ethics codes
- Quality management procedures

2.1 International Standards on Auditing

FAST FORWARD

International Standards on Auditing are set by the **International Auditing and Assurance Standards Board.**

2.1.1 Rules governing audits

We discussed in Chapter 1 the various stakeholders in a company, and the various people who might read a company's financial statements. Consider also that some of these readers will not just be reading a single company's financial statements, but will also be looking at those of a large number of companies, and making comparisons between them.

Readers want **assurance** when making comparisons that the **reliability** of the financial statements **does not vary from company to company**. This assurance will be obtained not just from knowing that each set of financial statements has been audited, but knowing that this has been done to **common standards**.

Hence there is a need for audits to be **regulated** so that auditors follow the same standards. As we will see in this chapter, auditors have to follow rules issued by a variety of bodies. Some obligations are imposed by governments in law or statute. Some obligations are imposed by the professional bodies to which auditors are required to belong, such as the AIA.

International Standards on Auditing (ISAs) are produced by the **International Auditing and Assurance Standards Board (IAASB),** a technical standing committee of the **International Federation of Accountants (IFAC),** which also issues standards relating to review engagements, other assurance engagements, quality management and related services.

The IAASB's objective is the development of a set of international standards that are accepted worldwide. The IAASB's pronouncements relate to audit, other assurance and related services that are conducted in accordance with international standards.

2.1.2 Relationship between ISAs and national regulation

ISAs do **not** override the local regulations referred to above governing the audit of financial or other information in a particular country.

(a) To the extent that ISAs **conform** with local regulations on a particular subject, the audit of financial or other information in that country in accordance with local regulations will automatically comply with the ISA regarding that subject.

(b) In the event that the local regulations **differ from**, or conflict with, ISAs on a particular subject, member bodies should comply with the obligations of members set forth in the IFAC Constitution as regards these ISAs (ie **encourage changes** in local regulations to comply with ISAs).

The IAASB also publishes other papers, such as **Discussion Papers**, to promote discussion on auditing, review, other assurance and related services and quality management issues affecting the accounting profession, present findings, or describe matters of interest relating to these engagements.

Case Study — UK ISAs

The UK versions of the International Standards of Auditing, known as **ISAs (UK)** are currently set by the FRC.

There are three categories of auditing pronouncement set by the FRC:

- Auditing Standards (quality management, engagement and ethical)
- Practice notes
- Bulletins

The FRC has adopted International Standards on Auditing. The ISAs (UK) are aligned with those issued by the IAASB. They are essentially the same standards with some extra sections included to cater for UK specific guidance.

Complying with the ISAs (UK) is a requirement when carrying out statutory audits.

2.1.3 Working procedures of the IAASB

A rigorous due process is followed by the IAASB to ensure that the views of all those affected by its guidance are taken into account. The following diagram summarises the process followed in the development of IAASB standards.

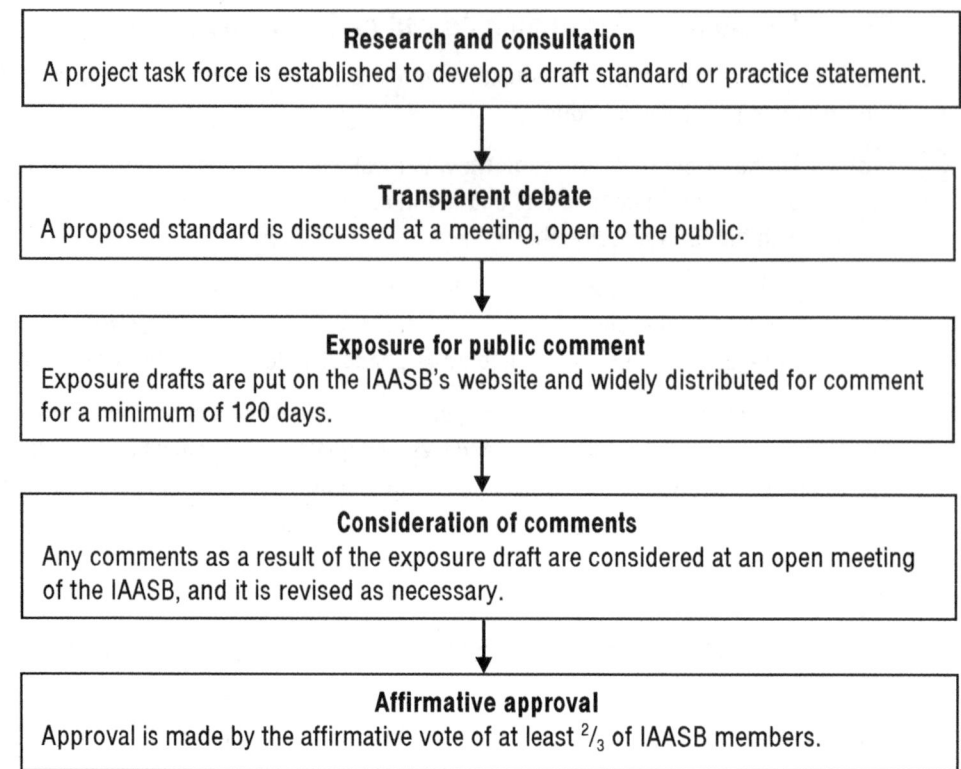

2.1.4 Current ISAs and other standards

We will touch on the content of some of the international auditing standards later in this chapter.

2.2 Professional ethics

2.2.1 The need for an ethical code

> **FAST FORWARD**
>
> Professional accountants need an ethical code because they are **relied upon** for their expertise.

Ethics can be defined as a set of principles of right conduct or a system of moral values. In its most basic form, it means knowing the difference between right and wrong and choosing to do what is right. Ethical dilemmas will naturally arise in the workplace and an ethical code provides **guidance** on the best course of action.

Members of all professions, including doctors, lawyers and accountants are **relied upon** for their expertise. Accountants are relied upon by their clients and other stakeholders such as employees, lenders and taxation authorities. Accountants must act, and be seen to act, in the **public interest** rather than in their own interest. By adhering to an ethical code, accountants help to maintain the **integrity** of their profession providing reassurance to both individual stakeholders and the wider community.

An ethical code also provides some **protection** for accountants if they have been accused of acting unethically. An accountant cannot be accused of acting differently from other accountants if they all follow the same ethical code.

2.2.2 Ethical guidance

> **FAST FORWARD**
>
> Sources of ethical guidance include the *Code of Ethics for Professional Accountants* issued by the International Ethics Standards Board for Accountants (the IESBA *Code*) and the FRC's *Ethical Standard*.

The AIA has adopted the **Code of Ethics for Professional Accountants issued by the International Ethics Standards Board for Accountants** (the **IESBA Code**). All AIA members and candidates are expected to follow this guidance. The International Ethics Standards Board for Accountants (IESBA) is an independent standard-setting board of IFAC which is responsible for developing and issuing high quality global ethical standards and other pronouncements. IFAC is the global organisation for the accountancy profession based in New York City. IFAC was founded in 1977 and one of its aims is to establish and promote adherence to high quality international standards. AIA's Code of Ethics fully complies with the IESBA Code and all members and candidates are expected to comply with it.

Some countries may have their own ethical guidance in additional to the IESBA Code. For example, in the UK, the Financial Reporting Council has issued its own **Ethical Standard** (FRC ES) – the 'Revised Ethical Standard 2024' – which provides an additional source of guidance.

2.2.3 IESBA *Code of Ethics for Professional Accountants*

FAST FORWARD

> The five **fundamental principles** of professional ethics are integrity, objectivity, professional competence and due care, confidentiality and professional behaviour.

The IESBA *Code of Ethics for Professional Accountants* (*Code*) sets out five fundamental principles of professional ethics and provides a conceptual framework for applying those principles.

The five fundamental principles are summarised in the table below.

IESBA *Code's* fundamental principles (IESBA *Code* para. 110.1 A1)	
Integrity	To be straightforward and honest in all professional and business relationships.
Objectivity	To exercise professional or business judgment without being compromised by: • Bias; • Conflict of interest; or • Undue influence of, or undue reliance on individuals, organisations, technology or other factors.
Professional competence and due care	To: • Attain and maintain professional knowledge and skill at the level required to ensure that a client or employer receives competent professional service, based on current technical and professional standards and relevant legislation; and • Act diligently and in accordance with applicable technical and professional standards.
Confidentiality	To respect the confidentiality of information acquired as a result of professional and business relationships.
Professional behaviour	To: • Comply with relevant laws and regulations; • Behave in a manner consistent with the profession's responsibility to act in the public interest in all professional activities and business relationships; and • Avoid any conduct that the professional accountant knows, or should know, might discredit the profession.

The ethics code has detailed guidance on the matters that could threaten the ethical conduct, but this is beyond the scope of this paper.

Accountants who fail to comply with the ethical codes may face disciplinary action.

PART B FOUNDATIONS OF AUDITING

2.3 Quality management

> As part of their self-regulation, audit firms need to have an effective **system of quality management**.

The International Standards on Quality Management (ISQMs) and ISA 220 (Revised) published by the IAASB provide guidance on quality management for audits.

The ISQMs are not examinable, but it is useful to look at the eight components that a system of quality management at an audit firm should address set out in ISQM 1 *Quality Management for Firms that Perform Audits or Reviews of Financial Statements, or Other Assurance or Related Services engagements* which will help you understand the quality management considerations for audit firms.

The risk assessment process	The firm should design and implement a risk assessment process to establish quality objectives, identify and assess quality risks and design and implement responses to address the quality risks.
Governance and Leadership	The firm should promote an internal culture based on the recognition that quality is essential in performing engagements. This includes devoting sufficient resources to quality management, and linking to performance evaluation, pay and promotion.
Relevant ethical requirements	There should be procedures designed to ensure that all staff adhere to the principles of integrity, independence, objectivity, confidentiality and professional behaviour.
	Examples: training sessions, appraisal sessions.
Acceptance and continuance of client relationships and specific engagements	Prospective clients should be evaluated and existing clients reviewed regularly. The firm should consider the integrity of senior personnel, competence of engagement team, any ethical barriers, problems in the past.
	Each time the firm takes on a new engagement (or is deciding on whether to continue on an engagement) an assessment of the client and of the firm's ability to perform the engagement in accordance with professional standards and applicable legal and regulatory requirements should take place.
Engagement performance	The firm should ensure that staff are properly directed and supervised and that their work is properly reviewed.
Resources	Resources to be considered include human resources, technological resources, intellectual resources (for examples access to accounting and auditing guidance) and resources from service providers.
	The firm should establish policies and procedures to ensure it recruits, trains and retains good quality staff.
	For technological and other resources, appropriate resources should be available to enable the operation of the firm's system of quality management and the performance of engagements.
Monitoring and remediation process	The firm should have procedures to monitor whether the quality management procedures are effective, including reviewing the files of a selection of completed audits and taking appropriate action when any issues are found.
Information and communication	The nature, timing and extent of the information communicated to the firm's staff should be sufficient to enable them to understand and carry out their responsibilities relating to quality management or to client engagements.
	Only relevant and reliable information should communicated to external parties. This is necessary, for example, when required by law, regulation or professional standards.

3 Statutory regulation

3.1 Appointment

The auditors should be appointed by and therefore **answerable** to the **shareholders**. The table below shows what the position should ideally be, using the **UK as an example**. The Companies Act 2006 sets out the rules for appointment of auditors. An auditor must be appointed for each financial year unless the directors reasonably resolve otherwise on the grounds that audited financial statements are unlikely to be required. The table summarises who can appoint auditors for UK public companies.

Auditor appointment (UK)	
Directors	Can appoint auditor: (a) Before company's **first period for appointing auditors** (b) Following a period during which the company **did not have an** auditor (as exempt), at any time before the next period for appointing auditors (c) To fill a **casual vacancy**
Members	Can appoint auditor by ordinary resolution: (a) During a **period for appointing auditors** (b) If company **should have** appointed auditor during a period for appointing auditors **but failed to do so** (c) If directors **fail to do so**
Secretary of State	Can appoint auditors if **no auditors** are **appointed** per above

3.2 Resignation and dismissal

> **FAST FORWARD**
>
> There are various legal and professional requirements on resignation and dismissal of auditors which must be followed.

The legal requirements for resignation and dismissal of auditors using the **UK as an example** are discussed below.

It is important that auditors know the procedures because as part of their client acceptance, they have a duty to ensure the old auditors were properly removed from office.

Resignation of auditors (UK)		
1	Resignation procedures	Auditors deposit **written notice** together with **statement of circumstances** relevant to members/creditors. A statement of circumstance must always be submitted for a quoted company, even if the auditor considers that there are no circumstances that should be brought to the attention of members or creditors.
2	Notice of resignation	Sent by **company** to regulatory authority.
3	Statement of circumstances	Sent by: (a) Auditors to regulatory authority (b) Company to everyone entitled to receive a copy of accounts
4	Convening of general meeting	**Auditors** can **require directors** to call an **extraordinary general meeting** to discuss circumstances of resignation. Directors must send out notice for meeting within **21 days** of having received requisition by auditors.
5	Statement prior to general meeting	**Auditors** may require company to circulate **statement of circumstances** to everyone entitled to notice of meeting.

Resignation of auditors (UK)		
6	Other rights of auditors	Can **receive all notices** that relate to: (a) A general meeting at which their term of office would have expired (b) A general meeting where casual vacancy caused by their resignation is to be filled Can **speak** at these meetings on **any matter** which **concerns them as auditors**.

Removal of auditors (UK)		
1	Notice of removal	**Either special notice** (28 days) with copy sent to auditor. **or** (in private company), **written resolution** to appoint a different auditor with copy sent to proposed and outgoing auditors. Directors must convene a meeting within a reasonable period of time.
2	Representations	**Auditors** can make **representations** on why they ought to stay in office. They may require company to state in notice that representations have been made and send copy to members.
3	If resolution passed	(a) Company must **notify** regulatory authority. (b) Auditors must **deposit statement of circumstances** at company's registered office **within 14 days** of ceasing to hold office. Statement must be sent to regulatory authority.
4	Auditor rights	Can **receive notice** of and **speak** at: (a) General meeting at which their term of office would have expired. (b) General meeting where casual vacancy caused by their removal is to be filled.

The UK's Companies Act 2006 places a requirement on auditors to notify the appropriate audit authority in certain circumstances on leaving office.

Under the UK Companies Act 2006, for a quoted (listed) company an auditor must always submit a **statement of circumstances** surrounding their leaving office, even where there are no matters which the auditor believes should be brought to the attention of members or creditors (Companies Act 2006: s.519).

In the case of a private company (or an unlisted public company), the auditor does not need to submit a statement if they are leaving because their term of office has come to an end. If they are leaving before this, then a statement must be submitted unless the reasons for leaving are 'exempt reasons' (eg the auditor is ceasing to practise as an auditor, or the company is now exempt from audit), and there is nothing that needs to be communicated (*Companies Act 2006*: s. 519(1)–(3)).

The appropriate audit authority in the UK is:

- Secretary of State or delegated body (such as the FRC's Conduct Committee) if a major audit
- Recognised Supervisory Body for other audits

Notice must inform the appropriate audit authority that the auditor has ceased to hold office and be accompanied by a statement of circumstances or no circumstances.

Question New auditors

You are a partner in Messrs Borg, Connors & Co, International Accountants. You are approached by Mr Nastase, the managing director of Navratilova Enterprises Ltd, who asks your firm to become auditors of his company. The existing auditors, Messrs Wade, Austin & Co, have not resigned but Mr Nastase informs you that they will not be re-appointed in the future.

Required

Are Messrs Wade, Austin & Co within their rights in not resigning when they know Mr Nastase wishes to replace them? Give reasons for your answer.

Answer

Wade, Austin & Co have every right not to resign even though they may be aware that Mr Nastase wishes to replace them. The auditors of a company are appointed by, and report to, the members of a company and the directors are not empowered to remove the auditors. If the reason for the proposed change arises out of a dispute between management and the auditors then the auditors have a right to put forward their views as seen above and to insist that any decision should be made by the members, but only once they have been made aware of all pertinent facts concerning the directors' wishes to have them removed from office.

PART B FOUNDATIONS OF AUDITING

Chapter roundup

- International Standards on Auditing are set by the International Auditing and Assurance Standards Board.
- Professional accountants need an ethical code because they are relied upon for their expertise.
- Sources of ethical guidance include the *Code of Ethics for Professional Accountants* issued by the International Ethics Standards Board for Accountants (the IESBA *Code*) and the FRC's *Ethical Standard*.
- The five fundamental principles of professional ethics are integrity, objectivity, professional competence and due care, confidentiality and professional behaviour.
- As part of their self-regulation, audit firms need to have an effective system of quality management.
- There are various legal and professional requirements on appointment, resignation and dismissal of auditors which must be followed.

Quick quiz

1. What is the function of IFAC?
2. Who produces ISAs?

   A   IAASB
   B   IFAC
   C   IESBA

3. What are the five fundamental ethical principles?
4. Of which ethical principle is this the definition?

   "Not to compromise professional or business judgments because of bias, conflict of interest or undue influence of others."

5. In order to ensure good quality management, an audit firm should establish policies and procedures to ensure it ...., ... and .... good quality staff.
6. Under UK law, who can appoint an auditor?

Answers to quick quiz

1. The function of IFAC is to initiate, co-ordinate and guide efforts to achieve international technical, ethical and educational pronouncements for the accountancy profession.
2. IAASB
3. Integrity, objectivity, professional competence and due care, confidentiality and professional behaviour.
4. Objectivity
5. In order to ensure good quality management, an audit firm should establish policies and procedures to ensure it recruits, trains and retains good quality staff.
6. Members can appoint the auditors (at each general meeting where accounts are laid).

    Directors can appoint the auditors (before the first general meeting where accounts are laid or to fill a casual vacancy).

    The Secretary of State can appoint the auditors (if no auditors are appointed/reappointed at the general meeting where accounts are laid).

End of chapter questions

9.1 Which international body aims to initiate, co-ordinate and guide efforts to achieve international technical, ethical and educational pronouncements for the accountancy profession?

　　A　IASB
　　B　IAASB
　　C　IESB
　　D　IFAC

9.2 Which international body issues a code of ethics which indicates a minimum level of conduct to which all accountants must adhere?

　　A　The United Nations
　　B　International Accounting Standards Board (IASB)
　　C　International Ethics Standards Board for Accountants (IESBA)
　　D　International Auditing and Assurance Standards Board (IAASB)

9.3 Which word best describes the fundamental principle of integrity ?

　　A　Objectivity
　　B　Impartiality
　　C　Trustworthiness
　　D　Straightforwardness

9.4 Which is the best description of the fundamental principle of professional behaviour?

　　A　Adherence to all accounting standards currently in force.
　　B　Not doing anything that might bring discredit to the profession.
　　C　Behaviour that is in accord with both the spirit and the letter of the ethical guidelines.
　　D　Behaviour which, if conducted to appropriate standards, would justify the charging of a fee.

9.5 Which of the following is not a circumstance in which the directors may appoint the auditor?

　　A　Before company's first AGM
　　B　Following a period during which the company did not have an auditor (as exempt due to small size), at any time before the next AGM
　　C　The auditor passes away
　　D　The shareholders do not appoint anyone at the AGM

PART B FOUNDATIONS OF AUDITING

The audit process

Topic list	Syllabus reference
1 The audit process	B2.6

Introduction

This is a very short chapter which gives an overview of the audit process, a few key explanations, and links to the chapters with more information on each area.

Students often find it hard to visualise how all the different aspects of auditing fit together, so keep referring to the diagram below as we move through the text to help you put all the different aspects into context.

PART A   FOUNDATIONS OF AUDITING

1 The audit process

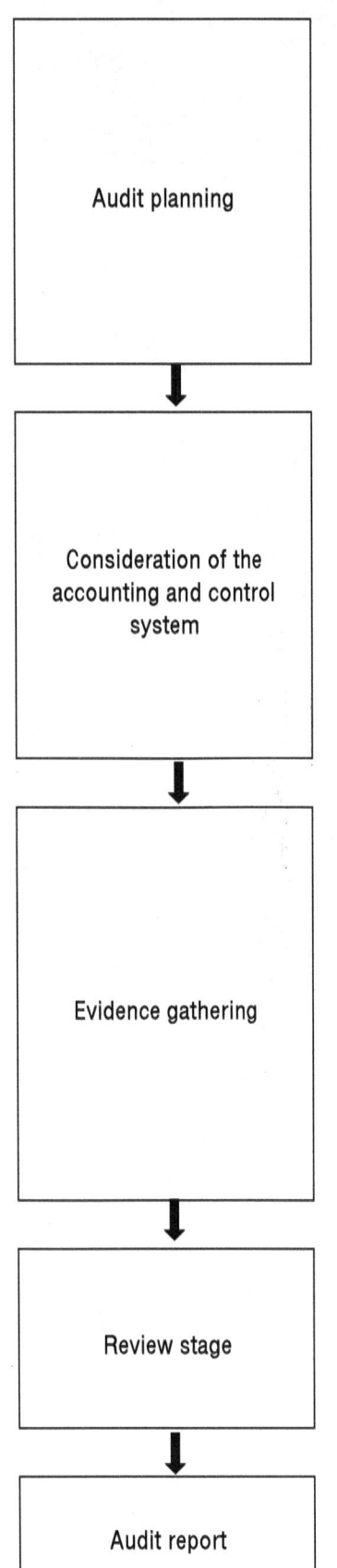

This involves gathering information about the client's business (eg major suppliers, customers, industry factors, financial performance, key staff) in order to decide on the audit approach.

A key consideration here is **risk** assessment, which we will consider in **Chapter 11**.

This process includes the use of **analytical procedures,** looking at the relationships between numbers in the accounts to help understand the business and understand risky areas. We consider these in **Chapter 11**.

This involves finding out about the client's system (and recording it in our audit working papers) and assessing the system and the risks relating to it. We will consider this in **Chapter 12**.

If the system is good we may decide to **rely** on the internal controls in the system, perform **tests of control** to confirm the controls are operating as expected and, if so, perform **lower amounts** of **substantive testing**.

If the system is poor we will not be able to rely on the controls and we will need to do **higher amounts** of substantive testing.

Audit evidence is the information the auditor obtains in order to form the audit opinion. It has to be sufficient (quantity) and appropriate (quality). We will consider audit evidence in **Chapter 13**.

Evidence is obtained from tests of control and substantive testing.

Tests of control are tests which the auditor performs to gain evidence about whether the system is operating effectively. These are covered in more detail in **Chapter 14**.

Substantive tests (or procedures) are tests to gain evidence as to whether amounts in the accounts are materially misstated. We will look at these in **Chapter 13**.

This is the stage where we're finalising the audit and thinking about our audit opinion. We do things like evaluating the impact of any errors we've found, considering impact of subsequent events, and considering whether the company is a going concern (ie is likely to be able to continue to trade). This stage is not covered in this paper.

We then produce our audit report. We had a brief look at this in Chapter 8, but detailed knowledge of the audit report is not required in this paper.

Risk assessment

Topic list	Syllabus reference
1 Introduction to risk	B2.6
2 Understanding the entity and its environment	B2.5, B2.6, B2.7
3 Assessing the risks of material misstatement	B2.6, B2.7
4 Responding to the risk of material misstatement	B2.6, B2.7

Introduction

This chapter covers the aspects of the external audit which will be considered at the earliest stages, during planning. The key issue here is risk.

Firstly, we introduce the concept of risk and look in detail at audit risk and its components (control risk, inherent risk and detection risk) and at how audit risk is managed by the auditor.

The importance of understanding the entity being audited and its environment is a key aspect of audit planning and helps the auditor to identify potential risk areas on which to focus. Various techniques can be used here such as inquiry, analytical procedures, observation and inspection. The risk assessment stage allows the auditor to respond with a proposed audit approach which may be a mixture of tests of controls and substantive testing or totally substantive.

PART B FOUNDATIONS OF AUDITING

1 Introduction to risk

FAST FORWARD

A **risk assessment** carried out under the ISAs helps the auditor to identify financial statement areas susceptible to material misstatement and provides a basis for designing and performing further audit procedures.

1.1 The risk-based approach

Auditors usually follow a **risk-based approach** to auditing as required by ISAs. In this approach, auditors analyse the risks associated with the client's business, transactions and systems which could lead to misstatements in the financial statements and then direct their testing to risky areas.

1.2 Audit risk

FAST FORWARD

Audit risk is the risk that the auditor expresses an inappropriate audit opinion when the financial statements are materially misstated. It is a function of the risk of material misstatement (**inherent risk** and **control risk**) and the risk that the auditor will not detect such misstatement (**detection risk**).

Key term

Audit risk is the risk that the auditor expresses an inappropriate audit opinion when the financial statements are materially misstated.

Audit risk has **two** major components. One is dependent on the entity, and is the risk of material misstatement arising in the financial statements (**inherent risk** and **control risk**). The other is dependent on the auditor, and is the risk that the auditor will not detect material misstatements in the financial statements (**detection risk**). We shall look in detail at the concept of materiality in the next section of this chapter.

1.2.1 Inherent risk

Key term

Inherent risk is the susceptibility of an assertion about a class of transaction, account balance or disclosure to a misstatement that could be material either individually or when aggregated with other misstatements, before consideration of any related controls.

(ISA 200: para. 13(n)(i))

In other words, inherent risk is the likelihood of a misstatement that could be material individually or when aggregated with other misstatements, assuming there were no related internal controls.

We'll look at the meaning of 'assertion' in Chapter 13.

Inherent risk is the risk that items will be misstated due to the characteristics of those items. For examples estimates have higher inherent risk as, being estimates, they may be estimated wrongly.

Inherent risk is also affected by the **nature of the entity**, for example the industry it is in and the regulations it falls under, and also the nature of the strategies it adopts. We shall look at more examples of inherent risks later in this chapter.

1.2.2 Control risk

The other element of the risk of material misstatements in the financial statements is control risk.

Key term

> **Control risk** is the risk that a material misstatement that could occur in an assertion about a class of transaction, account balance or disclosure and that could be material, either individually or when aggregated with other misstatements, will not be prevented, or detected and corrected, on a timely basis by the entity's internal control.
>
> (ISA 200: para. 13(n)(ii))

If a company has good internal controls there is low control risk. We shall look at control risk in more detail in Chapter 12 when we discuss internal controls.

1.2.3 Detection risk

Key term

> **Detection risk** is the risk that the procedures performed by the auditor to reduce audit risk to an acceptably low level will not detect a misstatement that exists and that could be material, either individually or when aggregated with other misstatements.
>
> (ISA 200: para. 13(e))

The third element of audit risk is detection risk. This is the component of audit risk that the auditors have a degree of control over, because, if risk is too high to be tolerated, the auditors can carry out more work to reduce this aspect of audit risk and, therefore, audit risk as a whole.

One way to decrease detection risk is to increase sample sizes; if more items are tested there is less chance of not detecting material misstatements.

However detection risk may also be reduced by performing the audit well, such as:

- Adequate planning
- Assignment of more experienced personnel to the engagement team
- The application of professional scepticism
- Increased supervision and review of the audit work performed.

All the above reduce the possibility that an auditor might select an inappropriate audit procedure, misapply an appropriate audit procedure or misinterpret the audit results.

1.3 Management of audit risk

ISA 200 *Overall Objectives of the Independent Auditor and the Conduct of an Audit in Accordance with International Standards on Auditing* states that 'to obtain reasonable assurance, the auditor shall obtain sufficient appropriate audit evidence to reduce audit risk to an acceptably low level and thereby enable the auditor to draw reasonable conclusions on which to base the auditor's opinion'.

As we have seen above, it is not in the auditors' power to affect inherent or control risk. These are risks integral to the client, and the auditor cannot change the level of these risks. The **auditors therefore manage overall audit risk by manipulating detection risk**, the only element of audit risk they have control over. This is because the more audit work the auditors carry out, the lower detection risk becomes, although it can never be entirely eliminated due to the inherent limitations of audit. The auditors will decide what level of **overall risk** is acceptable and then determine a level of audit work so that detection risk is as low as possible.

This links back to what we said in Chapter 10 when we looked at the audit process.

If the controls are good, this means there is **low control risk**, therefore the auditor can accept higher detection risk which means less substantive testing.

In contrast, if the controls are poor there is higher control risk, which means detection risk needs to be lower which requires more substantive testing.

Question | Audit risk

Hippo Co is a long established client of your firm. It manufactures bathroom fittings and fixtures, which it sells to a range of wholesalers, on credit. You are the audit senior and have recently been sent the following extract from the draft statement of financial position by the finance director.

	Budget		Actual	
	$'000	$'000	$'000	$'000
Non-current assets		453		367
Current assets				
Trade receivables	1,134		976	
Bank	–		54	
Current liabilities				
Trade payables	967		944	
Bank overdraft	9		–	

During the course of your conversation with the finance director you establish that a major new customer the company had included in its budget went bankrupt during the year.

Required

Identify any potential risks for the audit of Hippo and explain why you believe they are risks.

Answer

Potential risks relevant to the audit of Hippo

(1) **Credit sales.** Hippo makes sales on credit. This increases the risk that Hippo's sales will not be converted into cash. Trade receivables is likely to be a risky area and the auditors will have to consider what the best evidence that customers are going to pay is likely to be.

(2) **Related industry.** Hippo manufactures bathroom fixtures and fittings. These are sold to wholesalers, but it is possible that Hippo's ultimate market is the building industry. This is a notoriously volatile industry, and Hippo may find that their results fluctuate too, as demand rises and falls. This suspicion is added to by the bankruptcy of the wholesaler in the year. The auditors must be sure that accounts which present Hippo as a viable company are in fact correct.

(3) **Controls.** The fact that a major new customer went bankrupt suggests that Hippo did not undertake a very thorough credit check on that customer before agreeing to supply them. This implies that the controls at Hippo may not be very strong.

(4) **Variance.** The actual results are different from budget. This may be explained by the fact that the major customer went bankrupt, or it may reveal that there are other misstatements and problems in the reported results, or in the original budget.

(5) **Bankrupt wholesaler.** There is a risk that the result reported contains balances due from the bankrupt wholesaler, which are likely to be irrecoverable.

1.4 Materiality

Our definitions of risk above referred to the concept of materiality.

FAST FORWARD — An item is material if its omission or misstatement could influence the economic decisions of the users of the financial statements.

Material really just means important/significant, and items may be material due to their size or their nature. We looked at materiality in Chapter 8 in the context of materiality for the financial statements as a whole. A reminder of the definition is set out below.

Key term

> Misstatements, including omissions, are considered to be **material** if they, individually or in the aggregate, could reasonably be expected to influence the economic decisions of users taken on the basis of the financial statements. Judgements about materiality are made in light of surrounding circumstances, and are affected by the size or nature of a misstatement, or a combination of both.

ISA 320 *Materiality in Planning and Performing an Audit,* requires auditors to set materiality when establishing the strategy for the audit.

The materiality assessment will help the auditors to decide:

- **How many** and **what items** to examine
- Whether to use **sampling techniques**
- What **level of misstatement** is likely to lead to a modified audit opinion

When putting together the audit plan, the auditors should set performance materiality.

Key term

> **Performance materiality** is the amount or amounts set by the auditor at less than materiality for the financial statements as a whole (or individual balances if materiality has been set differently for them) to reduce to an appropriately low level the probability that the aggregate of uncorrected and undetected misstatements exceeds materiality for the financial statements as a whole.

As auditors are testing a sample of items, there is a risk that misstatements will be undetected by them. Auditors set performance materiality to be as sure as possible that undetected misstatements cannot be material to the financial statements.

Performance materiality may be set at planning materiality, but it is more likely to be reduced to, say 75% or even 50% of planning materiality to take account of sampling risk.

To set the materiality level the auditors need to decide the level of misstatement which would distort the view given by the accounts. This is a matter of **judgement** and, when setting benchmarks, auditors will consider:

- Elements of the financial statements (profit, assets, revenue etc)
- Whether there are key elements in the financial statements for users (for example, profit)
- The nature of the entity
- The ownership structure and finance
- The relative volatility of the benchmark chosen

The auditors may then set a percentage of the benchmark – for example 5% of profit.

Note that the auditors will often calculate a range of values, such as those shown below, and then take an average or weighted average of all the figures produced as the materiality level.

Value	%
Profit before tax	5
Gross profit	½–1
Revenue	½–1
Total assets	1–2
Net assets	2–5
Profit after tax	5–10

Materiality can be thought of in terms of the size of the business. Hence, if the company remains a fairly constant size, the materiality level should not change; similarly if the business is growing, the level of materiality will increase from year to year.

The size of a company can be measured in terms of turnover and total assets before deducting any liabilities both of which tend not to be subject to the fluctuations which may affect profit.

However, **materiality has qualitative, as well as quantitative**, aspects. You must not simply think of materiality as being a percentage of items in the financial statements.

This is why planning and performance materiality may be set differently for different balances and classes of transactions in the financial statements, depending on factors such as:

- Legal or reporting framework requirements relating to that matter
- Key disclosures in the industry
- Unusual matters in the financial statements (such as an acquisition)

For example, in the UK, matters relating to directors in financial statements are usually considered material due to the legal disclosures relating to directors' remuneration.

Audit materiality and performance materiality should be documented in the audit strategy.

2 Understanding the entity and its environment

FAST FORWARD

The auditor is required to obtain an **understanding** of the entity and its environment in order to be able to assess the risks of material misstatements.

2.1 Why, what, how?

Obtaining an understanding of the entity and its environment	
Why?	• To identify and assess the risks of material misstatement in the financial statements • To enable the auditor to design and perform further audit procedures • To provide a frame of reference for exercising audit judgement, for example, when setting audit materiality
What?	• Industry, regulatory and other external factors, including the applicable financial reporting framework • Nature of the entity, including operations, ownership and governance, investments, structure and financing • Entity's selection and application of accounting policies • Objectives and strategies and related business risks that might cause material misstatement in the financial statements • Measurement and review of the entity's financial performance • Internal control
How?	• Inquiries of management and others within the entity • Analytical procedures • Observation and inspection • Knowledge from having performed the audit previously • Knowledge gained in deciding whether to accept client • Discussion by the audit team of the susceptibility of the financial statements to material misstatement • Information from other engagements undertaken for the entity

11: RISK ASSESSMENT

As can be seen in the table, the reasons the auditor has to obtain an understanding of the entity and its environment are very much bound up with assessing risks and exercising audit judgement. We shall look at these aspects more in the next two sections of this chapter.

2.2 Analytical procedures

Key term

> **Analytical procedures** consist of the evaluations of financial information made by a study of plausible relationships among both financial and non-financial data. They also encompass the investigation of identified fluctuations and relationships that are consistent with other relevant information or deviate significantly from predicted amounts.

In the table above and also in Chapter 10 we mentioned analytical procedures.

Analytical procedures can be used at all stages of the audit. ISA 315 (Revised) *Identifying and Assessing the Risks of Material Misstatement* requires their use during the risk assessment stage of the audit. We will look at uses of analytical procedures for purposes other than planning later in this Workbook. Analytical procedures include:

(a) Comparing (financial and non-financial) information with:

- Similar information from prior periods
- Anticipated results of the entity, from budgets or forecasts
- Predictions prepared by the auditors
- Industry information

(b) Considering relationships between elements of financial information that are expected to conform to a predicted pattern based on the entity's experience, such as the relationship of gross profit to sales.

(c) Considering relationships between financial information and **relevant non-financial information**, such as the relationship of payroll costs to number of employees.

As well as helping to determine the nature, timing and extent of other audit procedures, such analytical procedures may also indicate aspects of the business of which the auditors were previously unaware. Auditors are looking to see if developments in the client's business have had the expected effects. They will be particularly interested in changes in audit areas where problems have occurred in the past.

Question — Analytical procedures

You are auditing the financial statements of Pumpkin Co for the year ended 31 March 20X9. Pumpkin Co is a chain of bakeries operating in five locations. The bakeries sell a range of cakes, pastries, bread, sandwiches, pasties and drinks which customers purchase in cash. The company has had a 'challenging' year, according to its directors, and is renegotiating its bank overdraft facility with its bank. The statement of profit or loss for the year ended 31 March 20X8 is shown below together with the draft statement of profit or loss for the year ended 31 March 20X9.

PUMPKIN CO: STATEMENTS OF PROFIT OR LOSS

	31 March 20X9	31 March 20X8
	$'000	$'000
Revenue	4,205	3,764
Cost of sales	(1,376)	(1,555)
Gross profit	2,829	2,209
Operating expenses		
Administration	(667)	(798)
Selling and distribution	(423)	(460)
Interest payable	(50)	(49)
Profit before tax	1,689	902

Required

As part of your risk assessment procedures for the audit of Pumpkin Co, perform analytical procedures on the draft statement of profit or loss to identify possible risk areas requiring further audit work.

Answer

In total, Pumpkin's profit for the year has increased by 87% which appears at odds with the revenue figure, which has only increased by 12% in comparison to the previous year. This may indicate that revenue has been inflated or incorrect cut-off applied, especially given the fact that the directors of Pumpkin have described the year as 'challenging'.

Revenue has increased overall by 12% but cost of sales has fallen by 12% – we would expect an increase in revenue to be matched by a corresponding increase in cost of sales. Again, this may indicate incorrect allocation of revenue in order for the bank to look favourably on the company and increase its overdraft facility. It could also indicate a misstatement in the valuation of closing inventory.

The gross profit has increased by 28% compared to the previous period. The audit will need to focus on this change which is significant, focusing on the revenue and costs of sales figures to establish the reasons for the increase.

Administration expenses have fallen in comparison to the previous year (decrease of 16%) which is unusual given that revenue has increased by 12%. We would expect an increase in costs to be in line with the increase in the revenue figure. This could indicate that expenses may be understated through incorrect cut-off or incorrectly capitalising expenditure which should be written off to the statement of profit or loss for the year.

A similar issue applies to selling and distribution costs which have fallen by 8% – they have not increased as expected in line with revenue. There could be legitimate reasons for the change but this area needs to be investigated further during the audit fieldwork stage.

Interest payable has stayed in line with the previous year (increase of 2%). This figure can be verified easily during the audit fieldwork by inspecting bank statements and other relevant documentation from the bank.

3 Assessing the risks of material misstatement

> **FAST FORWARD**
>
> When the auditor has obtained an understanding of the entity, they must assess the risks of material misstatement in the financial statements, also identifying significant risks.

3.1 Identifying and assessing the risks of material misstatement

ISA 315 (Revised) says that 'the auditor shall design and perform risk assessment procedures to obtain audit evidence that provides an appropriate basis for the identification and assessment of **risks of material misstatement**, whether due to fraud or error, at the **financial statement** and **assertion levels**'.

ISA 315 (Revised) requires the auditor to take the following steps:

Step 1 Identify risks throughout the process of obtaining an understanding of the entity (as already set out in Section 2).

Step 2 Assess the identified risks and whether they are pervasive to the financial statements.

Step 3 Relate the risks to what can go wrong at the **assertion** level taking account of the controls that the auditor intends to test.

Step 4 Consider the likelihood of the risks causing a misstatement and whether the risks are of a magnitude that could result in a **material** misstatement.

Key term

> **Assertions** are representations by management, explicit or otherwise, that are embodied in the financial statements, as used by the auditors to consider the different types of potential misstatements that may occur. We look at these in detail in Chapter 13.

3.2 Significant risks

FAST FORWARD

> **Significant risks** are complex or unusual transactions, those that may indicate fraud or other special risks.

Once the auditor has obtained an understanding of the entity and its environment, they shall assess the risks of material misstatement in the financial statements and identify significant risks. Where a risk is identified as **significant**, it presents **special audit considerations** for the auditors.

Key term

> A **significant risk** is a risk of material misstatement
> - For which the **assessment of inherent risk** is close to the **upper end** of the **spectrum of inherent risk** due to the degree to which inherent risk factors affect the combination of the likelihood of a misstatement occurring and the magnitude of the potential misstatement should that misstatement occur; or
> - That is to be treated as a significant risk in accordance with the requirements of other ISAs.
>
> (ISA 315 (Revised): para. 12l)

The auditor will begin simply by identifying risks, but **will then need to consider how severe each risk is** in terms of the 'spectrum of inherent risk'. Significant risks are essentially the most severe risks.

Routine, non-complex transactions are **less likely** to give rise to significant risks as client staff are likely to be more used to processing these transactions and such transactions are likely to be **subject to robust internal controls**.

Unusual and complex transactions and matters where **judgement** is required are **more likely to pose significant risk**.

4 Responding to the risk of material misstatement

FAST FORWARD

> The auditor shall **formulate an approach** to the assessed risks of material misstatement.

Once the auditor has assessed the risks of material misstatement, there must be a suitable response.

4.1 Overall responses

Overall responses to address the risks of material misstatement at the financial statement level will be changes to the general audit strategy or re-affirmations to staff of the general audit strategy. For example:

- Emphasising to audit staff the need to maintain professional scepticism
- Assigning additional or more experienced staff to the audit team
- Providing more supervision on the audit
- Incorporating more unpredictability into the audit procedures
- Making general changes to the nature, timing or extent of audit procedures

The evaluation of the control environment that will have taken place as part of the assessment of the client's internal control systems will help the auditor determine what type of audit approach to take.

Key term

> **Professional scepticism** is an attitude that includes a questioning mind, being alert to conditions which may indicate possible misstatements due to fraud or error, and a critical assessment of evidence.

4.2 Responses to the risks of material misstatement at the assertion level

ISA 330 *Responding to the risks of material misstatement* says that the auditor shall design and perform further audit procedures whose **nature**, **timing** and **extent** are based on and are responsive to the assessed risks of material misstatement at the assertion level. 'Nature' refers to the purpose and the type of test that is carried out, which include **tests of controls** and **substantive tests**.

4.2.1 Tests of controls

Key term

> **Tests of controls** are audit procedures designed to evaluate the operating effectiveness of controls in preventing, or detecting and correcting, material misstatements at the assertion level.

When the auditor's risk assessment includes an expectation that controls are operating effectively, the auditor shall design and perform tests of controls to obtain sufficient appropriate audit evidence that the controls were operating.

The auditor shall also undertake tests of controls when it will not be possible to obtain sufficient appropriate audit evidence simply from substantive procedures. This might be the case if the entity conducts its business using IT systems which do not produce documentation of transactions.

4.2.2 Substantive procedures

Key term

> **Substantive procedures** are audit procedures designed to detect material misstatements at the assertion level. They consist of tests of details of classes of transactions, account balances and disclosures, and substantive analytical procedures.

The auditor shall always carry out substantive procedures on material items. The ISA says that, irrespective of the assessed risk of material misstatement, the auditor shall design and perform substantive procedures for each material class of transactions, account balance and disclosure.

Substantive procedures fall into two categories: analytical procedures and tests of details. The auditor must determine when it is appropriate to use which type of substantive procedure. We discuss these in more detail in Chapter 13.

Chapter roundup

- A **risk assessment** carried out under the ISAs helps the auditor to identify financial statement areas susceptible to material misstatement and provides a basis for designing and performing further audit procedures.
- **Audit risk** is the risk that the auditor expresses an inappropriate audit opinion when the financial statements are materially misstated. It is a function of the risk of material misstatement (**inherent risk** and **control risk**) and the risk that the auditor will not detect such misstatement (**detection risk**).
- An item is **material** if its **omission or misstatement** could **influence the economic decisions** of the users of the financial statements.
- The auditor is required to obtain an **understanding** of the entity and its environment in order to be able to assess the risks of material misstatements.
- When the auditor has obtained an understanding of the entity, they must assess the risks of material misstatement in the financial statements, also identifying significant risks.
- **Significant risks** are complex or unusual transactions that may indicate fraud, or other special risks.
- The auditor shall **formulate an approach** to the assessed risks of material misstatement.

Quick quiz

1. Complete the definitions.

   .... risk is the risk that the .... may give an .... opinion on the financial statements.

   .... risk is the .... of an assertion to a .... that could be material, assuming there were no related ....

2. If control risk and inherent risk are assessed as sufficiently low, substantive procedures can be abandoned completely.

   True ☐   False ☐

3. Which procedures might an auditor use in gaining an understanding of the entity?

4. The audit team is required to discuss the susceptibility of the financial statements to material misstatements.

   True ☐   False ☐

5. An item is material if its .... or .... could influence .... of the users of the financial statements.

6. If a company has poor internal controls, control risk will be low.

   True ☐   False ☐

PART B FOUNDATIONS OF AUDITING

Answers to quick quiz

1 Audit risk is the risk that the auditors may give an inappropriate opinion on the financial statements.

   Inherent risk is the susceptibility of an assertion to a misstatement that could be material, assuming there were no related internal controls.

2 False

3 Inquiry, analytical procedures, observation and inspection.

4 True

5 An item is material if its omission or misstatement could influence the economic decisions of the users of the financial statements.

6 False. Poor controls means a higher risk that the controls will fail to prevent/detect/correct misstatements therefore higher control risk.

End of chapter questions

11.1 Your audit client XYZ Co has a new computerised inventory system. Which of the following procedures are relevant responses to the risk that inventory quantities are misstated by the new computerised inventory system?

   A Review a sample of purchase requisitions to determine whether the quantity of inventory held was checked before the requisition was approved.

   B Review the records of inventory counting and the level of corrections required to the quantities held on the inventory system.

   C Review sales prices of inventory sold after the year end to identify inventory where cost exceeds net realisable value.

   D Agree the cost of the new system to the purchase invoice.

11.2 Your client, XYZ Co, generates its revenue primarily in the form of cash. Which of the following statements are true with respect to audit risk?

   (1) Detection risk will increase due to the increased risk of cash donations being misappropriated and revenue being overstated.

   (2) Inherent risk will increase as the nature of XYZ's transactions means that revenue may be misstated either in error or deliberately.

   A (1) only
   B (2) only
   C (1) and (2)
   D Neither (1) nor (2)

11.3 Your client, Kind Co, is a charity operating a chain of charity shops. Which of the following statements are true with respect to audit risk?

   (1) Control risk will increase as internal controls may be weak due to the large number of volunteers used by Kind Co.

   (2) Audit risk will increase due to the large number of volunteers used by Kind Co.

   A (1) only
   B (2) only
   C (1) and (2)
   D Neither (1) nor (2)

11.4 Which of the following statements gives a true explanation of why ISA 315 (Revised) *Identifying and Assessing the Risks of Material Misstatement* requires a risk assessment to be carried out at the planning stage?

(1) The risk assessment will help the audit team gain an understanding of the entity for audit purposes.

(2) The risk assessment will enable the audit senior to produce an accurate budget for the audit assignment.

A (1) only
B (2) only
C (1) and (2)
D Neither (1) nor (2)

11.5 Which of the following statements gives a true explanation of why ISA 315 (Revised) *Identifying and Assessing the Risks of Material Misstatement* requires a risk assessment to be carried out at the planning stage?

(1) The risk assessment will form the basis of the audit strategy and the detailed audit plan

(2) Once the risks have been assessed, the auditor can select audit team members with sufficient skill and experience to maximise the chance of those risks being addressed.

A (1) only
B (2) only
C (1) and (2)
D Neither (1) nor (2)

PART B FOUNDATIONS OF AUDITING

Internal controls

Topic list	Syllabus reference
1 Internal control systems	B2.5
2 Internal controls in a computerised environment	B2.5
3 The use of internal control systems by auditors	B2.5
4 Recording accounting and control systems	B2.5
5 The evaluation of internal control components	B2.6

Introduction

The auditor generally seeks to rely on the internal controls within the entity in order to reduce the amount of testing of final balances.

The initial evaluation of a client's system is essential as the auditor gains an understanding of the entity, as we outlined in Chapter 11. In this chapter, we shall look at this in more detail.

The auditor will assess the risks of material misstatement arising and, as we discussed in Chapter 11, may respond to those risks by carrying out tests of controls. If the auditor concludes that they can rely on the controls in place, the level of substantive audit testing required can be reduced.

We shall examine the detailed controls that businesses operate in Chapter 14 and the tests that the auditors may carry out in specific areas. You should bear in mind the principles discussed in this chapter when considering the controls needed over specific accounting areas.

1 Internal control systems

FAST FORWARD

The auditors must **understand** the **accounting system** and **control environment** in order to determine their audit approach.

Key term

The **system of internal control** is the system designed, implemented and maintained by those charged with governance, management, and other personnel to provide reasonable assurance about the achievement of an entity's objectives with regard to reliability of financial reporting, effectiveness and efficiency of operations and compliance with applicable laws and regulations.

(ISA 315 (Revised), para. 12(m))

An understanding of internal control assists the auditor in identifying types of potential misstatements and factors that affect the risks of material misstatement, and in designing the **nature, timing and extent** of further audit procedures.

Initially, gaining an understanding of internal control helps auditors' to determine which internal controls are **relevant to the audit**. Many controls will relate to financial reporting, operations and compliance, but not all of the entity's objectives and controls will be relevant to the auditor's risk assessment.

Having determined which controls are relevant, and are adequately designed to aid in the prevention of material misstatements in the financial statements, the auditor can then decide whether it is more efficient to seek reliance on those controls and perform **tests of controls** in that area, or more efficient to perform **substantive testing** over that area.

ISA 315 (Revised) *Identifying and Assessing the Risks of Material Misstatement* deals with the whole area of controls.

A system of internal control has **five** components:

- The control environment
- The entity's risk assessment process
- The entity's process to monitor the system of internal control
- The information system and communication
- Control activities

Exam focus point

You should know these components and could be given four choices and asked to state which are (or are not) one of the components of internal control.

In obtaining an understanding of internal control, the auditor must understand the **design** of the internal control and the **implementation** of that control. In the following sub-sections, we look at each of the elements of internal control in turn.

1.1 Control environment

The control environment is the framework within which controls operate. The control environment is very much determined by the management of a business.

Key term

Control environment includes the governance and management functions and the attitudes, awareness and actions of those charged with governance and management concerning the entity's internal control and its importance in the entity.

A strong control environment does not, by itself, ensure the effectiveness of the overall internal control system, but can be a positive factor when assessing the risks of material misstatement. A weak control environment can undermine the effectiveness of controls.

The following table illustrates the elements that may be relevant when obtaining an understanding of the control environment.

Control Environment	
Communication and enforcement of integrity and ethical values	Essential elements which influence the effectiveness of the design, administration and monitoring of controls
Commitment to competence	Management's consideration of the competence levels for particular jobs and how those levels translate into requisite skills and knowledge
Participation by those charged with governance	• Independence from management • Experience and stature • Extent of involvement and scrutiny of activities • Appropriateness of actions and interaction with internal and external auditors
Management's philosophy and operating style	• Approach to taking and managing business risks • Attitudes and actions towards financial reporting • Attitudes towards information processing and accounting functions and personnel
Organisational structure	The framework within which an entity's activities for achieving its objectives are planned, executed, controlled and reviewed
Assignment of authority and responsibility	How authority and responsibility for operating activities are assigned and how reporting relationships and authorisation hierarchies are established
Human resource policies and practices	Recruitment, orientation, training, evaluating, counselling, promoting, compensation and remedial actions

The auditor shall assess whether these elements of the control environment have been implemented using a combination of **inquiries of management**, **observation** and **inspection**.

1.2 Entity's risk assessment process

ISA 315 (Revised) says the auditor shall obtain an understanding of whether the entity has a process for:

- Identifying business risks relevant to financial reporting objectives
- Estimating the significance of the risks
- Assessing the likelihood of their occurrence
- Deciding upon actions to address those risks

1.3 The entity's process to monitor the system of internal control

Key term

> **Monitoring of controls** is a process to assess the effectiveness of the performance of the system of internal control over time. It includes assessing the design and operation of controls on a timely basis and taking necessary corrective actions modified for changes in conditions.

The auditor shall obtain an understanding of the entity's process for monitoring the system of internal control relevant to the preparation of the financial statements. This includes ongoing and separate evaluations for monitoring the effectiveness of controls, and the identification and remediation of control deficiencies identified (this may well be carried out by an internal audit function).

If the entity has an **internal audit function**, the external auditors shall obtain an understanding of its **nature and responsibilities**, how it **fits** in the organisational structure, and the **activities** performed/to be performed.

The auditor shall also obtain an understanding of the **sources of the information** used in the monitoring activities and the **basis** on which management considers it reliable.

1.4 The information system and communication

> **Key term**
>
> The **information system** is a component of internal control that includes the financial reporting system, and consists of the procedures and records established to initiate, record, process and report entity transactions and to maintain accountability for the related assets, liabilities and equity.

The auditor is required to obtain an understanding of the entity's information system and communication relevant to the preparation of financial statements.

The auditor shall obtain an understanding of the entity's information processing activities, including its data and information, the resources to be used in such activities and the policies that define, for significant classes of transactions, account balances and disclosures:

- **How information flows through the entity's information system.** This includes how transactions are initiated, recorded, processed, corrected, incorporated in general ledger and reported in the financial statements and how information about events and conditions, other than transactions, is captured, processed and disclosed in the financial statements.

- The accounting records, specific accounts in the financial statements and other supporting records relating to the flows of information in the information system.

- The financial reporting process used to prepare the entity's financial statements, including significant accounting estimates and disclosures.

- The entity's resources, including the IT environment relevant to the points above.

The auditor shall obtain an understanding of how the entity **communicates** significant matters that support the preparation of the financial statements and related reporting responsibilities in the information system and other components of the system of internal control.

1.5 Control activities

> **Key term**
>
> **Control activities** are those policies and procedures that help ensure that management directives are carried out.

ISA 315 (Revised) states that the auditor shall obtain an understanding of control activities relevant to the audit and how the entity has responded to risks arising from IT.

Control activities include those activities designed to **prevent** or to **detect** and **correct misstatements**. Examples include activities relating to authorisation, performance reviews, information processing, physical controls and segregation of duties.

Examples of control activities	
Approval and control of documents	Transactions should be approved (signature or online/electronic approval) by an appropriate person. For example, overtime should be approved by departmental managers.
Controls over computerised applications	We shall look at computer controls later in this chapter.
Checking the arithmetical accuracy of records	For example, checking to see if individual invoices have been added up correctly.
Maintaining and reviewing	Control accounts bring together transactions in individual ledgers. Trial

Examples of control activities	
control accounts and trial balances	balances bring together unusual transactions for the organisation as a whole. Preparing these can highlight unusual transactions or accounts. Note that where an entity has a fully integrated accounting system the recording of sales and purchase invoices will automatically update the individual customer and supplier accounts and so control accounts will reconcile with these balances.
Reconciliations	Reconciliations involve comparison of a specific balance in the accounting records with what another source says the balance should be, for example, a bank reconciliation. Differences between the two figures should only be reconciling items.
Comparing the results of cash, security and inventory counts with accounting records	For example, in a physical count of petty cash, the balance shown in the petty cash book or petty cash ledger account should be the same as the amount held.
Comparing internal data with external sources of information	For example, comparing records of goods despatched to customers with customers' acknowledgement of goods that have been received.
Limiting physical access to assets and records	Only authorised personnel should have access to certain assets (particularly valuable or portable ones). For example, ensuring that the inventory store is only open when store personnel are there and is otherwise locked.

1.5.1 Segregation of duties

Segregation implies a **number of people** being involved in the accounting process. This makes it more difficult for fraudulent transactions to be processed (since a number of people would have to collude in the fraud), and it is also more difficult for accidental misstatements to be processed (since the more people are involved, the more checking there can be).

Segregation should take place in various ways:

(a) **Segregation of function.** The key functions that should be segregated are the **carrying out** of a transaction, **recording** that transaction in the accounting records and **maintaining custody** of assets that arise from the transaction.

(b) The various **steps** in carrying out the transaction should also be segregated. We shall see how this works in practice when we look at the major transaction cycles in Chapter 14.

(c) The **carrying out** of various **accounting operations** should be segregated. For example, the same staff should not record transactions and carry out the reconciliations at the period-end.

1.6 Emerging technology and automation bias

We have already stated that the auditor is required to obtain an understanding of the entity's systems relevant to the financial reporting process. Technology within client systems is evolving at an ever increasing rate with some complex IT tools, platforms and software being used to manage, automate and control financial accounting processes.

Technology increasingly used by audit clients include:

(a) **Cloud servers** and **cloud accounting software** where the accounting system is hosted by a third party on online servers. Clients pay a subscription (based on user numbers or business size) to use and access the system but a cloud service provider (CSP) manages the risks and controls over financial data and systems.

(b) **Machine learning** and **artificial intelligence tools**, for example to automate control processes. These are configured to automatically perform some of the processing or checking previously performed by staff and complex algorithms mean these tools can 'learn' and become more efficient over time.

(c) **Robotic process automation** runs with other programs and is configured to perform whole repeatable business processes (rather than just one task) using a series of rules. This includes data extraction, performing calculations and entering transactions.

There are other technologies used as well and the auditor will need to obtain the relevant expertise (internally through training or externally using an expert) to understand and evaluate client systems in order to perform an effective risk assessment.

In some cases this technology may make it more difficult for the auditor to fulfil their responsibilities. For example where an organisation uses a CSP to manage risks and controls over the finance system the auditor may find it more difficult to document and assess the system (backups, data recovery, automated processes etc).

One thing the auditor also has to be careful of here is to avoid **automation bias,** which is a human tendency to consider that information is correct just because something has been produced or by computer software or automated computer processes. This can result in a lower level of scrutiny being applied to these outputs that is applied to manually produced information.

Computers can be configured incorrectly or encounter computer errors so **professional scepticism** must be exercised when reviewing computer generated financial information.

1.7 Limitations of accounting and control systems

Any internal control system can only provide the directors with **reasonable assurance** that their objectives are reached, because of **inherent limitations**. These include:

- The costs of control **not outweighing** their **benefits**
- The potential for **human error**
- **Collusion** between employees
- The possibility of **controls** being **by-passed** or **overridden** by management
- Controls being **designed to cope** with **routine** and **not non-routine transactions**

These factors show why auditors cannot obtain all their evidence from tests of the systems of internal control. The key factors in the limitations of controls system are **human error** and **potential for fraud**.

The safeguard of segregation of duties can help deter fraud. However, if employees decide to perpetrate frauds in harness, or management commit fraud by overriding systems, the accounting system will not be able to prevent such frauds.

2 Internal controls in a computerised environment

FAST FORWARD

> There are special considerations for auditors when a system is computerised. IT controls comprise general controls and information processing controls.

Exam focus point

> A common exam question is to give a list of controls and asked to identify which is a general IT control, or instead to identify which or a list of controls is an information processing control.

The internal controls in a computerised environment include both manual procedures and procedures designed into computer programs. Such control procedures comprise two types of control, **general IT controls** and **information processing controls**.

12: INTERNAL CONTROLS

Key terms

> **General IT controls** are controls over the entity's IT processes that support the continued proper operation of the IT environment, including the continued effective functioning of information processing controls and the integrity of information (ie, the completeness, accuracy and validity of information) in the entity's information system.
>
> (ISA 315 (Revised): para. 12(d))
>
> **Information processing controls** are controls relating to the processing of information in IT applications or manual information processes in the entity's information system that directly address risks to the integrity of information (ie the completeness, accuracy and validity of transactions and other information).
>
> (ISA 315 (Revised): para. 12(e))

2.1 General controls

General controls	Examples
Development of computer applications	**Standards** over systems design, programming and documentation
	Full **testing procedures** using test data
	Approval by computer users and management
	Segregation of duties so that those responsible for design are not responsible for testing
	Installation procedures so that data is not corrupted in transition
	Training of staff in new procedures and availability of adequate **documentation**
Prevention or detection of unauthorised changes to programs	**Segregation of duties**
	Full records of program changes
	Password protection of programs so that access is limited to computer operations staff
	Restricted access to central computer by locked doors, keypads
	Maintenance of **programs logs**
	Virus checks on software: use of anti-virus software and policy prohibiting use of non-authorised programs or files
	Back-up copies of programs being taken and stored in other locations
	Control copies of programs being preserved and regularly compared with actual programs
	Stricter controls over certain programs (utility programs) by use of **read-only memory**
Testing and documentation of program changes	Complete **testing procedures**
	Documentation standards
	Approval of changes by computer users and management
	Training of staff using programs
Controls to prevent wrong programs or files being used	**Operation controls** over programs
	Libraries of programs
	Proper job scheduling

PART B   FOUNDATIONS OF AUDITING

General controls	Examples
Controls to prevent unauthorised amendments to data files	**Password protection** **Restricted access** to authorised users only
Controls to ensure continuity of operation	Storing **extra copies** of programs and data files off-site **Protection of equipment** against fire and other hazards **Back-up power sources** **Disaster recovery procedures** eg availability of back-up computer facilities **Maintenance agreements** and **insurance**

The auditors will wish to test some or all of the above general IT controls, having considered how they affect the computer applications significant to the audit.

General IT controls that relate to some or all applications are usually interdependent controls, ie their operation is often essential to the effectiveness of information processing controls. As information processing controls may be useless when general IT controls are ineffective, it will be more efficient to review the design of general IT controls first, before reviewing the information processing controls.

2.2 Information processing controls

The purpose of information processing controls is to establish **specific control procedures** over the accounting applications in order to provide reasonable assurance that all transactions are authorised and recorded, and are processed completely, accurately and on a timely basis.

Information processing controls include the following.

Information processing controls	Examples
Controls over **input: completeness**	Manual or programmed agreement of **control totals** **Document counts** **One-for-one checking** of processed output to source documents **Programmed matching** of input to an expected input control file **Procedures** over resubmission of rejected controls
Controls over **input: accuracy**	**Programmes to check data** fields (for example value, reference number, date) on input transactions for plausibility: • Digit verification (eg reference numbers are as expected) • Reasonableness test (eg sales tax to total value) • Existence checks (eg customer name) • Character checks (no unexpected characters used in reference) • Necessary information (no transaction passed with gaps) • Permitted range (no transaction processed over a certain value) **Manual scrutiny** of output and reconciliation to source Agreement of **control totals** (manual/programmed)
Controls over **input: authorisation**	**Manual checks** to ensure information input was: • Authorised

Information processing controls	Examples
	• Input by authorised personnel
Controls over **processing**	Similar controls to input must be in place when input is completed, for example, **batch reconciliations**
	Screen warnings can prevent people logging out before processing is complete
Controls over **master files and standing data**	**One-for-one checking**
	Cyclical reviews of all master files and standing data
	Record counts (number of documents processed) and **hash totals** (for example, the total of all the payroll numbers) used when master files are used to ensure no deletions
	Controls over the deletion of accounts that have no current balance

3 The use of internal control systems by auditors

FAST FORWARD

The auditors will assess the **adequacy** of the systems as a basis for the financial statements and identify **risks** of material misstatements to provide a basis for designing and performing further audit procedures.

Auditors are concerned with assessing policies and procedures which are relevant to the financial statements. Auditors are required to:

- **Assess the adequacy** of the accounting system as a basis for preparing the financial statements
- **Identify** the types of **potential misstatements** that could occur in the financial statements
- **Consider factors** that affect the **risk of misstatements**
- **Design appropriate audit procedures**

We have discussed the process of assessing the risks of material misstatement in Chapter 11. The assessment of the controls of an entity will have an impact on that risk assessment.

4 Recording accounting and control systems

FAST FORWARD

The auditors must keep a record of the client's systems which must be updated each year. This can be done through the use of narrative notes, flowcharts, questionnaires or checklists.

Method of recording	Key features
Narrative notes	System is recorded in typed or written notes (using word processing software or manually written).
Flowcharts	System is recorded in diagrammatic form.
Questionnaires	System is recorded by addressing questions about the system.
Checklists	Similar to questionnaires, but auditor ticks boxes when controls present.

5 The evaluation of internal control components

> **FAST FORWARD**
>
> If the auditors believe the system of controls is strong, they may choose to test controls to assess whether they can rely on the controls having operated effectively.

5.1 Confirming understanding

In order to confirm their understanding of the control systems, auditors will often carry out **walk-through tests**. This is where they pick up a transaction and follow it through the system to see whether all the controls they anticipate should be in existence were in operation with regard to that transaction.

5.2 Tests of control

Key term

> **Tests of control** are tests performed to obtain audit evidence about the effectiveness of the:
>
> - Design of the accounting and internal control systems, ie whether they are suitably designed to prevent, or detect and correct, material misstatement at the assertion level; and
> - Operation of the internal controls throughout the period.

Tests of control are distinguished from **substantive tests** which are designed to detect material misstatements in the financial statements. We discuss substantive tests in much greater depth in the next chapter.

Tests of control may include the following.

(a) **Inspection of documents** supporting controls or events to gain audit evidence that internal controls have operated properly, eg verifying that a transaction has been authorised (by signature or electronic approval).

(b) **Inquiries about internal controls** which leave no audit trail, eg determining who actually performs each function not merely who is supposed to perform it.

(c) **Reperformance of control procedures**, eg reconciliation of bank accounts, to ensure they were correctly performed by the entity.

(d) **Examination of evidence of management views**, eg minutes of management meetings.

(e) Testing of internal controls operating on **computerised systems** or over the overall IT function, eg access controls.

(f) **Observation of controls** to consider the manner in which the control is being operated.

5.3 Communication of deficiencies in internal control

> **FAST FORWARD**
>
> If the auditors detect weaknesses (deficiencies) in the design or operation of controls they advise the management of the company in writing so that they have an opportunity to address them.

Significant deficiencies in internal controls must be communicated in writing to those charged with governance in a **report to management** in accordance with ISA 265 *Communicating Deficiencies in Internal Control to Those Charged with Governance and Management* which states that the objective of the auditor is to communicate appropriately to those charged with governance and management deficiencies in internal control identified during the audit which the auditor considers are of sufficient importance to warrant their attention.

Chapter roundup

- The auditors must **understand** the **accounting system** and **control environment** in order to determine their audit approach.

- There are special considerations for auditors when a system is computerised. IT controls comprise **general** and **information processing** controls.

- The auditors will assess the **adequacy** of the systems as a basis for the financial statements and shall identify **risks** of material misstatements to provide a basis for designing and performing further audit procedures.

- The auditors must keep a record of the client's systems which must be updated each year. This can be done through the use of narrative notes, flowcharts, questionnaires or checklists.

- If the auditors believe the system of controls is strong, they may choose to test controls to assess whether they can rely on the controls having operated effectively.

- If the auditors detect weaknesses (deficiencies) in the design or operation of controls they advise the management of the company in writing so that they have an opportunity to address them.

PART B FOUNDATIONS OF AUDITING

Quick quiz

1. Complete the definition taking the words given below.

   The .... includes the governance and management functions and the.............., ... and .... of those charged with .... and management concerning the entity's internal .... and its .... in the entity.

   | attitudes | importance | control | environment | awareness | governance | actions | control |

2. Name two **key** inherent limitations of an internal control system.

   (1) ....

   (2) ....

3. Put the controls below in the correct category.

Information processing controls	General IT controls

One-for-one checking	Virus checks	Hash totals
Segregation of duties	Passwords	Program libraries
Review of master files	Training	Controls over account deletions
Back-up copies	Record counts	Back-up power source

4. Which of the following is not a test of control?

   A Inspection of documents
   B Reperformance of control procedures
   C Observation of controls
   D Verification of value to invoice

5. After the controls have been assessed, the audit plan may be modified.

   True ☐
   False ☐

6. What should the auditors do if, upon testing the controls, they discover that they are not operating as well as expected.

Answers to quick quiz

1. The control environment includes the governance and management functions and the attitudes, awareness and actions of those charged with governance and management concerning the entity's internal control and its importance in the entity.

2. (1) Human error
   (2) Possibility of staff colluding in fraud

3.

Information processing controls	General IT controls
One-for-one checking	Virus checks
Hash totals	Program libraries
Review of master files	Segregation of duties
Record counts	Passwords
	Controls over account deletion
	Training
	Back-up power source
	Back-up copies

4. D

5. True

6. (1) Consider the implications for the audit strategy
   (2) If the deficiency is significant, include details in the report to management

End of chapter questions

12.1 Internal control systems have five components.

Which of the following is not a component of an internal control system?

- A The control environment
- B The entity's risk assessment process
- C Communication system
- D Control activities

12.2 Which of the following is correct with respect to external auditors?

- A They design the system of internal control.
- B They do not report to management on the effectiveness of internal control.
- C They report to management any material deficiencies discovered in internal control.
- D They can insist that a client implements good internal controls.

12.3 The term 'segregation of duties' means that:

- A Certain different steps in a transaction should be carried out by different people.
- B The business should be organised into different functional departments.
- C All similar transactions should be collected together and dealt with as a batch.
- D Managers should perform directing and supervisory roles.

12.4 Which of the following is not an information processing control?

- A One-for-one checking of processed output to source documents
- B Passwords are required to access the system
- C Screen warnings to prevent people logging out before processing is complete
- D Manual or programmed agreement of control totals

12.5 The internal control system has five components. These are:

- A Control environment, the entity's risk assessment process, risk evaluation, control activities, and the entity's process to monitor the system of internal control
- B Control environment, the entity's risk assessment process, information system and communication, control activities, and the entity's process to monitor the system of internal control
- C Control design, risk assessment, information system and communication, control activities, and control effectiveness
- D Control effectiveness, control efficiency, control activities, control operation and control monitoring

Audit evidence

Topic list	Syllabus reference
1 Audit evidence	B2.4
2 Financial statement assertions	B2.4
3 Substantive procedures	B2.4, B2.6
4 Audit sampling	B2.4, B2.6

Introduction

In this chapter, we discuss the fundamental auditing concept of audit evidence. Audit evidence is required to enable the auditor to form an opinion on the financial statements. Therefore such evidence has to be sufficient and appropriate.

We also explain the financial statement assertions for which audit evidence is required. Audit tests are designed to obtain sufficient appropriate evidence about the assertions for each balance or transaction in the financial statements.

In Section 3 we talk a little about the types of evidence we might seek in some key areas.

In Section 4 we look briefly at audit sampling.

1 Audit evidence

FAST FORWARD — Auditors must design and perform audit procedures to obtain **sufficient appropriate** audit evidence.

1.1 The need for audit evidence

Remember that the objective of an audit of financial statements is to enable the auditor to express an opinion on whether the financial statements are prepared, in all material respects, in accordance with an identified financial reporting framework. In this section, we shall look at the **audit evidence** gathered, which enables the auditor to express his opinion.

Key term

> **Audit evidence** is all of the information used by the auditor in arriving at the conclusions on which the auditor's opinion is based.

Audit evidence includes the information contained in the accounting records underlying the financial statements and other information gathered by the auditors, such as confirmations from third parties. Auditors are **not expected to look at all the information** that might exist. They will often select **samples** to test, as we shall see later in this chapter.

1.2 Sufficient appropriate audit evidence

Key terms

> The **appropriateness** of audit evidence is the measure of the quality of it, that is, its relevance and its reliability in providing support for the conclusions on which the auditor's opinion is based.
>
> The **sufficiency** of audit evidence is the measure of the quantity of audit evidence. The quantity of audit evidence required is affected by the auditor's assessment of the risks of material misstatement and also by the quality of such audit evidence.

ISA 500 *Audit Evidence* requires auditors to 'design and perform audit procedures that are appropriate in the circumstances for the purposes of obtaining **sufficient appropriate** audit evidence'. 'Sufficiency' and 'appropriateness' are interrelated and apply to both tests of controls and substantive procedures.

- **Sufficiency** is the measure of the **quantity** of audit evidence.
- **Appropriateness** is the measure of the **quality** or **reliability** of the audit evidence.

The **quantity** of audit evidence required is affected by the **level of risk** in the area being audited. It is also affected by the **quality** of evidence obtained. If the evidence is high quality, the auditor may need less than if it were poor quality. However, obtaining a high quantity of poor-quality evidence will not cancel out its poor quality. The ISA requires auditors to consider the **relevance and reliability** of the information to be used as audit evidence when designing and performing audit procedures.

Relevance deals with the logical connection with the purpose of the audit procedure and the assertion under consideration (we look at assertions in the next section). The relevance of information may be affected by the direction of testing.

Reliability is influenced by the source and nature of the information, including the controls over its preparation and maintenance. The following generalisations may help in assessing the reliability of audit evidence.

Quality of evidence	
External	Audit evidence from **external sources** is more reliable than that obtained from the entity's records because it is from an independent source.
Auditor	Evidence obtained **directly by auditors** is more reliable than that obtained indirectly or by inference.
Controls	Evidence obtained from the entity's records is more reliable when the related **control system operates effectively**.
Written	Evidence in the form of **documents (paper or electronic)** are more reliable than oral representations.
Originals	**Original documents** are more reliable than photocopies or facsimiles.

2 Financial statement assertions

FAST FORWARD

Audit tests are designed to obtain evidence about the **financial statement assertions**. Assertions relate to **classes of transactions, events and related disclosures**, and **account balances and related disclosures**, at the period-end.

Key term

Assertions are the representations by management, explicit or otherwise, that are embodied in the financial statements, as used by the auditor to consider the different types of potential misstatements that may occur.

In simple terms, assertions are the characteristics of the items in the accounts that must be true in order for the financial statements to give a true and fair view. They are the characteristics that the directors imply when they produce financial statements which they say give a true and fair view. The auditors, therefore, have to check that this is the case.

Exam focus point

In your exam you could be tested on which assertions related to classes of transactions and events compared to assertions relating to account balances. In particular, you could be asked which of a given list of assertions does **not** relate to classes of transaction and events, or which of a given list of assertions does **not** relate to account balances.

ISA 315 (Revised) states that the auditor must use assertions for **classes of transactions, events, and related disclosures** (ie statement of profit or loss), and **account balances and related disclosures** (ie statement of financial position) in sufficient detail to form the basis for the assessment of risks of material misstatement and the design and performance of further audit procedures. It gives examples of assertions in these areas which are set out in the table that follows.

Assertions used by the auditor (ISA 315)	
Assertions about **classes of transactions and events, and related disclosures**, for the period under audit	**Occurrence**: transactions and events that have been recorded or disclosed, have occurred, and such transactions and events pertain to the entity. **Completeness**: all transactions and events that should have been recorded have been recorded, and all related disclosures that should have been included in the financial statements have been included. **Accuracy**: amounts and other data relating to recorded transactions and events have been recorded appropriately, and related disclosures have been appropriately measured and described. **Cut-off**: transactions and events have been recorded in the correct accounting period.

PART B FOUNDATIONS OF AUDITING

Assertions used by the auditor (ISA 315)	
	Classification: transactions and events have been recorded in the proper accounts.
	Presentation: transactions and events are appropriately aggregated or disaggregated and clearly described, and related disclosures are relevant and understandable in the context of the requirements of the applicable financial reporting framework.
Assertions about **account balances and related disclosures** at the period-end	**Existence**: assets, liabilities, and equity interests exist.
	Rights and obligations: the entity holds or controls the rights to assets, and liabilities are the obligations of the entity.
	Completeness: all assets, liabilities and equity interests that should have been recorded have been recorded, and all related disclosures that should have been included in the financial statements have been included.
	Accuracy, valuation and allocation: assets, liabilities, and equity interests are included in the financial statements at appropriate amounts and any resulting valuation or allocation adjustments have been appropriately recorded, and related disclosures have been appropriately measured and described.
	Classification: assets, liabilities and equity interests have been recorded in the proper accounts.
	Presentation: assets, liabilities and equity interests are appropriately aggregated or disaggregated and clearly described, and related disclosures are relevant and understandable in the context of the requirements of the applicable financial reporting framework.

2.1 Audit procedures to obtain audit evidence

FAST FORWARD

Audit evidence can be obtained by inspection, observation, inquiry and confirmation, recalculation, reperformance and analytical procedures. Auditors design audit plans for each item in the financial statements.

Exam focus point

You will be tested on audit procedures during the exam. You need to know the difference between substantive procedures and tests of controls, and the purpose of each type of procedure. Analytical procedures are a type of substantive procedure and you may be tested on which stages of the audit analytical procedures are commonly used, or must be used, under the ISAs.

The auditor obtains audit evidence by undertaking audit procedures to do the following:

- Obtain an understanding of the entity and its environment to assess the risks of material misstatement at the financial statement and assertion levels (**risk assessment procedures**)
- Test the operating effectiveness of controls in preventing, or detecting and correcting, material misstatements at the assertion level (**tests of controls**)
- Detect material misstatements at the assertion level (**substantive procedures**)

The auditor must **always** perform **risk assessment procedures** to provide a satisfactory assessment of risks.

Tests of controls, which were introduced in the previous chapter, are necessary to test the controls to support the risk assessment, and also when substantive procedures alone do not provide sufficient appropriate audit evidence. **Substantive procedures** must **always** be carried out for **material** classes of transactions, account balances and disclosures.

Key terms

> **Tests of controls** are performed to obtain audit evidence about the operating effectiveness of controls preventing, or detecting and correcting, material misstatements at the assertion level.
>
> **Substantive procedures** are audit procedures performed to detect material misstatements at the assertion level. They are generally of two types:
> - Substantive analytical procedures
> - Tests of detail of classes of transactions, account balances and disclosures

Procedures	
Inspection of tangible assets	Inspection of tangible assets that are recorded in the accounting records confirms existence, but does not necessarily confirm rights and obligations or valuation. Confirmation that assets seen are recorded in accounting records gives evidence of completeness.
Inspection of documentation or records	This is the examination of documents and records, both internal and external, in paper, electronic or other forms. This procedure provides evidence of varying reliability, depending on the nature, source and effectiveness of controls over production (if internal). Inspection can provide evidence of existence (eg a document constituting a financial instrument), but not necessarily about ownership or value.
Observation	This involves watching a procedure or process being performed (for example, post opening). It is of limited use, as it only confirms the procedure took place when the auditor was watching, and because the act of being observed could affect how the procedure or process was performed.
Inquiry	This involves seeking information from client staff or external sources. Strength of evidence depends on the knowledge and integrity of source of information. Inquiry alone does not provide sufficient audit evidence to detect a material misstatement at assertion level nor is it sufficient to test the operating effectiveness of controls.
Confirmation	This is the process of obtaining a representation of information or of an existing condition directly from a third party eg confirmation from bank of bank balances.
Recalculation	This consists of checking the mathematical accuracy of documents or records and can be performed through the use of IT.
Reperformance	This is the auditor's independent execution of procedures or controls that were originally performed as part of the entity's internal control.
Analytical procedures	Evaluating and comparing financial and/or non-financial data for plausible relationships. Also include the investigation of identified fluctuations and relationships that are inconsistent with other relevant information or deviate significantly from predicted amounts.

3 Substantive procedures

This paper does not require you to have a detailed knowledge of audit procedures in different areas, but it is worth spending a little bit of time practising thinking about how you might use the procedures discussed above to gain evidence in relation to the assertions above.

This table shows some typical tests:

Audit assertion	Type of assertion	Typical audit tests
Completeness	Classes of transactions Account balances	(a) Review of post year-end items (b) Cut-off testing (c) Analytical procedures (d) Confirmations (e) Reconciliations to control accounts
Rights and obligations	Account balances	(a) Reviewing invoices for proof that item belongs to the company (b) Confirmations with third parties
Accuracy, valuation and allocation	Account balances	(a) Matching amounts to invoices (b) Recalculation (c) Confirming accounting policy is consistent and reasonable (d) Review of post year-end payments and invoices (e) Expert valuation
Existence	Account balances	(a) Physical verification (b) Third party confirmations (c) Cut-off testing
Occurrence	Classes of transactions	(a) Inspection of supporting documentation (b) Confirmation from directors that transactions relate to business (c) Inspection of items purchased
Accuracy	Classes of transactions	(a) Recalculation of correct amounts (b) Third party confirmation (c) Analytical procedures
Classification	Classes of transactions Account balances	(a) Confirming compliance with law and accounting standards (b) Reviewing notes for understandability
Cut-off	Classes of transactions	(a) Cut-off testing (b) Analytical procedures
Presentation	Classes of transactions Account balances	(a) Reviewing financial statements

Now let's consider these general principles in relation to two key areas of non-current assets and receivables.

3.1 Non-current assets

Audit plan: tangible non-current assets	
Completeness	• **Compare non-current assets** in the general ledger with the **non-current assets register** and **obtain explanations** for **differences**. • For a sample of assets which physically exist agree that they are **recorded** in the **non-current asset register**.
Existence	• **Inspect assets**, concentrating on high value items and additions in-year. Confirm that items inspected: – Exist – Are in use – Are in good condition – Have correct serial numbers
Valuation	• **Verify valuation** of property to valuation certificate. • **Consider reasonableness** of **valuation**, reviewing: – Experience of valuer – Scope of work – Methods and assumptions used – Valuation bases are in line with accounting standards • **Reperform** calculation and accounting for revaluation surplus. • Confirm whether valuations of all assets that have been revalued have been **updated regularly** (full valuation every five years and an interim valuation in year three generally) by asking the Finance Director and inspecting the previous financial statements. • **Review depreciation** rates applied in relation to: – Asset lives – Residual values – Replacement policy – Past experience of gains and losses on disposal – Consistency with prior years and accounting policy – Possible obsolescence • **Review** non-current assets register to ensure that **depreciation** has been **charged on all assets** with a limited useful life. • For **revalued assets**, ensure that the charge for **depreciation** is based on the revalued amount by recalculating it for a sample of revalued assets. • **Reperform calculation** of depreciation rates to ensure it is correct. • **Compare ratios** of depreciation to non-current assets (by category) with: – Previous years – Depreciation policy rates • **Scrutinise** draft accounts to ensure that **depreciation policies** and rates are **disclosed** in the accounts.

Audit plan: tangible non-current assets	

Rights and obligations	• **Verify title** to land and buildings by inspection of:
	   – Title deeds
	   – Land registry certificates
	   – Leases
	• **Inspect registration documents** for vehicles held, confirming that they are in client's name.
	• **Examine documents** of title for other assets (including purchase invoices, architects' certificates, contracts, hire purchase or lease agreements).

Additions	These tests are to confirm **rights and obligations**, **valuation** and **completeness**. • Verify additions by inspection of architects' certificates, solicitors' completion statements, suppliers' invoices etc. • Check **additions** have been **recorded** by **scrutinising** the non-current asset register and general ledger.
Disposals	These tests are to confirm **rights and obligations**, **completeness**, **occurrence** and **accuracy**. • **Verify disposals** with supporting documentation, checking transfer of title, sales price and dates of completion and payment. • **Recalculate** profit or loss on disposal.
Classification and presentation	• **Review** non-current asset disclosures in the financial statements to ensure they meet IAS 16 criteria. • For a sample of **fully depreciated assets**, inspect the register to ensure no further depreciation is charged. • **Inspect** draft accounts to ensure that **depreciation policies and rates** are correctly **disclosed**.

3.2 Receivables

Audit plan: receivables	
Completeness	• **Agree** the balance from the individual sales ledger accounts to the aged receivables' listing and vice versa. • **Match** total of the aged receivables' listing to the sales ledger control account. • **Cast and cross-cast** the aged trial balance before selecting any samples to test. • **Trace** a sample of shipping documentation to sales invoices and into the sales and receivables' ledger. • **Compare** the gross profit % by product line with the previous year and industry data.

Audit plan: receivables	
Existence	• Perform a **receivables' confirmation** on a sample of year-end trade receivables. (This is where the auditor writes to the customer, asking them to confirm the balance owing.) • **Follow up** all balance disagreements and non-replies to the receivables' confirmation. • **Perform alternative procedures** for any exceptions and non-replies to the receivables' confirmation, such as: • **Review after-date cash receipts** by inspecting bank statements and cash receipts documentation. • Examine the **customer's account and customer correspondence** to assess whether the balance outstanding represents specific invoices and confirm their validity. • Examine the **underlying documentation** (purchase order, dispatch documentation, duplicate sales invoice etc).
Rights and obligations	• Make **inquiries of management, review** loan agreements and review board minutes for any evidence of receivables being sold (eg to factors).
Accuracy, valuation and allocation	• **Compare** receivables' turnover and receivables' days to the previous year and/or to industry data. • **Compare** aged analysis of receivables from the aged trial balance to prior year. • **Review** the adequacy of the allowance for uncollectable accounts through discussion with management. • **Compare** the bad debt expense as a % of sales to the previous year and/or to industry data. • Confirm adequacy of allowance by **reviewing correspondence** with customers and solicitors. • **Examine credit notes** issued after year-end for allowances that should be made against current period balances. • For a sample of old debts on the aged trial balance, obtain further information regarding their recoverability by **discussions** with management and **review** of customer correspondence.
Cut-off	• For a sample of sales invoices around the year-end, **inspect the dates** and compare with the dates of dispatch and the dates recorded in the ledger for application of correct cut-off.

4 Audit sampling

Auditors usually seek evidence from less than 100% of items of the balance or transaction being tested by using **sampling techniques**.

4.1 Introduction to audit sampling

The detail of audit sampling is beyond the scope of this paper. The purpose of this brief section is to give you an idea of some of the main concepts.

Key terms

> **Audit sampling** is the application of audit procedures to less than 100% of items within a population of audit relevance such that all sampling units have a chance of selection in order to provide the auditor with a reasonable basis on which to draw conclusions about the entire population. Audit sampling can be applied using either statistical or non-statistical approaches.
>
> The **population** is the entire set of data from which a sample is selected and about which the auditor wishes to draw conclusions.

Auditors do not normally examine all the information available to them as it would be impractical to do so and using audit sampling will produce valid conclusions.

Audit sampling can be done using either **statistical sampling** or **non-statistical sampling** methods.

Key terms

> **Statistical sampling** is an approach to sampling that involves random selection of the sample items, and the use of probability theory to evaluate sample results, including measurement of sampling risk.
>
> **Non-statistical sampling** is a sampling approach that does not have these characteristics.

4.2 Projection of misstatements

Having tested a sample of items, auditors then project the results of their testing to the entire population.

Chapter roundup

- Auditors must design and perform audit procedures to obtain **sufficient appropriate** audit evidence.
- Audit tests are designed to obtain evidence about the **financial statement assertions**. Assertions relate to **classes of transactions, events and related disclosures**, and **account balances and related disclosures**, at the period-end.
- Audit evidence can be obtained by inspection, observation, inquiry and confirmation, recalculation, reperformance and analytical procedures.
- Auditors design audit plans for each item in the financial statements.
- Auditors usually seek evidence from less than 100% of items of the balance or transaction being tested by using **sampling techniques**.

Quick quiz

1. Define sufficiency and appropriateness as they relate to audit evidence.
2. State the financial statement assertions.
3. Fill in the blanks.

    Audit evidence from external sources is ……………………… …………………….. than that obtained from the entity's records.

4. State five procedures which auditors can use to obtain audit evidence.
5. Explain what 'reperformance' is.
6. Audit sampling is the application of audit procedures to …………….. …………….. ……………..of items within a population of audit relevance such that all …………….. ……………. have a chance of selection in order to provide the auditor with a reasonable basis on which to draw conclusions about the ………….. …………….. Audit sampling can be applied using either ………….. or ………….. approaches.

PART B FOUNDATIONS OF AUDITING

Answers to quick quiz

1   Sufficiency is the measure of the quantity of audit evidence.

    Appropriateness is the measure of the quality/reliability of audit evidence.

2   Existence, rights and obligations, occurrence, completeness, valuation and allocation, accuracy, classification, cut-off and presentation.

3   Audit evidence from external sources is more reliable than that obtained from the entity's records.

4   Any five from:
    - Inspection
    - Observation
    - Inquiry
    - Confirmation
    - Recalculation
    - Reperformance
    - Analytical procedures

5   'Reperformance' is the auditor's independent execution of procedures or controls that were originally performed as part of the entity's internal control.

6   Audit sampling is the application of audit procedures to less than 100% of items within a population of audit relevance such that all sampling units have a chance of selection in order to provide the auditor with a reasonable basis on which to draw conclusions about the entire population. Audit sampling can be applied using either statistical or non-statistical approaches.

End of chapter questions

13.1   ABC & Co has performed analytical procedures on the financial statements of XYZ Co and discovered an increase in receivables collection period.

       Which of the following auditor responses to the increase in the receivables collection period of XYZ Co is the **least** relevant?

       A   Make enquiries of management to understand the likely reason why the receivables collection period exceeds the extended credit period

       B   Perform detailed substantive testing on the aged receivables listing, to determine whether any amounts should be written off

       C   Perform a trend analysis on current year and prior year monthly revenue, to identify whether revenue is overstated as a result of fraud or error

       D   Perform further working capital ratio analysis, to determine the effect of the extended credit on XYZ's cash position

13.2   The auditor of XYZ Co is performing audit procedures to confirm the company's ownership of motor vehicles.

       Which of the following would provide the most persuasive evidence of this?

       A   Physical inspection of the motor vehicles
       B   Inspection of vehicle registration documents
       C   Checking that the motor vehicles are recorded in the non-current asset register
       D   Review of vehicle insurance documentation

13.3 As part of the audit of receivables it is common for auditors to ask their client to write to their customers to obtain a reply confirming the debt. Which of the following assertions will this procedure address?

- (1) Existence
- (2) Valuation
- (3) Completeness
- (4) Rights and obligations

- A (2) and (3)
- B (1) and (4)
- C (2) and (4)
- D (1), (2), (3) and (4)

13.4 Which of the following is a test of control?

- A Carrying out analytical procedures
- B Tracing purchase invoices to the credit of supplier accounts
- C Performing a bank reconciliation where the client has not
- D Observing warehouse staff count goods as they are received.

13.5 Which of the following statements most accurately describes substantive audit procedures?

- A Substantive audit procedures consist of analytical procedures and tests of controls.
- B Substantive audit procedures are tests to obtain audit evidence about the design and operation of an entity's internal control system.
- C Substantive audit procedures are tests to obtain audit evidence to detect material misstatements in the financial statements.
- D Substantive audit procedures are only carried out when the internal control system is assessed as being strong.

PART B FOUNDATIONS OF AUDITING

Tests of controls

Topic list	Syllabus reference
1 Manual and computer based systems and controls	B2.5, B2.8
2 The sales system	B2.5, B2.8
3 The purchases system	B2.5, B2.8
4 The cash system	B2.5, B2.8
5 The payroll system	B2.5, B2.8

Introduction

We discussed internal controls in Chapter 12. In this chapter we will look at how tests of controls might be applied in practice. We will examine the sales, purchases, cash and payroll systems in a typical accounting system.

We have already stated that the auditors must establish what the accounting system and the system of internal control consist of. The auditors will then decide which controls, if any, they wish to rely on and plan tests of controls to obtain the audit evidence as to whether such reliance can be warranted. For each of the major transaction systems we will look at the system objectives the auditors will bear in mind while assessing the internal controls and give examples of common controls. We shall then go on to look at a 'standard' programme of tests of controls.

PART B FOUNDATIONS OF AUDITING

1 Manual and computer based systems and controls

For each system we cover in this chapter, starting with the sales system, we look at objectives, controls and tests of controls. As you review these please bear in mind that controls may be either carried out manually or, in a computerised system, electronically. This also means tests of control could require a review or inspection of printed documents or electronic documents on screen.

For example:

(a) Where recording transactions is mentioned, these could be manually inputted transactions or they could be imported or automatically posted from integrated systems.

(b) Where authorisation of documents is discussed approval could be in the form of a written signature on a printed document, or it could be an electronic/digital signature to approve electronic files or entries. This means the auditor may be reviewing a physical signature or software audit logs to see if a document is approved and who it was approved by.

(c) References to numerical sequencing or matching of documents could relate to manual numbering or matching, but there could instead be auto generated sequential numbering or electronic (or even automatic) matching of related documents (orders, GRNs and invoices for example).

(d) Sending of invoices, statements and other documents could be by post, by email or other electronic means (such as a customer portal).

It is not practical to duplicate every control and test of control in the sections throughout the chapter to cater for systems of varying levels of technology and automation. However, please note that where there are references to physical documents, authorisations or processes they could equally be electronic documents, authorisations or processes.

2 The sales system

FAST FORWARD

The tests of controls in the **sales system** will be based around:

- **Selling** (authorisation)
- **Goods outwards** (custody)
- **Accounting** (recording)

The following diagram illustrates the sales system.

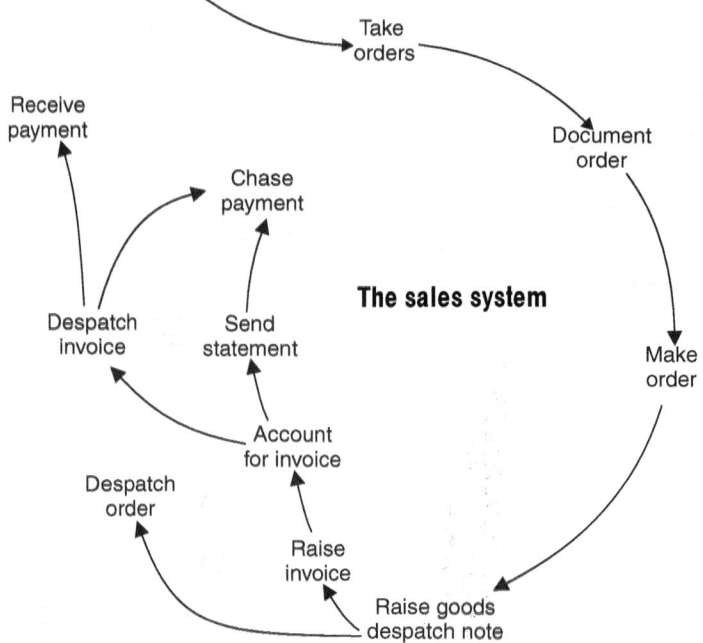

The sales system

2.1 Sales system: Control objectives, controls and tests of controls

Control objectives	Controls	Tests of controls
Assertion: occurrence and existence		
• To ensure that recorded sales transactions represent goods or services provided.	• The tasks of taking orders, recording sales and receiving payment are allocated to three different staff members.	• Observe the processing of orders through the sales cycle and inspect sign-offs to evaluate whether proper segregation of duties is operating.
	• Sales are only recorded if there is an approved sales order form and shipping/despatch documentation.	• For a sample of sales invoices, ensure there is a related sales order form that has been authorised and shipping documentation. • Examine information processing controls for authorisation.
	• Accounting for numerical sequences of invoices.	• Inspect invoices to confirm whether they are sequentially numbered.
	• Monthly customer statements sent out and customer queries and complaints handled independently.	• Review entity's procedures for sending out monthly statements and dealing with customer queries and complaints.
• To ensure that goods and services are only supplied to customers with good credit ratings.	• Authorisation of credit terms to customers (senior staff authorisation, references/credit checks for new customers, regular review of credit limits).	• Review entity's procedures for granting credit to customers.
	• Authorisation by senior staff required for changes in other customer data such as address etc.	• Examine a sample of sales orders for evidence of proper credit approval by the appropriate senior staff member.
	• Orders not accepted unless credit limits reviewed first.	• Examine application controls for credit limits. • Review new customer files to ensure satisfactory credit references were obtained.
• To ensure that goods and services are provided at authorised prices and on authorised terms. • To ensure that customers are encouraged to pay promptly.	• Authorised price lists and specified terms of trade in place.	• Verify that price lists and terms of trade are properly documented, authorised and communicated. • Examine information processing controls for authorised prices and terms.

Control objectives	Controls	Tests of controls
Assertion: completeness		
• To ensure that all revenue relating to goods despatched is recorded.	• Accounting for numerical sequences of invoices.	• Review and test entity's procedures for accounting for numerical sequences of invoices, and inspect invoices to confirm whether they are sequentially numbered.
• To ensure that all goods and services sold are correctly invoiced.	• Shipping/despatch documentation is matched to sales invoices.	• For a sample of shipping/despatch documents, ensure each has been matched to a related sales invoice that was subsequently recorded.
	• Sales invoices are reconciled to the daily sales report.	• Review a sample of reconciliations performed. Reperform a sample of reconciliations.
	• An open-order file is maintained and reviewed regularly.	• Inspect the open-order file for unfulfilled orders.
Assertion: accuracy		
• To ensure that all sales and adjustments are correctly journalised, summarised and posted to the correct accounts.	• Sales invoices and matching documents required for all entries and the date and reference of the entry are written on each document.	• Review supporting documents for a sample of sales entries to ensure they contain the details that indicate they were referred to when entered.
Assertion: cut-off		
• To ensure that transactions have been recorded in the correct period.	• All shipping documentation is forwarded to the invoicing section on a daily basis.	• Compare dates on sales invoices with dates of corresponding shipping documentation.
	• Daily invoicing of goods shipped.	• Compare dates on sales invoices with dates recorded in the sales ledger.
Assertion: classification		
• To ensure that all transactions are properly classified in accounts.	• Chart of accounts (COA) in place and is regularly reviewed for appropriateness and updated where necessary.	• Inspect any documentary evidence of review (such as emails requesting update to COA as a result of review).
	• Codes in place for different types of products or services.	• Test application controls for proper codes.

3 The purchases system

FAST FORWARD

The tests of controls in the **purchases system** will be based around:

- **Buying** (authorisation)
- **Goods inwards** (custody)
- **Accounting** (recording)

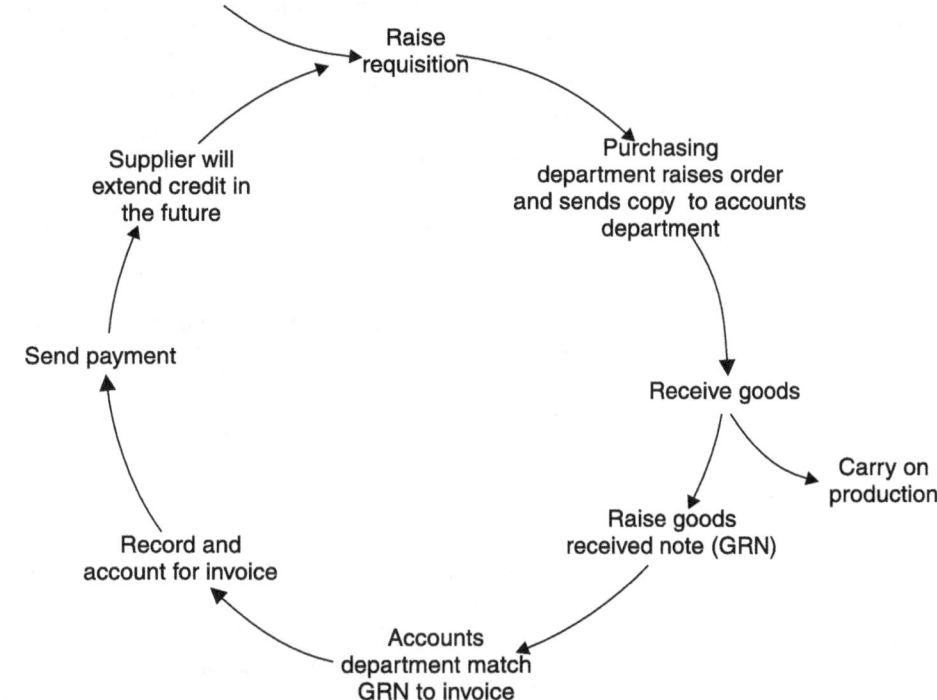

3.1 Purchases system: Control objectives, controls and tests of controls

Assertion	Control objectives	Controls	Tests of controls
Occurrence and existence	• To ensure that recorded purchases represent goods and services received.	• Authorisation procedures and policies in place for ordering goods and services.	• Inspect policies and procedures and enquire about them. • Observe the processing of purchase orders throughout the purchasing cycle and evaluate whether proper segregation of duties is operating.
		• The responsibility for placing the orders, recording the purchase order and making the payment is carried out by three different staff members.	

Assertion	Control objectives	Controls	Tests of controls
	• To ensure that recorded purchases represent goods and services received.	• Purchase orders raised for each purchase and authorised by appropriate senior personnel.	• Examine a sample of purchase orders to ensure they have been appropriately authorised. • Review the delegated list of authority for purchases.
		• Approved purchase order for each receipt of goods.	• For a sample of goods received notes (GRNs), ensure there is a related purchase order that has been properly approved.
		• Staff receiving goods check them to the purchase order.	• Observe receipt of goods by staff to confirm whether the check is done. • Inspect a sample to confirm whether stores staff undertake this check.
		• Stores clerks sign for goods received.	
		• Purchase orders and GRNs are matched with the suppliers' invoices.	• Examine supporting documentation to ensure it has been matched for a sample of invoices.
		• Supplier statements independently reviewed and reconciled to trade payable records.	• Review procedures for reconciling supplier statements and reperform a sample of reconciliations.
Completeness	• To ensure that all purchase transactions that occurred have been recorded.	• Purchase orders and GRNs are matched with the suppliers' invoices.	• For a sample of purchase orders in the year ensure each has been matched to a related invoice that was subsequently recorded.

14: TESTS OF CONTROLS

Assertion	Control objectives	Controls	Tests of controls
	• To ensure that all purchase transactions that occurred have been recorded.	• Periodic accounting for pre-numbered GRNs and purchase orders.	• Review entity's procedures for accounting for pre-numbered documents and inspect a sample of GRNs for sequential numbering.
		• Independent check of amount recorded in the purchase journal.	• Examine application controls. • Examine documentation for evidence of this check.
		• Supplier statements independently reviewed and reconciled to trade payable records.	• Review procedures for reconciling supplier statements and reperform a sample of reconciliations.
Rights and obligations	• To ensure that recorded purchases represent the liabilities of the entity.	• Purchase orders and GRNs are matched with the suppliers' invoices.	• Examine supporting documentation to ensure it has been matched for a sample of invoices.
Accuracy and classification	• To ensure that purchase transactions are correctly recorded in the accounting system.	• Purchase orders and GRNs are matched with the suppliers' invoices. • Mathematical accuracy of the supplier's invoice is verified. • Chart of accounts in place.	• Examine supporting documentation for a sample of invoices. • Review a sample of invoices for evidence the accuracy has been verified (eg signature or initials) and reperform the check. • Review reconciliations for evidence of this check. • Review purchases journal and general ledger for reasonableness.
Valuation and allocation	• To ensure that purchases are recorded at the correct amount and in the right account	• Amount posted to general ledger is reconciled to the purchases ledger.	• Review a sample of invoices for evidence that cost is accurate, and that items are included in the correct account

Assertion	Control objectives	Controls	Tests of controls
Presentation	• To ensure that purchases are properly classified in the financial statements.	• Chart of accounts. • Independent approval and review of accounts charged to purchases. • Purchasing budgets in place and reviewed by management.	• Review chart of accounts. • Review procedures for classifying purchases. • Review budgeting procedures.
Cut-off	• To ensure that purchase transactions are recorded in the correct accounting period.	• All goods received reports forwarded to accounts payable department daily. • Procedures in place that require recording of purchases as soon as possible after goods/services received.	• Compare dates on reports to dates on relevant vouchers. • Compare dates on vouchers with dates they were recorded in the purchases journal.

4 The cash system

Controls over bank and cash receipts and payments should prevent fraud or theft.

4.1 Cash system: Control objectives, controls and tests of controls

The following table sets out the control objectives, controls and possible tests of controls over bank and **cash payments**.

Assertion	Control objectives	Controls	Tests of controls
Occurrence	• To ensure that only valid payments are made.	• Separate responsibilities for the recording, payment and reconciliation of cash. • Supplier statements independently reviewed and reconciled to trade payable records. • Monthly bank reconciliations prepared and reviewed.	• Observe the processing of payments and review the entity's policies to evaluate whether proper segregation of duties is operating. • Review procedures for reconciling supplier statements. • Review reconciliations to confirm whether undertaken and reviewed.

14: TESTS OF CONTROLS

Assertion	Control objectives	Controls	Tests of controls
		• Only authorised staff can make electronic bank payments and issue cheques. • Electronic bank payments and cheques prepared only after all source documents have been independently approved.	• Review delegated list of authority for payments. • Inspect relevant documentation for evidence of approval by senior personnel.
Completeness	• To ensure that all payments that occurred are recorded.	• Separate responsibilities for the recording, handling and reconciliation of cash at bank. • Supplier statements independently reviewed and reconciled to trade payable records. • Monthly bank reconciliations prepared and reviewed. • Review of payments by manager before release. • Daily bank and cash payments reconciled to posting to payable accounts. • Use of pre-numbered cheques.	• Observe the processing of bank and cash payments and review the entity's policies to evaluate whether proper segregation of duties is operating. • Review procedures for reconciling supplier statements. • Review reconciliations to confirm whether undertaken and independently reviewed. • Inspect sample of listings for evidence of senior review. • Review a sample of reconciliations for evidence that they have been done. • Examine evidence of use of pre-numbered cheques.
Accuracy, classification and valuation	• To ensure that payments are recorded correctly in the ledger.	• Reconciliation of daily payments report to electronic payment transfers and cheques issued.	• Review reconciliation, to ensure performed, reviewed and any discrepancies followed up on a timely basis.

Assertion	Control objectives	Controls	Tests of controls
	• To ensure that payments are recorded correctly in the ledger.	• Supplier statements reconciled to payable accounts regularly. • Monthly bank reconciliations of bank statements to ledger account.	• Review reconciliations for a sample of accounts. • Review bank reconciliation for evidence it was done and independently reviewed. Reperform a sample of bank reconciliations.
	• To ensure that payments are posted to the correct payable accounts and to the general ledger.	• Supplier statements reconciled to payable accounts regularly. • Agreement of monthly payments journal to general ledger posting. • Payable accounts reconciled to general ledger control account.	• Review reconciliations for a sample of accounts. • Review postings from journal to general ledger. • Review reconciliation, to ensure performed, reviewed and any discrepancies followed up on a timely basis.
Cut-off	• To ensure that payments are recorded in the correct accounting period.	• Reconciliation of electronic funds transfers and cheques issued with postings to payments journal and payable accounts.	• Review reconciliation and check it is carried out regularly.
Presentation	• To ensure that payments are charged to the correct accounts.	• Chart of accounts. • Independent approval and review of general ledger account assignment.	• Review payments journal to assess reasonableness of charging of accounts. • Review assignment of general ledger account.

The following table sets out the control objectives, controls and possible tests of controls over bank and **cash receipts**.

Assertion	Control objectives	Controls	Tests of controls
Occurrence	• To ensure that all valid bank and cash receipts are received and deposited.	• Separate responsibilities for the recording, receipt and reconciliation of cash.	• Observe the processing of cash and review the entity's policies to evaluate whether proper segregation of duties is operating.
		• Use of electronic receipts transfer not received or deposited.	• Examine information processing controls for electronic receipts transfer.
		• Monthly bank reconciliations performed and independently reviewed.	• Review monthly bank reconciliations to confirm performed and reviewed.
		• Use of cash registers or point-of-sale devices.	• Observe cash sales procedures.
		• Periodic inspections of cash sales procedures.	• Enquire of managers about results of inspections.
		• Restrictive endorsement of cheques immediately on receipt.	• Observe mail opening, including endorsement of cheques.
		• Mail opened by two staff members.	• Observe mail opening procedures.
		• Immediate preparation of cash book or list of mail receipts.	• Observe preparation of bank and cash receipts' records.
		• Independent check of agreement of cash/cheques to be deposited at bank with register totals and receipts listing.	• Review documentation for evidence of independent check.
		• Independent check of agreement of bank deposit slip with daily cash summary.	• Review documentation for evidence of independent check.

Assertion	Control objectives	Controls	Tests of controls
Completeness	• To ensure that all bank and cash receipts are recorded.	• Separate responsibilities for the recording, receipt and reconciliation of cash.	• Observe the processing of cash and review the entity's policies to evaluate whether proper segregation of duties is operating.
		• Use of electronic receipts transfer not received or deposited.	• Examine information processing controls for electronic receipts transfer.
		• Monthly bank reconciliations performed and independently reviewed.	• Review monthly bank reconciliations to confirm performed and reviewed. Reperform a sample of the reconciliations.
		• Daily bank and cash receipts listing reconciled with posting to customer accounts.	• Review reconciliation.
		• Customer statements prepared and sent out on a regular basis.	• Enquire of management about handling of customer statements. • Examine a sample of customers and note frequency of statements.

14: TESTS OF CONTROLS

Assertion	Control objectives	Controls	Tests of controls
Accuracy, classification and valuation	• To ensure that bank and cash receipts are recorded at correct amounts.	• Daily remittance report reconciled to control listing of remittance advices. • Monthly bank statement performed and reviewed independently.	• Review reconciliations. • Review reconciliations for evidence they were performed and independently reviewed.
	• To ensure that bank and cash receipts are posted to correct receivables accounts and to the general ledger.	• Daily remittance report reconciled daily with postings to bank and cash receipts journal and customer accounts. • Monthly customer statements sent out. • Monthly bank and cash receipts journal agreed to general ledger posting. • Receivables' ledger reconciled to control account.	• Review reconciliations. • Review entity's procedures for sending out statements. • Review journal and posting to general ledger. • Review reconciliations.
Cut-off	• To ensure that bank and cash receipts are recorded in the correct accounting period.	• Bank reconciliation at period end.	• Review and test reconciliation.
Presentation	• To ensure that bank and cash receipts are charged to the correct accounts.	• Chart of accounts (COA) in place and is regularly reviewed for appropriateness and updated where necessary. • Codes in place for different types of receipt.	• Inspect any documentary evidence of review (such as emails requesting update to COA as a result of review). • Test application controls for proper codes.

PART B FOUNDATIONS OF AUDITING

5 The payroll system

FAST FORWARD

Key controls over **payroll** cover:

- **Documentation** and **authorisation** of staff changes
- **Calculation** of wages and salaries
- **Payment** of wages
- **Authorisation** of **deductions**

5.1 Payroll system: Control objectives, controls and tests of controls

Assertion	Control objectives	Controls	Tests of controls
Occurrence and existence	• To ensure that payment is made only to genuine employees of the entity.	• Segregation of duties between HR and payroll functions.	• Review payroll and HR job descriptions and company policies on payroll process, to evaluate whether proper segregation of duties is in place.
		• Personnel files held for all employees.	• Review a sample of starters and leavers in the year to ensure correct documentation is in place.
		• Authorisation procedures for hiring, terminating, time worked, wage rates, overtime, benefits etc.	• Review authorisation procedures in place and documentation for evidence of authorisation.
		• Any changes in employment status of employees (eg maternity, special leave) informed to HR department.	• Review policies and procedures in place for changing status and consider whether adequate.
		• Use of time clocks/electronic clock in to record time worked.	• Review personnel files for a sample of employees whose status changed in the year.

Assertion	Control objectives	Controls	Tests of controls
Occurrence and existence		• Clock cards approved by supervisor.	• Observe employees' use of time clocks.
		• Employee numbers assigned to each employee in the payroll master file. Only employees with valid employee numbers are paid.	• Inspect a sample of clock cards for evidence of approval by appropriate level of management.
		• Payroll budgets in place and reviewed by management.	• Review and test procedures for entering and removing employee numbers from the payroll master file.
• Review budgeting procedures.
Completeness	• To ensure that all payroll costs are recorded for work done by employees.	• Pre-numbered clock cards in use.	• Review numerical sequence of clock cards.
		• Regular reconciliations carried out of payroll records and employee costs recorded in the general ledger.	• Review a sample of reconciliations to ensure they are properly carried out. Reperform a sample of reconciliations.
		• Comparison of cheques and bank transfer list with payroll to ensure all employees paid have been recorded via payroll.	• Enquire whether comparisons are being made between payment records and payroll and inspect any documentary evidence of the review.
		• Preparation and authorisation of cheques and bank transfer lists.	• Examine paid cheques or a certified copy of the bank list for employees paid by cheque or bank transfer to ensure proper authorisation.

Assertion	Control objectives	Controls	Tests of controls
Accuracy, classification, valuation and allocation	• To ensure that all benefits and deductions (tax, pension etc) are computed correctly.	• Reperformance of a sample of payroll benefit and deduction calculations. • Payroll budgets in place and reviewed by management. • Agreement of gross earnings and total tax deducted with taxation returns.	• Review documentary evidence that recalculation occurred (eg spreadsheet printout). • Review budgeting procedures. • Inspect documentation for evidence of management's review.
	• To ensure that payroll transactions are correctly recorded in the accounting system.	• Changes to master payroll file verified through 'before and after' reports. • Payroll master file reconciled to general ledger.	• Review reconciliation of 'before and after' reports to payroll master file. • Review reconciliation of payroll master file to general ledger. Confirm whether discrepancies are followed up promptly and resolved.
Cut-off	• To ensure that payroll transactions are recorded in the correct accounting period.	• All starters, leavers, changes to salaries and deductions are reported promptly to payroll department and changes are updated in the payroll master file promptly.	• Review entity's procedures for reporting changes to the payroll department. • Verify sample of starters and leavers.
Presentation	• To ensure that payroll transactions are properly classified in the financial statements.	• Chart of accounts. • Independent approval and review of accounts charged to payroll. • Payroll budgets in place and reviewed by management.	• Review chart of accounts. • Review procedures for classifying payroll costs. • Review budgeting procedures.

Chapter roundup

- The tests of controls in the **sales system** will be based around:
  - **Selling** (authorisation)
  - **Goods outwards** (custody)
  - **Accounting** (recording)
- The tests of controls in the **purchases system** will be based around:
  - **Buying** (authorisation)
  - **Goods inwards** (custody)
  - **Accounting** (recording)
- Controls over bank and cash receipts and payments should prevent fraud or theft.
- Key controls over **payroll** cover:
  - **Documentation** and **authorisation** of staff changes
  - **Calculation** of wages and salaries
  - **Payment** of wages
  - **Authorisation** of deductions

Quick quiz

1 Complete the table, putting the sales system control considerations under the correct headings.

Ordering/credit approval	Dispatch/invoicing	Recording/accounting

   (a) All sales that have been invoiced have been put in the general ledger.
   (b) Orders are fulfilled.
   (c) Cut-off is correct.
   (d) Goods are only supplied to good credit risks.
   (e) Goods are correctly invoiced.
   (f) Customers are encouraged to pay promptly.

2 State five controls relating to the ordering and granting of credit process.

   1 ……………………………………………………..
   2 ……………………………………………………..
   3 ……………………………………………………..
   4 ……………………………………………………..
   5 ……………………………………………………..

PART B FOUNDATIONS OF AUDITING

3   Complete the table, putting the purchase system control considerations under the correct headings.

Ordering	Receipts/invoices	Accounting

(a) Orders are only made to authorised suppliers.
(b) Liabilities are recognised for all goods and services received.
(c) Orders are made at competitive prices.
(d) All expenditure is authorised.
(e) Cut-off is correctly applied.
(f) Goods and services are only accepted if there is an authorised order.

4   (a) State four examples of purchase documentation on which numerical sequence should be checked.

   (1) ....
   (2) ....
   (3) ....
   (4) ....

   (b) Why is numerical sequence checked?

5   List the five key aims of controls in the bank and cash system.

   (1) ....
   (2) ....
   (3) ....
   (4) ....
   (5) ....

6   Give five examples of tests to be performed on the cash payments book (or payments recorded in the bank general ledger account).

   (1) ....
   (2) ....
   (3) ....
   (4) ....
   (5) ....

7   State two controls that will help to ensure that payment is made only to genuine employees of the entity and two related tests of controls that will provide evidence the controls are operating effectively.

Controls	Tests of control

Answers to quick quiz

1.

Ordering/credit approval	Dispatch/invoicing	Recording/accounting
(b) (d) (f)	(e)	(a) (c)

2. Any five from:
   - Segregation of duties; credit control, invoicing and inventory dispatch
   - Authorisation of credit terms to customers
     - References/credit checks obtained
     - Authorisation by senior staff
     - Regular review
   - Authorisation for changes in other customer data
     - Change of address supported by letterhead
     - Deletion requests supported by evidence balances cleared/customer in liquidation
   - Orders only accepted from customers who have no credit problems
   - Sequential numbering of blank pre-printed order documents
   - Correct prices quoted to customers
   - Matching of customer orders with production orders and dispatch notes and querying of orders not matched
   - Dealing with customer queries

3.

Ordering	Receipts/invoices	Accounting
(a) (c)	(b) (f)	(d) (e)

4. (a) From: (1) purchase requisitions, (2) purchase orders, (3) goods received notes, (4) goods returned notes, (5) suppliers invoices

   (b) Sequence provides a control that sales are complete. Missing documents should be explained, or cancelled copies available.

5. (1) All monies received are recorded.
   (2) All monies received are banked.
   (3) Cash and cheques are safeguarded against loss or theft.
   (4) All payments are authorised, made to the correct payees and recorded.
   (5) Payments are not made twice for the same liability.

6. For a sample of payments:

   (1) Compare with paid cheques to ensure payee agrees.
   (2) Observe whether cheques are signed by the persons authorised to do so within their authority limits.
   (3) Match to suppliers' invoices for goods and services. Verify that supporting documents are signed as having been checked and passed for payment and have been stamped or marked 'paid'.
   (4) Match to suppliers' statements.
   (5) Agree to other documentary evidence, as appropriate (agreements, authorised expense vouchers, wages/salaries records, petty cash books, authorised electronic payment lists etc).

7 Two controls and related tests of control are shown below. See section 5 for further examples.

Controls	Tests of control
Segregation of duties between HR and payroll functions.	Review payroll and HR job descriptions and company policies on payroll process, to evaluate whether proper segregation of duties is in place.
Authorisation procedures for hiring, terminating, time worked, wage rates, overtime, benefits etc.	Review authorisation procedures in place and documentation for evidence of authorisation.

End of chapter questions

14.1 Which of the following helps ensure sales invoices are only raised for goods provided?

- A Checking that the related delivery note has been signed before raising an invoice
- B Checking that amounts included on invoices agree to price lists
- C Checking that a customer has not exceeded its credit limit before raising an invoice
- D Checking that there is a valid sales order before raising an invoice

14.2 Which of the following controls does not satisfy the objective of ensuring that sales are completely recorded?

- A Sequence tests on sales orders, despatch notes, invoices and credit notes to ensure that there are no missing numbers or two documents with the same number
- B Comparisons of despatch notes with order and invoices, ensuring documents are cross-referenced to each other
- C Matching posting of sales day book to receivables ledger control account and receivables ledger
- D Comparison of receivables accounts balances with credit limits

14.3 Why is it important to reconcile suppliers' statements to their payables account record?

- A To ensure that the correct goods have been invoiced for
- B To identify long overdue invoices so as to enable these to be promptly paid
- C To ensure that only approved suppliers send invoices
- D To identify discrepancies between the payables ledger and what the supplier says is owed

14.4 As part of your audit of the purchasing system of a client, you have recommended that the goods inwards department should ensure that the goods received are valid business purchases by matching all deliveries to an authorised order form before issuing a GRN.

Which of the following would be an appropriate test of control to confirm that the control is operating effectively?

- A For a sample of orders, check that there is a matching GRN
- B Check that the numerical sequence of purchase orders is complete
- C For a sample of GRNs check that there is an authorised purchase order
- D Check that the numerical sequence of GRNs is complete

14.5 Which of the following controls would not provide assurance that the correct amounts are paid to employees, in a system where employees are paid by the hour?

- A Automated recording of hours worked
- B Reperformance of payroll calculations
- C Comparing bank transfer list with payroll
- D Comparing payroll and income tax returns

PART B FOUNDATIONS OF AUDITING

Auditing and governance

Topic list	Syllabus reference
1 The relationship between auditing and governance	B2.9
2 The role and responsibilities of internal audit	B2.5, B2.9

Introduction

In this final chapter of the Workbook we bring everything together to discuss the relationship between auditing and corporate governance.

We also consider the role and responsibilities of internal audit, which we will look at in Section 2.

PART B FOUNDATIONS OF AUDITING

1 The relationship between auditing and governance

1.1 Introduction

> **FAST FORWARD**
>
> Audit is an important part of good corporate governance.

In this paper we have considered the importance and principles of corporate governance together with objectives and procedures of auditing. In this final chapter we bring it all together and consider the relationship between auditing and governance.

As we shall see there is a two-way relationship in that corporate governance has an input into auditing and auditing contributes to improved corporate governance.

1.2 External audit

As seen in Chapter 8, the historical development of auditing is linked to the growth in the use of the limited company as a business structure.

Limited companies may have many shareholders who are not involved in the management of the company. Management is therefore delegated to the directors of the company, who may not perform their role in the best interests of the shareholders.

The role of the auditor is to form an opinion on whether the financial statements prepared by the directors represent a true and fair view of the company's performance and position, ie to check the work done in producing the financial statements, thereby increasing the accountability of the directors. The audit therefore contributes to ensuring that the directors are accountable and that the company is well-managed, which is part of corporate governance. We looked at this in Chapter 1.

Corporate governance affects the audit, in that corporate governance codes require an audit committee to be set up for listed companies which liaises with the auditor and oversees the independence of the auditor. We looked at this in Chapter 5.

1.3 Internal audit

Corporate governance also affects internal audit in that, in many countries, corporate governance codes require the setting up of an internal audit department or, at least, a regular review of the need for one.

The presence of an internal audit department contributes to improving corporate governance in that internal audit is likely to be a key aspect of risk management.

We shall consider these relationships in more detail below.

1.4 The need for internal audit

> **FAST FORWARD**
>
> Companies should assess on an annual basis whether there is a need for an internal audit function.

In the UK, the FRC's Corporate Governance Code Guidance (that sits alongside the UK Corporate Governance Code 2024) outlines that the need for an internal audit function will vary depending on company specific factors. Senior management and the board may desire objective assurance and advice on risk and internal control. An adequately resourced internal audit function (or its equivalent where, for example, a third party is contracted to perform some or all of the work concerned) may provide such assurance. Given their size and complexity, FTSE 350 companies should consider having an internal audit function. (FRC's *Corporate Governance Code Guidance*, 2024, para. 96)

The UK Corporate Governance Code itself requires companies to consider the need for an internal audit function **at least annually**, so that the **need for internal audit is regularly reviewed** (FRC *UK Corporate Governance Code 2024*: Principle M, provision 25). Listed companies with an internal audit function should review annually its **scope, authority** and **resources**.

15: AUDITING AND GOVERNANCE

The Turnbull report played an important part in the subsequent development of the UK corporate governance codes and guidance. It set out guidance for best practice relating risk management and internal control, including considering the need for an internal audit function.

It gives a very useful summary of what should be considered when establishing how great the need for an internal audit function is, which will depend on:

Scale, diversity and complexity of the company's operations	The more complex the operations, the more that can go wrong, so there is a greater need for an independent internal audit department to look at the system as a whole, to see if risk management and internal controls are appropriately focused. Also where there is close scrutiny of the company's operations by regulators with the power to remove the company's licence to operate, the case for internal audit is much stronger.
Number of employees	Number of employees is generally used as a proxy for size. Investors would expect that the larger the company, the more formal the systems of internal control should be, including a separate internal audit department.
Cost-benefit considerations	As with other controls, the costs of internal audit (salary, management time lost dealing with internal audit) should not outweigh the benefits. The benefits however may be difficult to quantify (how do you quantify the errors that internal audit has prevented?).
Changes in organisational structure	A simplification of the organisational structure may often lead to a slimming down of the internal audit department. However a slimming down should really mean the opposite. The removal of the checks and balances implied by a bureaucratic structure would seem to increase the need for an effective internal audit function.
Changes in key risks	If the business is developing in new areas, an internal audit assessment of how effectively it is handling consequent changes in risk can be very significant.
Problems with the system of internal control	Internal audit assessment would help to determine how serious these problems are and what can be done to resolve them.
Increased number of unexplained or unacceptable events	This applies not just to events that cause problems with the accounting records, but also problems that delay production or result in inferior quality goods or services. The costs of internal audit may need to be weighed against the possibilities of lost sales.

Although there may be alternative means of carrying out the routine work of internal audit, those carrying out the work may be involved in operations and hence lack **objectivity**.

It seems likely that once the task of reviewing internal control and risk management systems becomes complex, a skilled and objective internal audit team will be needed to give the audit committee the evidence it needs about how systems are working.

1.5 The role of internal audit in risk management

FAST FORWARD Internal audit is a key part of a risk management system.

Internal audit will play a significant part in the organisation's risk management processes, being required to assess and advise on how risks are countered. Internal audit's work will be influenced by the organisation's **appetite** for bearing risks. Internal audit will assess:

- The **adequacy of the risk management and response processes** for identifying, assessing, managing and reporting on risk
- The risk management and control **culture**

- The appropriateness of **internal controls** in operation to **limit risks**
- The **operation and effectiveness** of the **risk management processes**, including the internal controls

Internal auditors should be **checking that day-to-day control procedures such as monitoring** of **transactions are being carried out**, rather than carrying out these control procedures themselves. If they had day-to-day responsibilities, they would be **part of the control system** rather than reviewers of it, and therefore be unable to give an independent opinion on its operation.

2 The role and responsibilities of internal audit

> **FAST FORWARD**
>
> Internal audit assists management in achieving the entity's corporate objectives, particularly in establishing good corporate governance.

2.1 Introduction

Key term

> The **Internal audit function** is a function of an entity that performs assurance and consulting activities designed to evaluate and improve the effectiveness of the entity's governance, risk management and internal control processes.

Internal auditing is an appraisal or monitoring activity established within an entity as a service to the entity. It functions by, amongst other things, examining, evaluating and reporting to management and the directors on the adequacy and effectiveness of components of the accounting system and system of internal control.

An Internal audit function is generally a feature of large companies. It is a function, provided either by employees of the entity or sourced from an external organisation, to assist management in **achieving corporate objectives**.

It is the responsibility of management and those charged with governance to prevent and detect fraud, and in this respect, internal auditors may have a role to play.

2.2 Internal audit and corporate governance

Established codes of corporate governance such as the UK Corporate Governance Code highlight the need for businesses to maintain **good systems of internal control** to manage the risks the company faces. **Internal audit** can play a key role in assessing and monitoring internal control policies and procedures.

The internal audit function can assist the board in other ways as well:

- By, in effect, acting as auditors for board reports not audited by the external auditors
- By being the experts in fields such as auditing and accounting standards in the company and assisting in implementation of new standards
- By liaising with external auditors, particularly where external auditors can use internal audit work and reduce the time and therefore cost of the external audit. In addition, internal audit can check that external auditors are reporting back to the board everything they are required to under auditing standards.

2.3 Distinction between internal and external audit

> **FAST FORWARD**
>
> Although many of the techniques internal and external auditors use may be similar, the basis and reasoning of their work is different.

The **external audit** is focused on the **financial statements**, whereas the **internal audit** is focused on the **operations of the entire business**.

Key term

> An **external audit** is an exercise whose objective is to enable auditors to express an opinion whether the financial statements give a true and fair view (or equivalent) of the entity's affairs at the period end and of its profit and loss for the period then ended and have been properly prepared in accordance with the applicable reporting framework.

Contrast the definition of external audit with the definition of internal audit given in Section 2.1. The external audit is focused on a very specific item, the financial statements, whereas the internal audit function is focused on the operations of the entire business.

The following table highlights the key differences between internal and external audit.

	Internal audit	External audit
Objective	Designed to add value and improve an organisation's operations.	An exercise to enable auditors to express an opinion on the financial statements.
Reporting	Reports to the board of directors, or other people charged with governance, such as the audit committee. Reports are private and for the directors and management of the company.	Reports to the shareholders or members of a company on the truth and fairness of the financial statements. Audit report is publicly available to the shareholders and other interested parties.
Scope	Work relates to the operations of the organisation.	Work relates to the financial statements.
Relationship	Often employees of the organisation, although sometimes the function is outsourced.	Independent of the company and its management. Usually appointed by the shareholders.
Planning and collection of evidence	Strategic long term planning carried out, to achieve objective of assignments, with no materiality level being set. Some audits may be procedural, rather than risk-based. Evidence mainly from interviewing staff and inspecting documents (ie not external).	Planning carried out to achieve objective regarding truth and fairness of financial statements. Materiality level set during planning (may be amended during course of audit). External audit work is risk-based. Evidence collected using a variety of procedures per ISAs to obtain sufficient appropriate audit evidence.

The table demonstrates that the **whole basis and reasoning** of internal audit work is **fundamentally different** to that of external audit work.

2.4 Internal audit assignments

FAST FORWARD

> Internal audit can be involved in many different assignments as directed by management. These can range from **value for money** projects to **special** assignments looking at specific parts of the business.

The work of internal audit can be anything required by management, but will generally fall into the following areas:

Review of the accounting and control systems	The internal auditor will review the design of the system, monitor the effectiveness of the system by risk assessment and tests of control, and recommend cost-effective improvements.
	There are similarities between the work of internal and external auditors. But the internal auditor will review both financial and non-financial controls.

Examination of financial and operating information	This will include detailed testing of transactions, balances and procedures.
	This is similar to the substantive testing performed by external auditors, but also includes operating information.
Review of economy, efficiency and effectiveness of operations. Also known as **Value For Money** (VFM) auditing.	The three Es can be defined as follows. • **Economy**: attaining the appropriate quantity and quality of physical, human and financial resources (**inputs**) at lowest cost. • **Efficiency**: this is the relationship between goods or services produced (**outputs**) and the resources used to produce them. • **Effectiveness**: this is concerned with how well an activity is achieving its policy objectives or other intended effects. The auditor will compare the current operations with alternatives to establish if there is value for money.
Compliance auditing	This involves reviewing evidence to establish if the company has complied with laws and regulations.
Review of the safeguarding of assets	Reviewing the procedures to prevent valuable, portable items being stolen.
Review of the risk management process	Reviewing the overall risk management policy and monitoring the risk management strategies to ensure they continue to operate effectively.
Special investigations into particular areas.	For example, the auditor could investigate suspected fraud to determine its occurrence and quantify losses.

2.5 Outsourcing

FAST FORWARD

Internal audit functions may consist of employees of the company, or may be **outsourced** to external service providers. The **advantages** of outsourcing the internal audit function include speed, cost and a tailored answer to internal audit requirements. One of the main **disadvantages** may include threats to independence and objectivity if the external audit service is provided by the same firm.

2.5.1 What is outsourcing?

Key term

Outsourcing is the use of external suppliers as a source of finished products, components or services. It is also known as sub-contracting.

2.5.2 Advantages and disadvantages of outsourcing internal audit

The advantages and disadvantages of outsourcing the internal audit function are set out in the following table.

Advantages of outsourcing	Disadvantages of outsourcing
• Staff do not need to be recruited, as the service provider has good quality staff. • The service provider has different specialist skills and can assess what management require them to do. • Outsourcing can provide an immediate internal audit department. • Associated costs, such as staff training, are eliminated. • The service contract can be for the appropriate time scale. • Because the time scale is flexible, a team of staff can be provided if required. • It can be used on a short-term basis.	• There will be independence and objectivity issues if the company uses the same firm to provide both internal and external audit services. • The cost of outsourcing the internal audit function might be high enough to make the directors choose not to have an internal audit function at all. • Company staff may oppose outsourcing if it results in redundancies. • There may be a high staff turnover of internal audit staff. • The outsourced staff may only have a limited knowledge of the company. • The company will lose in-house skills.

PART B FOUNDATIONS OF AUDITING

Chapter roundup

- Audit is an important part of good corporate governance.
- Companies should assess on an annual basis whether there is a need for an internal audit function.
- Internal audit is a key part of a risk management system.
- Internal audit assists management in achieving the entity's corporate objectives, particularly in establishing good corporate governance.
- Although many of the techniques internal and external auditors use may be similar, the basis and reasoning of their work is different.
- Internal audit can be involved in many different assignments as directed by management. These can range from **value for money** projects to **special** assignments looking at specific parts of the business.
- Internal audit functions may consist of employees of the company, or may be **outsourced** to external service providers. The **advantages** of outsourcing the internal audit function include speed, cost and a tailored answer to internal audit requirements. One of the main **disadvantages** may include threats to independence and objectivity if the external audit service is provided by the same firm.

Quick quiz

1 What is an internal audit function?

2 Name three key differences between internal and external audit.

   (1) ....
   (2) ....
   (3) ....

3 Link the value for money 'E' with its definition.

   (a) Economy
   (b) Efficiency
   (c) Effectiveness

   (i)   The relationships between the goods and services produced (outputs) and the resources used to produce them.
   (ii) The concern with how well an activity is achieving its policy objectives or other intended effects.
   (iii) Attaining the appropriate quantity and quality of physical, human and financial resources (inputs) at lowest cost.

4 It is possible to buy in an internal audit service from an external organisation.

   True ☐
   False ☐

5 Give three advantages of outsourcing internal audit.

6 Give three disadvantages of outsourcing internal audit.

Answers to quick quiz

1. The **Internal audit function** is a function of an entity that performs assurance and consulting activities designed to evaluate and improve the effectiveness of the entity's governance, risk management and internal control processes.

2. (1) External auditors report to members, internal auditors report to directors.

   (2) External auditors report on financial statements, internal auditors report on systems, controls and risks.

   (3) External auditors are independent of the company, internal auditors are often employed by it.

3. (a) (iii), (b) (i), (c) (ii)

4. True – this is known as outsourcing.

5. Any three from:
   - Staff do not need to be recruited, as the service provider has good quality staff.
   - The service provider has different specialist skills and can assess what management require them to do.
   - Outsourcing can provide an immediate internal audit department.
   - Associated costs, such as staff training, are eliminated.
   - The service contract can be for the appropriate time scale.
   - Because the time scale is flexible, a team of staff can be provided if required.
   - It can be used on a short-term basis.

6. Any three from:
   - There will be independence and objectivity issues if the company uses the same firm to provide both internal and external audit services.
   - The cost of outsourcing the internal audit function might be high enough to make the directors choose not to have an internal audit function at all.
   - Company staff may oppose outsourcing if it results in redundancies.
   - There may be a high staff turnover of internal audit staff.
   - The outsourced staff may only have a limited knowledge of the company.
   - The company will lose in-house skills.

PART B FOUNDATIONS OF AUDITING

End of chapter questions

15.1 XYZ Co's management is keen to increase the range of assignments that the company's internal audit department undertakes.

Which of the following assignments should the internal audit department be asked to perform by management?

- A Undertake 'mystery shopper' reviews, where they enter the store as a customer, purchase goods and rate the overall shopping experience
- B Assist the external auditors by requesting bank confirmation letters
- C Provide advice on the implementation of a new payroll package for the payroll department
- D Review the company's financial statements on behalf of the board

15.2 Which of the following best summarises the meaning of 'efficiency' in the context of a Value for Money audit as requested by KLE Co's management?

- A The lowest cost at which the appropriate quantity and quality of physical, human and financial resources can be achieved
- B Producing the required goods and services in the shortest time possible
- C The extent to which an activity is achieving its policy objectives
- D The relationship between goods and services produced and the resources used to produce them

15.3 Which two of the following characteristics apply to internal audit?

(1) The purpose is to improve the company's operations.
(2) Reports to shareholders on whether the financial statements give a true and fair view of affairs.
(3) Auditors may be employees of the company.
(4) Their duties are set by statute.

- A (1) and (3)
- B (2) and (4)
- C (1) and (4)
- D (2) and (3)

15.4 Which of the following internal audit assignments aims to monitor management's performance and ensure that company policy is followed?

- A Value for money
- B Fraud investigation
- C Financial
- D Operational

15.5 Which of the following is a limitation of the internal audit function?

- A The internal audit report is not circulated to the members.
- B Internal audit assignments are designed to meet the needs of the business.
- C Internal auditors may be employees of the company.
- D Internal auditors may report to an audit committee.

Answers to end of chapter questions

ANSWERS TO END OF CHAPTER QUESTIONS

Chapter 1

1.1	C	Internal auditors are employed by the directors to carry out the work they require, so are the agents of the directors.
1.2	B	A and C, while problematic, are not related to agency. D is a reason why agency relationships arise.
1.3	C	A and B are examples of stakeholders but not a definition. D is a definition of an agent rather than a stakeholder.
1.4	D	Power and dependence explain the impact of resources on relationships between firms. Scarcity and dependence determine the importance of a particular resource.
1.5	A	Auditors, directors and lawyers are all acting on behalf of the shareholders/company and so are agents. The shareholders are not agents and so dividends are not agency costs.

Chapter 2

2.1	D	The other statements are advantages of corporate governance. D relates to the legal requirement for auditors to give an opinion on the accounts.
2.2	C	The UK Corporate Governance Code (2024) is UK specific guidance, the Hampel Report (1998) recommended the production of a combined code, and the King Report provides guidelines for the governance structures and operation of companies in South Africa.
2.3	C	Corporate governance is the system by which companies are directed and controlled.
2.4	A	A is not an G20/OECD principle. The G20/OECD principle relating to protection of rights focuses on the protection of shareholders rather than directors. The relevant principle is: 'To protect and facilitate the exercise of shareholders' rights and ensure the equitable treatment of all shareholders'.
2.5	B	Criminal sanctions is a characteristic of a rule-based system.

Chapter 3

3.1	A	Preparing the financial statements is the responsibility of the finance director alone rather the board as a whole.
3.2	B	The unitary board structure is more common countries with accounting and laws based on the Anglo-Saxon model.
3.3	D	The others are characteristics of an effective board.
3.4	C	The nomination committee should be set up to select and appoint directors.
3.5	D	Companies in the UK and USA are more likely to have unitary boards. Japanese companies are less likely than the UK and USA to have a unitary board and may have the keiretsu model. German companies are likely to have a two-tier structure.

Chapter 4

4.1	B	The other roles have functional responsibility and therefore are executive directors.
4.2	C	Managing the board is the responsibility of the chair.
4.3	B	Hiring non-executive directors will cost the company more money.
4.4	A	The lawyer may have had a material business relationship with the company, but it ended four years ago (the limit is three).
4.5	C	Developing corporate strategy is the responsibility of the CEO. As directors should not be involved in setting their own remuneration, the chair should not set the remuneration of the non-executives as the chair is also a non-executive director.

ANSWERS TO END OF CHAPTER QUESTIONS

Chapter 5

5.1   A   The others are all common objectives of the audit committee.

5.2   B   The directors of listed companies (which have audit committees) do not normally give guarantees (A). C describes the role of the external auditor. The finance director should not be on the audit committee (D) as the role of the audit committee involves independent monitoring of the finance function.

5.3   C   The board as a whole has the task of supervising the CEO and other executive directors.

5.4   A   Directors should be put forward for re-election automatically after the specified period (B). The nomination committee is not involved in appointments other than to the board (C). The nomination committee should make nominations themselves rather than merely rubber stamp suggestions made by others (D).

5.5   C   C is the worst as there is an executive director chairing the committee, next worst is D as it has a representative from management who is not the chair. The best is A as all directors are independent.

5.6   B   Members of the sustainability committee should have the relevant mix of skills, experience and diversity. The membership should include a mix of executive and non-executive directors and ideally the majority of the members should be non-executive directors. Establishment of a sustainability committee is not mandatory for all listed entities but the trend is that companies are increasingly setting these up voluntarily due to the importance of ESG related issues to company stakeholders.

Chapter 6

6.1   B   Corporate citizenship refers to an organisation's responsibilities toward society. The goal of corporate citizenship is to produce higher standards of living and quality of life for the communities that surround them and still maintain profitability for stakeholders.

6.2   D   An entity must apply both of the current IFRS Sustainability Disclosure Standards in order to comply with IFRS Sustainability Disclosure Standards. Application of the standards is on a **voluntary basis** unless jurisdiction authorities decide to require application, so not all organisations have to apply the standards. The standards do not prescribe the disclosures be included in the notes to the financial statements. They are currently likely to be included within a **sustainability report** in the annual report.

6.3   A   Stakeholder engagement is the process of involving all parties affected by a company's operations in its decision-making processes.

Chapter 7

7.1   B   No system can provide absolute assurance (A), C is too narrow a definition, and D refers to corporate governance.

7.2   A   Responsibility for the effectiveness of a company's system of internal control lies with the board of directors.

7.3   B   The risk has been accepted as it is considered the cost of addressing the risk would outweigh the benefit from addressing it.

7.4   D   It makes sense that risks must be identified first, before being assessed and then managed.

7.5   A   B is incorrect because insurance would not be cost-effective in those circumstances, C is incorrect because accepting these risks could potentially destroy the business, D is incorrect because low likelihood, low impact risks generate little threat to the business and controls may not be cost effective.

Chapter 8

8.1 A The principal aim of the audit is not in relation to the control system in place or to identify other areas of deficiency, although deficiencies and recommendations may be suggested by the external auditors as a by-product of the external audit in a report to management at the conclusion of the audit.

8.2 B ISA 250 (Revised) distinguishes between regulations which have a direct effect on the financial statements and those which do not have a direct effect but can still have a material effect. The hygiene regulations do not have a direct effect but they may have a material effect. The external auditor must therefore perform audit procedures to help identify any non-compliance which might have a material effect on the financial statements, ie any breaches of the hygiene regulations that could result in material fines or restaurant closures.

8.3 A

8.4 C This is not required by statute therefore A is incorrect. XYZ Co is hiring an external firm therefore B is incorrect. Systems are not being checked therefore D is incorrect.

8.5 B The auditor must gain reasonable assurance as to whether the financial statements are materially misstated as a result of fraud.

Chapter 9

9.1 D

9.2 C

9.3 D Integrity requires straightforwardness and honesty in all business relationships.

9.4 B

9.5 D In these circumstances the Secretary of State would appoint an auditor.

Chapter 10

There are no end of chapter questions for chapter 10.

Chapter 11

11.1 B None of A, C or D relate to inventory quantities recorded on the system, which is what the risk relates to.

11.2 B As cash is susceptible to theft there is a risk it may be stolen and so cash (and the associated revenue) may be materially misstated, so increased inherent risk. Detection risk is inversely related to the risk of material misstatement (inherent risk and control risk combined) so the high inherent risk will result in low detection risk. This means the auditor will increase testing in this area.

11.3 D Controls are not weaker just because there are large numbers of volunteers. Audit risk is managed by the auditor to keep it to an acceptably low level by adjusting the level of detection risk. This prevents audit risk from increasing.

11.4 A Risks must be identified so they can be addressed as part of the audit strategy, the ISA is not concerned with the audit budget.

11.5 C These are both reasons.

Chapter 12

12.1 C

12.2 C

12.3 A

12.4 B Passwords are general IT controls.

12.5 B

Chapter 13

13.1 C An increase in revenue would result in a decrease, rather than increase, in receivables collection period.

13.2 B A relates to existence and C to completeness. Although D also relates to ownership, B is better evidence.

13.3 B

13.4 C This is an example of reperformance; reperforming the control to confirm the company did it properly.

13.5 C

Chapter 14

14.1 A Checking that there is a signed delivery note gives evidence the goods have been delivered to the customer. The customer will sign it to say they have received the goods.

14.2 D D would satisfy the objective of sales only being made to credit-worthy customers.

14.3 D Statement reconciliations identify discrepancies between the payables ledger balances and suppliers' versions.

14.4 C The direction of the test is important here. The sample is taken from goods received notes as these represent deliveries. The auditor can then check that each delivery is supported by a valid order. If the sample is chosen from purchase orders (as in the first option) the test would confirm whether orders have been fulfilled. The remaining options are tests of controls regarding completeness of accounting information.

14.5 D This gives evidence that the correct payments have been made to the tax authorities.

Chapter 15

15.1 A Bank confirmations should always be carried out by the external auditor to ensure they cannot be tampered with. Providing advice on the implementation of a new payroll system would impair the internal auditors' independence. Reviewing the financial statements on behalf of the board is the responsibility of the audit committee, not internal audit.

15.2 D A value for money audit focuses on three Es: Economy, Efficiency and Effectiveness. A describes economy. C describes effectiveness. B only describes one aspect of efficiency.

15.3 A 2 and 4 are characteristics of external audit.

15.4 D This is an operational audit assignment.

15.5 C As employees of the company the internal auditors may lack independence.

Practice question bank

Chapter 1 Corporate governance and agency theory

1   With regard to the concept of agency, which of the following statements is true?

   A   The CEO is the agent of the company as principal.

   B   Auditors are the principals with shareholders as their agents.

   C   Shareholders of a company are agents of the directors as principals.

   D   Parliamentary representatives are principals and citizens are their agents.

2   Which of the following has NOT been a contributing factor towards growing expectations for best practice in corporate governance?

   A   Shareholder activism

   B   The globalisation of markets

   C   Higher expectations of institutional investors that their investments are protected

   D   The de-listing of public companies and growth in the number of private companies

3   What term is used to refer to arrangements that seek to ensure that the actions of the board of directors and executive management are performed in the best interests of the company and its shareholders?

   A   Utilitarianism

   B   Stakeholder theory

   C   Corporate governance

   D   Corporate social responsibility

4   Which of the following statements expresses the relationship between a company and its shareholders?

   A   Shareholders delegate the power to manage the company to a board of directors.

   B   Directors are given powers under the company's constitution and cannot delegate these to management.

   C   Shareholders should expect to be involved in management of the company at times of financial crisis.

   D   Shareholders should not be consulted about new appointments to the positions of chair of the board or chief executive officer (CEO).

5   The relevance of agency theory to corporate governance for a large listed company is mainly a consequence of

   A   The globalisation of markets.

   B   Corporate social responsibility.

   C   The separation of ownership and control.

   D   The appointment of non-executive directors to the board.

6   Which of the following groups would be least likely to be considered to be stakeholders in the activities of a nuclear power station?

    A   Employees
    B   Local residents
    C   The government
    D   Animal rights pressure group

7   Companies are often said to have information asymmetry, meaning that there is unevenness of access to information.

    Which of the following is the best definition of information asymmetry, with regard to companies?

    A   Principals have better access to information than agents.
    B   Agents have better access to information than principals.
    C   Directors understand information better than shareholders.
    D   Institutional shareholders are more knowledgeable than other shareholders, and so are able to interpret published information better.

8   According to agency theory, the requirement for the annual financial statements of a company to be audited is an example of

    A   Residual loss.
    B   Bonding cost.
    C   Opportunity cost.
    D   Monitoring cost.

9   Where there is information asymmetry (unevenness) giving rise to agency costs, this is because

    A   Agents hold more information than third parties.
    B   Principals generally have more information than agents.
    C   Information held by agents exceeds that held by principals.
    D   Third parties generally have more information than principals.

10 In the context of agency costs, which of the following is an example of a monitoring cost?

    A   External audit
    B   A director's company car
    C   A loss on an ill-considered takeover
    D   The opportunity cost of a risky investment that is not made

Chapter 2 Overview of corporate governance

11 An employee has been asked to prepare a presentation for the company directors on good corporate governance. Which of the following is NOT likely to be included in the presentation?

　A　Internal controls
　B　Risk management
　C　Accountability to stakeholders
　D　Maximising shareholder wealth

12 Which of the following is often considered to be a feature of poor corporate governance?

　A　Supervision of staff in key roles
　B　Lack of focus on short-term profitability
　C　Domination of the board by a single individual
　D　Critical questioning of senior managers by external auditors

13 In most countries, what is the usual purpose of codes of practice on corporate governance?

　A　To provide a comprehensive framework for management and administration
　B　To establish legally binding requirements to which all companies must adhere
　C　To set down detailed rules to regulate the ways in which companies must operate
　D　To provide guidance on the standards of best practice that companies should adopt

14 Governance is the system by which organisations are directed and controlled by senior officers. Which of the following statements is true?

　A　Governance systems apply in sole operator enterprises.
　B　Governance is an issue for large commercial organisations only.
　C　Not-for-profit organisations are exempt from governance issues.
　D　Commercial organisations, not-for-profit organisations and state-owned corporations may all face issues of governance.

15 Corporate governance represents principles, policies and procedures that determine

　A　How an organisation is financed.
　B　How an organisation is structured and owned.
　C　How an organisation is directed and controlled.
　D　How an organisation decides on types of products and services to produce.

16 Some commentators claim that there is a need for sound corporate governance both from a corporate perspective and also from a public policy perspective. Which of the following might be a public policy reason for sound corporate governance?

　A　To encourage enterprise, but to ensure that returns to shareholders are not obtained at the expense of society as a whole
　B　To maximise value, subject to the company meeting its financial, legal and contractual objectives
　C　To attract foreign investment and to broaden and deepen domestic capital markets by attracting more local investors
　D　To protect the interests of those who supply external finance to a company from those who have effective control over the company

17 Which of the following reflects a rules-based approach to corporate governance?

  A Sarbanes-Oxley Act
  B UK Corporate Governance Code
  C OECD Principles of Corporate Governance
  D None of the above

18 Which of the following is NOT one of the aims of an effective corporate governance framework?

  A Consistency with the rule of law
  B Maximisation of returns on investment
  C Promotion of transparent and efficient markets
  D Clear division of responsibilities between regulatory, supervisory and enforcement agencies

19 Which of the following are advantages of corporate governance?

  (1) It helps to increase the confidence of capital markets
  (2) It helps to prevent misuse of resources
  (3) It increases accountability to shareholders and other stakeholders
  (4) It provides an independent opinion on whether the accounts give a true and fair view.

  A (1), (2) and (3)
  B (1), (2) and (4)
  C (1), (3) and (4)
  D (2), (3) and (4)

20 What was the name of the 2003 UK report which covered non-executive directors?

  A The Cadbury Report
  B The Hampel Report
  C The Greenbury Report
  D The Higgs Report

Chapter 3 The board

21 Who has the primary responsibility in a large listed company for building strategies?

   A   The CEO
   B   The board chair
   C   The shareholders
   D   The board of directors

22 It is good corporate governance practice that companies should provide all directors with appropriate professional development opportunities. What is the reason for this?

   A   To help recognise and manage risk
   B   To structure the board to add value
   C   To make timely and balanced disclosure
   D   To lay solid foundations for management and oversight

23 Many corporate governance codes include a recommendation that companies should establish a gender diversity policy for board membership and report on its attainment.

   To which of the following objectives is this recommendation related?

   A   Manage risks effectively
   B   Respect the rights of shareholders
   C   Promote ethical and responsible decision-making
   D   Lay solid foundations for management and oversight

24 Which of the following is a characteristic of an Anglo-Saxon based system of corporate governance?

   A   Extensive cross-shareholdings by listed companies
   B   Boards of directors with many family members
   C   A widespread representation of interests on the board of directors, including employees
   D   Widespread equity ownership and large shareholdings by investment institutions

25 Which of the following is a common characteristic of the European two-tier system of corporate governance?

   A   There are employee representatives on the supervisory board.
   B   Some directors are members of both the supervisory and the management boards.
   C   Long-term shareholdings are common and these increase the risk of hostile takeovers.
   D   The agency problem is more serious than in a unitary-board system of corporate governance.

PRACTICE QUESTION BANK

26 To ensure good corporate governance, the responsibility to develop the requisite mix of skills among directors falls to

   A   The CEO
   B   The board chair
   C   The shareholders
   D   The nomination committee

27 Who is ultimately responsible for a company's financial statements?

   A   External auditors
   B   Board of directors
   C   Internal auditors
   D   Audit committee

28 Which of the following would not be performed by the board as a whole?

   A   Monitoring the Chief Executive Officer
   B   Overseeing strategy
   C   Monitoring risks, control systems and governance
   D   Preparing the financial statements

29 Match the board structure with the country in which it most likely to be found

Board structure	Country
(1) Chaebol	(a) Australia
(2) Unitary	(b) Japan
(3) Two-tier	(c) Korea
(4) Keiretsu	(d) Austria

   A   1a, 2b, 3c, 4d
   B   1a, 2c, 3d, 4b
   C   1c, 2a, 3d, 4b
   D   1b, 2c, 3d, 4a

30 Which of the following are characteristics of an effective board?

   (1)   Character
   (2)   Competence
   (3)   Coherence
   (4)   Communication

   A   (1) and (2)
   B   (3) and (4)
   C   (1) and (3)
   D   (2) and (4)

Chapter 4 Board members (directors)

31 Various bodies that have issued guidelines on corporate governance have identified three major areas for a potential conflict of interest for executive directors. Which of the following is NOT one of these three areas?

   A   The audit

   B   Risk management

   C   Executive remuneration

   D   Nominations to the board

32 The *UK Corporate Governance Code* requires that the board should be supplied in a timely manner with information of a form and of a quality appropriate to enable it to discharge its duties. Whose responsibility should it be to ensure that all directors are properly briefed on issues arising at board meetings?

   A   The chair

   B   Management

   C   The chief executive

   D   The board collectively

33 Which of the following provides the best definition of a non-executive director?

   A   A consultant to the board

   B   A director with limited responsibilities as director

   C   A director who is not a member of a board committee

   D   A director who does not hold a management position within the company

34 Which of the following is normally a non-independent non-executive director in a listed company?

   A   Chief financial officer (CFO)

   B   The head of the internal audit team

   C   Nominee director for a major shareholder

   D   An executive director of another listed company

35 Aaron, Beth, Connor and Daisy are all directors of XYZ Co. Aaron worked as chief accountant for a rival company until two years ago. Beth is the chief financial officer of XYZ Co. Connor is the sister of Seth, who is the CEO of XYZ Co. Daisy owns a company called ABC Co, which supplies a large amount of products to XYZ Co.

   Which of the following would be considered an independent non-executive director of XYZ Co?

   A   Aaron

   B   Beth

   C   Connor

   D   Daisy

PRACTICE QUESTION BANK

36 Which of the following statements is true?

A All directors are independent of their company.
B No executive director is independent of their company.
C All executive directors are independent of their company.
D All non-executive directors are independent of their company.

37 To ensure transparency in setting directors' remuneration, a key governance principle is that

A An audit committee should set executive pay.
B A nomination committee should set executive pay.
C No individual should be involved in setting their own pay.
D The annual directors' report should contain a summary of directors' pay.

38 Which of the following arrangements for determining the remuneration of directors is consistent with the *UK Corporate Governance Code*?

A The remuneration committee should decide the remuneration of all board directors.
B The remuneration for all non-executive directors should reflect the time commitment and responsibilities of the role.
C The remuneration committee should recommend and monitor the remuneration of the external auditor.
D The performance-related element in the remuneration of executive directors should be limited and should not be a significant part of the total remuneration package.

39 Which of the following principles or provisions is included in the *UK Corporate Governance Code* with regard to leadership and board effectiveness?

A Boards of large companies should have at least four non-executive directors.
B The chair of the board of directors should not also be chair of the nomination committee.
C A majority of members of the nomination committee should be independent non-executive directors.
D The board of a large company should consist of equal numbers of independent non-executive directors and other directors, excluding the chair.

40 Which of the following features are corporate governance weaknesses which a company would need to address prior to a listing?

(1) The chairman has sole responsibility for liaising with shareholders.
(2) The company has not established an internal audit function.
(3) The chairman and all of the NEDs are former executive directors of the company.

A 1 and 2 only
B 1 and 3 only
C 2 and 3 only
D 1, 2 and 3

Chapter 5 Board committees

41 The proposed membership of the audit committee of XYZ Co is:

Aaron (chief internal auditor)

Beth (existing executive director with some financial expertise)

Connor (proposed new independent director)

Daisy (existing independent director)

Which of these people should be on the audit committee?

- A   Aaron, Beth and Connor
- B   Beth, Connor and Daisy
- C   Aaron, Connor and Daisy
- D   Connor and Daisy

42 Which of the following statements are true about audit committees?

- (1)   The audit committee should be made up of independent non-executive directors
- (2)   The audit committee normally appoints the external auditors at the AGM
- (3)   The audit committee monitors and reviews the internal audit function
- (4)   The audit committee sets out the scope of the external auditor's work

- A   (1) and (2)
- B   (3) and (4)
- C   (1) and (3)
- D   (2) and (4)

43 Which of the following statements are true?

- (1)   Listed companies should establish an audit committee with at least four directors.
- (2)   Listed companies must establish an internal audit department.
- (3)   If listed companies have an audit committee and an internal audit department, the head of the internal audit department should report to the audit committee.
- (4)   Directors should not rely on the external audit to inform them of deficiencies in internal controls.

- A   (1) and (2)
- B   (3) and (4)
- C   (1) and (3)
- D   (2) and (4)

PRACTICE QUESTION BANK

44 Lynne is the finance director of ABC Co and a non-executive director (NED) of DEF Co. She serves on the remuneration committee and the risk committee of DEF Co. Rodney is the chief executive officer (CEO) of DEF Co and a NED of ABC Co. He is a member of ABC Co's audit committee and remuneration committee.

Which of the following statements is correct in relation to improving corporate governance?

A Lynne should not be a member of the risk committee as she is a NED and will know nothing about operational risks

B Rodney should not be a NED of any company as he is DEF Co's CEO

C Either Lynne or Rodney should resign as a member of a remuneration committee

D Neither Lynne nor Rodney should serve on any more than one standing committee

45 Which of the following are included in the responsibilities of an audit committee?

(1) To review arrangements which allow staff to 'whistleblow' any frauds discovered

(2) To establish a rewards policy and financial package for existing directors

(3) To review the internal financial controls and risk management systems

(4) To recruit and review performance of directors

A (1) and (3)

B (1) and (4)

C (2) and (3)

D (2) and (4)

46 Which of the following describes the UK Corporate Governance Code recommendation concerning the composition of the nomination committee of the board?

A All the members of the committee should be independent and it should be chaired by the chair of the board.

B The majority of the members should be independent and it should be chaired by the finance director.

C The majority of the members should be independent and it should be chaired by an independent director.

D All the members of the committee should be independent and it should be chaired by an independent director.

47 Which of the following structures for the composition of an audit committee for a listed company is most likely to meet requirements for good practice in corporate governance?

A A committee consisting entirely of independent directors

B A committee consisting entirely of non-executive directors

C A committee with an executive director chair and all other members who are non-executive directors

D A committee with a non-executive chair, one representative of management and other members who are non-executive directors

48 The board of directors of TBF Ltd has decided to establish an audit committee which will be made up of three independent non-executive directors. As the company has six independent non-executive directors, three will serve on the committee in the first year and the other three will then serve for the next year. Of the six non-executive directors, only one has a comprehensive knowledge of financial operations. One of the non-executive directors will also serve as the chairman of the company for the next year and it has been decided that he will also be the chairman of the audit committee for this period.

According to best practice in corporate governance, which of the following statements is correct in relation to the above arrangements?

(1) It is inappropriate for the chairman of the company to be chairman of the audit committee at the same time

(2) The audit committee should be made up of a majority of non-executive directors.

(3) The audit committee will not have the necessary competences to discharge its responsibilities in the second year

(4) The non-executive directors should only serve one year, so no arrangements should be put in place in relation to the composition of the audit committee for the second year.

A   (1) and (3)

B   (2) and (4)

C   (1) and (2)

D   (3) and (4)

49 ABC Co is a large listed company. The finance department of ABC Co has completed the preparation of the draft financial statements.

To which of the following will these statements be submitted initially for scrutiny?

A   The external auditors

B   The audit committee

C   The board of directors

D   The internal auditors

50 Which of the following is NOT a reason for establishing committees of a board of directors in a listed company?

A   To distribute the workload of the board

B   To provide an independent perspective where conflicts of interest may arise

C   To provide the opportunity for specific issues to be discussed in greater detail

D   To take responsibility for decisions in matters where a conflict of interest may arise with executive directors

Chapter 6 Stakeholders, corporate social responsibility and sustainability

51 Which of the following is TRUE in relation to Corporate and Social Responsibility (CSR)

    A   In the context of CSR, social costs are the monetary amounts involved in complying with sustainability reporting requirements.

    B   A company that places emphasis on CSR recognises that managing relationships with multiple stakeholders is vital for long-term success.

    C   CSR is shareholder focussed, recognising the organisation exists to increase the wealth of these key stakeholders

    D   In the context of CSR, corporate citizenship refers to business partnerships with other organisations to form a corporate community targeting common goals.

52 A company's board should consider, manage and report on its sustainability related impacts and dependencies.

Which one of the following is a sustainability related dependency?

    A   Worker health

    B   Greenhouse gas emissions produced by the company

    C   Use of natural resources

    D   Waste produced by the company.

53 Which of the following should **NOT** be included in an effective annual sustainability report?

    A   ESG Key Performance measures

    B   The sustainability reporting framework adopted

    C   Narrative containing greenwashing

    D   A board statement including relevant actions taken

54 Which one of the following is false in relation to sustainability committees?

    A   Corporate governance codes, such as the UK Corporate Governance Code require listed entities to establish a sustainability committee made up of non-executive directors

    B   A benefit of establishing a sustainability committee is the potential to take advantage of commercial opportunities that may otherwise not have been recognised.

    C   The sustainability committee should review the entity's ESG-related reporting prior to approval, including the annual sustainability report.

    D   The number of members on a sustainability committee should be comparable with other board-level committees.

55 A government notices that one of the biggest corporate groups based in the region is taking advantage of a tax exemption by structuring its business in a particular way, allowing it to avoid paying tax on 30% of its revenues. As a result, the government forces through a change in tax legislation that will mean all revenues of the corporate group will be taxed in the next financial year.

This change in tax legislation can be categorised as which one of the following?

A   A connected stakeholder's response to a stakeholder risk

B   An entity's response to a connected stakeholder's risk

C   An external stakeholder's response to a stakeholder risk

D   An entity's response to an external stakeholder's risk

PRACTICE QUESTION BANK

Chapter 7 Risk and control

56 A principle of good corporate governance is that the board should maintain a sound system of risk management and internal control to safeguard shareholders' investment and the company's assets. The directors should therefore monitor the effectiveness of the company's system of internal control.

Which of the following would NOT be covered by this monitoring process?

A   Financial controls

B   Risk management

C   Operating and compliance controls

D   The effectiveness of the external auditors

57 Which of the following groups has responsibility for internal control within a company?

A   The internal audit department

B   The audit committee

C   The Board of Directors

D   The external auditor

58 Match the name of the risk with the definition.

Type of risk	Definition
(1) Business risks	(a) Risks that relate to the fundamental decisions that the directors take about the future of the organisation.
(2) Operational risks	(b) Risks that relate to the fundamental decisions that the directors take about the future of the organisation.
(3) Strategic risks	(c) The threat that an event or action will adversely affect a business's ability to achieve its ongoing objective. It can arise due to external and internal factors.

A   1a, 2b, 3c

B   1c, 2b, 3a

C   1b, 2c, 3a

D   1b, 2a, 3c

59 Which of the following statements are true about strategic objectives and business risk?

	Strategic objective	Business risk
A	Profit maximisation	Risk that operations will be inefficient
B	Increased market share	Risks that could damage ability to make profit
C	Profit maximisation	Risks that could damage ability to make profit
D	Increased market share	Risk that operations will be inefficient

PRACTICE QUESTION BANK

60 ABC Co has identified the following risks by the following means:

(1) The payroll clerk identified the risk that uncollected pay-packets could be stolen.

(2) The office manager identified the risk that items of office equipment could be damaged by misuse.

What type of risk identification approach is being used?

	Risk 1	Risk 2
A	Top-down	Bottom-up
B	Bottom-up	Top-down
C	Top-down	Top-down
D	Bottom-up	Bottom-up

61 You are reviewing a risk assessment performed at ABC Co.

(1) The payroll clerk identified the risk that uncollected pay-packets could be stolen. This risk was stated to be once in 5 years.

(2) The office manager identified the risk that items of office equipment could be damaged by misuse, amounting to an estimated potential loss of $2,000.

What is being assessed in relation to each of these risks?

	Risk 1	Risk 2
A	Likelihood	Impact
B	Impact	Likelihood
C	Likelihood	Likelihood
D	Impact	Impact

62 XYZ Co is a haulage company and has a fleet of vehicles. Which risk management strategies would be best for managing the risk of vehicle theft?

(1) Avoidance

(2) Mitigation

(3) Transfer

(4) Acceptance

A (1) and (2)

B (3) and (4)

C (1) and (4)

D (2) and (3)

63 What is the name of the diagram used to plot the likelihood and severity of risk?

A Risk graph

B Risk matrix

C Risk diagram

D Risk chart

64 Which of the following are examples of internal controls?
- (1) Internal audit
- (2) Insurance against theft
- (3) Locking up moveable assets
- (4) Training of accounting staff

A (1), (2) and (3)
B (1), (2) and (4)
C (1), (3) and (4)
D (2), (3) and (4)

65 Which of the following statements about the risk management committee are true?
- (1) The UK corporate governance code requires the formation of a risk management committee
- (2) The risk management committee should monitor overall exposure to risk and ensure it remains within limits set by the board
- (3) Internal audit should report to the risk management committee
- (4) The risk management committee should review reports on key risks prepared by business operating units, management and the board

A (1) and (2)
B (3) and (4)
C (1) and (3)
D (2) and (4)

Chapter 8 The nature and purpose of auditing

66 Which of the following statements best describes an auditor's responsibility regarding a client's compliance with laws and regulations which do not have a direct impact on the financial statements, in line with ISA 250 (Revised) *Consideration of Laws and Regulations in an Audit of Financial Statements*?

    A   The auditor should actively prevent and detect non-compliance with the regulations.

    B   The auditor should perform specific audit procedures to identify possible non-compliance.

    C   The auditor should obtain sufficient appropriate audit evidence about a client's compliance with all regulations.

    D   The auditor has no responsibility in respect to regulations which do not have a direct effect on the financial statements.

67 A partner in your audit firm has informed you that a particular engagement is an assurance engagement.

Which of the following would **NOT** have been relevant to the partner in forming this opinion?

    A   The existence of a three-party relationship

    B   The existence of suitable criteria

    C   The determination of materiality

    D   The subject matter

68 What is the level of assurance and type of opinion can be provided on a review engagement?

	Level of assurance	Report wording
A	Reasonable	Positive
B	Reasonable	Negative
C	Limited	Positive
D	Limited	Negative

69 Which **two** of the following are elements of an assurance engagement?

    (1)   A three-party relationship

    (2)   Suitable criteria

    (3)   Determination of materiality

    (4)   An engagement letter

    A   (1) and (2) only

    B   (1) and (3) only

    C   (2) and (3) only

    D   (1), (2) and (3)

PRACTICE QUESTION BANK

70 Which of the following statements best defines the external audit?

    A   The external audit is an exercise carried out by auditors in order to give an opinion on whether the financial statements of a company are fairly presented.

    B   The external audit is an exercise carried out in order to give an opinion on the effectiveness of a company's internal control system.

    C   The purpose of the external audit is to identify areas of deficiency within a company and to make recommendations to mitigate those deficiencies.

    D   The external audit provides negative assurance on the truth and fairness of a company's financial statements.

71 Which of the following is not a limitation of auditing?

    A   Sampling is used as an audit tool

    B   Internal control systems have inherent limitations

    C   Client staff may collude in fraud

    D   Unqualified staff may be used on audit assignments

72 External auditors express an opinion on a company's financial statements in an auditor's report. To whom is this addressed?

    A   The members

    B   Those charged with governance

    C   Senior management

    D   The board of directors

73 Who is responsible for the prevention and detection of fraud within an organisation?

    A   External auditor

    B   Directors

    C   Internal auditors

    D   Audit committee

74 Which of the following statements is true in respect of the external audit?

    A   An external audit is undertaken by the management of a company to assess the effectiveness of the internal controls.

    B   An external audit is carried out in order for auditors to report independently on the truth and fairness of a company's financial statements.

    C   An external audit is performed with the express purpose of reporting on deficiencies in internal control.

    D   An external audit must always consist of an interim audit visit and a final audit visit.

75 Which of the following statements explains one of the reasons why external audits provide reasonable, but not absolute, assurance?

    A   Some reliance is placed on the work of internal audit.

    B   Not all transactions and balances are examined.

    C   The audit has to be completed within a specific timeframe.

    D   Not all members of the audit team are fully qualified accountants.

Chapter 9 Regulation of audit

76 Which of the following is the correct definition of 'integrity' in accordance with the IESBA Code of Ethics?

    A   To not allow bias, conflicts of interest or undue influence of others to override professional or business judgements

    B   To maintain professional knowledge and skill at the level required to ensure that a client or employer receives competent professional services based on current developments in practice, legislation and techniques and act diligently and in accordance with applicable technical and professional standards

    C   To comply with relevant laws and regulations and avoid any action that discredits the profession

    D   To be straightforward and honest in all business and professional relationships

77 A professional accountant agrees to falsify accounting records to improve the results of his employer. Which fundamental principle of ethical behaviour is the accountant in breach of?

    A   Objectivity

    B   Integrity

    C   Confidentiality

    D   Professional competence

78 The fundamental principles are integrity, confidentiality, professional behaviour, professional competence and due care, and

    A   fairness.

    B   objectivity.

    C   impartiality.

    D   trustworthiness.

79 The fundamental principle of professional competence and due care is best defined as:

    A   Exercising reasonable judgment when making decisions.

    B   Adherence to all appropriate accounting standards and ethical rules.

    C   The provision of a quality of service that can reasonably be expected from a skilled and qualified practitioner.

    D   Refraining from performing any services that you cannot perform with reasonable care, competence and diligence.

80 The accountant's fundamental principle of confidentiality is best defined as:

    A   A duty to restrict access to all documents in your possession.

    B   A duty to control access to all documents and information for which you are responsible.

    C   A duty to keep confidential all potentially sensitive data to which one has gained access in the course of one's work.

    D   A duty to safeguard the security of information in your possession unless there is a legal or professional right or duty to disclose.

81 The fundamental principle of professional behaviour is best defined as:

   A   Adherence to all accounting standards currently in force.
   B   Not doing anything that might bring discredit to the profession.
   C   Behaviour that is in accord with both the spirit and the letter of the ethical guidelines.
   D   Behaviour which, if conducted to appropriate standards, would justify the charging of a fee.

82 An accountant takes work home to complete over a weekend to ensure the work is completed on time. During the weekend, in completing it, they spent considerably less time on the work than if they had done it in the office in normal working hours.

   Which of the fundamental principles is the member at risk of breaching?

   A   Integrity
   B   Objectivity
   C   Professional behaviour
   D   Professional competence and due care

83 Who normally appoints the external auditors of a company?

   A   Directors
   B   Shareholders
   C   Audit committee
   D   Those charged with governance

84 Which of the following statements, if any, are true?

   (1) The international body which oversees the accounting profession is the International Federation of Auditors (IFAC)
   (2) Global standards for auditors are issued by the International Auditing and Ethical Standards Board (IAESB).

   A   (1) only
   B   (2) only
   C   Both (1) and (2)
   D   Neither (1) nor (2)

85 Which of the following statements about the role of the International Audit and Assurance Standards Board (IAASB), if any, are true?

   (1) IAASB is committed to producing high quality audit standards and promoting international convergence in auditing practice.
   (2) IAASB is a constituent body of IFAC.

   A   (1) only
   B   (2) only
   C   Both (1) and (2)
   D   Neither (1) nor (2)

Chapter 10 The audit process

There are no questions on Chapter 10 specifically as it provides an overview of information covered in subsequent chapters.

Chapter 11 Risk assessment

86 The auditor of A Co wishes to reduce audit risk. Which of the following actions could the auditor take to achieve this?

   (1) Increase sample sizes

   (2) Reduce control risk

   (3) Assign more experienced staff to the engagement team

   A (1) only

   B (2) only

   C (1) and (3)

   D (2) and (3)

87 When gaining an understanding of the specific business operations of an audit client, which of the following matters would an auditor need to consider?

   A Accounting principles and industry specific accounting practices which are relevant to the client's business

   B Acquisitions or disposals of the client's business activities

   C Leasing of property, plant or equipment for use in the client's business

   D Products or services and markets of the client's business

88 Which of the following procedures must the auditor use to obtain an understanding of the entity and its environment in accordance with ISA 315 (Revised) *Identifying and Assessing the Risks of Material Misstatement*?

   (1) Analytical procedures

   (2) Inquiry

   (3) Confirmation

   (4) Reperformance

   A (1), (2) and (3)

   B (1) and (2)

   C (2), (3) and (4)

   D (1) and (4)

89 Which of the following is an example of an inherent risk factor?

   A The company is rapidly expanding.

   B There is no log in or password required to access the accounting system.

   C The company does not maintain a non-current asset register to record its assets.

   D No backups are taken of the computer system at the end of each day.

90 As part of audit planning, an audit team needs to obtain an understanding of the company's system of internal control.

Which of the following is **NOT** a component of an entity's system of internal control?

A   The control environment

B   Control activities relevant to the audit

C   The selection and application of accounting policies

D   The information system and communication relevant to the preparation of the financial statements

91 Which of the following statements does not illustrate an inherent risk?

A   The organisation is seeking to raise finance to diversify

B   The auditor uses samples when carrying out audit testing

C   Directors participate in a profit-related bonus scheme

D   The financial statements contain complex transactions

92 When gaining an understanding of the financial reporting systems of an audit client which of the following matters would an auditor need to consider?

A   Accounting principles and industry specific practices relevant to the client's business

B   Qualifications of the members of the audit committee

C   Major competitors

D   Products or services and markets of the client's business

93 Why do auditors need to obtain an understanding of the client and its environment?

A   To assist them in designing and performing further audit procedures

B   To help them estimate how much the audit will cost

C   To ascertain whether the auditor's report will be modified or not

D   To assist them when writing their report to management

94 What are the two elements of the risk of material misstatement at the assertion level?

A   Inherent risk and detection risk

B   Audit risk and detection risk

C   Inherent risk and control risk

D   Detection risk and control risk

95 During which of the following stages of the audit **MUST** analytical procedures be used, in accordance with International Standards on Auditing?

(1) Audit planning

(2) Audit fieldwork (as a substantive test)

(3) Audit completion

A   (1) and (3) only

B   (1), (2) and (3)

C   (1) only

D   (2) and (3) only

PRACTICE QUESTION BANK

96 The auditor of Berry Co, a manufacturing company, has noted an increase in total sales value but a decrease in the company's gross profit percentage for 20X1 as compared to the previous year.

Which of the following is consistent with, and adequately explains, the decrease?

(1) Sales volumes have decreased as compared to 20X0.

(2) During 20X1, due to a scarcity of supply the company had to pay higher prices when purchasing components.

(3) During 20X1, a major component supplier withdrew early settlement discounts previously granted.

A   (1) only

B   (1) and (2) only

C   (2) only

D   (3) only

97 Which of the following factors could be the reason for an **INCREASE** in reported gross profit in the financial statements of a company?

(1) A reduction in carriage outward costs for the period under review

(2) A reduction in carriage inward costs for the period under review

(3) An increase in the amount of discount received from suppliers of components for early payment of purchase invoices

A   (1) and (2) only

B   (2) only

C   (3) only

D   (1), (2) and (3)

98 Which of the following statements, if any, are true?

(1) Auditors are required to obtain an understanding of the entity and its environment only when the client is a new client.

(2) Auditors are required to obtain an understanding of the entity and its environment so that they are able to assess the risks relating to the audit.

A   (1) only

B   (2) only

C   Both (1) and (2)

D   Neither (1) nor (2)

PRACTICE QUESTION BANK

99 Which combination of the following definitions is correct?

Term	Definition
Inherent risk	(a) The risk that the system of internal control at the company does not detect, correct or prevent misstatements
Control risk	(b) The risk that auditors do not discover misstatements in the financial statements
Detection risk	(c) The risk arising as a result of the nature of the business, its transactions and environment.

A 1a, 2b, 3c

B 1b, 2c, 3a

C 1c, 2a, 3b

D 1b, 2a, 3c

100 The auditor takes a number of steps after gaining an understanding of a client and its environment.

Which ONE of the following steps would **NOT** be taken?

A Identify inherent and control risks while obtaining an understanding of the entity

B Relate identified risks to what could go wrong at a financial statement level

C Consider if the risks could cause material misstatement

D Identify detection risk as part of a review of audit firm procedure

101 An auditor has performed analytical procedures as part of the planning process. Match the finding with the most likely conclusion that should be drawn.

Finding	Conclusion
(1) Sales revenue has increased by 3% but the gross profit margin is down by 1.5%.	(a) More information required to draw a conclusion
(2) Sales in the last month of the year were 5% higher than in previous years, and also 4% higher than the average for a month for the company.	(b) Sales revenue may be overstated
	(c) Sales revenue may be understated

A 1a, 2b,

B 1a, 2c

C 1b, 2a

D 1b, 2c

250

102 Which of the following factors are likely to increase the risk of misstatement?

    (1) The company operates in a highly regulated industry.

    (2) The company has an internal audit function committed to monitoring internal controls.

    (3) The company has set ambitious growth targets for all its salesmen, to be judged at the end of the financial year.

    A   (1), (2) and (3)

    B   (1) and (2) only

    C   (1) and (3) only

    D   (2) and (3) only

103 Which of the following will lead to a decrease in control risk?

    (1) The role of sales ledger clerk has been filled by four different people during the year, following the retirement of a long-standing sales ledger clerk at the end of last year.

    (2) The financial controller is a qualified accountant, as are two of his high level staff.

    (3) The directors have a positive attitude towards controls and enforce them company-wide.

    A   (1), (2) and (3)

    B   (1) and (2) only

    C   (1) and (3) only

    D   (2) and (3) only

104 Which of the following statements about materiality are true?

    (1) Materiality means the importance of a matter to users.

    (2) It is relevant to auditors because they will only test items which are material.

    (3) Calculating materiality and selecting samples on the basis of materiality helps the auditor to reduce audit risk to an acceptable level.

    A   (1), (2) and (3)

    B   (1) and (2) only

    C   (1) and (3) only

    D   (2) and (3) only

105 Which of the following does not suggest a significant risk?

    A   A risk of fraud

    B   A complex transaction

    C   A significant transaction with a related party

    D   A transaction in the normal course of business for the entity

106 The auditor of Fig Co, which is a manufacturing company, has noted an increase in total sales value but a decrease in the company's gross profit margin for 20X5, as compared to the previous year.

Which of the following is consistent with, and adequately explains, the decrease in the gross profit margin?

- A   The number of units sold has decreased as compared to 20X4.
- B   Wage bonuses payable to the company's sales force increased in relation to sales values as compared to 20X4.
- C   During 20X5, the company had to pay higher prices when purchasing components.
- D   During 20X5, a major component supplier withdrew early settlement discounts previously granted.

107 When planning an audit of financial statements, the external auditor is required to consider how factors such as the entity's operating environment and its system of internal control affect the risk of misstatement in the financial statements.

Identify whether each of the following factors are likely to increase or reduce the risk of misstatement by selecting the appropriate option.

Factor	Increase or decrease
(1) Directors communicate and enforce integrity and ethical values.	(a) Increase
(2) Top managers are offered profit related bonuses, which are scaled according to the level of profit achieved.	(b) Decrease
(3) The entity has not taken any action about matters raised in the report to management from the previous three audits.	

- A   1a, 2a, 3a
- B   1b, 2b, 3b
- C   1a, 2b, 3b
- D   1b, 2a, 3a

108 Identify whether each of the following factors are likely to increase or reduce control risk by selecting the appropriate option.

Factor	Increase or decrease
(1) There is a large staff in the accounting department, and key areas are segregated between different staff.	(a) Increase
(2) Financial statements are produced by the financial controller after he has carried out a large number of journals to get things in order.	(b) Decrease

- A   1a, 2a
- B   1b, 2b
- C   1a, 2b
- D   1b, 2a

109 Which of the following factors are likely to lead to the auditor assessing that there is an decrease in control risk?

(1) The financial controller submits detailed budgets to the managing director and scrutinises variances from actual in detail.

(2) The company has a detailed set of control procedures which staff are required to follow.

(3) The directors ensure there is good segregation of duties at the company

A (1), (2) and (3)

B (1) and (2) only

C (1) and (3) only

D (1) and (2) only

110 Which of the following must the auditor use to obtain an understanding of the entity and its environment in accordance with ISA 315 (Revised) *Identifying and Assessing the Risks of Material Misstatement*?

A Analytical procedures

B Tests of detail

C Confirmation

D Recalculation

PRACTICE QUESTION BANK

Chapter 12 Internal controls

111 You are the audit manager of ABC, a charity. You have noted in the detailed audit plan that ABC's control environment may be weak.

Which of the following statements are valid reasons as to why ABC may have a weak control environment?

(1) ABC has a detailed constitution which explains how the charity's income can be spent.

(2) ABC finance department relies on volunteers who may not have accounts experience.

(3) A high proportion of the income of ABC is cash.

(4) Understaffing in the finance department at certain times is due to the ad hoc nature of volunteer working hours.

A (1) and (2)
B (3) and (4)
C (1) and (3)
D (2) and (4)

112 With respect to the achievement of the company's objectives, the internal control system should provide:

A Absolute assurance
B Reasonable assurance
C No assurance, because internal control is nothing to do with achieving objectives
D Negative assurance, because positive assurance is not a realistic objective

113 Which of the following is correct with respect to external auditors?

(1) They may rely on internal controls in order to reduce substantive procedures.

(2) They do not report to management on the effectiveness of internal control.

(3) They report to management any material deficiencies discovered in internal control.

(4) They can insist that a client implements good internal controls.

A (1) and (2)
B (3) and (4)
C (1) and (3)
D (2) and (4)

114 Which of the following is an example of a preventative control?

A Working out gross profit percentages of each shop in a business that has a number of similar shops
B Taking regular back-ups of the accounting system
C Regular inventory counts
D Keeping inventory in a secure location

115 Which of the following is *not* an objective of a system of internal control?

    A   To increase the efficiency of operations

    B   To increase the effectiveness of operations

    C   To provide reasonable safeguarding of the organisation's assets

    D   To prevent and detect all fraud

116 Which of the following controls would be designed to ensure accuracy over input of data?

    A   A range check

    B   A sequence check

    C   Password protection

    D   Authorisation

117 What are the two classifications of control procedures in an IT environment?

    A   General controls and information processing controls

    B   System controls and information processing controls

    C   Edit controls and sequence controls

    D   General controls and specific controls

118 Information processing controls are manual or automated procedures that operate over accounting applications to ensure that all transactions are complete and accurate.

Which of the following are Information processing controls?

    (1)   Password protection of programs

    (2)   Existence checks

    (3)   One for one checking

    (4)   Regular back up of programs

    A   (1) and (4)

    B   (3) and (4)

    C   (1) and (2)

    D   (2) and (3)

119 What is the correct order for the following steps to be taken during an audit?

    (1)   Perform walkthrough tests

    (2)   Complete flowcharts and internal control evaluation questionnaires

    (3)   Revise the audit strategy and audit plan

    (4)   Perform tests of control

    A   1, 2, 3, 4

    B   4, 3, 2, 1

    C   2, 1, 4, 3

    D   3, 2, 4, 1

120 Which of the following are examples of good internal control within a company?

(1) Internal audit department
(2) Segregation of duties
(3) External audit
(4) Audit committee

A (1), (2), (3) and (4)
B (1), (3) and (4) only
C (1), (2) and (4) only
D (2) and (3) only

121 Which of the following statements describe the **PRIMARY** purpose of an external auditor evaluating and testing the internal controls of a limited liability company?

A To be in a position to advise management of any deficiencies in internal control
B To be able to assess control risk and determine the level of substantive procedures required
C To be able to confirm in their auditor's report that management have maintained an adequate system of internal control during the period
D To demonstrate that they have a proper understanding of their audit client

122 Which of the following is a component of an entity's system of internal control?

A Information system and communication relevant to financial reporting
B Internal control questionnaires
C The head of internal audit reporting to the audit committee
D Segregation of duties

123 Which of the following is **NOT** an example of a control activity?

A Bank reconciliations are prepared each month by the accountant.
B Entry to the inventory store room is by keypad.
C Senior managers have to authorise all purchase order requests.
D There is an IT policy handbook in place.

124 Which of the following is the correct definition of general IT controls?

A Controls that are preventative or detective in nature and are designed to ensure the integrity of the accounting records
B Policies and procedures that relate to many applications and support the effective functioning of information processing controls
C Programmes designed for auditors which carry out audit procedures automatically
D Controls which isolate a sample of transactions for testing by the internal audit function to determine whether controls are operating as per the IT manual

125 Which of the following is **NOT** an example of a general IT control?

    A   All computer users must change their log-on password every six weeks.

    B   Information on computer servers is backed up every day.

    C   The accounting system has a program installed which produces control totals.

    D   The computer system has a firewall installed.

126 Which of the following statements is a **NOT** a valid reason to explain the inherent limitations of control systems?

    A   There is potential for human error.

    B   The auditors cannot test every transaction and balance.

    C   Controls can be bypassed or overridden.

    D   The cost of controls does not outweigh their benefit.

127 What is the primary purpose of the report to management (letter on internal control)?

    A   It sets out management's responsibilities and those of the auditor.

    B   It sets out deficiencies found in the internal control system and makes recommendations to overcome those deficiencies.

    C   It states the audit fee for the audit.

    D   It states whether the financial statements are true and fair.

128 Which of the following is **NOT** a recognised method for recording a company's accounting and control systems?

    A   Questionnaires

    B   Disclosure checklists

    C   Narrative notes

    D   Flow charts

129 Which of the following statements, if any, are true?

    (1)   The control environment is the attitudes, awareness and actions of management and those charged with governance about internal control and its importance.

    (2)   If the directors follow control activities themselves and encourage others to do so, if they promote an attitude in a company that internal control is important, and encourage staff to monitor their own performance and the performance of others in observing control, then they can contribute to an excellent control environment.

    (3)   If directors override controls in a company and give other staff the impression that controls are not important, then they will be strongly contributing to a good control environment.

    A   (1), (2) and (3)

    B   (1) and (2) only

    C   (1) and (3) only

    D   (2) and (3) only

PRACTICE QUESTION BANK

130 Which of the following, if any, is a computerised information system?

(1) An information system that is heavily documented in physical ledgers.

(2) A system which is retained predominantly in electronic format.

A (1) only

B (2) only

C (1) and (2)

D Neither (1) nor (2)

131 What is the correct matching of control and control type?

Control	Type of control
(1) A company will not place an order for goods until a senior member of staff has confirmed that order.	(a) Physical controls
(2) A company locks the storeroom so that raw materials cannot be accessed.	(b) Information processing
(3) An accounts department is organised so that Debbie is in charge of invoicing and Phil is in charge of receipts.	(c) Segregation of duties

A 1a, 2b, 3c

B 1b, 2c, 3a

C 1a, 2c, 3b

D 1b, 2a, 3c

132 Which of the following will not contribute to a strong control environment?

(1) Directors document control policies and procedures and communicate them to all staff.

(2) Directors demand staff push themselves to obtain goals and promote the concept of 'by any means possible'.

(3) A director has perpetrated a fraud.

A (1) only

B (2) only

C (1) and (2)

D (2) and (3)

133 Which of the following is not an inherent limitation of systems of internal control?

A Employees may make mistakes implementing controls.

B Controls may have been badly designed by management.

C Employees and third parties may collude to circumvent controls.

D Controls may be too expensive to operate on a daily basis.

134 Your audit junior is seeking to understand when deficiencies in internal control would be judged to be significant and therefore should be reported to those charged with governance.

Which of the following factors would influence your judgement of whether the control deficiencies identified at Swan are significant?

(1) The likelihood of material misstatement resulting
(2) The fact that a system is new
(3) The number of deficiencies identified

A (1), (2) and (3)
B (1) and (2) only
C (1) and (3) only
D (2) and (3) only

135 In the context of a computer-based accounting system, which of the following are general information technology controls?

(1) Document counts
(2) Virus checks on software
(3) Maintenance of program logs

A (1) only
B (1) and (2) only
C (2) and (3) only
D (3) only

Chapter 13 Audit evidence

136 ISA 520 *Analytical Procedures* states that where analytical procedures identify fluctuations or relationships that are inconsistent with other relevant information or that differ significantly from the expected results, the auditor shall investigate the reason for this.

Which of the following auditor responses to the increase in the receivables collection period of a client is the **LEAST** relevant?

A Make enquiries of management to understand the likely reason why the receivables collection period exceeds the extended credit period

B Perform detailed substantive testing on the aged receivables listing, to determine whether any amounts should be written off

C Perform a trend analysis on current year and prior year monthly revenue, to identify whether revenue is overstated as a result of fraud or error

D Perform further working capital ratio analysis, to determine the effect of the extended credit on the cash position

137 As part of the audit of receivables it is common for auditors to ask their client to write to their customers to obtain a reply confirming the debt. Which of the following assertions will this procedure address?

(1) Existence

(2) Valuation

(3) Completeness

(4) Rights and obligations

A 2 and 3

B 1 and 4

C 2 and 4

D 1, 2, 3 and 4

138 Which of the following is a test of control?

A Carrying out analytical procedures.

B Tracing purchase invoices to the credit of supplier accounts.

C Performing a bank reconciliation where the client has not.

D Observing warehouse staff count goods as they are received.

139 The auditor of M Co has agreed a sample of non-current assets selected by physical inspection back to the non-current asset register.

For which of the following assertions does this test provide assurance?

A Completeness

B Existence

C Rights and obligations

D Accuracy and valuation

140 Which of the following statements most accurately describes substantive audit procedures?

- A Substantive audit procedures consist of analytical procedures and tests of controls.
- B Substantive audit procedures are tests to obtain audit evidence about the design and operation of an entity's internal control system.
- C Substantive audit procedures are tests to obtain audit evidence to detect material misstatements in the financial statements.
- D Substantive audit procedures are only carried out when the internal control system is assessed as being strong.

141 Which of the following is **NOT** a financial statement assertion relating to transactions and events and related disclosures?

- A Completeness
- B Occurrence
- C Existence
- D Presentation

142 Which of the following financial statement assertions are relevant to account balances at the period end and related disclosures?

- (i) Rights and obligations
- (ii) Cut-off
- (iii) Existence

- A (i) only
- B (i) and (ii)
- C (i) and (iii)
- D (iii) only

143 Which of the following factors influence the auditor's judgement as to what constitutes sufficient, appropriate audit evidence?

- (1) Risk
- (2) Cost
- (3) Materiality
- (4) Experience from prior audits

- A (1), (2) and (3)
- B (1), (3) and (4)
- C (3) and (4)
- D (2), (3) and (4)

PRACTICE QUESTION BANK

144 Which of the below factors influence the auditor's judgement regarding the sufficiency of the evidence obtained?

(1) The materiality of the account
(2) The size of the account
(3) The source and quality of the evidence available
(4) The amount of time allocated to the audit

A   1 and 3
B   2 and 4
C   2 and 3
D   1 and 4

145 Which of the following procedures is most reliable in confirming the valuation of a client's bank balance?

A   Inspecting the cash book
B   Inspecting the bank reconciliation
C   Inspecting the bank statement
D   Inspecting the bank letter (letter written by auditor to bank)

146 The payables ledger clerk at a client compares supplier statements with payables ledger accounts on a monthly basis. This action is most useful in supporting which of the following assertions?

A   Classification
B   Rights and obligations
C   Existence
D   Completeness

147 Which of the following statements most accurately describes tests of control?

A   Tests of control consist of analytical procedures and tests of detail.
B   Tests of control are tests to obtain audit evidence about the design and operation of an entity's internal control system.
C   Tests of control are tests to obtain audit evidence to detect material misstatements in the financial statements.
D   Tests of control are only carried out when the internal control system is assessed as being weak.

148 Which of the following are financial statement assertions relating to transactions and events and related disclosures?

(1) Completeness
(2) Occurrence
(3) Existence

A   (1) and (2)
B   (1) and (3)
C   (2) and (3)
D   All three

149 Which of the following financial statement assertions are not relevant to account balances at the period end and related disclosures?

  (1) Rights and obligations
  (2) Cut-off
  (3) Existence

  A (1) only
  B (2) only
  C (1) and (3)
  D (3) only

150 Which of the following factors should not influence the auditor's judgement as to what constitutes sufficient, appropriate audit evidence?

  (1) Risk
  (2) Cost
  (3) Materiality
  (4) Experience from prior audits

  A (1), and (3) only
  B (2) and (4) only
  C (1) only
  D (2) only

151 Which of the following are examples of 'reperformance' in the context of procedures carried out by an auditor to obtain audit evidence?

  (1) Carrying out arithmetical checks of copy sales invoice documentation
  (2) Carrying out an end of year bank reconciliation
  (3) Extracting a trial balance from the general ledger of the audit client

  A (1) and (2) only
  B (2) and (3) only
  C (1) and (3) only
  D All of the above

152 Which of the following audit procedures is a valid test for the existence of tangible non-current assets?

  A Inspecting title deeds to buildings
  B Agreeing figures on the valuation certificate for a building to the general ledger
  C Agreeing a sample of assets selected by physical inspection back to the non-current assets register
  D Physically inspecting a sample of assets selected from the non-current assets register

PRACTICE QUESTION BANK

153 For which of the following financial statement assertions does the receivables' confirmation not provide adequate assurance?

(1) Existence
(2) Completeness
(3) Valuation
(4) Rights and obligations

A (2) and (3) only
B (1) and (4) only
C (1), (2) and (4) only
D (2) and (4) only

154 Which of the following techniques for collecting audit evidence, is generally accepted to be very reliable when testing for the 'existence' of a freehold building?

A Inspection
B Inquiry
C Observation
D Confirmation

155 Which of the following populations should the auditor start from when testing for the completeness of reported revenue of a manufacturing company?

A Sales receipts
B Sales invoices
C Goods despatch notes
D Sales day book

156 Which of the following sources of evidence would be most appropriate to confirm the existence of year-end trade receivables balances?

A External confirmations
B Written confirmation from management
C Verification of balances to invoices
D Review of board meeting minutes

157 Which of the following procedures carried out at an inventory count by an auditor is a test primarily for overstatement of inventory, ie to check that inventory is not overvalued?

A Sequence check of pre-numbered inventory sheets at the conclusion of the count.
B Identify slow-moving or obsolete inventory lines.
C Vouch third party responses to confirm that inventory held at third party locations is included in the count.
D Agree items that have been counted (including items of high value) from physical inventory to inventory sheets.

158 Which of the following correctly describes the stages of an audit during which the auditor must make use of analytical procedures?

    A   As a risk assessment procedure at the planning stage, and the results of analytical procedures must be used at the overall review stage of the audit

    B   At all stages of an audit other than the planning stage

    C   In the closing stages of the audit only, when conducting the overall review of the financial statements

    D   At the planning stage and the substantive procedures stage of the audit

159 Which of the following statements about evidence, if any, are true?

    (1)   An auditor needs to obtain sufficient, appropriate evidence.

    (2)   Sufficient means evidence from at least two sources.

    A   (1) only

    B   (2) only

    C   Both (1) and (2)

    D   Neither (1) nor (2)

160 Which of the following audit procedures are substantive procedures?

    (1)   Observation of inventory count

    (2)   Inspection of invoices to vouch cost of new non-current assets

    (3)   Recalculation of depreciation charge

    A   (1), (2) and (3)

    B   (1) and (2)

    C   (1) and (3)

    D   (2) and (3)

161 Which of the following audit procedures are tests of control?

    (1)   A test to verify the operation of procedures designed to safeguard the business

    (2)   A comparison of financial and non-financial information by the auditor

    (3)   A test to verify an assertion made in the financial statements

    A   (1) only

    B   (2) only

    C   (1) and (3)

    D   (2) and (3)

162 Which of the following statements about audit approaches, if any, are true?

(1) The auditor may take a combined approach, where he will test controls and then reduce his subsequent substantive testing (although he must always carry out tests of detail on material items).

(2) The auditor may take a substantive approach, where he does not test controls, but instead renders control risk as high and conducts more tests of detail instead.

A (1) only
B (2) only
C Both (1) and (2)
D Neither (1) nor (2)

163 Which of the following assertions are relevant to the audit of tangible non-current assets?

(1) Existence
(2) Occurrence
(3) Classification
(4) Presentation

A (1), (2) and (3)
B (1), (2) and (4)
C (1), (3) and (4)
D (2), (3) and (4)

164 An audit junior plans to obtain the following evidence in respect of bank and cash.

(1) Bank reconciliation carried out by the client's cashier
(2) Bank confirmation report from client's bank
(3) Verbal confirmation from the directors that the overdraft limit is to be increased
(4) Cash count carried out by the audit junior himself

What is the correct order of ranking of reliability of these sources of evidence, most reliable first?

A (1), (3), (2), (4)
B (2), (4), (1), (3)
C (3), (1), (4), (2)
D (4), (2), (3), (1)

165 As part of substantive audit procedures, you perform a sequence check on the sales invoice numbers issued by a client over the year.

What is the purpose of the sequence check you have performed?

A To give assurance that cut-off has been applied accurately
B To give assurance over the occurrence of the sales transactions recorded
C To provide audit evidence over the completeness of the recording of sales
D To provide audit evidence that the sales figure has been calculated accurately

Chapter 14 Tests of controls

166 What is the main control objective of a payroll system?

    A   To ensure all employees are well-paid

    B   To minimise wage and salary costs

    C   To maximise employee motivation

    D   To avoid under- or over-payments of wages and salaries

167 Which of the following is the most important reason to reconcile HR records and payroll records?

    A   To ensure all employees are on the payroll

    B   To ensure only current employees are paid

    C   To ensure employees are not being paid too little

    D   To ensure that wages are in line with the organisation's budget

168 Who should normally approve overtime payments?

    A   The employee himself or herself

    B   The chief executive officer

    C   The employees' managers

    D   The payroll officer

169 To prevent a non-existent employee being added to the employee master file in order to pay into an account fraudulently, the master file should be checked against:

    A   Appointment letters

    B   Payroll summary reports

    C   Payroll detailed reports

    D   Payslips

170 Which of the following controls would not provide assurance that the correct amounts are paid to employees, in a system where employees are paid by the hour?

    A   Automated recording of hours worked

    B   Reperformance of payroll calculations

    C   Comparing bank transfer list with payroll

    D   Comparing payroll and income tax returns

171 One of the control objectives of the sales system of B Co is to ensure that goods and services are sold to credit-worthy customers.

Which of the following control activities would assist B Co in achieving this objective?

    A   All sales orders are based on authorised price lists.

    B   Credit limits are checked before sales orders are accepted.

    C   Overdue debts are chased each month by the credit controller.

    D   The aged-debt listing is reviewed by the finance director on a monthly basis.

172 A control objective of the purchases system of D Co is to ensure that all liabilities for purchases are valid obligations of the company.

Which of the following control activities would help to ensure that this objective is achieved?

- A Reconciliation of the payables control account to the purchase ledger
- B Matching of suppliers' invoices to purchase orders and goods received notes
- C Checking of the mathematical accuracy of the supplier invoice
- D Sequential numbering of goods received notes

173 Which of the following controls helps to ensure that payroll payments are only made to bona fide employees?

(1) Personnel records maintained for all employees
(2) Comparison of bank transfer listing with payroll
(3) Segregation of duties between staff involved in human resources and payroll functions
(4) Reperformance of the calculation of a sample of payroll deductions

- A (1) and (2)
- B (1) and (3)
- C (2) and (4)
- D (3) and (4)

174 An internal auditor has been examining the purchases system and has been asked by the manager of the internal audit department to describe and explain the purpose of the procedures that should be applied to a supplier's invoice when received. Which of the following responses is best?

- A The invoice should be checked to the goods received note (GRN) and the GRN should be checked to the invoice.
- B Details on the invoice should be compared to details on the GRN, then invoices should be entered into a purchases day book before posting to the supplier's account.
- C Each invoice should be matched with and compared to a GRN to ensure that the goods being invoiced have been received.
- D Invoices should be attached to related GRNs and then credited to the supplier's account in the payables ledger.

175 Which of the following control activities would satisfy the objective of preventing/detecting a material misstatement if it is operating effectively?

(1) All orders are recorded on pre-printed, three-part sequentially numbered order forms. One copy is kept by the sales clerk, one copy is forwarded to the warehouse for the dispatch of inventory, and one copy is sent to the customer as evidence of the order.
(2) The sales clerk regularly performs reviews of the standing data on the system, matching the price of flowers against an up to date price list.
(3) To ensure completeness of orders, a sequence check is performed on the sales invoices manually by the sales clerk and any missing documents are investigated.
(4) Sales invoices are posted on a weekly basis to the sales day book and accounts receivable ledger.

- A (1) and (2)
- B (3) and (4)
- C (2) only
- D (3) only

176 You instruct the audit junior to confirm whether the post is opened by more than one individual.

Over which of the following internal control objectives would this provide assurance?

(1) Cash receipts are not misappropriated

(2) All cash receipts that occurred are recorded

(3) Cash receipts are recorded at the correct amounts in the ledger

(4) Cash receipts are posted to the correct receivables accounts and to the general ledger

A (1) only

B (2) only

C (3) and (4)

D (1) and (4)

177 During the course of the audit, the audit team identified numerous deficiencies in internal control relating to the sales system. The amounts exposed to the deficiencies were high and you have concluded that it is likely that the deficiencies would result in material misstatements in the financial statements. A deficiency was also identified in the purchases system but further investigation showed this to be a minor, isolated issue.

Which of the following statements is correct regarding the deficiencies which must be included in the report to management?

A The deficiencies identified in the sales system only

B The deficiencies identified in the purchases system only

C The deficiencies identified in the sales and purchases system

D Neither the deficiencies identified in the sales system nor the purchases system

178 'To ensure that goods and services are only supplied to customers with good credit ratings'.

This statement describes a:

A Risk

B Control objective

C Control activity

D Test of controls

179 While reviewing a company's purchases cycle, you identified that goods received notes for raw material purchases are not sequentially numbered.

Which of the following areas would you consider to be most at risk of material misstatement, as a result of this internal control deficiency?

A Rights and obligations of inventory

B Valuation of payables

C Existence of inventory

D Completeness of payables

PRACTICE QUESTION BANK

180 Which of the following is a control objective relating to the sales system?

    A   Credit notes are only issued for valid reasons.

    B   Sales invoices are checked to Goods Despatched Notes by accounts staff.

    C   Customer accounts are scrutinised to see if credit limits have been observed.

    D   Orders are made only to authorised suppliers.

181 Which of the following is **NOT** a control activity relating to the purchases system?

    A   All orders are authorised by a senior staff member.

    B   Blank order forms are kept in a secure location with restricted access.

    C   All goods and services received are accurately recorded.

    D   Order forms are sequentially pre-numbered.

182 Which of the following audit procedures is a test of controls over inventory?

    A   Recalculating the year-end inventory figure

    B   Physically inspecting a warehouse owned by the company to store inventory

    C   Inspecting a sample of inventory movement records for authorisation

    D   Matching the last Goods Received Notes of the period to the relevant purchase invoices

183 Which of the following controls would provide the most positive assurance as to the completeness of the sales figure recorded in the financial statements of a manufacturing company?

    A   Segregation of duties between the preparation of goods despatched notes and the preparation of the sales invoices

    B   The issue of pre-numbered sales invoices for every sales transaction and internal checking for completion of processing

    C   The use of a pre-numbered goods despatched note for every sales transaction and internal checking for completeness of processing

    D   Authorisation of all sales invoices by the sales manager prior to processing

184 Which of the following controls would provide assurance that the wages paid to employees of a company are only for work carried out?

    (1)   Written authorisation from an authorised personnel officer in respect of employee additions to and deletions from the payroll, and in respect of changes to rates of pay

    (2)   Segregation of duties between the processing of the wages payroll and the entering of the wages transactions into the accounting records

    (3)   Segregation of duties between the authorisation of employee clock cards and the processing of the wages payroll

    A   (1) and (3) only

    B   (2) only

    C   (2) and (3) only

    D   (3) only

185 Identify each of these statements as control objective, risk or control procedure.

Statement	Objective, risk, procedure?
(1) Customers do not pay for the goods	(a) Control objective
(2) Customers should pay promptly for goods	(b) Risk
(3) Customers are allocated credit limits	(c) Control procedure

A   1a, 2b, 3c

B   1b, 2c, 3a

C   1a, 2c, 3b

D   1b, 2a, 3c

186 Identify each of these statements as control objective, risk or control procedure.

Statement	Objective, risk, procedure?
(1) A company intends to invoice all despatches correctly	(a) Control objective
(2) A company can match despatch notes with invoices prior to invoices being sent out	(b) Risk
(3) A company can send out goods and not invoice them	(c) Control procedure

A   1a, 2b, 3c

B   1b, 2c, 3a

C   1a, 2c, 3b

D   1b, 2a, 3c

187 Identify each of these statements as control objective, risk or control procedure.

Statement	Objective, risk, procedure?
(1) The company should pay employees for work done	(a) Control objective
(2) The company could make incorrect payments to the tax authority	(b) Risk
(3) The company reviews payroll against budgets	(c) Control procedure

A   1a, 2b, 3c

B   1b, 2c, 3a

C   1a, 2c, 3b

D   1b, 2a, 3c

188   Identify each of these statements as control objective, risk or control procedure.

Statement	Objective, risk, procedure?
(1) The company buys assets it does not need	(a) Control objective
(2) Depreciation rates should reflect the useful life of an asset	(b) Risk
(3) The company keeps a non-current assets register	(c) Control procedure

A   1a, 2b, 3c
B   1b, 2c, 3a
C   1a, 2c, 3b
D   1b, 2a, 3c

189   Identify each of these statements as control objective, risk or control procedure.

Statement	Objective, risk, procedure?
(1) Goods inwards are checked and recorded	(a) Control objective
(2) Goods may be used for personal gain	(b) Risk
(3) Goods are available when required for use in the business	(c) Control procedure

A   1a, 2b, 3c
B   1b, 2c, 3a
C   1c, 2a, 3b
D   1c, 2b, 3a

190   Which of the following procedures within a sales system are strengths?

(1)   Julie raises the sales invoices on the basis of the goods received notes she is sent by the warehouse. She inputs the information, prints the invoices, and sends them out. No other procedures are carried out.

(2)   Statements are sent to customers on a monthly basis.

A   (1) only
B   (2) only
C   Both (1) and (2)
D   Neither (1) nor (2)

191   Which of the following procedures within a purchases system are strengths?

(1)   Sandra reconciles supplier statements with the purchase ledger as she receives them.

(2)   Payments, which are approved by a director after reviewing supporting documentation, are made on a monthly basis on the basis of a printout of due items from the purchase ledger.

A   (1) only
B   (2) only
C   Both (1) and (2)
D   Neither (1) nor (2)

192 Which of the following procedures within a payroll system are strengths?

(1) Each member of staff is allocated a personnel file on arrival, which is updated for any changes in pay rates or hours.

(2) The payroll is created by the wages clerk on the last Thursday of a month. She runs the payroll package which automatically produces a bank payments list and notifies the bank to pay the salaries.

A (1) only

B (2) only

C Both (1) and (2)

D Neither (1) nor (2)

193 Identify which risk each of the following control procedures should mitigate

Internal control procedure	Risk mitigated
(1) Credit checks are run on new customers.	(a) Customers are invoiced incorrectly.
(2) Despatches are checked for quality before leaving the warehouse.	(b) Customers are issued credit notes incorrectly.
	(c) Customers are not good credit risks.
	(d) Customers don't pay promptly.

A 1a, 2d

B 1b, 2a

C 1c, 2b

D 1d, 2c

194 Identify which control procedure should mitigate each risk.

Risk mitigated	Internal control procedure
(1) Company pays for poor quality goods	(a) Company only purchases from approved suppliers
(2) Company pays for the same invoice twice	(b) Company provides supporting evidence of payments before approval
	(c) Company records payments promptly on the purchases ledger
	(d) Company reviews all goods inwards for condition

A 1a, 2d

B 1b, 2a

C 1c, 2b

D 1d, 2c

195 Identify how an auditor would best test these controls by matching each control with the appropriate tests below

Controls	Tests of control
(1) Hours worked are reviewed.	(a) Observe staff arriving at work
(2) Payroll is prepared by a director.	(b) Observe the director preparing payroll
	(c) Review clock cards
	(d) Review payroll

A 1c, 2d
B 1d, 2a
C 1a, 2b
D 1b, 2c

Chapter 15 Auditing and governance

196 Which of the following activities should the internal audit function **NOT** be involved in?

    A   Assessing compliance with health and safety regulation

    B   Reviewing adequacy of management information for decision-making purposes

    C   Taking responsibility for the implementation of a new payroll system

    D   Monitoring of management's performance

197 The board of Tangerine is considering establishing an internal audit function.

Which of the following factors would be relevant in making this decision?

    (1)   It would help the audit committee to discharge its responsibilities for monitoring internal control.

    (2)   The board would no longer need to take responsibility for the prevention and detection of fraud and error.

    (3)   The costs of establishing an internal audit function should be considered against the benefits gained.

    A   1 and 2 only

    B   1 and 3 only

    C   2 and 3 only

    D   1, 2 and 3

198 Which of the following are advantages of outsourcing the internal audit function?

    (1)   Greater availability of specialist industry skills as required

    (2)   Flexibility regarding staff numbers in response to changing circumstances

    (3)   Elimination of direct training costs

    (4)   Development of skills increasing the human resource strength of the entity

    A   (1), (2) and (3)

    B   (1), (3) and (4)

    C   (1), (2) and (4)

    D   (2), (3) and (4)

199 Which of the following internal audit assignments is described below?

The examination of the economy, efficiency and effectiveness of activities and processes.

    A   Regulatory compliance audit

    B   Value for money audit

    C   Financial audit

    D   IT audit

PRACTICE QUESTION BANK

200 Which **two** of the following characteristics apply to internal audit?
- (1) The purpose is to improve the company's operations.
- (2) Reports to shareholders on whether the financial statements give a true and fair view of affairs.
- (3) Auditors may be employees of the company.
- (4) Their duties are set by statute.

A (1) and (3)
B (2) and (4)
C (1) and (4)
D (2) and (3)

201 Which of the following internal audit assignments aims to check whether there are errors in transactions and balances?

A Value for money
B Fraud investigation
C Financial
D Operational

202 Which of the following is not a limitation of the internal audit function?
- (1) The internal audit report is not circulated to the members.
- (2) Internal audit assignments are designed to meet the needs of the business.
- (3) Internal auditors may be employees of the company.
- (4) Internal auditors may report to an audit committee.

A (1), (2) and (3)
B (1), (2) and (4)
C (1), (3) and (4)
D (2), (3) and (4)

203 Which of the following best summarises the meaning of 'effective' in the context of a Value for Money audit?

A The lowest cost at which the appropriate quantity and quality of physical, human and financial resources can be achieved
B Producing the required goods and services in the shortest time possible
C The extent to which an activity is achieving its policy objectives
D The relationship between goods and services produced and the resources used to produce them

204 Which of the following statements about the responsibilities of internal auditors with regards to fraud, if any, are true?

(1) The internal auditor must always consider the potential of management overriding controls and modify their audit procedures accordingly when performing internal audit engagements.

(2) The work of internal auditors in reviewing the company's internal control systems helps management to fulfil its responsibility for preventing and detecting fraud.

A (1) only
B (2) only
C Both (1) and (2)
D Neither (1) nor (2)

205 In the absence of an audit committee, which of the following recommendations are appropriate in increasing the independence of an internal audit department?

(1) The chief internal auditor should be appointed by the board of directors.
(2) The chief internal auditor should report to the board of directors.
(3) The finance director should decide on the scope of the internal audit work.

A (1) and (2) only
B (1) and (3) only
C (2) and (3) only
D (1), (2) and (3)

Practice answer bank

Chapter 1 Corporate governance and agency theory

1   A   A CEO acts as the company's agent. Citizens are the principals for parliamentary representatives, while directors are the agents of shareholders. Finally, auditors are agents of the shareholders rather than vice versa.

2   D   Expectations of good practice in corporate governance have grown with the globalisation of stock markets and investment. Institutional investors, especially in the USA, have increased their investments in global markets and they expect high standard of corporate governance to protect their investment. This has been accompanied by growing shareholder activism in response both to perceived weaknesses in corporate governance practices and also to criticisms that shareholders are not doing enough to exercise their rights and hold management to account. Although there are some codes of corporate governance for unlisted companies, the focus of attention is on listed companies, not private companies.

3   C   The description in the question refers to the traditional 'shareholder' view of corporate governance.

4   A   Shareholders do not become involved in day-to-day management, even at times of crisis. Shareholders should expect to be consulted about new appointments to the positions of chair of the board or CEO. Shareholders delegate the power to manage the company to a board of directors. The powers of directors may be stated in its constitution (articles of association) and many of these powers are delegated to management.

5   C   The separation of ownership (by the equity shareholders) and control (by the board of directors and management) creates conflicts of interest. Directors should act in the best interests of the company and its shareholders, but this is sometimes in conflict with their self-interest. Rules or principles of best corporate governance practice have been developed mainly to address this problem.

6   D   The animal rights pressure group would be the least likely to be considered a stakeholder in this instance. Although the nuclear power station is likely to attract the attention of pressure groups, these are more likely to be those concerned with environmental issues. The other groups have a legitimate stake in the enterprise: the government as a regulator, employees as participants in the business, and local residents because of potential impacts.

7   B   Information asymmetry occurs when one group has better access to relevant information than other groups. It is not so much concerned with how the available information is understood and interpreted. A feature of information asymmetry is that agents (management) have better access to information than principals (shareholders).

8   D   Monitoring costs are costs that are incurred by the principal (shareholders) to monitor the activities and performance of agents (directors), to ensure that they are acting in their interests.

9   C   Information held by third parties is not an issue in agency theory. Information asymmetry arises because agents hold more and better information than principals.

10   A   The cost of the external audit is a monitoring cost as it is a cost incurred specifically so the shareholders can be assured that their agents, the directors, are acting properly.

PRACTICE ANSWER BANK

Chapter 2 Overview of corporate governance

11	D	The objective of corporate governance is overall performance, enhanced by good supervision and management, within best practice guidelines. Business is to be conducted in a way that is both ethical and effective from the perspective of all stakeholders – not just shareholders.
12	C	Domination of the board by a single individual is often considered a feature of poor corporate governance because it allows for self-interested decision-making. The other features of corporate governance in the question may 'look' like negatives, but are in fact the opposite of three other features of poor corporate governance: lack of independent scrutiny, lack of supervision, and an emphasis on short-term profitability (which can cause pressure to conceal problems or manipulate accounts).
13	D	Codes of practice are usually associated with a principles-based approach (rather than a rules-based approach) and so options B and C should have been easily eliminated. The words 'guidance' and 'should adopt' were the key words to lead to the correct option.
14	D	Although governance is mostly discussed in relation to large quoted companies, it is an issue for all large organisations including government boards and agencies and also not-for-profit organisations such as charities.
15	C	Corporate governance is the system by which organisations are directed and controlled by senior officers.
16	A	The public policy reason for needing sound corporate governance is to encourage business enterprise, but to prevent the benefits for business being gained at the expense of social considerations. The other reasons relate to different categories of stakeholder rather than the public as a whole.
17	A	This should be fairly apparent, since the Sarbanes-Oxley Act is a law and the others are principles or principle-based codes.
18	B	Maximisation of returns on investment may be the strategic objective of an individual corporation, but the corporate governance framework looks much wider than that. It seeks to promote transparent and efficient markets as a whole, whilst remaining consistent with the rule of law and ensuring there is a clear division of responsibilities between regulatory, supervisory and enforcement agencies.
19	A	(4) is the role of the external auditor rather than an advantage of corporate governance.
20	D	

Chapter 3 The board

21	A	The CEO (and the management team) has primary responsibility for building strategies. The board of directors should approve the strategies and is accountable to shareholders for any strategy failure.
22	B	A principle is that the board should be structured in a way that adds value to the company. Directors on the board should therefore receive relevant training and development.
23	D	The requirement for gender diversity is intended to lay solid foundations for management and oversight.
24	D	Widespread share ownership, with many shares in the hands of institutional investors, is a feature of the Anglo-Saxon based system of corporate governance. This is found in countries such as the UK, Australia and New Zealand.

25	A	In Germany, for example, employee representation on the supervisory board is a legal requirement for large companies.
26	B	It is the chair of the board who must develop the requisite mix of skills among directors by ensuring the right people are appointed, they receive adequate induction, training and development, and they are properly informed. The board chair should also review directors' performance, and whether the board needs refreshing.
27	B	The board is responsible for the preparation of the financial statements, although the audit committee may perform a preliminary review over them.
28	D	Preparing the financial statements is the task of the finance director alone rather the board as a whole
29	C	Keiretsu and chaebols are typical of Japan and Korea respectively. Australia follows the Anglo-Saxon unitary model and Austria the European two-tier model.
30	A	Communication and coherence are not characteristics of an effective board

Chapter 4 Board members (directors)

31	B	This is why audit, nomination and remuneration committees are required by the UK Corporate Governance Code. Risk management committees are not compulsory and are less common.
32	A	The provisions of the UK's Code state that management has an obligation to provide the board with appropriate and timely information, but this is unlikely to be sufficient in all circumstances and directors should make further enquiries where necessary. However, the Chair is responsible for ensuring that all directors are properly briefed on issues arising at board meetings.
33	D	Non-executive directors are directors without executive responsibilities in the company. They have full responsibility, along with executive directors, as directors of the company, and they are directors, not consultants. Non-executives make up all or the majority of the membership of various board committees.
34	C	The nominee director representing a major shareholder is non-executive, but not independent (because he represents a major shareholder). A CFO is an executive director. An executive director of another listed company is non-executive, and should normally be independent. The head of the internal audit team should also be independent, even if they are directly employed by the organisation itself. In many organisations the head of internal audit is not a director.
35	A	The fact that Aaron worked for a rival company until fairly recently does not affect his independence. He would not be considered independent if he had been a chief accountant of XYZ Co. Connor has a close family connection and Daisy is the owner of a major supplier to XYZ Co, and so are not independent. Beth is an executive director.
36	B	Because directors direct and control a company it is impossible for them all to be independent of it, and indeed no executive directors (who by definition 'do' things in the name of the company for its benefit) can be said to be independent of their company. It is not necessary for all non-executive directors to be independent of their company; some are independent and some are non-independent non-executive directors. The only true statement, therefore, is that no executive director is independent of the company.
37	C	While many jurisdictions do have statutory legislation which requires disclosure of directors' remuneration in an annual report (often in considerable detail) the key corporate governance principle in this area is that no individual should be involved in setting their own pay. For this reason, executive directors do not sit on the remuneration committee. (The nomination and audit committees have no role in remuneration.)

38	B	The remuneration for all non-executive directors should reflect their time commitment and executive responsibilities of the role. The remuneration committee should decide the remuneration of all executive directors and the chair, but not the other non-executive directors (because no directors should decide their own pay). The performance-related element in the remuneration of executive directors should be 'a significant proportion' of their total remuneration.
39	C	A majority of members of the committee should be independent non-executive directors. This supports the principle that appointments to the board should be subject to a formal, rigorous and transparent procedure. Boards of large companies should have at least three non-executive directors, not four. The chair of the board of directors should not chair the nomination committee only when it is dealing with the appointment of their successor. At least half of the board of a large company (excluding the chair) should consist of independent non-executive directors but the proportion could be higher.
40	B	The board as a whole should take on the responsibility for liaising with shareholders, not just the chairman. As the chairman the NEDs are former executive directors they were previously employed by the company and as a result this raises questions about their independence. The company is not required to have an internal audit function (however, where there is no internal audit function, the company is required annually to consider the need for one).

Chapter 5 Board committees

41	D	The audit committee has a monitoring role and should therefore comprise at least three independent non-executive directors, one of whom should have relevant financial expertise. Aaron is the chief internal auditor and so should not be part of the audit committee because he manages the team that will report to the audit committee. Whilst Beth has some financial experience, she is already an executive director and so should not be a member of the audit committee as well. The two new independent directors should be appointed to the audit committee provided that they have the relevant skills.
42	C	The audit committee makes recommendations about the appointment of external auditors but the shareholders are responsible for appointing them at the AGM. The scope of the external auditor's work is determined by the audit engagement partner on the basis of the requirements of auditing standards. The scope of the audit may be discussed with the audit committee but the audit committee does not set out the scope of the work as the audit must be an independent exercise.
43	B	Listed companies should establish an audit committee with at least three independent non-executive directors. Listed companies do not need to have an internal audit department but should review at least annually the need for one.
44	C	As Rodney is the CEO and Lynne is the finance director, this would be a problem if they are members of each other's company's remuneration committees. Such a "cross directorship" creates a threat to objectivity; there is a potential self-interest threat as both might be inclined to promote each other's financial interests as members of boards responsible for considering director remuneration.
45	A	An audit committee's responsibilities encompass financial statements and control, external auditors and internal auditors. Reviewing arrangements which allow staff to 'whistleblow' is an aspect of the audit committee's responsibility for internal audit. Reviewing the internal financial controls and risk management systems concerns financial statements and controls.

46	C	The majority of the members of the nomination committee should be independent, chaired by an independent director. The chair is allowed to chair the nomination committee except when appointing their successor.
47	A	Audit committees should consist of independent non-executive directors.
48	A	The audit committee should be made up entirely of independent non-executive directors and should not be chaired by the chair of the board. As only one NED had adequate knowledge of financial matters, but would only serve on the audit committee every other year, this would result in the committee having no financial expertise whatsoever. Directors are re-elected annually but can be directors for more than one year.
49	B	The most important word in the question is "initially". Although external auditors have a statutory verification role and the board of directors is ultimately accountable for the company's financial statements, the audit committee has a vital initial scrutiny role with respect to the draft financial statements.
50	D	Board committees are used to spread the work load of the board, so that matters can be studied and discussed in more detail than if the entire board had to be involved in everything. Board committees can also provide objectivity and independence when a conflict of interest would otherwise arise, such as in decisions on executive director remuneration and the financial report. Committees do not take full responsibility for decisions: they make recommendations to the board or refer decisions to the board for approval.

Chapter 6 Stakeholders, corporate social responsibility and sustainability

51	B	Companies placing emphasis on CSR recognise that managing relationships with multiple stakeholders, not just shareholders, is vital for long-term success. Social costs are a reflection of the costs to society of the organisation's activities, not the monetary costs to the organisation. Corporate citizenship refers to an organisation's responsibilities toward society, and does not relate to business relationship with other corporations.
52	A	An organisation is dependent on the health of its workforce. The remaining choices are all **impacts** of the organisation rather than dependencies.
53	C	Greenwashing is where the impression is given that the company is managing sustainability effectively, when in reality little action is being taken. It is an attempt at keeping stakeholders happy through sustainability reporting without fulfilling ESG obligations.
54	A	The UK Corporate Governance Code (and others) do not yet **require** sustainability committees to be set up. Some entities may choose to, for example, place accountability with an existing committee (such as the audit committee) but increasingly companies are establishing dedicated sustainability committees.
55	C	The risk of loss of tax revenue is a risk to the government (an external stakeholder), so the legislation to ensure tax is collected is that external stakeholder's response to the stakeholder risk it faces. This of course conflicts with the company's goal to increase overall profits and the wealth of the shareholders.

Chapter 7 Risk and control

56	D	The work done by the external auditors will be considered as part of the board's responsibility for the audit and presenting a true and fair view of the financial statements, but is not a requirement for the review of internal control.
57	C	The Board of Directors is responsible for maintaining a system of internal control. The Internal auditors will examine elements of the system of internal control but it is not their responsibility. The audit committee will meet regularly with the head of internal audit department but they are not responsible for the system of internal control. The external auditor has no responsibility for the design of the system of internal control but must have an understanding of it in order to assess the risk of material misstatement in the financial statements.
58	B	
59	C	The objective of most firms is profit maximisation, which then increases shareholders' wealth. Business risk is anything which could affect the firm's ability to achieve this.
60	D	Both of these illustrate the bottom-up approach as they start from the operational level of the business.
61	A	The frequency stated in (1) refers to likelihood. The quantification in (2) refers to impact.
62	D	The company should insure the vehicles (transfer) and keep them locked (mitigation). Avoidance would not be appropriate as the company needs the vehicles to operate its business. Acceptance would not be appropriate as without management there could be many thefts which could result in a large financial loss.
63	B	This is known as a risk matrix.
64	C	Insurance is an example of transferring risk rather than mitigating it by introducing an internal control.
65	D	Risk management committees are not required by the code, and the internal auditors should report to the audit committee.

Chapter 8 The nature and purpose of auditing

66   B   ISA 250 (Revised) distinguishes between regulations which have a direct effect on the financial statements (in the sense of directly affecting the determination of balances) and those which do not have a direct effect but can still have a material effect (such as an operating licence). For regulations which do not have a direct effect, the external auditor must perform audit procedures to help identify any non-compliance which might have a material effect on the financial statements.

67   C   There are five elements to an assurance engagement: criteria, report, evidence, subject matter and three-party relationship.

68   D   A review engagement is an assurance engagement where the practitioner carries out limited procedures. As the procedures are limited, the practitioner will gain only enough evidence to provide a negative expression of opinion.

69   A   There are five elements in total: Criteria, Report, Evidence, Subject matter and Three-party relationship (remember CREST).

70   A   The external audit is carried out by external auditors, who are independent of the company so that they can provide an independent opinion on whether the company's financial statements are prepared, in all material respects, in accordance with an applicable financial reporting framework. The principal aim of the audit is not in relation to the control system in place or to identify other areas of deficiency, although deficiencies and recommendations may be suggested by the external auditors as a by-product of the external audit in a report to management at the conclusion of the audit.

71   D   This increases detection risk but is not an inherent limitation.

72   A

73   B   The directors of a company are responsible for the prevention and detection of fraud. They can do this in various ways, one of which is to have an internal audit department in place. The head of the internal audit department should report to the audit committee.

74   B   The external audit is an exercise undertaken to provide an independent opinion on the truth and fairness of the financial statements. It is not done by the management of the company itself – this would not provide an independent view. Its primary aim is to report on the truth and fairness of the financial statements, not on the system of internal control. A report to management on deficiencies in internal control is issued at the end of the audit, but this is a by-product of the audit, the main outcome of which is the auditor's report with the auditor's opinion. The external audit does not have to comprise an interim audit visit as well as a final audit visit.

75   B   The external audit assignment provides reasonable assurance as to the truth and fairness of the financial statements and one of the reasons for this is because the auditors do not test every single transaction and balance – this would make the audit far too time-consuming and costly. The other statements are not valid reasons.

Chapter 9 Regulation of audit

76   D   Statement A is the definition of objectivity. Statement B is the definition of professional competence and due care. Statement C is the definition of professional behaviour.

77   B   Integrity is defined as follows: 'Members shall be straightforward and honest in all their professional and business relationships'.

78   B   The fundamental principles are integrity, confidentiality, professional behaviour, professional competence and due care, and objectivity.

79	D	Professional competence also includes a duty to remain technically up to date.
80	D	Confidentiality also means not using information obtained in the course of work for personal advantage.
81	B	The key test for professional behaviour is whether one's actions are likely to bring the profession into disrepute.
82	D	Members are obliged to spend enough time on a piece of work to complete it thoroughly. It is unlikely that this would be the case if they spent considerably less time on the work at home than they would have done if they were in the office.
83	B	The shareholders of the company usually appoint the auditors at a shareholders' annual general meeting. In rare circumstances, the directors may appoint the auditors (Companies Act 2006: s. 475).
84	D	IFAC stands for International Federation of Accountants. International auditing standards are issued by the International Auditing and Assurance Standards Board (IAASB) and the ethics code is the responsibility of the International Ethics Standards Board for Accountants (IESBA)
85	C	Both statements are true.

Chapter 10 The audit process

There are no questions and answers on Chapter 10 specifically as it provides an overview of information covered in subsequent chapters.

Chapter 11 Risk assessment

86	C	The auditor cannot affect control risk or inherent risk. The auditor can reduce audit risk by manipulating detection risk. Both increasing sample sizes and assigning more experienced staff to the audit will reduce detection risk and therefore audit risk.
87	D	The matters mentioned in option D relate specifically to business operations. The matters mentioned in the other options relate specifically to financial reporting (A), investments (B) and financing (C).
88	B	ISA 315 (Revised) requires auditors to use analytical procedures and inquiry when obtaining an understanding of the entity and its environment. In addition, they should also use observation and inspection.
89	A	The fact that the company is rapidly expanding is an example of an inherent risk factor. The other statements are all examples of control risk factors.
90	C	The selection and application of accounting policies is one of the areas in which the auditor is required to gain an understanding, as part of the auditor's risk assessment procedures. It is not a component of internal control. The other components of internal control are the entity's risk assessment process and process to monitor the system of internal control.
91	B	This illustrates detection risk.
92	A	B relates to monitoring/oversight and C and D relate to business operations.
93	A	Auditors need to obtain an understanding of their audit client and its environment to help them design and perform further audit procedures. In addition to this, understanding the client helps them identify the risks of material misstatement and provides a frame of reference for exercising audit judgement.
94	C	The risk of material misstatement at the assertion level is made up of inherent risk and control risk.

PRACTICE ANSWER BANK

95	A	Analytical procedures must be used during audit planning and review, in accordance with ISA 315 (Revised) paragraph 6(b) and ISA 520 paragraph 6. They can **optionally** also be used as substantive procedures during audit fieldwork.
96	C	Sales volumes combined with other factors could also be accompanied by an increased gross profit percentage. Any settlement discounts received should not be accounted for in the trading account and should therefore, not affect reported gross profit. An increase in the cost of sales would be consistent with the noted decrease in gross profit.
97	B	Neither carriage outwards costs nor early payment discounts should be reflected above the gross profit line. They would therefore not impact the company's gross profit. Carriage inward costs are part of costs of sales, so a reduction in these will cause the gross profit to increase.
98	B	The auditor should obtain this understanding for all clients, new and existing.
99	C	
100	D	Detection risk is not so much identified as calculated based on the risk of material misstatement identified at the client. It is specific to the particular audit.
101	A	
102	C	The risk of material misstatement is made up of inherent risk and control risk. (1) and (3) will lead to an increase in inherent risk but (2) will lead to a decrease in control risk.
103	D	(1) is an indication of poor control, which will lead to an increase in control risk.
104	C	Auditors will test some immaterial as well as material items.
105	D	This does not suggest a significant risk – a significant risk might be indicated by a transaction outside the normal course of business for an entity.
106	C	An increase in the cost of sales as explained would be consistent with the noted decrease in gross profit. A sales volume decrease would result in a corresponding fall in cost of sales which combined with the increase in sales value would result in an increased gross profit margin. Wage bonuses paid to the company's sales force, and settlement discounts received should not be accounted for in the trading account and should therefore, have no effect on reported gross profit.
107	D	
108	D	
109	A	All of these factors will improve controls and therefore decrease control risk.
110	A	ISA 315 (Revised) requires auditors to use analytical procedures when obtaining an understanding of the entity and its environment. In addition, they should also use inquiry, observation and inspection

Chapter 12 Internal controls

111	D	The fact that ABC has a detailed constitution which explains how the charity's income can be spent is a positive influence on the control environment, as it indicates that there is a benchmark in place against which the suitability of ABC's expenditure can be measured.
		The fact that the income of ABC is primarily cash increases inherent risk but does not automatically mean that the control environment is weak.
112	B	The system of internal control should provide reasonable assurance with regard to achieving company objectives.

PRACTICE ANSWER BANK

113	C	External auditors will investigate the system of internal control as part of their audit procedures and will report on material deficiencies found. They may choose to reply on these controls to reduce their substantive testing.
114	D	Working out gross profit percentages of each shop in a business that has a number of similar shops would allow inventory theft or incorrect accounting to be detected, but would not prevent theft or incorrect accounting from occurring. Taking regular back-ups of the accounting system allows correction should something go wrong, but will not prevent a systems failure from occurring. Regular inventory counts would detect inventory irregularities, but not prevent them from occurring. Keeping inventory in a secure location would help to prevent theft.
115	D	Internal controls only provide reasonable assurance that efficiency and effectiveness are improved and that assets are safeguarded. Internal controls do not have an objective of preventing or detecting all fraud.
116	A	A range check helps to confirm that the data has been input correctly. A sequence check is a completeness control. Password protection and authorisation are general controls and therefore they do not impact directly on the input of data.
117	A	The two classes are general controls (the environment) and information processing controls (business process level).
118	D	Password protection and backups both relate to many applications at the same time, therefore they are both examples of general IT controls, not information processing controls.
119	C	The first step should be to document the system of internal control – this is done using the flowchart and internal control evaluation questionnaire. The second step should be to confirm the auditor's understanding of the system – this is done with a walkthrough test. Tests of control are then performed to obtain audit evidence about the effectiveness of the design and operation of internal controls. Finally, if controls testing reveals any deficiencies in internal controls that have not been previously identified, the audit strategy and the audit plan should be revised as required.
120	C	Having an internal audit department, implementing segregation of duties and the presence of an audit committee are all indicative of good internal control.
121	B	The principal purpose of evaluating and testing the internal controls of a limited liability company is to provide the auditor with the opportunity to assess the strength of the client's system of internal control and determine the level of control risk. If control risk is deemed sufficiently low, then the auditor will be able to reduce the level of substantive procedures performed. However it should be noted that whilst, evaluating and testing a company's internal controls does also enable an auditor to report to management on the deficiencies of those controls, this is not the primary purpose.
122	A	A system of internal control has five components in accordance with ISA 315 (Revised) *Identifying and Assessing the Risks of Material Misstatement* which are the control environment, the entity's risk assessment process, the information system and communication system, control activities, and the entity's process to monitor the system of internal control.
123	D	Having an IT policy in place is an example of the control environment, not a control activity. The others are all examples of control activities.
124	B	A relates to information processing controls, whilst C is the definition of audit software, a type of automated tool and technique used by the auditor. D describes an embedded test facility

125	C	Control totals are an example of an information processing control. All the other statements are examples of general IT controls.
126	B	This is not a valid reason to explain the inherent limitations of control systems, rather it is an inherent limitation of external audit.
127	B	The report to management sets out deficiencies in internal control found during the audit and makes recommendations to mitigate those deficiencies.
128	B	Questionnaires, narrative notes and flow charts can be used to document a company's system of internal control. Disclosure checklists are used during the completion stage of the audit to ensure that the financial statements contain all relevant information and disclosures.
129	B	(3) is a sign of a weak control environment
130	B	
131	D	
132	D	(1) contributes to a strong control environment, (2) and (3) do not.
133	D	
134	C	The likelihood of material misstatement occurring is a key factor in determining whether the deficiency is significant. The number of deficiencies is a factor, as deficiencies may become significant if there is a significant combination of deficiencies. A deficiency is a deficiency regardless of whether the related control is new or not. In fact, an old deficiency might be more significant than a new one if, say, it had been previously reported and not acted on.
135	C	Both program logs and virus checks are general controls to prevent unauthorised changes. Document counts are information processing controls.

Chapter 13 Audit evidence

136	C	An overstatement of revenue would result in a reduction, not an increase in the receivables collection period.
137	B	This procedure will not give evidence that the amount will be paid (valuation) nor will it give evidence that receivables are complete (you would only write to those you know about).
138	D	A, B and C do not test controls: these are substantive tests. D tests the control that client staff are carrying out a check on goods received.
139	A	For the test to provide evidence of existence (B) the sample should be selected from the asset register ie the auditor would be looking to confirm that all assets recorded on the register exist. Rights and obligations (ownership) (C) would be tested by reference to purchase/legal documentation. Accuracy and valuation would be tested by inspecting purchase documentation (D).
140	C	Substantive audit procedures consist of both analytical procedures and tests of detail, not tests of control (A). B describes tests of controls. Substantive audit procedures must be carried out in all audits, whether the internal control environment is weak or strong (D).
141	C	Existence is an assertion relating to account balances at the period-end. The others all relate to transactions and events and related disclosures.
142	C	Rights and obligations and existence relate to account balances and related disclosures. Cut-off is relevant to transactions and events and related disclosures.

143	B	Risk, materiality and experience from prior audits are all factors that can influence the auditor's judgement as to what constitutes sufficient, appropriate audit evidence. The source and reliability of information available is also another factor to consider. Cost, however, should not be a relevant factor.
144	A	Material items will require more evidence to support them than immaterial items, which might be tested by comparative analytical review only. If the evidence is of high quality, then less may be required than if it were of poorer quality. Time and budget constraints should never influence the auditor's judgement regarding the sufficiency of audit evidence. The size of the account is considered in determining materiality (ie materiality may be determined as 5% of profit before tax) but the absolute size of an account will be material in some circumstances and not others.
145	D	This is third party evidence direct from the third party. The other items are created by or could have been tampered with by the client.
146	D	This helps the auditor have comfort about the completeness assurance. The test also provides evidence over existence, rights and obligations and accuracy.
147	B	A and C relate to substantive tests. D is incorrect – tests of control are performed when the system is thought to be strong
148	A	Existence is an assertion relating to account balances at the period-end.
149	B	Rights and obligations and existence relate to account balances and related disclosures. Cut-off is relevant to transactions and events and related disclosures.
150	D	Risk, materiality and experience from prior audits are all factors that can influence the auditor's judgement as to what constitutes sufficient, appropriate audit evidence. The source and reliability of information available is also another factor to consider. Cost, however, should not be a relevant factor.
151	B	Reperformance is defined by the IAASB's Glossary of Terms as the 'independent execution of procedures or controls that were originally performed as part of the entity's internal controls', whereas recalculation is 'checking the mathematical accuracy of documents and accounting records'. (1) is therefore an example of recalculation, whereas (2) and (3) are examples of reperformance.
152	D	Inspecting title deeds is a test for rights and obligations. Agreeing figures on the valuation certificate to the general ledger is a test for valuation. Agreeing a physical sample of assets back to the non-current asset register is a test for completeness.
153	A	The receivables' confirmation provides assurance over rights and obligations and existence of year-end receivables balances. It does not provide assurance over completeness and valuation.
154	A	The most reliable source of audit evidence is that which auditors themselves generate. There is no more reliable evidence with regard to verifying the existence of a freehold building than that of the auditor physically inspecting the property. Note that 'observation' describes the procedure whereby auditors watch a process or procedure being performed.
155	C	Revenue is usually recognised when goods have been despatched to the customer as this is the point at which ownership transfers to the customer. In order to test for completeness of revenue, auditors should therefore start from the goods despatched notes.
156	A	An external confirmation in the form of a trade receivables' confirmation would be most appropriate to test the existence of year-end trade receivables. Verification of balances to invoices and review of board meeting minutes are both internal sources of evidence and therefore not as reliable as an external confirmation. Written confirmation from management is less reliable as it is internally generated.

157 B This is a test for overstatement in that the auditor is seeking, subsequent to the count, to ensure that slow-moving and obsolete inventory lines have correctly been written down to the lower of cost and net realisable value. The other procedures are all tests for understatement of inventory.

158 A Analytical procedures must be applied as a risk assessment tool at the planning stage of the audit and to assist in understanding the business. The results of the analytical procedures must also be used in the overall review stage at the end of the audit when forming an overall conclusion as to whether the financial statements are consistent with the auditor's knowledge of the business

159 A

160 D

161 A

162 C

163 C Existence, classification and presentation are all assertions related to tangible non-current assets. Completeness and accuracy, valuation and allocation are also relevant assertions (ISA 315 (Revised)). Occurrence and classification relate to classes of transactions and events recorded in profit or loss (ISA 315 (Revised).

164 B Third-party evidence is the most reliable, followed by auditor-generated evidence. Client-generated evidence is deemed to be less reliable – more so when the evidence is verbal.

165 C Sequence checks on sales invoices provide evidence on the completeness of sales.

Chapter 14 Tests of controls

166 D Other choices might be considered as part of human resource management.

167 B If employees are not being paid, or are being paid too little, they will presumably complain. The HR/payroll reconciliation is little to do with budgets and targets. The main purpose would be to identify payments being made to people who are not employees.

168 C The employees' managers are best-placed to authorise overtime and to ensure that the extra work was carried out.

169 A The payroll reports and payslips are based on the employee data held in the master file. The appointment letters are an independent source.

170 D This gives evidence that the correct payments have been made to the tax authorities

171 B This means that customers are not able to exceed their credit limits and are therefore more likely to be able to pay. It helps to ensure that goods are sold at the right price. C & D are effective controls regarding the recovery of debts but do not prevent sales being made to customers who are unlikely to pay as the sale has already been made by this stage.

172 B Matching of suppliers' invoices to purchase orders and goods received notes ensures that liabilities are only recognised for goods which have been received by the company. The reconciliation of the payables control account and purchase ledger and checking of calculation of invoices are accuracy checks. Sequential numbering of documentation helps to ensure completeness.

173 B Personnel records are documentary evidence of the existence of an employee. Segregation of duties between staff involved in HR and payroll helps to prevent the creation of bogus employees with subsequent payroll payments being made.

174	C	This is the only response which explains the purpose of the control, ie it includes the words "to ensure that".
175	D	A sequence check of the invoices is an effective control, be it carried out manually or electronically. Order forms should have four, not three, parts. No copy of the order is sent to the accounts receivables clerk – as a result, the recording of receivables may be incomplete or delayed, and outstanding balances may remain uncollected. The sales clerk should not be reviewing the standing data themselves – this review should be performed by an independent, senior member of staff. Sales invoices should be posted automatically to the sales day book and the accounts receivables ledger immediately after the order is taken.
176	A	This simply reduces the risk that cash will be misappropriated. It does not provide any assurance that subsequent recording will be complete or accurate.
177	A	ISA 265 *Communicating Deficiencies in Internal Control to those Charged with Governance and Management* requires the auditor to communicate significant deficiencies in internal control. The fact that the amounts exposed to the deficiencies in the sales system were high and that it is likely that the deficiencies would result in material misstatements in the financial statements are indicators that the deficiencies are significant.
178	B	
179	D	The fact that goods received notes (GRNs) are not sequentially numbered means that GRNs may be omitted from accounting records and it would be difficult to trace the unrecorded GRNs. As a result, the risk is that payables (and inventory) are not complete.
180	A	B is a control activity, not a control objective. C is a test of controls, not a control activity and D is a control objective relating to the purchases system, not the sales system.
181	C	This statement is not a control activity, it is a control objective relating to the purchases system. The other statements are all control activities.
182	C	This is the only procedure which describes a test of control for inventory. A and D are substantive audit procedures for inventory, not tests of controls and B is a substantive audit procedure for non-current assets, not inventory.
183	C	A sale should be recognised as soon as goods have been safely despatched to a customer and every despatch should be accompanied with a goods despatched note. Consequently to obtain assurance about the completeness of sales, the auditor needs to be confident that all despatch notes have been recorded in the accounting system. The existence of segregation of duty controls does not in itself provide assurance as to completeness of recording of sales transactions. Checking that all sales invoices have been processed merely confirms that 'all sales invoices have been processed' and similarly the existence of authorisation controls merely provides assurance as to whether transactions have been authorised.
184	D	The control detailed in item (3) is the only option that actually deals with ensuring that no extra time/hours can be claimed and therefore ensures that staff can only be paid for hours actually worked.
185	D	
186	C	
187	A	
188	D	
189	D	

190 B (1) is not a strength as Julie does not check the invoices prior to sending to check they are correct.

191 C

192 A (2) is not a strength as the payroll does not appear to be authorised by a senior member of staff.

193 C

194 D

195 A

Chapter 15 Auditing and governance

196 C The internal audit function is a review and monitoring function. It should not take operational responsibility for any part of the system.

197 B The board is responsible for a company's system of internal control. The establishment of an internal audit function is one of the practical ways in which the board can meet its responsibility to monitor and review internal controls. However, as with all key decisions, costs versus benefits will be assessed too.

The directors are responsible for the prevention and detection of fraud. Whilst the internal audit function may assist the directors in this, the directors retain the ultimate responsibility.

198 A Where the internal audit department is outsourced to an external firm, a company is likely to benefit from specialist industry skills and will benefit from the greater flexibility in staffing numbers as the team can be modified depending on the workload at a particular point in time. A company will also be shielded from the direct costs of training staff. However, if the staff are employed by a company, this increases the skills held within the business and therefore increases the value of the workforce which is a strength of the company.

199 B Economy, efficiency and effectiveness are sometimes referred to as the '3E's' of VFM audits.

200 A 2 and 4 are characteristics of external audit.

201 B This is a financial audit assignment.

202 B As employees of the company the internal auditors will lack independence, which is a limitation. This means that the other statements are not limitations.

203 C A relates to economy and B and D to efficiency.

204 B Statement (1) is true of external rather than internal auditors.

205 A In the absence of an audit committee the work of the internal audit department should be directed by the board. The scope being set by the finance director reduces independence.

PRACTICE ANSWER BANK

Exam Question Bank

November 2021

1. Identify which of the following describes the main purpose of an external audit:

    A   To provide assurance to new investors regarding the financial health of a company.

    B   To provide assurance to the public that no fraud is taking place within the company.

    C   To provide assurance to the shareholders of the company in relation to the financial statements.

    D   To provide assurance to lenders that the company is financially sound.

2. Jane has set up her own car wash business and goes to clients' homes where she cleans their cars. She decides to buy a van costing £15,000 to carry her equipment. Her friend George has agreed to invest this amount in the business. Jane will incorporate her business into a company. Jane will be the director of the company and receive a salary. George will receive dividends on the shares issued to him in return for his £15,000 contribution.

    At the end of a year, Jane sends George a set of financial statements. George is disappointed to see that profits are lower than expected and therefore he will receive a very small dividend as a return for his investment.

    Required

    Which of the following theories best explains the problem facing George in terms his relationship to Jane:

    A   Agency theory.
    B   Internal audit theory.
    C   Stakeholder theory.
    D   Incorporation theory.

3. Identify which of the following describes the term *Corporate Governance*:

    A   The relationships between a company's directors, shareholders and government
    B   The relationships between the company directors, its shareholders and stakeholders
    C   The relationships between the company shareholders, stakeholders and government
    D   The relationships between the company's directors, stakeholders and government

4. Identify which of the following define features of a principles-based approach to corporate governance?

    i.   It is easy for users to apply a set of rules.
    ii.   It can be applied to any jurisdiction and any legal system.
    iii.   It deters a 'tick box' approach to corporate governance.

    A   i and ii only.
    B   i and iii only.
    C   ii and iii only.
    D   i, ii and iii.

5   Which of the following statements are recognised as valid in relation to internal control and directors' responsibilities?

   i.   Directors must appoint an internal audit function to perform reviews of the system of internal control.
   ii. Directors must appoint an external auditor to design and implement a system of internal control.
   iii. Directors must assess the risks facing the business, so that a system of internal control can be designed to ensure those risks are avoided.
   iv. Directors must perform reviews of the system of internal control.

   A   i and ii only.
   B   i and iii only.
   C   ii and iv only.
   D   iii and iv only.

6   Corporate governance rules and codes include aspects relating to the composition of boards and their committees. Select which of the following is the recommended membership of the Nomination Committee:

   A   Wholly or mainly executive directors of the company.
   B   Wholly or mainly non-executive directors.
   C   Wholly or mainly independent, non-executive directors.
   D   Wholly or mainly employees drawn from the company's workforce.

7   The *UK Corporate Governance Code* describes the purpose of the Audit Committee. Select which of the following is true:

   A   The board should set up an Audit Committee of independent, non-executive directors, with at least two members for both large and small companies.
   B   A member of the Audit Committee should be the Chair of the board.
   C   The board should assure itself that one or more members has up to date and appropriate financial experience.
   D   The whole Audit Committee should have knowledge in a range of industry sectors.

8   In different parts of the world there are different structures of company governance and boards of directors.

   Identify which of the following describes the Keiretsu structure:

   A   A structure in which organisations are linked by taking small stakes in each other to reinforce their already close business relationship.
   B   A structure with a supervisory board and a management board.
   C   A structure which is centred on the family, with close family control.
   D   A structure with a board of directors and independent, non-executive directors.

9   Select which of the following statements illustrate the 'expectations gap' in relation to a company's financial statements after examination by an external auditor:

   i.   The statement of financial position is a valuation of the company.

   ii. The amounts in the financial statements are stated exactly.

   iii. An unmodified auditor's opinion indicates that no frauds have happened in the year to date.

   A   i and ii only.
   B   i and iii only.
   C   ii and iii only.
   D   All of the above.

10 Identify which of the following statements defines the role and scope of an external audit?

   A   The external audit is performed to offer an opinion on the strength and quality of a company's internal controls.

   B   The external audit is conducted to provide an opinion on whether the financial statements of a company are fairly presented (give a true and fair view).

   C   The external audit's purpose is to identify areas of weakness within a company and to offer advice to help address those weaknesses.

   D   The external audit is carried out to provide a 'value for money' opinion on the performance of the directors.

11 Identify which of the following is correct in relation to external audit:

   A   The external auditor's opinion is NOT one of absolute correctness of the financial statements.
   B   The external auditors opinion is a guarantee of correctness of the financial statements.
   C   The definition of 'True and fair' is stated clearly in legal and auditing rules.
   D   External auditors do NOT give opinions on the financial statements.

12 Select which of the following is a definition of audit risk:

   A   Audit risk is the risk that the auditor expresses an inappropriate audit opinion when the financial statements are materially misstated.

   B   Audit risk is the risk that the financial statements are incorrect due to circumstances beyond the director's or auditor's influence.

   C   Audit risk is the risk that the controls put in place by directors are not working.

   D   Audit risk is the risk that the auditor will not get paid.

13 Identify which of the following are components of internal control according to ISA 315 (Revised) *Identifying and Assessing the Risks of Material Misstatement*:

   i.   The control environment.
   ii. The entity's risk assessment process.
   iii. The information system relevant to business risk.
   iv. Control activities.

   A   i, ii and iii only
   B   i, ii and iv only
   C   i, iii and iv only
   D   ii, iii and iv only

EXAM QUESTION BANK

14 In the United Kingdom external auditors have rights defined in statutory law.

Which of the following is an accurate statement of the external auditor's rights in relation to Resignation of Auditors in the United Kingdom:

- A Auditors can receive all notices that relate to a general meeting where a permanent vacancy caused by their resignation is to be filled.
- B Auditors can receive all notices that relate to Board of Directors meetings where a casual vacancy caused by their resignation is to be filled.
- C Auditors can speak at Board of Directors meetings on any matter which concerns them as auditors.
- D Auditors can receive all notices that relate to a general meeting at which their term of office would have expired.

15 In relation to corporate governance, different countries have responded to financial scandals in a variety of ways. In the United States of America, a significant piece of corporate governance legislation was introduced.

Identify which of the following describes characteristics of the Sarbanes-Oxley Act of 2002:

- A Sarbanes-Oxley shifts responsibility for financial integrity and accuracy to the Finance Director.
- B An Audit Committee, under the Sarbanes-Oxley Act, typically comprises three independent directors.
- C The Sarbanes-Oxley Act 2002 was the response of the US government to the Parmalat scandal.
- D Sarbanes-Oxley maintains the same financial statement disclosures requirements in place before the Act was introduced.

16 Which of the following definitions is true in relation to risks faced by a company?

- A Strategic risks are the threats that the auditor's planning of the audit fails to focus on the balances and accounts which are most likely to be misstated.
- B Operational risks relate to the threat posed by the auditor if he or she gives a negative opinion on the financial statements.
- C Independence risks are the threats to the existing directors if the shareholders appoint a director who owns shares in the company.
- D Business risks are the threats that an event or action will adversely affect a business's ability to achieve its ongoing objectives.

17 Select the control objective below which is relevant to the occurrence and existence assertions for the purchases system:

- A To ensure that recorded purchases represent goods received.
- B To ensure that all purchase transactions that occurred have been recorded.
- C To ensure that recorded purchases represent the liabilities of the entity.
- D To ensure that purchases are recorded at the correct amount and in the right account.

18 Identify which of the following statements is true with regard to an external auditor's purpose:

A The auditor's work is performed in order to provide absolute assurance regarding the financial statements.

B The auditor's work is performed in order to provide reasonable assurance regarding the financial statements.

C Auditor's reports with modified opinions occur when there are any misstatements in the financial statements.

D Auditor's reports with modified opinions occur when the auditor has not had time to obtain sufficient appropriate audit evidence.

19 A key factor of an assurance engagement is a three-party relationship.

Select which of the following are the parties in this relationship:

i. A practitioner.
ii. A responsible party.
iii. A regulatory body.
iv. An intended user.

A i, ii and iii only.
B i, iii and iv only.
C i, ii and iv only.
D ii, iii and iv only.

20 The UK Corporate Governance Code is a good example of a typical corporate governance code. Before this came about, there were several developments in corporate governance including the Cadbury Report of 1992.

Identify which of the following statements describes the main area(s) covered in the Cadbury Report:

A Directors' salaries.
B Non-executive directors.
C Composition and the role of boards.
D Risk management and internal control.

21 Identify which of the following statements is correct in relation to a Remuneration Committee according to the UK Corporate Governance Code:

A It must be staffed by a minimum of two non-executive directors.

B It can include the CEO of the organisation.

C It must seek to pay directors the lowest possible amount in order to protect the interests of shareholders.

D It must be staffed by independent non-executive directors.

22 An external auditor selects a sample of inventory from the storeroom, notes down the details of each, and traces these items to the inventory recorded in the accounting records.

Identify which of the following accurately describes this test procedure:

A A substantive test for existence of inventory.
B A substantive test for completeness of inventory.
C A test of control for inventory.
D A walk-through test for inventory.

23 Select which of the following statements is true, in relation to regulations for appointing an auditor in the UK:

- A Auditors must be appointed before the company's first period has commenced.
- B Auditors must be appointed after the company's first period has commenced.
- C The Secretary of State can appoint auditors.
- D Only directors can appoint auditors.

24 An auditor of a manufacturing company wishes to confirm whether the company owns motor vehicles.

Select which of the following sources of evidence is most persuasive for this:

- A Inspection of vehicle registration documents.
- B Physical inspection of the motor vehicles.
- C Checking that the motor vehicles are recorded in the non-current asset register.
- D Review of vehicle insurance documentation.

25 Select which of the following is a general control in terms of an entity's internal control within a computerised environment:

- A Manual or programmed agreement of control totals.
- B Reasonableness test (for example, sales tax as a percentage of total value).
- C Cyclical reviews of all master files and standing data.
- D Standards over systems design and programming.

May 2022

26 Identify which of the following describes the main features of Corporate Governance:

    A   Corporate governance is the system by which companies are directed and controlled.

    B   Corporate governance is about how companies are controlled by the government.

    C   Corporate governance is about relationships between a company's directors and government.

    D   Executive directors are responsible for the governance of their companies.

27 Identify which of the following features of a rule- or principles-based approach to corporate governance is correct.

    i.   In a rule-based approach, the law requires total compliance in all details.

    ii.   In a principles-based approach, listed companies are required by the law to meet certain standards of compliance.

    iii.   In a rule-based approach, it is investors who monitor and punish transgression.

    iv.   In a principles-based approach, the shareholders assess the transgression and take appropriate action.

    A   i and ii only.
    B   i and iv only.
    C   ii and iii only.
    D   ii and iv only.

28 Identify which of the following features of a 'Comply or Explain' basis of UK Corporate Governance Code is NOT true:

    A   Listed companies are expected to align with the Principles of the Code.

    B   Listed companies may choose whether or not to comply with its Provisions.

    C   While a departure from the Code could achieve effective corporate governance, an explanation is not necessary.

    D   Companies should provide full and meaningful explanations to define why they did not comply and discuss the rationale for the departure and any potential risks associated with it.

29 According to the UK Corporate Governance Code, which of the following statements are valid in relation to the board and its membership?

    i.   The board should include a combination of executive and non-executive directors.
    ii.   The roles of chair and chief executive should not be the same individual.
    iii.   All the non-executive directors need to be independent.

    A   i and ii only.
    B   i and iii only.
    C   ii and iii only.
    D   All of the above.

30 The UK Corporate Governance Code suggests that the board should establish a Nomination Committee to lead the process for appointments. Identify which of the following is the recommended membership of the Nomination Committee:

    A   All of the members should be executive directors.
    B   All of the members should be independent non-executive directors.
    C   Majority of the members should be independent non-executive directors.
    D   Majority of the members should be executive directors.

31 The UK Corporate Governance Code set up principles and provisions for the composition of boards and the committees. Identify which of the following is the recommended membership of the Remuneration Committee:

   A   All members should be executive directors of the company.
   B   All members should be non-executive directors of the company.
   C   All members should be independent, non-executive directors of the company.
   D   The chair of the board should be a member regardless of his/her independence.

32 Select which of the following statements illustrate the responsibility of the Audit Committee:

   i.   Monitoring the integrity of the financial statements of the company.
   ii.   Preparing the annual report and accounts.
   iii. Monitoring and reviewing the effectiveness of the company's internal audit function.
   iv.   Reviewing the effectiveness of the company's external audit process.

   A   i, ii and iii.
   B   i, ii and iv.
   C   ii, iii and iv.
   D   i, iii and iv.

33 Which of the following statements about the composition of the Audit Committee is true according to the UK Corporate Governance Code?

   A   An audit committee should be established with a minimum of two independent non-executive directors for large and small companies.
   B   The chair of the board should be a member.
   C   At least one member needs to have recent and relevant financial experience.
   D   Every member of the Audit Committee shall have competence to a range of business sectors.

34 Which of the following is a statutory right of the auditors of a limited liability company?

   A   A right to access all information that management and those charged with governance are aware is relevant to the preparation of the financial statements.
   B   A right to attend any general meetings and speak at the general meetings on any part of the business.
   C   A right to attend all directors' meetings and receive all notices and communications relating to such meetings.
   D   A right to speak at directors' meetings and take part in executive decisions on behalf of the company.

35 Identify which of the following statements is correct in relation to the audit of financial statements:

   A   The audited financial statements provide information about the company's future performance.
   B   The audit of financial statement enhances the degree of confidence of intended users in the financial statements.
   C   The audited financial statements accurately indicate the valuation of the company.
   D   The audited financial statements with an unmodified auditor's opinion indicate all the information is accurate.

36 Identify which of the following statements defines the role and scope of an external audit?

    A   The external audit constitutes an assurance engagement with respect to the future viability of the audited entity.

    B   The external audit provides assurance on the efficiency or effectiveness with which the board has conducted the affairs of the entity.

    C   The external audit is carried out to provide an opinion on the quality and effectiveness of a company's internal controls.

    D   The external audit is conducted to provide an opinion on whether the financial statements, in all material respects, give a true and fair view in accordance with an applicable financial reporting framework.

37 The concept of materiality is applied both in planning and performing the audit, and in evaluating the effect of identified misstatements. Select which of the following statements is NOT true:

    A   The auditor is responsible for the detection of misstatements that are material to the financial statements.

    B   Misstatements are considered to be material if they could be expected to influence the economic decisions of users taken on the basis of the financial statements.

    C   Judgments about materiality are made by the management of the company.

    D   The size or nature of a misstatement could affect the auditor's judgement about materiality.

38 For the purpose of International Standards on Auditing, which of the following definitions of audit evidence is correct?

    A   Audit evidence includes the information contained in the accounting records for financial statements only.

    B   Audit evidence is the information used by the auditor to conclude the auditor's opinion.

    C   The quality of audit evidence is affected by auditor's assessment of the risks of material misstatement.

    D   Appropriateness of audit evidence is the measure of the quantity of audit evidence.

39 Identify which of the following statements about audit risk are accurate:

    i.   Audit risk is the risk that the auditor expresses an inappropriate audit opinion when the financial statements are materially misstated.

    ii.   Audit risk is a function of the risks of material misstatement and control risk.

    iii.   Audit risk means that the procedures performed to reduce audit risk will not detect the existence of material misstatement.

    A   i only.
    B   ii only.
    C   iii only.
    D   i and ii only.

EXAM QUESTION BANK

40 Select which of the following statements is true, in relation to the appointment of an auditor in the UK:

A   The auditors could only be appointed by the directors.

B   The auditors should be answerable to the directors.

C   The auditors could be appointed by the Secretary of State.

D   The auditors do not need to be appointed for the first period of the company's commencement and directors do not need to resolve otherwise on the grounds that audited financial statements are unlikely to be required.

41 Simon and Kevin set up an online delivery business to provide delivery service for local restaurants and shops. Since Simon has a full time job, they have decided that when setting up the limited company, Simon makes an initial investment for the business, and owns the majority of the shares and is entitled to dividends; and Kevin is the managing director and will be paid a salary for his work. At the end of the first year of trading as a limited company, Simon received a copy of the financial statements. He is disappointed at the profit, as his dividend will not be as large as expected. While Kevin is paid a salary which was decided at the beginning.

Which of the following statements about this scenario is true:

A   Simon and Kevin are both shareholders of the business.

B   According to agency theory, Simon acts as the agent in his relationship to Kevin.

C   According to agency theory, Simon acts as the principle in his relationship to Kevin.

D   The best theory to explain the problem facing Simon in terms of his relationship to Kevin is Stewardship theory.

42 Identify which of the following is NOT an element of an assurance engagement performed by a practitioner:

A   A two party relationship.
B   A subject matter.
C   An assurance report.
D   Suitable criteria.

43 A small manufacturing company pays its staff in cash and by bank transfer. The payroll is maintained on the laptop owned by the chief accountant, who reports to the managing director. The chief accountant is the only member in the payroll department. As the auditor of this company, which of the following describes the internal control objectives that should be in place for the payroll department:

i.   To ensure that gross pay and deductions from gross pay have been calculated correctly.
ii. To ensure that only genuine staff are paid for what is performed.
iii. To ensure that the correct employees are paid what they are entitled to.
iv. To ensure that right amounts due for tax and national insurance are paid on a timely basis.

A   i, ii, and iii.
B   i, ii, and iv.
C   i, iii, and iv.
D   All of the above.

44 Under which of the following occasions would the net realisable value of inventory be likely to fall below cost:

i. An increase in selling price.
ii. Error in production or purchasing.
iii. Products from discontinued lines.
iv. A marketing decision to sell products at a loss.

A i, ii, and iii.
B i, ii, and iv.
C i, iii, and iv.
D ii, iii, and iv.

45 The internal control procedures in a computerised environment comprise two types of control; general controls and information processing controls. Select which of the following is an information processing control:

A Password protection of programs so that access is limited to computer operations staff.
B Virus checks on software.
C Cyclical review of all master files and standing data.
D Storing extra copies of programs and data files off-site.

46 Identify which of following statements is true, in relation to modified opinions in auditor's reports:

A A disclaimer of opinion is issued when the auditor cannot obtain sufficient appropriate audit evidence but concludes that the possible effects on the financial statements of undetected misstatements could be material but not pervasive.

B A qualified opinion is issued when the auditor cannot obtain sufficient appropriate audit evidence and concludes that the possible effects on the financial statements of undetected misstatements could be both material and pervasive.

C A qualified opinion is issued when the auditor concludes that misstatements are pervasive, but not material, to the financial statements.

D An adverse opinion is issued when, having obtained sufficient appropriate audit evidence, the auditor concludes that misstatements are both material and pervasive to the financial statements.

47 Identify which of the following could be issues reflecting the 'expectations gap' of auditors and the users of audited financial statements:

i. The amounts in the financial statements are stated precisely.

ii. The auditors provide absolute assurance that the figures in the financial statements are correct.

iii. The audited financial statements will guarantee that the entity will continue to exist.

iv. The auditors check all the documents and evidence.

A i, ii, and iii.
B i, ii, and iv.
C ii, iii, and iv.
D All of the above.

48 Select which of following procedures provide evidence concerning the completeness of the vehicles owned by the company:

A Compare vehicles in the general ledger with the vehicle register.
B Confirm that the company physically inspects all the vehicles in the register each year.
C Confirm all vehicles are used for the client's business.
D Reconcile opening and closing vehicles by numbers as well as amounts.

49 Inspecting the title deeds of a property provides audit evidence concerning which one of the following financial statement assertions?

   A   Occurrence.
   B   Completeness.
   C   Rights and obligations.
   D   Valuation.

50 When auditing the financial statements of a company using e-commerce, the auditor needs to have a good understanding of the business to assess the significance of e-commerce and its effect on audit risk. Which of the following are the specific risks affecting entities that engage in e-commerce:

   i.   Systems and infrastructure failures or crashes.
   ii. Over-reliance on e-commerce.
   iii. Security risks.
   iv. Outsourcing arrangements.

   A   i, ii, and iii.
   B   i, iii, and iv.
   C   ii, iii, and iv.
   D   All of the above.

November 2022

51 Identify which of the following best describes the definition of Corporate Governance:

A   Corporate governance is about how companies are supervised and controlled by the government.

B   Corporate governance is about making sure that companies are supervised and controlled to protect the interests of directors.

C   Corporate governance is about making sure that companies are supervised and controlled to protect the interests of shareholders only.

D   Corporate governance is about making sure that companies are supervised and controlled to protect the interests of shareholders and other stakeholders.

52 Identify which of the following statements related to an agency problem is correct:

A   Auditors being related to the management of the companies that they audit is not an agency problem.

B   The agency problem refers to the problem that the auditors do not act in the management of companies' interests.

C   The agency problem refers to the issue that managers do not consider the impact of business decisions on a wide range of groups in society, but only for their shareholders.

D   The agency problem can be addressed by offering company managers reward incentives depending on the achievement of ownership goals.

53 Shareholder activism refers to the way that "shareholders assess their power as owners of the company to influence its behaviour" (European Corporate Governance Institute). Identify which of the following are the possible drivers for shareholder activism:

i.   Failure to comply with laws and regulations, or corporate governance codes.
ii. Poor operational performance of key business segments.
iii. Concerns of excessive levels of directors' remuneration.
iv. Poor attitudes toward corporate social responsibility such as poor working conditions.

A   i, ii, and iii only.
B   ii, iii, and iv only.
C   i, iii, and iv only.
D   All of the above.

54 Identify which of the following statements describing the international corporate governance guidance is true:

A   The OECD has developed a set of rules-based corporate governance codes that countries and companies need to achieve.

B   According to OECD corporate governance code, minority shareholders and overseas shareholders should be treated differently from other shareholders.

C   The Sarbanes-Oxley Act (2002) adopts a rules-based approach that applies to all companies that file periodic reports with the Securities and Exchange Commission.

D   Sarbanes-Oxley Act (2002) requires all listed companies to establish a remuneration committee.

55 Identify which of the following features of a rules- or principles-based approach to corporate governance is NOT true:

- A Principles-based approaches focus on objectives rather than how the objectives are achieved.
- B Principles-based corporate governance codes are usually enforced on a 'comply or explain' basis.
- C A rules-based approach allows flexibility for different circumstances and organisations with different sizes or in different stages of development.
- D Rules-based corporate governance codes must be complied with by the companies, or they will face penalties.

56 Castle Co. is a company seeking a listing on the London Stock Exchange. The board of Castle Co. includes a CEO who is also acting as the Chair with four additional executive directors and one non-executive director. Identify which of the following statements is correct in relation to the board composition according to the UK Corporate Governance code:

- A Castle Co. should appoint only one more non-executive director.
- B Castle Co. should appoint four more independent non-executive directors, including a new Chair.
- C Castle Co. should reappoint two of its executive directors as non-executive directors.
- D Castle Co. should reappoint one of its executive directors as independent Chair.

57 You are an audit manager in Auditgo & Co. One of your clients, ABB Plc. is a company recently listed on the London Stock Exchange and asks your advice regarding achieving appropriate compliance with corporate governance best practice in the UK.

Ms Abby has been the CEO and Chair of the board of ABB for five years. The company maintains a board of five executive and one non-executive directors. The board sets performance targets for the senior managers in the company, but no formal targets are set for each director and no review of board policies is carried out. Ms Abby decides the salaries of all the board members, including herself, based on her own assessment every year. Identify which of the following actions would improve ABB's corporate governance compliance regarding the board:

- A ABB should establish a remuneration committee responsible for the appointment of new directors.
- B ABB should appoint a new Chair.
- C All the board members of ABB should be involved in the evaluation of its directors' performance and remuneration.
- D As the CEO and Chair of ABB, Ms Abby should review board policies every four years.

58 According to the UK Corporate Governance code, identify which of the following persons could be appointed as an independent non-executive director of a listed company:

- A A loyal employee who has worked for the company for the last ten years.
- B The current CEO's son.
- C A previous employee who is a member of the company's pension scheme.
- D The company's former sales manager who resigned five years ago.

59 Identify which of the following statements is true regarding the directors' salaries, as suggested by the UK Corporate Governance code:

   A   CEO should decide directors' salaries based on their actual performance.

   B   A remuneration committee, headed by the CEO, should be established to set directors' salaries.

   C   A remuneration committee composed of independent non-executive directors should be established to set CEO's salaries.

   D   A nomination committee composed of independent non-executive directors should be established to set directors' salaries.

60 Identify which of the following statements regarding the nomination committee is true according to the UK Corporate Governance code:

   A   All the members of the nomination committee should be executive directors.

   B   All the members of the nomination committee should be independent non-executive directors.

   C   The majority of nomination committee members should be independent non-executive directors.

   D   The CEO should also be the Chair of the nomination committee.

61 An audit committee is a sub-committee of the board. According to the UK Corporate Governance code, which of the following statements relating to the audit committee is true?

   A   The Chair of the board should be a member of the audit committee.
   B   The majority of the audit committee members should be non-executive directors.
   C   The audit committee should supervise internal audit and review the annual accounts.
   D   All members of the audit committee should have relevant financial experience.

62 Identify which of the following statements about risk are accurate:

   i.   Strategic risks relate to events or actions that could adversely affect a business's ability to achieve its ongoing objectives.

   ii.   Operational risks relate to daily matters that can go wrong while the business is operating.

   iii. Business risks relate to the fundamental decisions that the board make about the future strategic direction of the organisation.

   A   i only.
   B   ii only.
   C   iii only.
   D   i and ii only.

63 Identify which of the following statements is correct in relation to the purpose and scope of external auditing:

   A   External audit provides assurance to the shareholders and other stakeholders of a company on the financial statements.

   B   External audit gives an opinion on the correctness of the financial statements.

   C   External audit provides recommendations to the directors on improvements to the company's corporate governance.

   D   External audit aims to detect fraud in the financial statements.

64 Identify which of the following is a test of control:

  A Reviewing an invoice for proof that items belong to the company.
  B Reperform the calculation and accounting treatment for a revaluation surplus.
  C Verify the valuation of property to against a valuation certificate.
  D Inspection of purchase order documentation to confirm that it has been correctly authorised.

65 Which of the following are methods used to obtain audit evidence?

  i.   Inspection and observation.
  ii. Recalculation and reperformance.
  iii. Inquiry and external confirmation.
  iv. Analytical procedures.

  A i, ii, and iii only.
  B ii, iii, and iv only.
  C i, ii, and iv only.
  D All of the above.

66 Identify which of the following statements about audit sampling is NOT true:

  A When using audit sampling, all sampling units should have an equal chance of selection.
  B Audit sampling could be applied using statistical sampling or non-statistical sampling approaches.
  C Statistical sampling involves random selection of items.
  D Non-statistical sampling uses probability theory to evaluate results.

67 Inspection of vehicles that are recorded in the accounting records confirms which of the following financial statement assertions?

  A Existence.
  B Rights and obligations.
  C Valuation.
  D Classification.

68 Identify which of the following audit tests could be used to gain evidence in relation to the completeness of receivables:

  A Perform a receivables' confirmation on a sample of trade receivables.
  B Review board minutes for evidence of receivables being factored.
  C Trace a sample of shipping documentation to sales invoices and into the sales and receivables' ledger accounts.
  D Compare the bad debt expense as a percentage of sales to the previous year.

69 Internal audit plays an important role in a company's risk management. Select which of the following is NOT a function of internal audit:

  A Assessing the operation and effectiveness of the risk management processes.
  B Working for external auditors to reduce the time and cost of external auditing.
  C Assisting the implementation of new auditing and accounting standards.
  D Assessing the appropriateness of internal controls in operations.

70 Select which of the following statements are true about the differences between internal and external audit:

i. The audit report provided by internal auditors is publicly available.
ii. The external auditors are usually appointed by the shareholders.
iii. External audit adds value and improves a company's operation.
iv. Internal auditors report to the board of directors and/or the audit committee.

A i and ii.
B i and iii.
C ii and iii.
D ii and iv.

71 Internal audit could be outsourced to external providers. Select the accurate statement in relation to outsourcing internal audit:

A Outsourcing internal audit to the same firm that provides external audit services could improve the independence of the services.

B Service providers from outsourced suppliers would have specialist skills.

C Service providers from outsourced suppliers have better knowledge of the company.

D Outsourcing internal audit can only be used for long-term contracts.

72 Select which of the following examples of sales system controls matches the correct category:

i. Checking credit limits before accepting new orders is a Preventative control.
ii. Performing a control account reconciliation is a Corrective control.
iii. Following up slow-payers and adjusting credit limits as necessary is a Detective control.

A i only.
B ii only.
C iii only.
D None of the above.

73 ABC Co. keeps perpetual inventory records. Identify which of the following activities will contribute to the assertions of valuation and allocation of inventory recorded in the financial statements:

i. Procedures to identify obsolete and damaged inventory.
ii. Comparison of cost of inventory with selling price.
iii. Reconciliation of inventory records to results of inventory counts.
iv. Physical safeguards to protect inventory from theft.

A i and ii.
B i and iii.
C ii and iii.
D ii and iv.

74 ABC Co. is a gallery and has plenty of paintings. Select which risk management strategies would be the best for managing the risk of theft:

i. Avoidance.
ii. Mitigation.
iii. Transfer.
iv. Acceptance.

A i and ii.
B iii and iv.
C i and iv.
D ii and iii.

75 Select the two elements of risk of material misstatement at the assertion level:

i. Inherent risk.
ii. Detection risk.
iii. Audit risk.
iv. Control risk.

A   i and ii.
B   ii and iii.
C   i and iv.
D   ii and iv.

May 2023

76 Identify which of the following statements about the definition of Corporate Governance is correct:

- A Corporate governance is about making sure that companies are directed and controlled by the directors to maximize their own wealth.
- B Corporate governance is about making sure that companies are monitored and controlled by the government.
- C Corporate governance is about making sure that companies are supervised and controlled to improve companies' accountability to shareholders and to non-shareholding stakeholders.
- D Corporate governance is the system by which companies are directed aiming to attract capital investment into companies.

77 Nowadays, very few large businesses are managed by their owners. The separation of ownership from control provides the context of agency theory. Identify which of the following statements related to agency theory is correct:

- A In corporate entities, agency theory is concerned with resolving the problems between stakeholders (the principals), and the executives (the paid agents).
- B In the context of a business organisation, the executives and managers of the business are accountable to the creditors to act in their best interests.
- C One of the key problems agency theory addresses, is how to motivate the managers in a company to grow the company in a way that maximises their personal power and wealth, rather than in a way that generates value for the shareholders.
- D Agency costs are incurred when shareholders provide reward incentives to try to ensure that managers execute their duties in a way that increases shareholder value.

78 Identify which of the following statements related to stakeholders and stakeholder theory is correct:

- A Directors and managers need to be aware of the interests of stakeholders in governance, because they are also principals of the firm.
- B Stakeholders are any group that can affect or be affected by the achievements of an organisation's objectives.
- C All stakeholder groups have similar expectations about their wants and similar claims upon the organisation.
- D Stakeholders have no influence over the organisation, so it is not important to acknowledge claims made by the stakeholders.

79 Identify which of the following statements relating to the OECD corporate governance guidance and the Sarbanes-Oxley Act (2002) in the US is correct:

- A The OECD developed a set of corporate governance rules that governments could apply as the corporate governance code in their countries.
- B The OECD corporate governance guidance suggests that the board could choose when and what to disclose regarding the company, with only the financial situation and risk factors considered as material matters.
- C The OECD corporate governance guidance led to the formation of The Public Company Accounting Oversight Board (PCAOB), to oversee the audit of public companies.
- D The Sarbanes-Oxley Act (2002) is an example of a rules-based approach to corporate governance.

80 The UK Corporate Governance Code is an example of a typical corporate governance code, which has been developed for decades. Identify which of the following statements describing the UK Corporate Governance Code is correct:

   A   The UK Corporate Governance Code adopts a principles-based approach, which allows companies more flexibility to apply the codes based on their own circumstances.

   B   The UK Corporate Governance Code emphasises the mechanisms to achieve targets rather than focusing on the objectives themselves.

   C   The UK Corporate Governance Code requires all companies to comply with the rules or face penalties.

   D   The most recent update to the UK Corporate Governance Code is the UK Stewardship Code published in 2019, which mainly covers guidance on good practice for institutional investors.

81 There are different board structures in different countries. Identify which of the following statements regarding board structure is correct:

   A   In a unitary board, all directors are executive directors.

   B   The board of directors in a UK listed company normally consists of executive directors and independent non-executive directors.

   C   The two-tier board system consists of both the supervisory board and the management board. The management board appoints the supervisory board.

   D   In the traditional Japanese business network model (Keiretsu), the board is large in size with a majority of independent external directors.

82 You are an audit manager in BESTAUDIT & Co. One of your clients, HOMERUN Co. is a company seeking to list on the London Stock Exchange and asks your advice on effective boards. Identify which of the following could improve the board effectiveness:

   i.   Have a balance of executive and non-executive directors on board.

   ii. Increase the diversity of expertise and background of board members.

   iii. The CEO should assess the performance of the board, its committees, and individual directors once a year.

   iv. Every director needs to receive appropriate training when first appointed, but no subsequent trainings are necessary.

   A   i and ii only.
   B   i and iii only.
   C   iii and iv only.
   D   ii and iii only.

83 Mr Dickenson is the CEO and Chair of the board of HOMEBUY Co. and has held these positions for the last ten years. The company maintains a board of five executive directors (including the CEO) and one non-executive director. According to the UK Corporate Governance Code, identify which of the following actions would improve HOMEBUY's corporate governance compliance regarding the board composition:

    A   HOMEBUY Co. should reappoint two of its executive directors as independent non-executive directors.

    B   HOMEBUY Co. should reappoint the existing non-executive director as independent chair.

    C   HOMEBUY Co. should appoint an independent non-executive director as the new chair and three more independent non-executive directors.

    D   HOMEBUY Co. should appoint two more independent non-executive directors.

84 According to the UK Corporate Governance Code, identify which of the following statements is true regarding the directors' remuneration:

    A   The company does not need to disclose their remuneration policy or the remuneration package of individual directors.

    B   Directors' remuneration should be decided based on individual performance only.

    C   Directors' remuneration should be set by a remuneration committee consisting of independent non-executive directors and the CEO.

    D   The remuneration committee should consider stakeholders' opinions and ethical considerations when determining packages.

85 The nomination committee is responsible for recommending the appointment of directors to the board. Identify which of the following statements regarding the nomination committee is true:

    A   According to the UK Corporate Governance Code, the nomination committee should be wholly comprised of independent non-executive directors.

    B   According to the UK Corporate Governance Code, all directors should be subject to re-election every three years.

    C   The UK Corporate Governance Code states that the chair of the board should always chair the nomination committee.

    D   The UK Corporate Governance Code suggests using external search agencies and open advertising when appointing a non-executive director.

86 The board has overall responsibility for risk management as an essential part of its corporate governance responsibilities. Identify which of the following statements describing the risk management committee is correct:

    A   All boards should establish a separate risk committee for monitoring and supervising risk identification and management.

    B   Under the UK Corporate Governance Code, if the board doesn't have a separate risk committee, the audit committee should be responsible for risk management.

    C   A risk management committee should consist of non-executive directors only.

    D   The risk management committee is responsible for reviewing all the company's statements on internal control.

87 Identify which of the following statements regarding risk management is correct:

    A   The correct order for the risk management process is identification, assessment, and then management.

    B   Risk with low likelihood of occurrence but serious impact should be accepted.

    C   Risk with high likelihood of occurrence and high impact could be transferred.

    D   Insurance is a way to avoid risk.

88 According to the UK Corporate Governance Code, which of the following statements regarding the audit committee is true:

    A   The chair of the board should be a member of the audit committee.

    B   The board should establish an audit committee of independent non-executive directors, and all members should have recent financial experience.

    C   The audit committee should be responsible for reviewing the external auditor's independence.

    D   The audit committee should be responsible for preparing the annual reports and accounts.

89 Identify which of the following statements best describes the objective of the external audit:

    A   The purpose of the external audit is to prevent material fraud.

    B   The external audit provides negative assurance on the correctness of a company's financial statements.

    C   The purpose of the external audit is to give an opinion on the effectiveness of a company's system of internal control.

    D   The purpose of the external audit is to give an opinion on whether the financial statements of a company give a true and fair view.

90 Identify which of the following assignments could be carried out by the internal auditors:

    i.   Financial and operational audits.
    ii.   Information technology (IT) audit.
    iii.   Social and environmental audits.
    iv.   Value for money (VFM) audits.

    A   i, ii, and iii.
    B   i, iii, and iv.
    C   i, ii, and iv.
    D   i, ii, iii, and iv.

91 Identify which of the following could be example of an 'expectations gap':

    i.   The public believe that the audited financial statement will guarantee that the entity concerned will continue to exist.

    ii.   The public believe that an unmodified auditor's opinion means that no fraud has occurred in the period.

    iii.   The public believe that the auditors check all the receipts and figures.

    iv.   The public believe that internal audit is part of external audit.

    A   i, ii, and iii.
    B   i, iii, and iv.
    C   i, ii, and iv.
    D   ii, iii, and iv.

92 Identify which of the following statements regarding the appointment of auditors is true:

    A   For UK public companies, only directors can appoint auditors.
    B   The auditors should be appointed by and therefore answerable to the directors.
    C   An auditor must be appointed for each financial year.
    D   The Secretary of State can appoint auditors by ordinary resolution.

93 Identify which of the following statements regarding audit risk is true:

    A   Audit risk has two major components - inherent risk and control risk.
    B   Inherent risk is the risk that items will be misstated due to the characteristics of those items.
    C   Control risk could be reduced by increasing sample size or performing the audit well.
    D   Detection risk could be reduced by improved internal controls.

94 Identify which of the following is an information processing control:

    A   Manual checks to ensure information input was authorised.
    B   Virus checks on software.
    C   Segregation of duties.
    D   Full record of program changes.

95 The auditor of SDR Co is performing audit procedures to confirm the existence of equipment. Which of the following would provide the most persuasive evidence?

    A   Physical inspection of the equipment.
    B   Examine documents of title for the equipment such as purchase invoices.
    C   Checking that the equipment is recorded in the non-current asset register.
    D   Review non-current asset disclosure in the financial statements.

96 Which of the following procedure(s) should the auditor carry out if wages are paid in cash?

    i.   Examine receipts given by employees and confirm that unclaimed wages are recorded by inspection of the unclaimed wages book.
    ii.   Arrange to attend the pay-out of wages to confirm that the official procedures are being followed.
    iii.   Observe employees' use of time clocks.
    iv.   Confirm that no employee receives more than one wage packet by attending the pay-out.

    A   i, ii, and iii.
    B   i, ii, and iv.
    C   i, iii, and iv.
    D   ii, iii, and iv.

97 Identify which of the following tests of controls could NOT be used to satisfy the objective of ensuring that all the cash receipts are recorded.

    A   Observe the processing of cash and review the entity's policies to evaluate whether proper segregation of duties is operating.
    B   Examine information processing controls for electronic cash receipts transfer.
    C   Observe cash sales procedures.
    D   Enquire of management about handling of customer statements.

98 Identify which of the following describes the best reason for reviewing the delegated list of authority for purchases:

- A To ensure that recorded purchases represent goods and services received.
- B To ensure that all purchase transactions that occurred have been recorded.
- C To ensure that recorded purchases represent the liabilities of the entity.
- D To ensure that purchase transactions are correctly recorded in the accounting system.

99 Identify which of the following statements describing the internal and external audit is correct:

- A Internal audit relates to the financial statements.
- B External audit reports are publicly available to the shareholders and other interested parties.
- C Internal auditors report to the board of directors and shareholders.
- D Internal audit work is always risk-based.

100 The internal audit department may be outsourced to external service providers. Identify which of the following statements could describe the disadvantages of outsourcing:

- A The service provider has different specialist skills.
- B Associated costs are reduced.
- C The company will lose in-house skills.
- D The external service could be used on a short-time basis.

November 2023

101 Agency theory is used to understand the relationships between agents (such as directors) and principals (such as shareholders). Agency problems occur when the interests of principals and agents come into conflict. In a corporate context, corporate governance is highlighted to address agency problems. Identify which of the following statements describing how corporate governance codes resolve agency problems in corporate entities is correct:

- A Corporate governance codes alleviate the different attitudes towards risk between shareholders and directors by requiring disclosure of corporate social responsibility reports.
- B Corporate governance codes alleviate the problem of conflicting interests between shareholders and directors by aligning directors' remuneration with customer satisfaction.
- C According to the corporate governance codes, accountability could be enhanced by the creation of a nomination committee.
- D Corporate governance codes ensure directors fulfil their responsibilities as agents by suggesting they be rewarded on the basis of corporate performance.

102 The notion of stakeholder theory highlights the need for corporate entities to consider the implication of business decisions on a wide range of groups in society, rather than just to their shareholders. Identify which of the following statements related to stakeholder theory is correct:

- A Stakeholders include any person or groups that can be affected by a corporate entity's activities and objectives. It is a single-directional relationship.
- B In the context of a corporate entity, the executives and managers of the business need to be accountable to a number of stakeholders, as they all have legitimate interests in the corporate entity.
- C Each stakeholder group has different expectations from the corporate entity, but their relationship with the corporate entity is the same.
- D Only human interests are recognised as stakeholders as they are the parts of society that provide resources for the corporate entities.

103 Identify which of the following statements about the definition and advantages of corporate governance is correct:

- A Corporate governance is the system used to direct and control the companies to protect the interests of the directors.
- B Corporate governance is about the relationship between a company's directors, its shareholders and other stakeholders.
- C Corporate governance provides detailed guidance for an organisation to implement its strategy and offers safeguards against misuses of resources.
- D Corporate governance helps to increase accountability to the government and aims to attract new investment into companies.

104 The UK Corporate Governance Code is a good example of a typical corporate governance code. Identify which of the following statements about the historical development of the UK Corporate Governance Code is correct:

A   The main areas covered by Greenbury Report (1995) were about composition and role of the board.

B   The Turnbull Report (1999) mainly covered the area of non-executive directors.

C   The Higgs Report (2003) focused on risk management and internal control.

D   The Combined Code became the UK Corporate Governance Code in 2010.

105 Due to the increasing international trade and cross-border links, various international corporate governance codes were developed. Identify which of the following statements related to the international codes are correct:

A   The OECD developed a set of rules of corporate governance that countries and companies have to follow.

B   The US government issued the Sarbanes-Oxley Act (2002), which is an example of a principles-based approach to corporate governance.

C   The OECD codes are grouped into five broad areas including the right of shareholders, the equitable treatment of shareholders, the role of stakeholders, disclosure and transparency, and the responsibilities of the board.

D   The Sarbanes-Oxley Act (2002) applies to all companies that are required to file periodic reports with the Securities and Exchange Commission (SEC), but has no implications for overseas subsidiaries of those companies.

106 Many governance codes have adopted a principles-based approach, while others have a rules-based approach. Identify which of the following statements about the characteristics of these two approaches are correct:

A   A principles-based approach focuses on objectives rather than mechanisms.

B   Rules-based approaches can be applied across different legal jurisdictions.

C   Rules-based approaches are usually enforced on a comply or explain basis.

D   A principles-based approach allows no flexibility for different circumstances, which makes the enforcers difficult to deal with questionable situations.

107 The South African King Report provides a summary of the role of the board. The King Report stresses that the board is responsible for ensuring the company follows its strategic plan. Identify which of the following are the tasks that should be performed by the board of directors in relation to the King Report:

i.   Monitoring risks, control systems and governance.
ii. Managing potential conflicts of interest.
iii. Preparing the financial statements.
iv. Monitoring the Chief Executive Officer.

A   i, ii, and iii.
B   i, ii, and iv.
C   ii, iii, and iv.
D   i, iii, and iv.

108 All governance reports acknowledge the importance of having a division of responsibilities at the head of an organisation. Identify which of the following statements about board membership and roles are correct:

  i. The CEO is an executive director who leads the management team in the running of the organisation's business.

  ii. Non-executive directors do not have day-to-day operational responsibility for the company, but are employees of the company.

  iii. Non-executive directors should have no business, financial or other connection with the company.

  iv. The role of the chair is to lead the board of directors. It is recommended by the UK Corporate Governance Code that the chair should be the same individual as the CEO so that power could be centralised.

  A i and ii only.
  B ii and iii only.
  C i and iii only.
  D iii and iv only.

109 It is important that the best qualified candidates are appointed to the board. Identify which of the following statements about appointment of directors is correct:

  A A nomination committee should be established to recommend the appointment of new directors to the board.

  B The nomination committee should be made up wholly of executive directors.

  C The UK Corporate Governance Code states that all directors should be subject to annual re-election, but not the CEO.

  D An external consultancy firm should be hired to regularly review the structure, size and composition of the board, and keep under review the leadership needs of the company.

110 HOMETREE Co. is a company preparing for an IPO and seeking advice on effective boards. The directors of HOMETREE Co. read about the benefits of board diversity in the European Commission's Green Paper (2011), which could improve board efficiency. Identify which of the following statements about board diversity is correct:

  i. Diversified boards could bring a broad range of knowledge to the company.

  ii. A company committed to diversity has a better chance to access the wider talent pool.

  iii. Diversity in boards could result in lower cohesion and trust, unless members are trained to work together.

  iv. The Tyson report (2003) on Women on Boards in the UK highlights the benefits of greater female representation, and in the US, legislation required all listed companies to raise the proportion of women on their boards to 40% by 2008.

  A i, ii, and iii only.
  B i, ii, and iv only.
  C ii, iii, and iv only.
  D All of the above.

EXAM QUESTION BANK

111 According to the UK Corporate Governance Code, identify which of the following statements is true regarding remuneration committees and directors' remuneration:

A The remuneration committee is responsible for advising on executive director remuneration policy, however, the remuneration packages of individual directors should be decided by the shareholders.

B Remuneration committees should comprise independent non-executive directors.

C Remuneration packages of directors should be designed to attract and retain individuals of sufficient calibre, so should be as high as possible.

D Directors' remuneration should not be disclosed in the financial statements.

112 An audit committee is a sub-committee of the board of directors. Identify which of the following statements regarding the composition, role and function of the audit committee is correct based on the UK Corporate Governance Code:

A The members of an audit committee should all be independent non-executive directors, with relevant financial experience.

B The chair of the board should be a member of the audit committee.

C The committee is responsible for preparing the annual reports and accounts.

D The committee is responsible for reviewing and monitoring the external auditor's independence and objectivity.

113 Different risk management techniques will be appropriate in different circumstances. One should always consider whether the cost of introducing a risk management technique exceeds the benefit. DISKCO Co. is a family-owned IT training company based in India. One risk identified by the company is the risk that movable equipment could be stolen. Select which of the following is the most reasonable response to manage this risk, which has a high likelihood of occurrence but the impact would not be financially significant to the business.

A The company should accept the risk and do nothing.
B This risk should be managed by avoiding using movable equipment.
C This risk should be transferred by insurance.
D This risk should be mitigated by locking the training rooms and premises after use.

114 Risk is bound-up with doing business. It is important to implement effective risk management in the organisations. Select which of the following statements about risk management responsibilities is correct:

A Everyone who works for the organisation has responsibilities for risk management.

B Only members of the risk committee have responsibility for risk management.

C According to the UK Corporate Governance Code, if the board doesn't have a separate risk management committee, the remuneration committee will bear responsibility for risk management.

D Both internal and external auditors are responsible for risk management.

115 Identify which of the following statements best describes the objectives of the internal and external audit:

   i. Internal audit ensures the company's risk management system operates effectively.

   ii. External audit ensures that strategies implemented in respect of business risks operate effectively.

   iii. The purpose of an external audit is to enable auditors to give an independent opinion on the financial statements.

   iv. The internal audit provides assurance to the shareholders and other stakeholders of a company on the financial statements.

   A   i and ii only.
   B   i and iii only.
   C   ii and iii only.
   D   ii and iv only.

116 Analytical procedures are required during the risk assessment stage of the audit. Select which of the following are analytical procedures:

   i. Comparing financial information of the entity with industry information.

   ii. Comparing financial information of the entity with predictions prepared by the auditors.

   iii. Considering relationships between financial information and relevant non-financial information.

   iv. Considering relationships between elements of financial information that are expected to conform to a predicted pattern based on the entity's experience.

   A   i, ii, and iii only.
   B   ii, iii, and iv only.
   C   i, iii, and iv only.
   D   All of the above.

117 You are the external auditor for ROOMTOUR Co. which sells large furniture. Since COVID, ROOMTOUR Co. has struggled with supply chain and delivery and has a large amount of inventory stored in the warehouse. Identify which of the following procedures are relevant responses to the risk that inventory has a lower net realisable value than cost and is therefore overstated:

   A   Review the records of inventory counting and the level of corrections required to the quantities held on the inventory system.

   B   Increase sample sizes for inspecting recorded inventory, ensuring any material assets are verified.

   C   Increase the emphasis on reviewing the year-end aged inventory analysis for evidence of slow-moving inventory.

   D   Agree the cost of the newly purchased inventory to the purchase invoice.

118 Auditors shall obtain an understanding of control activities relevant to the audit and how the entity has responded to risks arising. Identify which of following examples of control activities relates to segregation of duties:

A   Approval and control of documents.

B   Checking the arithmetical accuracy of records.

C   Authorisation for access to computer programs and data files.

D   Assigning different people the responsibility of authorising transactions, recording transactions and maintaining custody of assets.

119 Internal audit can be involved in many different assignments as directed by management. Identify which of the following are examples of assignments that internal auditors can undertake:

i.   Assess the levels of customer service by visiting stores and pretending to be customers.
ii. Investigate specific instances of suspected fraud.
iii. Testing of controls over inventory counting or cash counting.
v.   Review controls over other computer systems that supply data to the accounting system.

A   i, ii, and iii only.
B   i, iii, and iv only.
C   i, ii, and iv only.
D   All of the above.

120 Audit evidence is all the information gathered and used by the auditor to reach the conclusion on which the auditor's opinion is based. Identify which of the following statements about the quality of audit evidence is true:

A   Sufficiency is the measure of the quality of audit evidence.

B   Audit evidence obtained from the entity's records is more reliable than that obtained from external sources.

C   Audit evidence obtained from the entity's records is more reliable when the related control system operates effectively.

D   Audit evidence obtained indirectly by auditors or by inference is more reliable than that obtained directly.

121 Auditors do not normally examine all the information available to them, and they use audit sampling to produce valid conclusions. It is important that the auditor selects a representative sample. Identify which of the following statements about sample selection methods is correct:

A   Systematic selection involves selecting items using a constant interval between selection, the first interval having a random start.

B   Block selection ensures that all items in the population have an equal chance of selection.

C   Random selection should not be used if auditors are carrying out statistical sampling.

D   Haphazard selection may be used to check whether certain items have particular characteristics.

122 Identify which of the following controls does NOT satisfy the objective of ensuring that cash payments are recorded in the correct accounting period.

- A Independent approval and review of the general ledger account assignment.
- B Reconciliation of electronic funds transfers and cheques issued with posting to cash payments journal and payable accounts.
- C Reconciliation of the daily payments report to electronic cash payment transfers and cheques issued.
- D Agreement of monthly cash payments journal to the general ledger posting.

123 Identify which of the following controls would NOT provide assurance that payment is made only to bona fide employees of the entity.

- A Use of time clocks to record time worked.
- B Segregation of duties between HR and payroll functions.
- C Comparison of cheques and bank transfer list with payroll records.
- D Review personnel file of employees whose status changed during the year.

124 Identify which of following audit procedures could be used to provide evidence for the existence of receivables.

- A Compare receivables' turnover and receivables' days to the previous year.
- B Perform a receivables' circularisation on a sample of year-end trade receivables.
- C Examine large customer accounts individually and compare to the previous year's balances.
- D Trace a sample of shipping documentation to sales invoices and into the sales and receivables' ledger.

125 As part of your audit of the purchasing system of a client, you have recommended that the goods inwards department should ensure that recorded purchases represent goods and services received. Select which of the following would be an appropriate test of control to confirm that the control is operating effectively.

- A For a sample of purchase orders in the year, check that each has been matched to a related invoice that was subsequently recorded.
- B Review purchases journal and general ledger for reasonableness.
- C Observe receipt of goods by staff to confirm staff receiving goods check them to the purchase order.
- D Review entity's procedures for accounting for prenumbered documents.

Exam Answer Bank

November 2021

1   C   The shareholders appoint the external auditor to undertake a statutory audit in order to give them assurance on the financial statements.

Distractors

- A   New investors are not the existing shareholders. They don't normally have the right to rely on the auditor's opinion.
- B   External auditors are only obliged to identify fraud where it has caused a material misstatement in the financial statements.
- D   Lenders are not the shareholders. While they might be interested in an external audit, they don't normally have the legal right to rely on the auditor's opinion.

2   A   George is subject to the agency theory. The agency theory refers to the problem that agents will pursue their personal interests, sometimes at the expense of making profits for the principals.

Distractors

- B   Internal auditing provides value to governing bodies and senior management as an objective source of independent advice.
- C   Stakeholder theory relates to the view that management should consider the needs of all relevant parties to a business - whether they are shareholders or not.
- D   Incorporation refers to the steps taken to form a company in law.

3   B   The relationships between the company directors, its shareholders and stakeholders. This definition captures the full range of parties included in the relationships of Corporate Governance.

Distractors

- A   Corporate governance includes relationships with a range of stakeholders not just those mentioned in A.
- C   Corporate governance includes relationships with the directors.
- D   Corporate governance includes the relationships with the shareholders.

4   C   A principles-based approach to corporate governance has the advantage of being applicable to any jurisdiction and any legal system. It also deters a 'tick box' approach to corporate governance.

Distractors

- A   While it can be applied to any jurisdiction and any legal system, a principles-based approach to corporate governance is not always straight-forward in terms of applying a set of rules.
- B   While a principles-based approach to corporate governance deters a 'tick box' approach it is not always easy for users to apply a set of rules.
- D   A principles-based approach can be applied to any jurisdiction and any legal system and can also deter a 'tick box' approach to corporate governance. However, it does not lend itself to the easy application by users of a set of rules.

EXAM ANSWER BANK

5   D   This defines the duties of directors in relation to their responsibilities for maintaining a sound system of internal control.

Distractors

- A   It is not always obligatory for directors to appoint an internal audit function and they are under no obligation to appoint external auditors to design and implement a system of internal control.
- B   It is not always obligatory for directors to appoint an internal audit function.
- C   Directors are not obliged to appoint an external auditor to design and implement a system of internal control.

6   C   A key purpose of the nomination committee is to ensure that directors are appointed based on their qualifications and experience rather than because of their relationship with the executive directors. Thus, the qualities of independent and non-executive directors reinforce this purpose.

Distractors

- A   Executive directors are not independent and therefore should not comprise wholly or mainly the Nomination Committee.
- B   The requirement is for independent, non-executive directors to form, wholly or mainly, the Nomination Committee if they are not independent then this would negate the purpose of the Nomination Committee.
- D   Employees of the entity's workforce are not independent, non-executive directors and so should not form the Nomination Committee.

7   C   The board should satisfy itself that at least one member has recent and relevant financial experience. This is a requirement of the UK Corporate Governance code.

Distractors

- A   The board should establish an Audit Committee of independent, non-executive directors, with a minimum membership of THREE, or in the case of smaller companies, TWO.
- B   The Chair of the board should NOT be a member of the Audit Committee.
- D   The Audit Committee as a whole shall have competence relevant to the sector in which the company operates.

8   A   A structure in which organisations are linked by taking small stakes in each other to reinforce their already close business relationship. This describes the Japanese network model where close ties between businesses (eg suppliers and buyers) lead to ways of working which are mutually beneficial.

Distractors

- B   A structure with a supervisory board and a management board is known as the two tier structure, used in Germany and other European countries.
- C   A structure which is centred on the family, with close family control typifies the Asian family-based model.
- D   A structure with a board of directors and independent, non-executive directors is known as a Unitary structure – typical in countries such as the UK, USA, Ireland, Australia and Canada.

EXAM ANSWERS BANK

9   D   Each of these statements are examples of misunderstandings about the role of external audit.

Distractors

- A   The statement of financial position represents a true and fair view of the company's financial position - it is not materially misstated. The amounts stated in the financial statements may, or may not, be stated precisely but it is not possible for an external audit to give this level of assurance.
- B   The statement of financial position represents a true and fair view of the company's financial position - it is not materially misstated. An unmodified auditor's opinion means that, in the auditor's opinion, the financial statements are not materially misstated whether due to fraud or error.
- C   The amounts stated in the financial statements may, or may not, be stated precisely but it is not possible for an external audit to give this level of assurance. An unmodified auditor's opinion means that, in the auditor's opinion, the financial statements are not materially misstated whether due to fraud or error.

10   B   The external audit is conducted to provide an opinion on whether the financial statements of a company are fairly presented (give a true and fair view).

The opinion is the ultimate reason for the external audit. The scope being the financial statements (and any other items required and agreed by the shareholders).

Distractors

- A   The external audit is carried out in order to give an opinion on the truth and fairness of the financial statements. The external auditor will, by taking a risk based audit approach, assess the effectiveness of controls with the aim of making an opinion about whether the financial statements are materially misstated or not.
- C   The external audit is performed in order to make an opinion about the truth and fairness of the financial statements. The external auditor will, while conducting the audit, identify areas of weakness within a company and make recommendations to address those weaknesses in order to help the company strengthen its controls.
- D   The external audit is carried out in order to give an opinion on the truth and fairness of the financial statements and not to provide a 'value for money' opinion on the performance of the directors.

11   A   The external auditor's opinion is not one of absolute correctness of the financial statements.

This highlights that the auditor's opinion reflects the need for sample testing, for example. It is not possible in most cases for the auditor to verify every balance and transaction.

Distractors

- B   The external auditor's opinion is an opinion – meaning it cannot be a guarantee of correctness of the financial statements.
- C   'True and fair' are not currently defined clearly in law and audit guidance.
- D   External auditors give opinions on the financial statements.

12   A   Audit risk is the risk that the auditor expresses an inappropriate audit opinion when the financial statements are materially misstated. This is the most complete definition of audit risk.

Distractors

- B   Audit risk is the risk that the auditor expresses an inappropriate opinion. The correctness of the financial statements is one of the responsibilities of the directors.
- C   Control risk is the risk that the controls put in place by directors are not working.
- D   An engagement acceptance risk is the risk that the auditor will not get paid.

13	B	Options i, ii and iv are all included in ISA 315 (Revised).

Distractors

- A The control environment and the entity's risk assessment process are correctly stated and included in ISA 315 (Revised). ISA 315 (Revised) lists the information system as a component 'relevant to the preparation of the financial statements'.
- C The control environment and control activities are correctly stated and included in ISA 315 (Revised). ISA 315 (Revised) lists the information system as a component 'relevant to the preparation of the financial statements'.
- D The entity's risk assessment process and control activities are correctly stated and included in ISA 315 (Revised). ISA 315 (Revised) lists the information system as a component 'relevant to the preparation of the financial statements'.

14	D	Auditors can receive all notices that relate to a general meeting at which their term of office would have expired.

Distractors

- A Auditors can receive all notices that relate to a general meeting where a **casual** vacancy caused by their resignation is to be filled.
- B Auditors can receive all notices that relate to a **general meeting** where a casual vacancy caused by their resignation is to be filled.
- C Auditors can speak at **general meetings** on any matter which concerns them as auditors.

15	B	An audit committee, under the Sarbanes-Oxley Act, typically comprises three independent directors.

Distractors

- A Sarbanes-Oxley shifts responsibility for financial integrity and accuracy to the board's audit committee.
- C The Sarbanes-Oxley Act 2002 was the response of the US government to the Enron scandal.
- D Sarbanes-Oxley requires companies to increase the financial statement disclosures in place before the Act was introduced.

16	D	**Distractors**

- A Strategic risks are the threats that the businesses' strategic goals are not met.
- B Operational risks are the threats faced by businesses in relation to their operational goals.
- C Independence risks are the risks arising if an external auditor is not independent or seen to be independent of the directors of the company.

17	A	To ensure that recorded purchases represent goods received.

This objective seeks to make sure that all receipts are recorded in the accounting records.

Distractors

- B To ensure that all purchase transactions that occurred have been recorded is an occurrence objective. However, existence of goods (existence) requires the receipt of the goods to be recorded.
- C To ensure that recorded purchases represent the liabilities of the entity is (partly) valid as an objective for **payables**.
- D To ensure that purchases are recorded at the correct amount and in the right account is an objective for **accuracy**.

EXAM ANSWERS BANK

18 B The auditor plans and performs an audit to obtain reasonable assurance.

Distractors

- A The auditor performs an audit to obtain **reasonable** assurance.
- C Auditor's reports with modified opinions may arise when there are **material** misstatements in the financial statements.
- D Auditor reports with modified opinions arise when there are material misstatements in the financial statements. The auditor is required to obtain sufficient appropriate audit evidence before forming an opinion.

19 C Only a practitioner, a responsible party and an intended user are included in the formal definition of the three party relationship.

Distractors

- A A practitioner and a responsible party are two parties in the formal definition of the three party relationship. A regulatory body is not party to the relationship.
- B A practitioner and an intended user are two parties in the formal definition of the three party relationship. A regulatory body is not party to the relationship.
- D A responsible party and an intended user are two parties in the formal definition of the three party relationship. A regulatory body is not party to the relationship.

20 C Composition and the role of boards are the main areas of the Cadbury Report of 1992.

Distractors

- A Directors' salaries (remuneration) was the main area covered by the Greenbury Report.
- B Non-executive directors was the main area covered by the Higgs Report.
- D Risk management and internal control was the main area covered by the Turnbull Report.

21 D The Remuneration Committee must be staffed by independent, non-executive directors. The Corporate Governance Code requires Remuneration Committee directors to be non-executive directors.

Distractors

- A A Remuneration Committee must be staffed by a minimum of two independent, non-executive directors.
- B A Remuneration Committee cannot include the CEO of the organisation.
- C Adequate remuneration (for example, in line with market norms) has to be paid to directors in order to attract and retain individuals of sufficient calibre.

22 B Tracing an asset to its record in the accounting records is a test of completeness which would be performed at the substantive 'tests of details' procedures of the audit.

Distractors

- A A substantive test for existence of inventory would include noting a sample from the inventory record and tracing it to the storeroom.
- C A test of control involves assessing whether a control exists and/or is operating effectively throughout the period being audited.
- D A walk-through test takes a sample of transactions and traces them through the client's system to assess whether the auditor has an accurate understanding of the system and its internal controls.

EXAM ANSWER BANK

23	C	This is the only true statement in the options provided.

Distractors

- A   There may be circumstances where auditors may not be appointed before the company's first period has commenced.
- B   Auditors may be appointed before the company's first period has commenced.
- D   Other parties can, in some circumstances appoint auditors – for example the Secretary of State in the UK.

24	A	Inspection of vehicle registration documents gives the best evidence as it is 3rd party evidence and will also reflect if the vehicle is still owned by the company.

Distractors

- B   Physical inspection of the motor vehicles will offer assurance as to existence but does not provide evidence of ownership.
- C   Checking that the motor vehicles are recorded in the non-current asset register is a test of completeness.
- D   Review of vehicle insurance documentation will offer some evidence of ownership but not if the asset has been sold since the insurance document was issued by the insurer.

25	D	This is a general control as standards are a form of policy or procedure which supports the effective working of a range of information processing controls.

Distractors

- A   Manual or programmed agreement of control totals is an information processing control relating to the accuracy and completeness of data input to the system.
- B   Reasonableness test (for example, sales tax to total value) is an information processing control relating to accuracy and completeness of data processed within the system.
- C   Cyclical reviews of all master files and standing data is an information processing control relating to the accuracy and completeness of data in the system.

May 2022

26	A	**Distractors**	
		B	Corporate governance is a system which companies are directed and controlled.
		C	Corporate governance is about relationships between directors and other stakeholders.
		D	Boards of directors are responsible for the governance of their companies.

27 B **Distractors**

A, C and D: ii. In a principles-based approach, listed companies are required by the stock exchange to meet certain standards of compliance.

iii. in a rule-based approach, it is judiciary rather than investors which monitors and punishes transgression.

28 C **Distractors**

A, B, D are true features of a 'Comply or Explain' basis of UK Corporate Governance Code.

29 A **Distractors**

B, C and D: At least half of the board, excluding the chair, should be non-executive directors whom the board considers to be independent.

30 C **Distractors**

A, B and D. Majority of the members in Nomination Committee should be independent non-executive directors.

31 C **Distractors**

A and B All members should be independent, non-executive directors. D The chair of the board can only be a member if they were independent on appointment.

32 D **Distractors**

A, B and C: ii Audit committee is responsible for providing advice on whether the annual report and accounts is fair, balanced and understandable.

33	C	**Distractors**	
		A	An audit committee should be established with a minimum of three independent non-executive directors for large companies, and two for smaller companies.
		B	The chair of the board should not be a member.
		D	The committee as a whole shall have competence relevant to the sector in which the company operates.
34	A	**Distractors**	
		B	The auditor has the right to speak at general meetings on any part of the business that concerns them as auditors.
		C	The auditor does not have the right to attend all directors' meetings.
		D	The auditor does not have the right to speak at directors' meetings and should not take part in any executive decisions on behalf of the company.

EXAM ANSWER BANK

35	B	**Distractors**

A The audited financial statements provide information about the company's past performance.

C The audited financial statements do not indicate the valuation of the company.

D The audited financial statements with an unmodified auditor's opinion indicate all the material information is presented in a true and fair view.

36	D	**Distractors**

A The external audit does not constitute an assurance engagement with respect to the future viability of the audited entity.

B The external audit does not provide an assurance on the efficiency or effectiveness with which the board has conducted the affairs of the entity.

C The external audit does not provide on opinion on the quality and effectiveness of a company's internal controls.

37	C	**Distractors**

A, B, D are true statements about materiality.

38	B	**Distractors**

A Audit evidence includes both the information contained in the accounting records for financial statements and other information.

C The quantity of audit evidence is affected by auditor's assessment of the risks of material misstatement.

D Appropriateness of audit evidence is the measure of the quality of audit evidence.

39	A	**Distractors**

B, C and D ii. Audit risk is a function of the risks of material misstatement and detection risk

iii. Detection risk means that the procedures performed to reduce audit risk will not detect the existence of material misstatement.

40	C	**Distractors**

A The auditors could be appointed by the directors, members and Secretary of State..

B The auditors should be answerable to the shareholders.

D The auditors must be appointed for each financial year or the directors need to resolve otherwise on the grounds that audited financial statements are unlikely to be required.

41	C	**Distractors**

A Only Simon is the shareholder of the business.

B According to agency theory, Simon acts as the principal in his relationship to Kevin.

D The best theory explains the problem facing Simon in terms of his relationship to Kevin is Agency theory.

42	A	**Distractors**

A, C, D are elements of an assurance engagement performed by a practitioner

A A two party relationship is not an element of an assurance engagement.

EXAM ANSWERS BANK

43	D	**Distractors**

A, B, C statements i, ii, iii, and iv all describe the internal control objectives that should be in place for the payroll department.

44	D	**Distractors**

A, B and C i. A decrease in selling price would be likely to make the net realisable value of inventory fall below cost.

45	C	**Distractors**

A, B and D are general controls.

46	D	**Distractors**

A   A qualified opinion is issued when the auditor cannot obtain sufficient appropriate audit evidence but concludes that the possible effects on the financial statement of undetected misstatements could be material but not pervasive.

B   A disclaimer of opinion is issued when the auditor cannot obtain sufficient appropriate audit evidence and concludes that the possible effects on the financial statement of undetected misstatements could be both material and pervasive.

C   A qualified opinion is issued when the auditor concludes that misstatements are material, but not pervasive to the financial statements.

47	D	**Distractors**

A, B, C i, ii, iii, iv all could be issues reflecting the 'expectation gap' of auditors and users of audited financial statements.

48	A	**Distractors**

B   Confirm that the company physically inspects all the vehicles in the register each year – Existence of vehicles.

C   Confirm all vehicles are used for the client's business – Rights and obligations of vehicles.

D   Reconcile opening and closing vehicles by numbers as well as amounts – Existence of vehicles.

49	C	**Distractors**

A, B, D The title deeds of a property provides audit evidence concerning Right and obligations.

50	A	**Distractors**

B, C and D: iv Outsourcing arrangements is not a specific risk affecting entities that engage in e-commerce.

November 2022

51 D Distractors

A Corporate governance is not about how companies are supervised and controlled by the government.

B and C Corporate governance is about making sure that companies are supervised and controlled to protect the interests of all stakeholders, not just shareholders or directors.

52 D Distractors

An agency problem is a conflict of interest where one party, motivated by self-interest, is expected to act in another's best interests, therefore the distractors are as follows:

A   Auditors being related to the management of the companies that they audit is an agency problem.

B   The agency problem refers to the problem that the managers (rather than the auditors) do not act in the management of companies' (ie: the owners') interests.

C   The agency problem does not refer to the issue that managers do not consider the impact of business decisions on a wide range of groups in society, but only for their shareholders.

53 D Distractors

All the statements i, ii, iii, and iv could be possible reasons for shareholder activism.
A, B and C do not include all the possible reasons.

54 C Distractors

A   The OECD has developed a set of principles of corporate governance that countries and companies should aim to achieve.

B   According to OECD corporate governance code, minority shareholders and overseas shareholders should be treated from the same as other shareholders.

D   Sarbanes-Oxley Act (2002) requires all listed companies to establish an audit committee.

55 C Distractors

A and B are true features of principles-based approaches to corporate governance.

D is a true feature of rules-based corporate governance codes.

56 B Distractors

A   Castle Co. should appoint four more independent non-executive directors, as the board requires a balance of executive and non-executive directors.

C   Castle Co. should not reappoint executive directors as non-executive directors.

D   Castle Co. should not reappoint an executive director as independent Chair as they cannot be independent.

57	B	**Distractors**	
		A	ABB should establish a nomination committee responsible for the appointment of new directors, not a remuneration committee.
		C	The remuneration committee should be involved in the evaluation of directors' performance and remuneration.
		D	The board should review board policies, not just Ms Abby.
58	D	**Distractors**	
			A, B and C are not independent of management or they have a business relationship that could interfere with the exercise of their unfettered and independent judgement.
59	C	**Distractors**	
		A	CEO should not decide directors' salaries whether based on their actual performance or not.
		B	CEO should not be the Chair of the remuneration committee.
		D	A remuneration committee (rather than a nomination committee) composed of independent non-executive directors should be established to set directors' salaries.
60	C	Majority of the members in a nomination committee should be independent non-executive directors, therefore the distractors are as follows:	

Distractors

	A	Executive directors are not independent.
	B	Majority, but not necessarily all, of the members in a nominated committee should be independent non-executive directors.
	D	The CEO should not be the Chair of the nominated committee, as the CEO is not independent.

61	C	**Distractors**	
		A	The Chair of the board should not be a member of the audit committee.
		B	All members in the audit committee should non-executive directors not just the majority.
		D	Rather than all members in the audit committee having relevant financial experience, at least one should have per the UK Corporate Governance Code.
62	B	**Distractors**	
			A, C and D: Statement i describes Business risk and statement iii describes Strategic risk.
63	A	**Distractors**	
		B	External audit is not a guarantee of accuracy so does not give an opinion on the correctness of the financial statements.
		C	External audit may provide recommendations to the directors on improvements to the company's corporate governance, but this is not the purpose of external auditing.
		D	External audit does not aim to detect fraud of the financial statements but is planned to provide reasonable evidence that the financial statements are free from material misstatement whether caused by fraud or error.

EXAM ANSWER BANK

64   **D**   **Distractors**

A, B and C are all substantive procedures (tests of detail rather than control).

65   **D**   **Distractors**

Methods i, ii, iii and iv could all be used to obtain audit evidence, hence all should be included.

A, B and C do not include all the correct methods.

66   **D**   **Distractors**

Statements A, B and C are true about audit sampling.

67   **A**   **Distractors**

B, C and D: Inspection confirms the existence of vehicles, not necessarily rights and obligations, valuation, or classification.

68   **C**   **Distractors**

- A   This is for existence of receivables.
- B   This is for rights and obligations of receivables.
- D   This is for accuracy of receivables.

69   **B**   **Distractors**

A, C and D are functions of internal audit; in some situations, internal auditors can perform some work to assist the external auditor but they do not work for them.

70   **D**   **Distractors**

A, B and C: Statements ii and iv are true on the differences between internal and external audit. Statements i and iii are not true because an internal auditor's report is an internal document and not publicly available and internal auditors (rather than external auditors) should add value to a company and improve their operations.

71   **B**   **Distractors**

- A   Outsourcing internal audit to the same firm that provides external audit services could cause an independence issue.
- C   Service providers from outsourced suppliers would not have the same level of knowledge as an internal auditor working within the organisation.
- D   Outsourcing internal audit can be used on a short-term basis for various projects.

72   **A**   **Distractors**

B, C and D: Example ii and iii are wrong. Performing control account reconciliations is a Detective control; and following up slow-payers and adjusting credit limits as necessary is a Corrective control.

73   **A**   **Distractors**

B, C and D: iii and iv are controls on existence.

74   **D**   **Distractors**

A, B and C: Strategy i and iv are not the best ways for managing the risk of theft because the company needs to sell paintings so avoidance is not appropriate, and acceptance could cause more theft.

75   **C**   **Distractors**

A, B and D: The risk of material misstatement at the assertion level is inherent risk and control risk.

May 2023

76 C Distractors

- A Corporate governance is about making sure that companies are supervised and controlled to protect the interests of shareholders and other stakeholders, not directors.
- B Corporate governance is not about how companies are monitored and controlled by the government.
- D Corporate governance is the system by which companies are directed and controlled, to improve companies' accountability to shareholders and to non-shareholding stakeholders. Companies with good corporate governance could attract investment, but this is the consequence rather than aim.

77 D Distractors

- A In corporate entities, the principals are shareholders, not stakeholders; and the executives are the paid agents.
- B In the context of a business organisation, the executives and managers of the business are accountable to the shareholders, not creditors, to act in their best interests.
- C One of the key problems agency theory addresses is how to motivate the managers in a company to grow the company in a way that generates value for the shareholders, rather than in a way that maximizes their personal power and wealth.

78 B Distractors

- A Directors and managers need to aware of the interests of stakeholders in governance because they could influence the achievements of an organisation's objectives, but they are not principals of the firm.
- C Each stakeholder group has different expectations about what it wants and different claims upon the organisation.
- D Stakeholders have influence over the organisation, so it is important to acknowledge claims made by the stakeholders.

79 D Distractors

- A The OECD developed a set of principles of corporate governance that governments could apply to improve the corporate governance code in their countries.
- B The OECD corporate governance guidance suggests that the corporate governance framework should ensure that **timely and accurate disclosure is made on all material matters** regarding the corporation, including the financial situation, performance, ownership, and governance of the company.
- C The PCAOB was formed after the Sarbanes-Oxley Act, not the OECD corporate governance guidance.

80 A Distractors

- B The UK Corporate Governance code adopts a principles-based approach, which focuses on objectives rather than mechanisms by which these objectives will be achieved.
- C According to the UK Corporate Governance Code, listed companies have to comply with corporate governance provisions or provide an explanation if they have not.
- D The UK Stewardship Code is not an update to the UK Corporate Governance Code. The UK Governance Code was last updated in 2024.

EXAM ANSWER BANK

81   B   **Distractors**

    A   In a unitary board, the board of directors consists of executive directors and independent non-executive directors.

    C   In the two-tier board system, the supervisory board appoints the CEO.

    D   In the traditional Japanese business network model (Keiretsu), the independent directors did not typically feature on the board of directors. In recent years it has become more acceptable to include independent directors on the board. It is still rare, however, for them to constitute a majority.

82   A   **Distractors**

B, C and D iii. The assessment of the board performance should be conducted by an external third party who can bring objectivity to the process. iv. Every director needs to receive appropriate training when first appointed, and subsequent training as necessary.

83   C   **Distractors**

    A   HOMEBUY Co. should not reappoint executive directors as non-executive directors as they cannot be independent.

    B   HOMEBUY Co. should not reappoint the current non-executive director as independent chair as he/she is not independent as a representative of a significant shareholder.

    D   HOMEBUY Co. should appoint four more independent non-executive directors as the board requires a balance of executive and non-executive directors.

84   D   **Distractors**

    A   The company should disclose the remuneration policy or the remuneration package of individual directors in the accounts.

    B   Directors' remuneration should be decided based on the organisation and individual performance.

    C   Directors' remuneration should be set by a remuneration committee consisting of independent non-executive directors only, without the CEO.

85   D   **Distractors**

    A   According to the UK Corporate Governance Code, the nomination committee should be mainly comprised of independent non-executive directors, not necessarily wholly.

    B   According to the UK Corporate Governance Code, all directors should be subject to annual re-election.

    C   The UK Corporate Governance Code states that the chair of the board should not chair the nomination committee when dealing with the appointment of their successor.

86   B   **Distractors**

    A   Not all boards are required to establish a separate risk committee for monitoring and supervising risk identification and management.

    C   A risk management committee can be staffed by executive directors.

    D   The risk management committee is responsible for reviewing the company's statements on internal control with reference to risk management, in conjunction with the audit committee.

EXAM ANSWERS BANK

87	A	**Distractors**	
		B	Risk with low likelihood of occurrence but serious impact should be transferred.
		C	Risk with high likelihood of occurrence and serious impact could be avoided.
		D	Insurance is a way to transfer risk.

88 C **Distractors**

- A The chair of the board should not be a member of the audit committee.
- B The board should establish an audit committee of independent non-executive directors, and at least one member should have recent financial experience.
- D Audit committees should be responsible for monitoring and providing advice on the preparation of the annual report and accounts.

89 D **Distractors**

- A The external audit could not prevent material fraud.
- B The external audit provides reasonable assurance as to whether the financial statements are materially misstated.
- C The external audit does not give an opinion on the effectiveness of a company's system of internal control.

90 D **Distractors**

A, B and C: All the assignments i, ii, iii, and iv could be carried out by internal auditors.

91 A **Distractors**

B, C and D: Statement iv is not an example of 'expectations gap' as it does not describe the difference between the actual and the public perception of responsibilities of external auditors.

92 C **Distractors**

- A For UK public companies, directors, members and the Secretary of State can appoint auditors.
- B The auditors should be appointed by and therefore answerable to the shareholders.
- D The Secretary of State can appoint auditors if no auditors are appointed by directors or members.

93 B **Distractors**

- A Audit risk has two major components; one is dependent on the entity (inherent risk and control risk) and the other is dependent on the auditor (detection risk).
- C Detection risk could be reduced by increasing sample size or performing the audit well.
- D Control risk could be reduced by improved internal controls.

94 A **Distractors**

B, C and D are general IT controls.

95 A **Distractors**

- B This provides the evidence for rights and obligations.
- C This provides the evidence for completeness.
- D This provides the evidence for classification and presentation.

| 96 | B | **Distractors** |

A, C and D. Procedure (iii) is not related to wages paid in cash.

| 97 | C | **Distractors** |

A, B and D are the possible tests of controls to ensure that all cash receipts are recorded. C is to ensure that all valid cash receipts are received and deposited.

| 98 | A | **Distractors** |

B, C and D: Reviewing the delegated list of authority for purchases is to ensure that recorded purchases represent goods and services received. It could not ensure that B all purchase transactions occurred have been recorded, or C recorded purchases represent the liability of the entity, or D purchase transactions are correctly recorded in the accounting system. To achieve the control objectives of B, C and D, other tests of controls should be conducted.

| 99 | B | **Distractors** |

- A   External audit relates to the financial statements.
- C   Internal auditors report to the board of directors or audit committee, external auditors report to the shareholders.
- D   External audit work is risk-based.

| 100 | C | **Distractors** |

A, B and D: These are the advantages of outsourcing the internal audit department, not disadvantages.

EXAM ANSWERS BANK

November 2023

101 D **Distractors**

    A   Corporate governance codes alleviate the different attitudes towards risk between shareholders and directors by requiring disclosure of risk management processes.

    B   Corporate governance codes alleviate the problem of conflicting interests between shareholders and directors by aligning directors' remuneration with corporate performance, not customer satisfaction.

    C   Accountability could be enhanced by the creation of an audit committee, rather than a nomination committee.

102 B **Distractors**

    A   Stakeholders include any person, group or possibly non-human entity that can affect or be affected by the achievements of a corporate entity's objectives. It is a bi-directional relationship.

    C   Each stakeholder has different expectations from the corporate entity, and their relationship with the corporate entity can also vary (including conflict, support, regular dialogue or joint enterprise).

    D   Not only human interest, but also animals and other non-human interests are recognised as stakeholders.

103 B **Distractors**

    A   Corporate governance is the system by which companies are directed and controlled to protect the interests of shareholders and other stakeholders, not for the interests of the directors.

    C   Corporate governance only provides a framework for an organisation to pursue its strategy and offers safeguards against misuses of resources.

    D   Corporate governance helps to increase accountability to shareholders and other stakeholders, not to the government. Good corporate governance could attract new investment as a consequence, but not as an aim.

104 D **Distractors**

    A   The main areas covered by Greenbury Report (1995) were about directors' remuneration.

    B   The Turnbull Report (1999) mainly covered the areas of risk management and internal control.

    C   The Higgs Report (2003) focused on non-executive directors.

105 C **Distractors**

    A   The OECD developed a set of principles (not rules) of corporate governance that countries and companies should work towards, but the OECD code is non-binding.

    B   The US government issued the Sarbanes-Oxley Act (2002), which is an example of a rules-based approach to corporate governance.

    D   The Sarbanes-Oxley Act (2002) applies to all companies that are required to file periodic reports with the Securities and Exchange Commission (SEC) and also has implications for overseas subsidiaries of those companies.

106	A	**Distractors**	
	B	Principles-based approaches can be applied across different legal jurisdictions rather than being founded in the legal regulations of one country.	
	C	Principles-based approaches are usually enforced on a comply or explain basis.	
	D	A rules-based approach allows no flexibility for different circumstances, which makes the enforcers difficult to deal with questionable situations.	

107 B **Distractors**

A, C, D. iii. Preparing the financial statements is not a task for the board of directors, but for financial accountants, however, the board need to ensure that the financial statements are prepared as required by Company Law.

108 C **Distractors**

A, B, and D. ii. Non-executive directors do not have day-to-day operational responsibility for the company, and they are not employees of the company; iv. The role of the chair is to lead the board of directors. It is recommended by the UK Corporate Governance Code that the chair should not be the same individual as the CEO to avoid one person having too much power.

109	A	**Distractors**	
	B	The nomination committee should be made up wholly or mainly of independent non-executive directors.	
	C	The UK Corporate Governance Code states that all directors should be subject to annual re-election, including the CEO.	
	D	The nomination committee should regularly review the structure, size and composition of the board, and keep under review the leadership needs of the company.	

110 A **Distractors**

B, C and D. iv. The UK Davies report (2011) on Women on Boards highlighted the advantages of greater female representation, not the Tyson report (2003). In Norway legislation required all listed companies to raise the proportion of women on their boards to 40% by 2008, not in the US.

111	B	**Distractors**	
	A	The remuneration committee is responsible for advising on executive director remuneration policy and the remuneration packages of individual directors.	
	C	Remuneration packages of directors should be designed to attract and retain individuals of sufficient calibre, but also need to ensure that individuals are motivated to achieve performance levels, hence should not be as high as possible.	
	D	Directors' remuneration should be disclosed in the financial statements with full transparency.	

EXAM ANSWERS BANK

112   D   **Distractors**

     A   The members of an audit committee should all be independent non-executive directors, with at least one member having recent and relevant financial experience.

     B   The chair of the board should not be a member of the audit committee.

     C   The committee is responsible for providing advice on whether the annual reports and accounts as a whole are fair. They are not responsible for preparing the annual reports and accounts.

113   D   **Distractors**

     A   This risk has high likelihood of occurrence, so acceptance is not the most reasonable technique.

     B   Avoiding using movable equipment is not the most cost-effective way to manage this risk and could impact on the ability of the company to run its business.

     C   Since the likelihood of occurrence of this risk is high but the impact is not significant, insurance may not be the most cost-effective.

114   A   **Distractors**

     B   Everyone who works for the organisation has responsibilities for risk management, and the primary responsibility belongs to the whole board. A separate risk committee could be established to monitor and supervise risk identification and management.

     C   According to the UK Corporate Governance Code, if the board doesn't have a separate risk management committee, the audit committee will be responsible for risk management.

     D   The internal audit department could be responsible for the overall risk management process or the controls that are being operated; but external auditors will be concerned only with those risks that could affect the financial statements, and are not responsible for risk management.

115   B   **Distractors**

A, C and D. ii. Internal audit ensures that strategies implemented in respect of business risks operate effectively; iv. The external audit provides assurance to the shareholders and other stakeholders of a company on the financial statements.

116   D   **Distractors**

A, B and C. i, ii, iii and iv are all analytical procedures used during the risk assessment stage of the audit.

117   C   **Distractors**

     A   This response is related to the risk that inventory quantities are misstated by the inventory system.

     B   This response is related to the risk that inventory is susceptible to theft leading to a risk that recorded inventory does not exist.

     D   This response is related to the risk that the cost of the new inventory is over- or understated.

118	D	**Distractors**	
		A	This is an example of control activity relating to authorisation.
		B	This is an example of control activity relating to performance review.
		C	This is an example of control activity relating to physical controls.
119	D	**Distractors**	
			A, B and C. All the assignments i, ii, iii, and iv could be carried out by internal auditors.
120	C	**Distractors**	
		A	Appropriateness is the measure of the quality of audit evidence.
		B	Audit evidence obtained from external sources is more reliable than that obtained from the entity's records because it is from an independent source.
		D	Audit evidence obtained directly by auditors is more reliable than that obtained indirectly or by inference.
121	A	**Distractors**	
		B	Random selection ensures that all items in the population have an equal chance of selection.
		C	Haphazard selection should not be used if auditors are carrying out statistical sampling.
		D	Block selection may be used to check whether certain items have particular characteristics.
122	B	**Distractors**	
		A	The objective of this control is to ensure that cash payments are charged to the correct accounts.
		C	The objective of this control is to ensure that cash payments are recorded correctly in the ledger.
		D	The objective of this control is to ensure that cash payments are posted to the general ledger.
123	C	**Distractors**	
			A, B and D. are controls which provide assurance that payment is made only to bona fide employees of the entity, while C is to ensure that all payments have been made to employees included in the payroll system and there could be unidentified fictitious employees in the system.
124	B	**Distractors**	
		A	This audit procedure provides evidence for valuation and allocation of receivables.
		C	This audit procedure provides evidence for valuation and allocation of receivables.
		D	This audit procedure provides evidence for completeness of receivables.
125	C	**Distractors**	
		A	This is a test of control to ensure that all purchase transactions that occurred have been recorded.
		B	This is a test of control to ensure that purchase transactions are correctly recorded in the accounting system.
		D	This is a test of control to ensure that all purchase transactions that occurred have been recorded.

Mock exam 1
questions and answers

MOCK EXAM 1 QUESTIONS

1   Which theory states that management has a duty of care, not just to the owners of the company in terms of maximising shareholder value, but also the wider community of interest?

    A   Agency theory

    B   Stakeholder theory

    C   Governance theory

    D   Stewardship theory

2   Which of the following are OECD principles of corporate governance?

    (1)   To protect directors' rights and ensure all directors are treated fairly

    (2)   To promote transparency, fair markets and efficient allocation of resources

    (3)   To allow timely and accurate disclosure of material matters

    (4)   To ensure companies' objectives are met

    A   (1) and (2)

    B   (3) and (4)

    C   (1) and (4)

    D   (2) and (3)

3   Which of the following are characteristics of a principles-based approach?

    (1)   Comply or explain

    (2)   Criminal sanctions

    (3)   Flexibility

    (4)   Focus on aims

    A   (1), (2) and (3)

    B   (1), (2) and (4)

    C   (1), (3) and (4)

    D   (2), (3) and (4)

4   Which of the following is the correct definition of 'integrity' in accordance with the IESBA Code of Ethics?

    A   Members should not allow bias, conflicts of interest or undue influence of others to override professional or business judgements.

    B   Members should act diligently and in accordance with applicable technical and professional standards when providing professional services.

    C   Members should comply with relevant laws and regulations and should avoid any action that discredits the profession.

    D   Members should be straightforward and honest in all business and professional relationships.

5   Difficulty in aligning the interests of the company and its directors/managers is known as:

    A   The agency problem.

    B   The principal problem.

    C   The stakeholder problem.

    D   The stewardship problem.

MOCK EXAM 1 QUESTIONS

6   Which of the following is generally NOT an advantage of having non-executive directors on the company board?

   A   They provide reassurance to shareholders.

   B   They can provide a wider perspective than executive directors.

   C   They have more time to devote to the role than executive directors.

   D   They may have external experience and knowledge which executive directors do not possess.

7   All control systems are subject to limitations, hence the auditor cannot rely solely on controls testing.

   Identify the type of limitation for each weakness described.

Weakness	Type of limitation
(1) The payroll clerk and the human resources manager, who authorises the payroll on a monthly basis, are working together to defraud the company by benefiting from the salaries of two false employees.	(a) Collusion
(2) Sales made to Dixie, a major customer, are always processed at a special discount not recognised by the computer controls, so the sales director always has to process Dixie's sales, and 'fix' the problem.	(b) Human error
	(c) Management override

   A   1a, 2b

   B   1b, 2c

   C   1a, 2c

   D   1b, 2a

8   The *UK Corporate Governance Code* provides that the board should identify in the annual report each non-executive director it considers to be independent. Which of the following circumstances is LEAST likely to impair, or could appear to impair, a non-executive director's independence?

   A   He is or has been an employee of the company or group within the last five years.

   B   He has close family ties with the company's directors or senior employees.

   C   He represents a significant shareholder.

   D   He has served on the board for five years from the date of his first appointment.

9   Which of the following is a characteristic of a European-style system of corporate governance?

   A   Extensive cross-shareholdings by listed companies

   B   Boards of directors with many family members

   C   A widespread representation of interests on the board of directors, including employees

   D   Widespread equity ownership and large shareholdings by investment institutions

10 Which of the following statements is true about audit committees?

(1) It is acceptable for the chairman to chair the audit committee.

(2) Only one member of the audit committee must have relevant financial experience.

A 1 only

B 2 only

C 1 and 2

D Neither 1 nor 2

11 Which of the following is NOT a board committee that a listed company is required to have under corporate governance codes, such as the UK Corporate Governance Code?

A Audit

B Investment

C Nomination

D Remuneration

12 The expectation gap is said to arise because the role and responsibility of the external auditor is frequently misunderstood.

Which of the following is NOT a misunderstanding about the role of the auditor?

A Auditors are not required to detect all fraud within a company.

B Auditors are the agents of the directors.

C Auditors are responsible for the system of internal control within a company.

D Auditors comment on the value of the company.

13 Which of the following aspects of the board is not a key feature in ensuring competence?

A Appointment procedures

B Unitary structure

C Training of directors

D Appraisal of directors

14 You are reviewing a risk assessment performed at XYZ Co.

(1) The sales manager identified the risk that delivery vehicles could be stolen, amounting to an estimated loss of $50,000 per theft.

(2) The warehouse manager identified the risk that items of inventory could be stolen, categorising the risk as manageable.

What is being assessed in relation to each of these risks?

	Risk 1	Risk 2
A	Likelihood	Impact
B	Impact	Likelihood
C	Likelihood	Likelihood
D	Impact	Impact

15 Which of the following is **NOT** one of the fundamental principles of IESBA's Code of Ethics and Conduct?

   A   Integrity
   B   Objectivity
   C   Independence
   D   Confidentiality

16 You are the auditor of a charity whose income is derived wholly from voluntary donations. Sources of donations include the public in the form of cash collected in buckets by volunteers in shopping areas. A risk has been identified that income may be understated in the financial statements. You are concerned that not all income may be recorded.

   Which of the following procedures is **NOT** an appropriate valid response to this audit risk?

   A   Obtain a breakdown of the income recorded from the cash that was collected in buckets, and vouch a sample of entries back to the volunteer in order to determine which volunteer collected the relevant donations.
   B   Perform analytical procedures on the level of donations in shopping areas per volunteer.
   C   Review the internal controls relating to cash collected in buckets to determine whether buckets are sealed, sequentially numbered and signed in and out by the volunteers.
   D   Observe the counting and recording of proceeds from collections, to determine whether appropriate segregation of duties is in place.

17 Which of the following procedures **must** the auditor use to obtain an understanding of the entity and its environment in accordance with ISA 315 (Revised) *Identifying and Assessing the Risks of Material Misstatement*?

   (1) Analytical procedures
   (2) Inquiry
   (3) Observation
   (4) Reperformance

   A   (1), (2) and (3)
   B   (1) and (2) only
   C   (2), (3) and (4)
   D   (1) and (4)

18 XYZ Co maintains a petty cash balance of $100. Which risk management strategies would be best for managing the risk of theft?

   (1) Avoidance
   (2) Mitigation
   (3) Transfer
   (4) Acceptance

   A   (1) and (2)
   B   (3) and (4)
   C   (1) and (3)
   D   (2) and (4)

19 Which of the following methods are auditors unlikely to use to record company systems?

    A   A graph

    B   A flowchart

    C   Narrative notes

    D   A questionnaire

20 Which of the following is **NOT** a financial statement assertion relating to account balances and related disclosures, in accordance with ISA 315 (Revised) *Identifying and Assessing the Risks of Material Misstatement*?

    A   Classification

    B   Completeness

    C   Rights and obligations

    D   Occurrence

21 What primary audit objective is an auditor seeking to confirm when carrying out a physical inspection of the plant and equipment of a company?

    A   Ownership of the assets

    B   Existence of the assets

    C   Ownership and existence of the assets

    D   Valuation of the assets

22 Identify each of these statements as control objective, risk or control procedure.

Statement	Control objective, risk or procedure?
(1) A Company pays for goods it has not received	(a) Control objective
(2) A Company only accepts goods it has ordered	(b) Risk
(3) A Company compares invoices to purchase orders and GRNs	(c) Control procedure

    A   1a, 2b, 3c

    B   1b, 2c, 3a

    C   1a, 2c, 3b

    D   1b, 2a, 3c

23 The sales invoices of Z Co are matched to dispatch notes, with any mismatched items investigated before they are recorded in the sales day book.

Which of the following control objectives does this help to achieve?

    A   It ensures that sales and receivables are valid and accurate.

    B   It ensures that all goods dispatched are recognised as sales and receivables.

    C   It ensures that all goods ordered by customers are dispatched.

    D   It ensures that customers do not exceed their credit limits.

24 You are aware that a company is considering establishing an internal audit department. With which of the following activities should the internal audit function **NOT** be involved?

A   Monitoring of management's performance
B   Reviewing adequacy of management information for decision-making purposes
C   Taking responsibility for the implementation of a new sales ledger system
D   Assessing compliance with relevant regulations

25 The roles of internal and external audit differ and below is a list of key characteristics. Match the following characteristics to the appropriate auditor.

Characteristic	Type of auditor
(1) Report to audit committee	(a) Internal auditor
(2) Reports are publicly available to shareholders	(b) External auditor
(3) Review effectiveness of internal controls to improve operations	
(4) Express an opinion on the truth and fairness of the financial statements	

A   1a, 2b, 3a, 4b
B   1b, 2a, 3b, 4a
C   1a, 2a, 3a, 4a
D   1b, 2b, 3b, 4b

MOCK EXAM 1 ANSWERS

1	B	Stakeholder theory is effectively a development of the notion of stewardship, stating that management has a duty of care, not just to the owners of the company in terms of maximising shareholder value, but also to the wider community of interest or stakeholders.
2	D	The OECD principles are not intended to protect directors' rights nor to ensure that companies' objectives are met.
3	C	Criminal sanctions are a characteristic of a rules-based approach, the rest are characteristics of a principles-based approach.
4	D	A is the definition of objectivity, B is the definition of professional competence and due care and C is the definition of professional behaviour.
5	A	The agency problem arises when the enterprise has difficulty in aligning the interests of the company with those of its directors/managers.
6	C	Time availability can actually be problematic for non-executive directors. Non-executive directors often have limited time to devote to the role as they are likely to have other time-consuming commitments.
7	C	
8	D	The UK Corporate Governance Code sets the period for serving on the board at more than nine years. The other options are circumstances which are likely to impair, or could appear to impair, a non-executive director's independence.
9	C	The European two-tier boards will often have a representative of the employees on the supervisory board.
10	D	The chairman should not be a member of the audit committee. At least one member must have recent and relevant financial experience, so more than one is acceptable.
11	B	Audit, nomination and remuneration are board committees required by corporate governance codes.
12	A	Statement A is true about the auditor's role therefore it is not a misunderstanding.
13	B	A unitary structure is not required for competence.
14	D	Both statements refer to impact but (1) is quantified in monetary terms.
15	C	
16	A	This will provide evidence of the occurrence of income, but the key risk here is completeness of income.
17	A	ISA 315 (Revised) requires auditors to use analytical procedures, inquiry and observation when obtaining an understanding of the entity and its environment. In addition, they should also use inspection.
18	D	The company could introduce internal controls (mitigation) such as locking the cash away. However, since the potential loss is small another option might be to accept the risk and do nothing.
19	A	The others are all commonly used methods.
20	D	Occurrence is a financial statement assertion that relates to classes of transactions and events and related disclosures, not to account balances and related disclosures at the period end.
21	B	The primary objective of a physical inspection of plant and equipment is 'existence'. The auditor may obtain corroborative evidence to support the ownership and valuation assertions when carrying out a physical inspection of such assets, but they should carry out other more pertinent tests to gain assurance in support of them.

22	D	
23	A	The control helps to ensure sales are valid as sales are only recognised for goods which have been dispatched.
24	C	The internal audit function is a review and monitoring function. It should not take operational responsibility for any part of the accounting or information systems.
25	A	Internal audit reports to the audit committee and it is the role of internal audit to review the effectiveness and efficiency of internal controls to improve operations. External audit looks at the operating effectiveness of internal controls on which they may rely for audit evidence and a by-product may be to comment on any deficiencies they have found but this is not a key function of the role.

The external auditor's report is publicly available to the shareholders of the company (internal audit reports are addressed to management/those charged with governance) and the external auditor provides an opinion on the truth and fairness of the financial statements.

Mock exam 2
questions and answers

MOCK EXAM 2 QUESTIONS

1. Which of the following is the agent in the agency relationship with a company?

    A   Citizens

    B   Suppliers

    C   Directors

    D   Shareholders

2. According to stakeholder theory, which of the following would be an expression of stakeholder power?

    A   A decision by a company to re-locate operations to another country where labour costs are cheaper

    B   A boycott by consumers on the purchase of goods made by a company whose major suppliers use child labour

    C   A decision by senior management to implement an IT system which will make many of the employees redundant

    D   A decision by a bank to withdraw overdraft facilities from a customer who has continually breached its overdraft limit

3. Which of the following is NOT a feature of the role of non-executive directors?

    A   Direction and control of day-to-day management

    B   Contributing to, and challenging the direction of strategy

    C   Satisfying themselves that financial information is fairly presented

    D   Scrutinising the performance of management in meeting goals and objectives

4. In order to be consistent with the principles of corporate governance, what should non-executive director remuneration be based on?

    A   Past performance of the company

    B   A fixed base plus an incentive-based element

    C   Reasonable return for the time dedicated to the job

    D   Increase in share price achieved in past financial year

5. Which of the following is a limitation of an audit committee?

    A   Its members may not have sufficient financial knowledge or experience.

    B   The committee and management may have different views about the financial report or the audit.

    C   It has power to make decisions without approval of the full board, reducing the board's authority.

    D   The absence of executive members on the committee means that it cannot discuss issues with management.

6. According to the *UK Corporate Governance Code*, an audit committee:

    A   Should consist of at least three members.

    B   Should be chaired by the chair of the board.

    C   Should consist of a majority of independent directors.

    D   May include non-executive members who are not directors.

7   Which of the following is not a limitation of auditing?

   A   The fact that the directors make subjective judgements in preparing the financial statements and there are instances where a range of values could be acceptable

   B   The fact that the directors might not provide the auditors with all the information they need, either intentionally or unintentionally

   C   The fact that fraud may be being concealed, even by falsifying documents which might reasonably appear genuine

   D   The fact that accounting systems are subject to human error

8   Which of the following fundamental principles of ethical behaviour is defined as follows?

   'Members shall:

   - Comply with relevant laws and regulations;
   - Behave in a manner consistent with the profession's responsibility to act in the public interest in all professional activities and business relationships; and
   - Avoid any conduct that the member knows might discredit the profession.'

   A   Integrity
   B   Objectivity
   C   Confidentiality
   D   Professional behaviour

9   Which of the following are aspects of good corporate governance?

   (1)   Internal controls
   (2)   Risk management
   (3)   Accountability to stakeholders
   (4)   Maximising shareholder wealth

   A   (1), (2) and (3)
   B   (1), (2) and (4)
   C   (1), (3) and (4)
   D   (2), (3) and (4)

10 An AIA member decides that they are not required to follow AIA's requirement for continuing professional development (CPD), as their job has not changed since they qualified.

   Which of the fundamental principles is the member at risk of breaching?

   A   Integrity
   B   Objectivity
   C   Confidentiality
   D   Professional competence and due care

11 You are reviewing a risk assessment performed at XYZ Co.

   (1)   The board identified the risk that a key member of staff might leave. This risk was stated to be once in every two years.

   (2)   The office manager identified the risk that the building could burn down. This was identified as low.

What is being assessed in relation to each of these risks?

	Risk 1	Risk 2
A	Likelihood	Impact
B	Impact	Likelihood
C	Likelihood	Likelihood
D	Impact	Impact

12 You are an audit senior of ABC Co which operates a chain of supermarkets. The company has recently installed a new till (cash register) system in the supermarkets. The audit engagement partner has said that she has is concerned that the new till system may not be reliable, and that consequently not all sales have been recorded, resulting in an understatement of revenue.

Which of the following audit procedures represent valid responses to this audit risk?

(1) Perform analytical procedures by comparing daily/weekly sales by store with both the prior year and with expectations, in order to determine whether any unusual patterns have occurred following the installation of the new system.

(2) Vouch the sales revenue per the system to the till receipts to confirm the accuracy of the sales.

(3) Obtain a copy of the training manual relating to the new till system and discuss with directors the extent of the training which staff have received on the new system.

(4) Agree sales revenue from till receipts to the cashbook to determine the accuracy of till receipts.

A (1) and (2)
B (3) and (4)
C (1) and (3)
D (2) and (4)

13 Which of the following are examples of inherent risk factors?

(1) The company is rapidly expanding.
(2) The company has lots of cash sales.
(3) The company does not maintain a non-current asset register to record its assets.
(4) No backups are taken of the computer system at the end of each day.

A (1) and (2)
B (3) and (4)
C (1) and (3)
D (2) and (4)

14 Which of the following will contribute to good corporate governance?

(1) Supervision of staff in key roles.
(2) Lack of focus on short-term profitability.
(3) Directors' remuneration entirely in the form of share options.
(4) A thorough appointment procedure for directors.

A (1), (2) and (3)
B (1), (2) and (4)
C (1), (3) and (4)
D (2), (3) and (4)

15 Which of the following is a characteristic of a Japanese style of board?

- A   Extensive cross-shareholdings by listed companies
- B   Boards of directors with many family members
- C   A widespread representation of interests on the board of directors, including employees
- D   Widespread equity ownership and large shareholdings by investment institutions

16 The external auditor may seek to place reliance on internal controls in order to restrict substantive testing.

In which of the following circumstances is the auditor likely to place reliance on controls?

(1) A company where there is an internal audit function which monitors controls on a systematic and regular basis.

(2) A small company where the owner-manager has virtual control over all accounting transactions, aided by his part-time, unqualified wife.

- A   (1) only
- B   (2) only
- C   Both (1) and (2)
- D   Neither (1) nor (2)

17 XYZ Co has set up an internal audit department. Of which risk management strategy is this an example?

- A   Avoidance
- B   Mitigation
- C   Transfer
- D   Acceptance

18 Which of the following factors contribute to a strong control environment?

(1) Management communicate controls values to staff and ensures new staff are thoroughly training in controls procedures.

(2) Management emphasises the importance of targets over procedures.

(3) Management includes adherence to company procedures in annual appraisals for staff members.

- A   (1), (2) and (3)
- B   (1) and (2) only
- C   (1) and (3) only
- D   (2) and (3) only

19 Which of the following is not a financial statement assertion relating to classes of transactions and events and related disclosures, in accordance with ISA 315 (Revised) *Identifying and Assessing the Risks of Material Misstatement*?

- A   Occurrence
- B   Completeness
- C   Valuation
- D   Presentation

20 Which of the following are key features in ensuring the competence of directors?

   (1) Appointment procedures
   (2) Age
   (3) Training
   (4) Appraisal of directors

   A (1), (2) and (3)
   B (1), (2) and (4)
   C (1), (3) and (4)
   D (2), (3) and (4)

21 Which of the following would provide the most persuasive evidence of a company's ownership of a freehold office building?

   A Inspection of the purchase documentation
   B Inspection of recent expense invoices for extensive repairs to the building, paid for by the company
   C Inspection of the title deeds to the building
   D Inspection of a directors' board minute confirming ownership of the building

22 Identify each of these statements as control objective, risk or control procedure.

Statement	Objective, risk or procedure?
(1) A company wants to pay the right amount for goods purchased	(a) Control objective
(2) A company reconciles supplier statements to the purchase ledger	(b) Risk
(3) A company may pay for goods which are used for personal purposes	(c) Control procedure

   A 1a, 2b, 3c
   B 1b, 2c, 3a
   C 1a, 2c, 3b
   D 1b, 2a, 3c

23 The auditor of Q Co has identified that Q Co does not match dispatch notes to sales invoices as part of the controls in the sales system.

   What is the potential consequence of this deficiency?

   A Customer orders may not be fulfilled accurately.
   B Sales and trade receivables may be overstated.
   C Sales and trade receivables may be understated.
   D Sales invoices may be posted inaccurately in the receivables control account.

24 Which of the following best summarises the meaning of 'economy' in the context of a Value for Money audit?

- A The lowest cost at which the appropriate quantity and quality of physical, human and financial resources can be achieved
- B Producing the required goods and services in the shortest time possible
- C The extent to which an activity is achieving its policy objectives
- D The relationship between goods and services produced and the resources used to produce them

25 Which of the following is not a benefit of assurance?

- A Users of financial statements will have more confidence that they are presented fairly.
- B Potential fraudsters might be deterred by regular scrutiny of the financial records.
- C Management might be motivated to operate systems properly by the thought of a regular review of these systems.
- D Investors will know the company is financially secure.

MOCK EXAM 2 ANSWERS

1   C   In relation to a company, directors are the agents who act on behalf of the shareholders who are the principals.

2   B   The withdrawal of an overdraft facility, the implementation of the IT system and the decision to re-locate operations are commercial decisions taken by the organisation, and are not the result of stakeholder pressure. The consumer boycott of products creates pressure on the company to change supplier or force the supplier to end the use of child labour. This is an example of stakeholder pressure from consumers.

3   A   Day-to-day management is the role of the executive directors, not the non-executives.

4   C   Non-executive directors should only be paid a reasonable return for the time dedicated to the job. If they are incentivised by profits of changes in share price it may adversely affect their independence.

5   A   A criticism of audit committees is that its members often lack the financial knowledge to deal adequately with the responsibilities of the committee. The audit committee cannot make decisions independently but must make recommendations to the board or submit decisions to the board for approval such as decisions about awarding non-audit work to the auditors. A function of the audit committee is to monitor the financial statements and the audit, and it is to be expected that disagreements may occasionally arise between the committee and management. If they did not, the purpose of having an audit committee could be questioned.

6   A   According to the UK Corporate Governance Code, an audit committee should consist of at least three members. The members should all be independent non-executive directors and the committee should not be chaired by the chair of the board.

7   D   This is more indicative of an inherent limitation in a system of internal control.

8   D

9   A   Corporate governance is not concerned with maximising shareholder wealth.

10 D   AIA members are obliged to remain technically up to date to ensure their professional competence.

11 A   The first statement refers to likelihood and the second to impact.

12 C   The audit risk relates to the concern that the system may not be reliable, that not all invoices have been recorded and that staff may not be familiar with the system.

Vouching the revenue per the system back to till receipts is not a valid response to the audit risk. Given that one concern is that revenue is understated, testing should be from the till receipts to the system to ensure that all sales have been recorded. Similarly, agreeing revenue from till receipts to the cashbook is also the wrong way around – this test should begin with the cashbook in order to test for completeness.

13 A   Rapid expansion leads to the risk of overtrading and going concern problems, cash is susceptible to theft.

14 B   If directors are paid entirely in share options it may encourage them to focus on short term goals to the detriment of long-term goals, contributing to poor corporate governance.

15 A   In Japan a feature of the kereitsu system is multiple cross shareholdings.

16 A   The owner would be able to override controls and collude with his wife, this increasing control risk.

17 B   Internal audit is part of the internal control system, and internal controls mitigate risks.

18 C

19 C   Valuation is a financial statement assertion that relates to account balances at the period end, not to classes of transactions.

MOCK EXAM 2 ANSWERS

20	C	Age is not a feature of competence.
21	C	The deeds provide independent reliable confirmation of ownership. The other options may provide corroborative evidence as to the ownership of the freehold office building but the evidence they provide is insufficient and not as reliable as that provided by inspecting the title deeds to the building.
22	C	
23	C	The matching of dispatch notes to an invoice ensures that for all goods dispatched an invoice has been raised. If this is not the case sales and trade receivables may be understated. For answer B an appropriate control would be to match invoices to dispatch notes. Matching dispatch notes and invoices would not prevent orders being dispatched incorrectly A or prevent invoices being input incorrectly D.
24	A	B and D relate to efficiency and C to effectiveness.
25	D	The other factors are benefits of assurance.

Bibliography

Acknowledging non-human stakeholders in designing for sustainable food systems (2014) (Authors: Jessica Frawley and Laurel Dyson).

Cadbury Committee (1992) *Report of the committee on the financial aspects of corporate governance.* London, Gee.

Chartered Governance Institute UK & Ireland (2024) *Governing Sustainability: Are sustainability committees the answer?* [Online]. Available from: https://www.cgi.org.uk/knowledge/research/governing-sustainability-apr24 [Accessed 11 July 2024].

Companies Act 2006. (2006) [Online]. Available from: www.legislation.gov.uk/ [Accessed 11 July 2024]. http://www.nationalarchives.gov.uk/doc/open-government-licence/version/3/ Contains Parliamentary information licensed under the Open Parliament Licence v3.0.

Financial Reporting Council (2021) *Board Diversity and Effectiveness in FTSE 350 Companies* [Online]. Available from: https://media.frc.org.uk/documents/FRC_Board_Diversity_and_Effectiveness_in_FTSE_350_Companies.pdf [Accessed 11 July 2024].

Financial Reporting Council (2023) *Audit Committees and the External Audit: Minimum Standard.* [Online]. Available from: https://www.frc.org.uk/news-and-events/news/2023/05/frc-publishes-minimum-standard-for-audit-committees/ [Accessed 11 July 2024].

Financial Reporting Council (2024) *Corporate Governance Code Guidance.* [Online]. Available from: https://www.frc.org.uk/library/standards-codes-policy/corporate-governance/corporate-governance-code-guidance/ [Accessed 11 July 2024].

Financial Reporting Council (2024) *UK Corporate Governance Code.* [Online]. Available from: https://www.frc.org.uk/library/standards-codes-policy/corporate-governance/uk-corporate-governance-code/ [Accessed 11 July 2024].

Financial Reporting Council (2019) *UK Stewardship Code.* [Online]. https://www.frc.org.uk/library/standards-codes-policy/stewardship/uk-stewardship-code/ [Accessed 11 July 2024].

Greenbury Committee (1995) *Directors' remuneration – report of a study group.*

Hampel Committee (1998) *Committee on corporate governance – final report.* London, Gee.

Higgs (2003) *Review of the role and effectiveness of non-executive directors.* London, The Stationery Office.

International Federation of Accountants (2023) *International Code of Ethics for Professional Accountants.* [Online]. Available from: https://www.ethicsboard.org/iesba-code [Accessed 11 July 2024].

King Reports on Corporate Governance (n.d.) [Online]. Available from: https://www.iodsa.co.za/page/king-iv [Accessed 11 July 2024].

New York Times (2023) *Apple Reaches Deal With Investors to Audit Its Labor Practices* [Online]. Available from: https://www.nytimes.com/2023/01/17/business/economy/apple-labor.html [Accessed 11 July 2024].

New York Times (2021) *Climate Activists Defeat Exxon in Push for Clean Energy* [Online]. Available from: https://www.nytimes.com/2021/05/26/business/exxon-mobil-climate-change.html [Accessed 11 July 2024].

Organisation for Economic Co-operation and Development (2023) G20/OECD *Principles of Corporate Governance* [Online]. Available from: https://www.oecd-ilibrary.org/governance/g20-oecd-principles-of-corporate-governance-2023_ed750b30-en [Accessed 11 July 2024].

Principles of External Auditing (2014), by Brenda Porter (Author), Jon Simon (Author), David Hatherly (Author), Wiley, 4th edition.

BIBLIOGRAPHY

Principles for Responsible Investment (PRI) (2018) *PRI Reporting Framework Main definitions* [Online]. Available from: https://www.unpri.org/Uploads/i/m/n/maindefinitionstoprireportingframework_127272_949397.pdf [Accessed 11 July 2024].

Sarbanes-Oxley Act 2002. (2002) [Online]. Available from: www.sec.gov/about/laws/soa2002.pdf [Accessed 11 July 2024].

Smith Committee (2008) *Consultation on proposed changes to guidance on audit committees*. London, Financial Reporting Council.

Spencer Stuart UK Board Index 2023 [Online]. Available from: https://www.spencerstuart.com/research-and-insight/uk-board-index [Accessed 11 July 2024]

Spencer Stuart US Board Index 2023 [Online]. Available from: https://www.spencerstuart.com/research-and-insight/us-board-index [Accessed 11 July 2024].

Starik, M. (1995). Should Trees Have Managerial Standing? Toward Stakeholder Status for Non-Human Nature. *Journal of Business Ethics, 14*(3), 207-217. Available from: https://www.jstor.org/stable/25072639?seq=1 [Accessed 11 July 2024]

Turnbull Committee (1998) *Combined code – principles of good governance and code of best practice*. London, The Stationery Office.

Turnbull Committee (1999) *Internal control – guidance for directors on the combined code*. London, The Stationery Office.

Wikipedia (2024) *List of corporate collapses and scandals*. [Online]. Available from: https://en.wikipedia.org/wiki/List_of_corporate_collapses_and_scandals [Accessed 03 July 2024].

Index

INDEX

> Note. **Key Terms** and their page references are given in **bold**.

Accountability, 110, 111
Accountability and audit, 17
Agency theory, 4
Agents, 110
AIA's Code of Ethics, 135
Analytical procedures, 151, 177
Appointment of auditors, 137
Appropriateness, 174
Assertions, 153, 175
Assurance, 109, 110, 116, 117, 127
Assurance engagement, 116, 127
Assurance over sustainability reporting and disclosures, 74
Audit, 110, 213
Audit committee, 20, 50
Audit Committees and the External Audit: Minimum Standard, 51
Audit evidence, 174
Audit procedures, 176
Audit risk, 146, 147
Audit sampling, 181, 182, 183, 184
Auditor's report, 112
Best value audits, 118
Board diversity, 31

Business risks, 94

Cash system, 194
Chair, 42
Chief Executive Officer (CEO), 38
Combined Code, 18, 34, 100, 101
Confidentiality, 135
Confirmation, 177
Consumer groups, 83
Consumerism, 83
Control activities, 162
Control environment, 160, 172
Control objectives, controls and tests of controls, 200
Control risk, 147, 147
Corporate governance, 16, 111
Corporate Governance Code, 43
Corporate social reporting, 67
Corporate social responsibility (CSR), 62, 80
CSR Strategy, 64
Customers, 80

Detection risk, 146, **147**
Directors' remuneration, 44
Director-shareholder relationship, 41
Discussion Papers, 133
Dismissal of auditors, 137
Double materiality, 73

Economic responsibilities, 65
Employees, 80
Enron, 20
Entity's risk assessment, 161
Environmental, Social and Governance (ESG), 55, 69
Ethical codes of conduct, 66
Ethical responsibilities, 66
Ethical safeguards, 82
Ethics, 134
European Sustainability Reporting Standards (ESRSs), 73
European Union's Corporate Sustainability Reporting Directive (CSRD), 73
Executive directors, 38
Executive Share Options Plans (ESOPs), 89
Expectations gap, 120, 125
External audit, 111, 112, 116, 117, 127, **213**

Fair, **112**, 115
Financial statement assertions, 175, 183
Fraud, 119, 124, 164
Fraudulent financial reporting, 120
FRC *Corporate Governance Code Guidance*, 39, 78
FRC's Corporate Governance Code Guidance, 210
Fundamental principles of professional ethics, 135, 140

G20/OECD Principles of Corporate Governance, 19
Global Reporting Initiative (GRI), 72
Government, 84
GRI Standards, 73

Higgs report, 41, 53

INDEX

IESBA Code of ethics, 134, 135
IFRS S1: *General Requirements for Disclosure of Sustainability-related Financial Information*, 74
IFRS S2: *Climate-related Disclosures*, 74
IFRS Sustainability Disclosure Standards, 74
IFRS Sustainability reporting standards and statutory audit, 74
Information processing controls, 165, 166
Information system, 162
Information technology (IT) audit, 118
Inherent risk, 146
Inquiry, 177
Inspection, 177
Institutional shareholders, 83
Integrity, 135
Internal audit committee, 49
Internal audit function, 217
Internal auditing, 117, 212
Internal auditors, 52
internal control, 98
Internal control, 160
International Auditing and Assurance Standards Board, 132
International Federation of Accountants, 132
International Standards on Auditing, 132, 133
ISA 200 *Overall Objectives of the Independent Auditor and the Conduct of an Audit in Accordance with International Standards on Auditing*, 147
ISA 240 *The Auditor's Responsibilities Relating to Fraud in an Audit of Financial Statements*, 121
ISA 250 (Revised) *Consideration of Laws and Regulations in an Audit of Financial Statements*, 122
ISA 265 *Communicating Deficiencies in Internal Control to Those Charged with Governance and Management*, 168
ISA 315 (Revised) *Identifying and Assessing the Risks of Material Misstatement*, 121, 151, 160
ISA 320 *Materiality in Planning and Performing an Audit*, 149
ISA 500 *Audit Evidence*, 174

King report, 28

Law and regulations, 122
Legal responsibilities, 65
Limitations of accounting and control systems, 163, 164
Limitations of audit, 124
Limitations of controls system, 164
Long-term creditors, 88
Long-term shareholder interest, 63

Managerial objectives, 5
Managing stakeholders, 78
Material, 115, 149
Materiality, 115
Mendelow's matrix, 85
Misappropriation of assets, 120
Mission statements, 66
Monitoring of controls, 161
Multiple stakeholder obligations, 63

Negative stakeholder power, 86
Nomination committee, 49, 52, 57
Non-executive directors, 39, 40, 46, 47
Non-statistical sampling, 182
Non-statutory audits, 116

Objectives of the auditor, 111
Objectivity, 135
Observation, 177
Operational risks, 94
Opinion, 111, 112, 127
Organisation for Economic Co-operation and Development (OECD), 19
Outsourcing, 214
Overall responses, 153

Payroll system, 200
Performance materiality, 149
Pervasiveness, 115
Philanthropic responsibilities, 66
Population, 182
Principles-based approach, 21, 22
Professional behaviour, 135
Professional competence and due care, 135
Professional scepticism, 153
Profit-making organisations, 83
Profit-related pay, 89
Projection of misstatements, 182
Public Company Accounting Oversight Board (PCAOB), 20
Purchases system, 191

Quality management, 136

Reasonable assurance, 115
Recalculation, 177

Receivables' confirmation, 181
Recognised Supervisory Bodies, 138
Recording accounting and control systems, 167
Removal of auditors, 138
Remuneration committee, 49, 54
Remuneration packages, 55
Reperformance, 177
Reputation risk, 65
Resignation of auditors, 137
Resource dependency theory, 9
Review, 110
Review engagement, 117
Risk committee, 100
Risk-based approach, 146
Rules-based approach, 22

Sales system, 188
Sarbanes-Oxley Act 2002, 20
Satisficing, 5
Securities and Exchange Commission (SEC), 20
Security, 89
Segregation of duties, 163
Self regulation, 90
Share option scheme, 89
Shareholder activism, 10
Shareholder theory, 7
Shareholders, 80, 83
Short-term shareholder interest, 63
Significant risk, 153
Social accounts, 67
Social cost, 62
Social responsibility, 62
Stakeholder analysis, 85
Stakeholder bargaining strength, 81, 82
Stakeholder conflict, 88
Stakeholder engagement, 86
Stakeholder influence, 86
Stakeholder mapping, 85, 86
Stakeholder objectives, 80
Stakeholder risks, 81
Stakeholder theory, 6, 8

Stakeholders, 7, 65, 66, 79, 88, 110
Statement of circumstances, 137
Statistical sampling, 182
Statutory audit, 116
Stewardship, 110
Stockholder theory, 7
Strategic CSR, 64
Strategic risks, 94
Substantive procedures, 154, 177
Substantive tests, 168
Sufficiency, 174
Suppliers, 84
Sustainability, 55, 68
Sustainability and governance, 75
Sustainability committee, 55, 76
Sustainability impacts and dependencies, 69
Sustainability reporting and governance, 67
System of internal control, 98

Tests of control, 168, 177
Tests of controls, 154
the International Sustainability Standards Board (ISSB), 74
True, 112, 115
Truth and fairness, 112
Turnbull report, 211

UK Corporate Governance Code, 17, 34, 50, 210, 212
UK Stewardship Code, 18
Unmodified opinion, 112

Value for money (VFM) audits, 118
Voluntary code of conduct, 90

Walk-through tests, 168
Working procedures of the IAASB, 133

INDEX